Frontiers in Economic History

Series Editors

Claude Diebolt, Faculty of Economics, BETA, CNRS, University of Strasbourg, Strasbourg, France

Michael Haupert, University of Wisconsin–La Crosse, La Crosse, WI, USA

Economic historians have contributed to the development of economics in a variety of ways, combining theory with quantitative methods, constructing new databases, promoting interdisciplinary approaches to historical topics, and using history as a lens to examine the long-term development of the economy. Frontiers in Economic History publishes manuscripts that push the frontiers of research in economic history in order to better explain past economic experiences and to understand how, why and when economic change occurs. Books in this series will highlight the value of economic history in shedding light on the ways in which economic factors influence growth as well as social and political developments. This series aims to establish a new standard of quality in the field while offering a global discussion forum toward a unified approach in the social sciences.

Giovanni B. Pittaluga • Elena Seghezza

An Economic Historiography of Germany, 1918-1931

How Inflation and Foreign Capital Inflows Allowed the Weimar Republic to Survive

Springer

Giovanni B. Pittaluga
Department of Political Science
University of Genoa
Genoa, Italy

Elena Seghezza
Department of Political Science
University of Genoa
Genoa, Italy

ISSN 2662-9771 ISSN 2662-978X (electronic)
Frontiers in Economic History
ISBN 978-3-031-70349-2 ISBN 978-3-031-70347-8 (eBook)
https://doi.org/10.1007/978-3-031-70347-8

This Springer imprint is published by the registered company Springer Nature Switzerland AG
The registered company address is: Gewerbestrasse 11, 6330 Cham, Switzerland

To Léon

Foreword

The interwar years in Germany are certainly one of the most often analyzed periods in economic history. The hyperinflation of 1923, featuring even in novels and movies, continues to be analyzed in scholarly work to this day and frequently serves as the background for a discussion of the stabilization of high rates of inflation in transition and emerging market countries. Interwar trade and exchange rate policies as well as the spillovers of banking crises continue to be used for comparisons, and international debt and the capacity (or willingness) to pay have given rise to a large comparative literature on the "transfer problem" at least since the 1980s debt crises in Latin America. More recently, reparations and sanctions regain attention in the current debate about economic statecraft and "geoeconomics." Weimar Germany, last but not least, is also a political warning how internal and international political and economic conflicts can lead a democratic country on the road to economic and political populism, dictatorship, violence, and war.

Despite Weimar Germany being so often analyzed, it is not easy to make sense of so many parallel developments that extend over more than a decade before the struggle between progressive forces and their enemies was decided for the worse. There still is a lively debate, as this book shows, about the interaction of political and economic crises, the relative role of home-grown or imported problem, and whether the causality ran from monetary policy to depreciation or whether it was the other way round?

In this book, Giovanni Battista Pittaluga and Elena Seghezza contribute to the debate and put forward a coherent interpretation of why Weimar Germany ultimately failed. They take a clear position in the debate and provide original contributions on the stabilization of the currency and the role of external capital flows, among others. Their interpretation is indeed able to make sense of and work out the direct connection between monetary policy in the 1920s and the depression that led the Nazi party to power. Where the authors depart from most existing work is that they put internal developments in Germany at the center of their narrative and analysis. The main drivers of events and economic and political decisions are identified in distributional conflicts among different societal groups. Choosing a political economy perspective allows the authors to coherently interpret events as a struggle between powerful interest groups.

The causality of hyperinflation in 1923 thus runs from political disorder that made it impossible to find a consensus on how to deal with the consequences of war and how to organize economic reconstruction. Conflicts were mitigated by increased public spending, leading to deficits, current account imbalances, and high inflation. That inflation could rage for so long was partly due to the fact that the "productive classes" benefited from it and that even workers were compensated by strong wage increases. The situation could no longer be controlled when capital inflows dried up and strong deprecations accelerated inflation. The exchange rate takes center stage because eventual inflation stabilization depended mainly on the stabilization of the exchange rate as well. But stabilization, and the Dawes plan of 1924, led to a resurgence of capital inflows which continued to finance budget deficits and current account imbalances. They also undermined competitiveness through appreciating the real exchange rate, however. Germany became vulnerable to sudden stops and when capital flows indeed dried up the Brüning government had no alternative but to implement fiscal austerity, paving the way for the rise of the Nazi government. In this view, internal conflicts and the impossibility to solve them adequately led to a series of temporary rather than sustainable solutions, and unresolved political economic conflicts are ultimately at the root of Weimar Germany's collapse.

Conflicts between capital and labor, between employers and workers, and between different sectors in Weimar Germany have been used before as an illustration of the war-of-attrition model where inflation is ultimately the equilibrium outcome because conflicting groups cannot agree on sharing the costs of necessary adjustment. As the structural change cannot be agreed upon to come from higher taxation or lower spending, the budget is financed through money creation. Yet while this view has been advanced before, Pittaluga and Seghezza argue that inflation was not only the default outcome because other ways of solving the war of attrition could not be found, but stress that at least for some groups inflation was a preferred instrument and not just the unwanted equilibrium outcome of a non-cooperative game. This interpretation offers interesting perspectives and potential lessons for current processes of high inflation in other countries as well. Stabilization is certainly more difficult to achieve if inflation is not, if to varying degrees, a burden on all groups but actually the preferred instrument of some.

The second current debate that Pittaluga and Seghezza offer a novel perspective on is the idea that capital inflows can lead to a Dutch disease problem. They show that following hyperinflation and the Dawes Plan of 1924, capital inflows mostly went to the non-tradable sectors of the economy. They identify a reverse Balassa–Samuelson effect because, in this case, wages and prices in the non-tradable sector increased faster than in the tradable sector and pushed up the real exchange rate. This resulted in a loss of international competitiveness for German products, made investments less attractive, and finally contributed to a reverse of capital flows. That negative consequence of large capital inflows can be widely observed in particular in resource-rich economies is widely known. It is less well known, however, that the Balassa–Samuelson effect can also work in reverse, yet having the same consequences as the original version.

Coming from a political science and an economic background respectively, Giovanni Pittaluga and Elena Seghezza are able to provide new interpretations of well-known events and to develop a fresh perspective on the political economic factors that drove Germany from losing one war to starting a second in only two decades. Not everyone will agree with all their views or give the same weight to different parts of the story, but readers will certainly come away with new perspectives and ideas.

University of Siegen,
Siegen, Germany

Carsten Hefeker

Acknowledgments

The project to write a book on a reconsideration of the Weimar economy has developed over the years from papers we presented in various Silvaplana Political Economy Workshops coordinated by Arye Hillman and Heinrich Ursprung. We are pleased to acknowledge our debt to the many friends and colleagues who in those Workshops and on other occasions commented on several parts of the manuscript.

Particular thanks go to Luca Beltrametti, Franco Bruni, Carsten Hefeker, Realino Marra, and Pierluigi Morelli for their comments, observations, and suggestions which helped to significantly improve the book.

Contents

List of Figures

List of Tables

Chapter 1
Introduction: The Main Political Economy Features of the Weimar Republic

The economic historiography of the Weimar Republic has focused almost exclusively on a few dramatic events that characterized the German economy in the 1920s and early 1930s. In particular, the 1923 hyperinflation, the 1931 currency and banking crisis, and Brüning's fiscal austerity policy.

Indeed, the weakening and eventual collapse of the Weimar Republic has typically been traced to precisely these events. However, as Feldman (1993) points out, by limiting the analysis in this way the underlying socio-political causes of the collapse are ignored leading one to attribute it to exclusively economic causes.

In fact, the dramatic events mentioned above cannot be considered, as has generally been done, in isolation from the wider social context. Although limiting his scope to Brüning's fiscal policy, Borchardt (1991b) himself emphasized the importance of dedicating attention to this. Indeed, he, like other scholars, such as James (1986), Kruedener (1990) and Ritschl (2002), argued that Brüning's margins of choice were limited given the prevailing institutional and socio-economic constraints in Germany. These scholars highlight how a large part of these limits and constraints were the result of policy choices that had enabled the Weimar Republic to maintain social stability and, hence, for the republic to survive. Regarding these constraints the Dawes Plan, in particular, imposed the convertibility of the Reichsmark and the independence of the Reichsbank, and at the same time facilitated Germany's renewed access to international financial markets which, thanks to the "transfer protection clause,"[1] triggered a huge inflow of foreign capital between 1924 and 1928.

Between 1925 and 1929, this inflow allowed the German government not only to pay the annual Reparations under the Dawes Plan without burdening the Reich's budget,[2] but also enabled it to cover its persistent budget deficits. Indeed, it was thanks to the massive foreign debt incurred in the latter half of the 1920s that the

[1] This clause gave commercial credits de facto seniority over Reparation claims. See Ritschl (1996).
[2] See Schuker (1988).

G. B. Pittaluga, E. Seghezza, *An Economic Historiography of Germany, 1918-1931*, Frontiers in Economic History, https://doi.org/10.1007/978-3-031-70347-8_1

Weimar Republic was able to maintain reasonable social stability and political consensus.

However, these massive foreign capital inflows had, over time, negative repercussions on the economic and political stability of the Weimar Republic. This for two main reasons, firstly, while borrowing from abroad allowed governments to expand public spending and pay for Reparations without recourse to domestic resources, it also led to an appreciation of the Reichsmark in real terms. Between 1924 and 1929, this led to the German economy being afflicted by a form of *Dutch disease*, which encouraged a significant expansion of non-tradables at the expense of tradables. As a result of this process, the increase in labor productivity in those years was, like output, extremely low. Secondly, the high level of foreign debt made German economic policy entirely dependent on international financial markets, exposing it to sudden stops. Indeed, from 1929 onwards, primarily due to changes in American monetary policy, capital flows from abroad diminished before drying up entirely, leaving the German government faced with the problem of how to deal with a persistent balance of payment and public spending deficits. In an effort to redress these imbalances, Brüning's center-right government, which in 1930 took over from the Grand Coalition government headed by Muller, introduced a series of tax changes that included spending cuts and tax increases.

However, the unpopularity of these measures led the government to attempt to distract domestic public attention and gain support among nationalists by adopting a more aggressive foreign policy. In international circles this policy shift was seen as an indication that Germany did not intend to fulfill its commitments under the Young Plan and expectations of a possible default resulted in a massive sudden stop which threatened the convertibility of the Reichsmark. Since a large proportion of the deposits of the large Berlin banks were held by non-residents, their sudden withdrawal severely impacted the liquidity of this important segment of the German banking system, provoking potential widespread insolvency.[3] The currency crisis thereby became compounded by a banking crisis.

In this context, the Reichsbank found itself, on the one hand, defending the stability of the Reichsmark by pledging a large part of its gold reserves and raising money market interest rates, and, on the other hand, injecting money into the banking system in order to guarantee adequate liquidity to the big banks. The simultaneous pursuit of these two objectives was contradictory: the banks, having liquidity at their disposal, were able to meet the demand for loans that were often used in speculation against the Reichsmark.

When it became clear that the Reichsbank's interventions in support of the banks could not continue, marked by the bankruptcy of the country's second largest bank, the currency crisis also became a banking crisis and these two crises began to feed off each other. In mid-July 1931, to counter the risk of a chain of bank failures, the government announced a 2-day bank holiday and, shortly afterwards, introduced exchange controls; effectively abandoning the convertibility of the Reichsmark.

[3] See Schnabel (2004).

As a result of the Brüning government's severe austerity measures and the credit crunch that followed the banking crisis, the German economy entered a phase of deflation, marked by a pronounced fall in output and a rise in unemployment to a level unknown in other European countries at the time. The result was a widespread discontent that paved the way to Hitler's rise to power. In light of this, while it is clear that the dramatic economic crisis that struck Germany between 1931 and 1932 was the result of the country's extreme dependence on the foreign capital inflows in the preceding years, it is also true that it was these capital inflows that had enabled the Weimar governments to maintain otherwise unsustainable levels of domestic spending and which had therefore, ultimately, allowed the Republic to survive.

Similar considerations to those concerning the 1931 crisis and Brüning's policy can be made about the hyperinflation of 1923. This cannot be seen as the isolated outcome of particular policy choices or of the burden of Reparations, but rather as the final outcome of the inflationary process that characterized Germany after the end of the First World War.

Recourse to inflation was, in fact, the most politically acceptable option open to the governments of the period. The failure of Erzberger's tax reform had showed that the Weimar Republic could not count on a level of consensus and social cohesion which would allow the government to adopt unpopular measures. The absence of this consensus, typical of solid democracies, was rooted in the widespread belief in conspiracy theories and myths that had led the German people into a kind of "fantasy land."[4] This, combined with post-war political propaganda, consolidated in the German people's minds the idea that Germany had not been "defeated" but rather "stabbed in the back." Thus, this myth, the so-called Dolchstoss myth, was born that Germany's defeat was due to traitors and defeatists, identified as pacifists, Jews and communists.[5]

The "stabbed in the back" myth prevented public acceptance of necessary tax reforms aimed at solving the serious economic deficits which Germany suffered from after the First World War. These beliefs led the various social groups to reject the sacrifices which would normally have been perceived as being necessary for the "general good," instead viewing any proposed tax increase or reduction in public spending as a further act of betrayal.

In this context, only the use of inflation could enable the German government to obtain, through seigniorage, the necessary resources to cover the deficits resulting from high public expenditure and insufficient tax revenue. The use of inflation for this purpose was actively supported by industrialists whose main concern, after the fall of the imperial regime, was to avert a Bolshevik revolution similar to the Russian one and, in order to marginalize the radical left, they supported the first Social Democratic-led governments of the Republic. Under pressure from industrialists, the

[4]As Bessel (1990, p. 127) writes: "Responsible politics remained a hostage to myths about First World War and Weimar democracy eventually had to pay the price."

[5]Field Marshal Paul Hindenburg himself expressed this view when testifying before the Untersuchungsausschuss für schuldfragen (the Committee of Inquiring into Guilt).

economic policy of German governments in the early 1920s was directed toward keeping unemployment low and maintaining state welfare spending high. In a context where reforms to increase tax revenues were hindered by the "myths" mentioned above, these goals could only be pursued through policies of budget deficits covered through seigniorage from high inflation.

The trade unions, for their part, were not adverse to inflation if it allowed the maintenance of high levels of employment, high levels of welfare support for workers and, critically, that workers purchasing power was preserved through wage indexation mechanisms.

The outcome of this type of policy was a higher output growth and a significantly lower unemployment rate than in other advanced countries, such as the United Kingdom and the United States. Appropriately, Feldman (1983, p. 390) argues that in those years inflation exercised a function of "... social pacification in Germany, a matter of particular importance during the war and in the revolutionary phase which followed it."

The fact that inflation enabled the German elite to minimize social discord and allow the Republic to survive has led some economists to emphasize the beneficial short-term effects of inflation on the German economy.[6]

These scholars, however, tend to overlook its social and economic costs, starting with the substantial "destruction" of large sections of the middle class. As Kunz (1986, p. 4) writes: "... political and social historians alike had until recently dealt almost exclusively with the impact of the hyperinflation of 1923 and with its connection to the crisis of the Weimar state in that fateful year. By doing so, they generally failed to perceive inflation as a long-term process."

In fact, the high increase in prices in the years following the First World War, even if fostered social peace and the survival of Weimar Republic, led the unions to ask for an increasingly effective wage indexation mechanism.

The gradual reduction of the time delay with which wages were adjusted to prices significantly increased the degree of persistence of German inflation, the level of which became increasingly dependent on its past level. The conditions were created for an explosive run-up between exchange rates, prices, and wages.

From mid-1922, following a violent sudden stop and the subsequent fall of the exchange rate of the mark, this run-up became tumultuous and inflation turned into hyperinflation. This weakened not only the structure of the German economy but also the moral, social, and political foundations on which the Weimar Republic was based.[7] However, it is fundamental to not forget that it was the inflation that preceded it that had enabled the Weimar Republic to survive.

---

[6]Regarding this "optimistic" view as early as 1930 Graham (1930, p. 320) claimed that "... domestic [German] production seems on the whole to have been greater than it would have been attained if the currency had been solidly based on gold."

[7]Various reasons have been given for the negative effects of hyperinflation on the solidity of the Weimar Republic according to Bresciani-Turroni (1937). Several other scholars argued, however, that hyperinflation, having eroded the financial wealth of rentiers and flattened wages and salaries differentials, had humiliated and proletarianized the middle class. The consequences of this are well

From this perspective, the hyperinflation of 1923, like the crisis of 1931 and Brüning's fiscal policy, can be seen as the degeneration of a process that had allowed the Weimar regime to manage the social and political conflict that would otherwise have undermined its existence.

The historical experience of the Weimar Republic is full of indications for situations we experience today. It is useful to explain the causes and consequences of sudden stops, i.e. sudden changes in the direction of capital flows from abroad: an experience which in this phase of globalization has affected several emerging economies and, more recently, advanced countries.

The Weimar experience certainly helps to understand how forms of persistent inflation that in the past decades have characterized and still characterize emerging countries, particularly in Latin America, can transform into hyperinflation, and the importance in these cases of foreign financial support. This support, however, has temporary effectiveness if it is not associated with the resolution of internal social conflicts. When this does not happen and social consensus is not consolidated, political and economic imbalances re-emerge with destructive effects also on an institutional level. Commitments in the management of economic policy, such as the independence of central banks or international agreements' constraints, are not sufficient to guarantee optimal economic choices. Politics in all its components, domestic and foreign, has the upper hand over the economy and inspires choices that appear irrational, not responsive to the well-being of society.

The rest of the book is divided into six chapters. Chapter 2 is dedicated to inflation in the years immediately following the First World War. The high inflation of these years, even if, as Feldman (1993) claims, had its origins in the methods of financing the war, guaranteed relative social peace. In Chap. 3, we show how in the long run, following the increasingly efficient indexation of wages, inflation became persistent. Chapter 4 traces the origin of the hyperinflation of 1923 to a sudden stop. Price growth took on an explosive character when, following the initial acceleration of inflation, a vicious circle began between wages, prices, and the exchange rate. Chapter 5 shows how the stabilization of late 1923 and early 1924, unlike what Sargent (1982) claimed, had non-negligible economic and social costs in the medium-long term. The relative stagnation of the German economy in the second half of the 1920s is analyzed in Chap. 6 and is traced back to a form of Dutch disease due to the huge inflows of capital from abroad which Germany benefited from in those years. In Chap. 7, we focus on the currency and banking crisis of 1931. The interpretation of this crisis first of all as a currency crisis allows us to reconsider the *Borchardt debate*, taking into account the political constraints of an internal and foreign nature that conditioned the choices of Brüning's policy.

---

illustrated by Lionel Robbins (1937, p. 6) when he writes: "... It [hyperinflation] destroyed the wealth of the more solid elements in German society: and it left behind a moral and economic disequilibrium, apt breeding ground for the disasters which have followed. Hitler is the foster-child of the inflation."

References

Bessel, R. (1990). Why did the Weimar Republic collapse? In I. Kershaw (Ed.), *Weimar: Why did German democracy fail?* St. Martin's Press.

Borchardt, K. ([1980], 1991b). The economic causes of the collapse of the Weimar Republic. In K. Borchardt (Ed.), *Perspectives on Modern German Economic History and Policy*, Cambridge University Press. English translation from K. Borchardt (1980), Wirtschaftliche Ursachen des Scheiterns der Weimarer Republik, in K.D. Erdmann, & H. Schulze (Eds.), *Weimar, Selbstpreisgabe eimer Demokratie. Eine Bilanz heute*, Droste. Reprinted in 1982 in K. Borchardt (Ed.), *Wachstum, Krisen, und Hundlungsspielräume der Wirtschaftspolitik.* Vandenhoeck & Ruprecht.

Bresciani-Turroni, C. (1937). *The economics of inflation: A study of currency depreciation in post-war Germany.* Allen & Unwin.

Feldman, G. D. (1983). The historians and the German inflation. In N. Schmukler & E. Marcus (Eds.), *Inflation through the ages: Economic, social, psychological and historical aspects.* Columbia University Press.

Feldman, G. D. (1993). *The great disorder: Politics, economics, and society in the German Inflation, 1914–1924.* Oxford University Press.

Graham, F. D. (1930). *Exchange, prices, and production in hyper-inflation: Germany, 1920–1923.* Princeton University Press.

James, H. (1986). *The German slump, politics and economics, 1924–36.* Clarendon Press.

Kruedener, J. B. (1990). Introduction: The 'Borchardt Debate' on the failure of economic policy at the end of the Weimar Republic. In J. B. Kruedener (Ed.), *Economic crisis and political collapse: The Weimar Republic 1924–1933.* St. Martin's Press.

Kunz, A. (1986). *Civil servants and the politics of inflation in Germany, 1914–1924.* De Gruyter.

Ritschl, A. (1996). *Was Schacht right? Reparations, the Young plan and the great depression in Germany.* Available on line at https://personal.lse.ac.uk/ritschl/pdf_files/schacht2.pdf

Ritschl, A. (2002). *Deutschlands Krise und Konjunktur, 1924–1934: Binnenkonjunktur, Auslandsverschuldung und Reparationsproblem zwischen Dawes-Plan und Transfersperre.* Akademie Verlag.

Robbins, L. (1937). Foreword. In C. Bresciani-Turroni. *The economics of inflation.* Allen & Unwin.

Sargent, T. J. (1982). The ends of four big hyperinflations. In R. E. Hall (Ed.), *Inflation: Causes and effects.* University of Chicago Press.

Schnabel, I. (2004). The German twin crisis of 1931. *Journal of Economic History, 64*, 822–871.

Schuker, J. A. (1988). American 'Reparations' to Germany, 1919-33: Implications for the Third-World debt crisis. Princeton Studies in International Finance, 61.

Chapter 2
The Inflation of the Early Years of the Weimar Republic

2.1 Introduction

At the end of October 1918, as the First World War was coming to an end, an attempt was made to turn Germany into a parliamentary monarchy. In the following days, about a thousand sailors were arrested for mutiny and strikes and riots spread throughout the country. Councils, modelled on the soviets of the 1917 Russian Revolution, made up of soldiers and workers were formed and took power in many German cities. In this climate of widespread unrest, and under pressure from US President Wilson, on 9 November Kaiser Wilhelm II abdicated. On the same day, a Republic was proclaimed and the role of head of the government was given to Friedrich Ebert, leader of the SPD (Sozialdemokratische Partei Deutschlands: Social Democratic Party) (Table 2.1).

The more radical component of the SPD, the USPD (Unabhängige Sozialdemokratische Partei Deutschlands: Independent Social Democratic Party), had already separated from the main group, and counter proposed the establishment of a socialist republic. On 11 November, Germany signed the armistice declaring its surrender and, after several months of negotiations, the Allies signed the Treaty of Versailles on 28 June 1919, which was ratified by Germany on the 9 July. However, the harshness of the terms of the Treaty shocked the German public, who saw it as an unjust humiliation inflicted on Germany. The press blamed Minister Erzberger for signing it, and organizations on both right and left joined in the condemnation, helping to instill in the people the idea that the German army had not been defeated on the battlefield, but rather had been "stabbed in the back." From this perspective, the Reparations to the German people not only appeared unjust, but also humiliating. This belief made the various interest groups unwilling to accept sacrifices to pay for Reparations, since the acceptance of these sacrifices would have meant, in fact, the implicit recognition of the Treaty of Versailles. In large sections of the population, the government representatives who had accepted and signed the Armistice of Compiègne and the Treaty were perceived as traitors to the fatherland.

G. B. Pittaluga, E. Seghezza, *An Economic Historiography of Germany, 1918-1931*, Frontiers in Economic History, https://doi.org/10.1007/978-3-031-70347-8_2

Table 2.1 German governments during the early years of Weimar Republic (1919–1922)

Chancellor	Date of entry into office	USPD	SPD	Zentrum	DDP	DVP	BVP	DNVP	WP	NSDAP	% of Parliament seats
Ebert	11/9/1919	R	X								–
Scheidemann	2/13/1919		X	R	R						78.1
Bauer	6/21/1919		X	R							60.3
Muller	3/27/1920		X	R	R						78.1
Fehrenbach	6/25/1920			X	R	R					36.6
Wirth	5/10/1921		R	X	R						44.7
Wirth	10/26/1921 11/14/1922		R	X	R						44.7

Source: Notermans (2000). Legenda: X, Party of Prime Minister; R, Party represented in coalition. USPD, Unabhängige Sozialdemokratische Partei Deutschlands (Independent Social Democratic Party); SPD, Sozialdemokratische Partei Deutschlands (Social Democratic Party); Zentrumpartei (Center Party: a Catholic party); DDP, Deutsche Democratische Partei (German Democratic Party: a liberal-socialist party); DVP, Deutsche Volkspartei (German People's Party: a center-right party supporting right-liberalism); BVP, Bayerische Volkspartei (Bavarian People's Party: a conservative party based mainly in Bavaria); DNVP, Deutschnationale Volkspartei (German National People's Party: an authoritarian and radical right party); WP, Wirtschaftspartei (Business Party: a tough conservative party; NSDAP, Nationalsozialistische Deutsche Arbeiterpartei (National Socialist German Workers' Party: the Nazi party)

The issue of Reparations heavily influenced German policy in the years following the First World War. Inevitably, the question of whether Germany was unable or unwilling to pay the sums that the Allies had imposed was, and remains, the subject of much debate. For a long time, the thesis put forward by Keynes in *The Economic Consequences of Peace* prevailed, however in more recent years the hypothesis of those who believe that Germany, irrespective of whether it could support the Reparations financially, could not support them politically, has found increasing credence. This unwillingness to pay was the result of myths promulgated and widely accepted in German society regarding the reasons for Germany's defeat linked with the bitter social and political conflicts that threatened the survival of the Republic. Until 1923, the struggle between interest groups over the distribution of income was blunted by the use of high inflation, which enabled the state to maintain a reasonable level of social calm and allowed the Weimar Republic to survive.

2.2 The Economic Implications of the November 1918 Revolution and the Weimar Constitution

The First World War ended on November 11, 1918 when representatives of the Allies and Germany signed the Armistice Agreement. A few days earlier, on 9 November to be precise, the German Republic had been proclaimed. In the Reichstag the Social Democratic Party (SPD) had a relative majority. The leaders of this party started negotiations with the radical left-wing component, the Independent Social Democratic Party (USPD) for the formation of a purely socialist government of the German Reich. On the basis of this, a provisional government called the Council of People's Deputies was formed on 10 November.[1]

The economic and social situation was critical. "Food, fuel, and clothes were very scarce immediately after the war, and when the blockade ceased and imports might have filled the gaps, the low level of real wages prevented much improvement in the standard of living."[2]

Faced with the risk of a "Bolshevik" revolution, the bourgeoisie and, in particular, industrialists, chose to collaborate with the SPD and the General German Trade Union (Allgemeiner Deutscher Gewerkschaftsbund: ADGB), i.e., the trade union that supported the SPD, in order to marginalize the USPD and the radical left.[3]

Out of this collaboration came the Stinnes–Legien Agreement, signed on 15 November 1918, which included the industrialists' acceptance nationwide of the unions as legitimate workers' organizations, instituted collective bargaining, and limited the working day to 8 h. In addition to this, industrialists and trade unions joined together in the so-called Central Labor Council

[1] See Breitman (1981) and Huber (1988).

[2] See Kuczynski (1925, p. 7).

[3] See, among others, Winkler (1987).

(Zentralarbeitsgemeinschaft—ZAG), whose aim was to institutionalize collaboration between these interest groups and to make the government face the fact that in Germany the power was of "the united employers and workers."[4] These arrangements represented the start of an implicit alliance between the productive classes, in particular between industrialists and workers. The latter had as their main objective to recover the pre-war real wage. Industrialists were relatively supportive of this goal, seeing it as the price to be paid to prevent the spread of discontent among workers reducing support for the radical left and averting a potential Bolshevik revolution. "... [C]ollaboration between capital and labor in the early years of the Weimar Republic was facilitated by industry's fear that something far more disastrous than welfare reform, namely outright revolution, might confront it in the absence of compromise."[5]

The Stinnes–Legien agreement illustrated the views of most of the leaders of the SPD and unions, who believed that a socialist economy could not be established immediately, but only after a long process of evolution and that, to achieve this, maintaining good relations between workers and employers was crucial.

A minority part of the SPD, the USPD and the radical left were, on the other hand, in favor of revolutionary changes in the economy, in particular the extensive use of nationalization and the "socialization" of the production process. On 18 November, the Council of People's Deputies decided that the socialization of the main branches of the economy should be initiated.

A commission consisting of economists and representatives of employers and employees was set up for this purpose with the task of suggesting concrete measures to be taken. In the Work Programme of the Socialization Commission published on December 11, 1918, it was specified that the prerequisite for the reorganization of the economy was the resumption of production and that socialization would only affect those sectors where monopoly conditions prevailed.

A significant proportion of the members of the Socialization Commission, including Hilferding and Kautsky, insisted that mineral resources, in particular coal-mining, should be nationalized immediately. These enterprises were to be expropriated and managed by a single autonomous economic cooperative (the Deutsche Kohlengemeinschaft: the German Coal Association) which was to be controlled by the management of the firms, their employees, the state, and the purchasers of coal.

The government considered this proposal of the Socialization Commission to be too radical and tried to slow down the implementation of the Commission's proposals. There were two main reasons for this. Firstly, the government considered it a priority to increase coal production to meet public demand and was well aware that the proposed management changes resulting from nationalization would jeopardize this objective. Secondly, the results of the January 1919 elections, in which the SPD and USPD had obtained 37.9 and 7.6% of the vote, respectively, shifted the balance

[4] See Feldman (1977, p. 82).

[5] See Geary (1990, p. 99).

in favor of the moderate socialists, i.e. those who preferred the consolidation of a parliamentary democracy rather than a soviet-style council system.[6]

The shift of the political balance within the left also marked the end of the Socialization Commission, which resigned on 3 February 1919. Although this Commission did not lead to concrete policy measures,[7] it did, however, have a significant indirect influence on the Weimar Constitution. Section five of this document, i.e. the section on the economy, was significantly influenced by these ideas. Indeed, the idea that, in the economic sphere, politics should play a predominant role in the allocation of resources pervaded the constitution of the Weimar Republic as approved by the German parliament on 11 August 1919.[8]

In fact, Article 151 of the new Constitution stated: "The management of economic life must correspond to the principles of justice with the goal of securing a basis of existence that encompasses human dignity. Within this limit, the economic freedom of individuals is to be secured." On the basis of this general principle, Article 153 provided that for the pursuit of the "general good," private property could be expropriated either with or without financial compensation.

The Weimar Constitution also allowed the government and parliament to intervene not only in the allocation of resources, but also in the distributive process, facilitating the resolution of conflicts between different interest groups. Article 156 stipulated that "[t]he Reich may also in case of urgent necessity for socioeconomic interests, by law effect a combination of economic enterprises and associations on the basis of self-administration with the object of securing the cooperation of all working elements of the population, of allowing employers and employees a share in the management and regulating the production, fabrication, distribution, utilization, price fixing ...".

With this in mind, farmers expected the government to set favorable food prices. Business leaders demanded subsidies to support foreign competition. Workers and their representatives demanded that wages be set not by the market, but by government arbitration of labor disputes. One of the SPD leaders, the economist Rudolf Hilferding, even proposed the introduction of the "political wage."

The above picture shows how the solution of social conflict in the Weimar Republic was, to a large extent, entrusted to the government. Dissatisfaction with the solutions to conflicts provided by the political class over time became distrust of democratic institutions themselves and was one of the causes of their collapse.

The ideology underlying the Socialization Commission was also behind the takeover by the state administration of enterprises operating in sectors of "public" interest which resulted in the transfer into the ownership of the Reich, states, and

---

[6] See Winkler (1993) and Frambach (2019).

[7] The failure of the Socialization Commission can be traced to several causes. Firstly, to the absence of a clear political majority in favour of the socialization of the means of production. Secondly, there was the realization that managerial skills were lacking in the trade unions and bureaucracy. The expropriation of big business would have led to the collapse of the German economy. See Frambach (2019).

[8] See, among others, Bessel (1997, p. 241) and James (2007).

municipalities of enterprises that operated public services and utilities, such as railways, local transport, gas, and waterworks.[9]

2.3 The Effects of the Treaty of Versailles and Reparations on German Politics and Economy

In the first days of November 1918, the imperial government under Prince Max von Baden entrusted Matthias Erzberger of the Zentrum, the Catholic Centre Party, with the task of negotiating an armistice with the Allies, which was signed on 11 November and included a commitment that the peace Treaty would bring about a fair peace in accordance with the 14 points set out by President Wilson. The Peace Treaty, the outcome of the Versailles negotiations, was submitted to the Germans for signature on 7 May 1919. It foresaw the surrender of substantial territorial control,[10] limits on the number of naval vessels and German army personnel. In addition, Article 231 of the Treaty stipulated that all responsibilities for the war and its material and immaterial costs fell on Germany, which was therefore obliged to pay substantial Reparations to the Allies. The severity of the Treaty's terms shocked politicians and the German public, who considered it very far from the "fair peace" that the Allies had promised when the Armistice was signed.

Art. 231 legitimized the Allies demand for huge Reparations from Germany stating: "The Allied and associated governments... require, and Germany undertakes, that she will make compensation for all damage done to the civilian population of the Allied and Associated Powers and to their property during the period of belligerency ..."

Unlike on past occasions, this article required Germany to pay not only the war costs incurred by the Allies, but also the damage that the war had inflicted on the civilian population of these countries. The detailed list of these types of damage was contained in Annex I to the Treaty. The monetary amount of the damage, although left to be determined by an Inter-Allied Commission—called the Reparations Commission—by May 1, 1921 (Art. 233), was clearly vast.[11] Because of this, the head of the German delegation Brockdorff-Rantzau refused to sign it and shortly afterwards, on 20 June, resigned as Foreign Minister. The Treaty was then signed on 28 June by German Finance Minister Erzberger.

---

[9] See Stolper (1967).

[10] Germany was forced to cede territory to Belgium, Czechoslovakia, and Poland, to return Alsace and Lorraine to France, and to cede the government of its colonies to the League of Nations. At the same time, the Treaty provided for Danzig to become a Free City, for the Rhineland to be demilitarized, and for the Saar region to be under French control. Finally, it was stipulated that the future of certain regions, such as Upper Silesia, would be decided by plebiscites.

[11] See Fulda (2009, p. 50ff).

The Treaty of Versailles and the Reparations had major effects on both German politics and its economy. Politically, the prevailing myths about the reasons for the defeat and about Article 231 of the Treaty conditioned the entire life of the Republic and the policy choices of its governments. Economically, the Reparations, especially for the first few years, were a very significant burden on the German economy, though scholars are still divided on the question of whether Germany was economically unable to pay them, given their onerousness, or more simply did not want to pay them, considering them unjust.

2.3.1 The Treaty of Versailles and the Myth of Germany Being "Stabbed in the Back"

The conditions of the Treaty of Versailles were seen by the German people, regardless of political viewpoint, as humiliating and unjustified. This view was shared across the entire political spectrum[12] and was fueled by widely believed delusions, the main one being the "stabbed-in-the-back" myth. The German High Command had hidden the increasing difficulties of its army from the public[13] so the call for an armistice on 3 October fell like a thunderbolt on an incredulous German people, who, since they had had no warning and had never seen enemy troops on their own soil, could not accept that the demand for an armistice and the eventual surrender be explained simply as a defeat.

Re-enforcing this incredulity, the German command claimed that the army had not been beaten on the battlefield and that the reasons for the defeat were non-military. Ludendorff, the de facto highest commander of Germany's troops, said in a confidential conversation with his officers that at some point it had become impossible to continue the war because of the pacifist poison of "Marxist-Socialist propaganda."[14] On December 10, 1918, Friedrich Ebert, the Social Democratic chairman of the provisional government, speaking to the troops also supported the idea that the German army had not been defeated on the battlefields with these words: "Let me extend a cordial welcome to your soldiers ... No enemy defeated you: It was only when the superior strength of the adversary grew overwhelming, we had to give up." These words, at least in part, indicate an acceptance of the "stabbed-in-the-back" theory (the Dolchstoßlegende).[15]

The theory was also fed by Field Marshall Paul Hindenburg in his testimony on 18 November 1919 to the Commission on the Causes of Defeat, when he claimed

[12] See, among others, Heinemann (1983).

[13] See Deist (1986).

[14] See Barth (2003, p. 81–84).

[15] Appropriately, Barth (2003, p. 212 ff.) notes that Ebert's words are a confirmation of the secret alliance between the Social Democratic and the military leadership against the German Bolsheviks.

that the stabbed-in-the-back image had been suggested to him by a senior British officer.[16]

In this climate, it is not surprising that the armistice was seen by the German public as a victory for the defeatists,[17] and that, a few months later, the government's acceptance of the Treaty of Versailles appeared to the public as a further example of being "stabbed-in-the-back."[18]

The other widely held belief that marked the years of the Weimar Republic was the rejection of "war guilt," the disavowal of Article 231 of the Treaty. This article, added to the Treaty by the Allies to legitimize the demand for Reparations, was seen by the German public, besides unjust, as an unjust humiliation.[19] Throughout the Paris negotiations, the German government was unanimous in demanding the deletion of the article[20] a demand which the Allies rejected.

Both the "stabbed-in-the-back" and the "war guilt" myths soon became major issues in German politics and impacted heavily on government decision-making, as well as later being used by Hitler in his rise to power.[21] The Germans, widely believing these myths, remained in a sort of "delusional state," a condition which was actively encouraged by politicians who, to gain support, simply repeated what the public wanted to hear. As Bessel (1993, p. 283) wrote: "Instead of facing the uncomfortable fact that the war and its legacy had limited their options, Germans retreated into an illusory world in which their problems were invariably the fault of others and, by extension, would be eliminated if only the external burden, imposed by the vengeful Allies, could be lifted."

The two myths described above led to "... the internal rejection of the Paris peace"[22] and convinced the German public that the Reparations demanded by the Allies should not be paid.[23] The result was widespread resistance to the adoption of fiscal adjustment measures: acceptance of the burdens of these measures implicitly amounted to recognition of the Treaty and its requests of Reparations.

Public opinion in the Allied countries was radically different, where, given the war damage suffered, the public called for exemplary punishment for Germany. As noted by Marks (1998, p. 339): "Curiously, it was usually in the political interests of both German and Allied leaders to obscure reality and to present Reparations demands as more onerous than they actually were. Leaders of continental victor

[16] Krumeich (2001, p. 593) quotes Hindenburg's words: "Our repeated request for the maintenance of stern discipline and the strict application of the law met with no results. Our operations in consequence failed, as they were bound to, and the collapse became inevitable. The Revolution was merely the last straw. As an English general has very much said: the German Army was stabbed in the back."

[17] See Hiller von Gaertringen (1963, p. 124–126).

[18] See Hiller von Gaertringen (1963, p. 139).

[19] See Marks (2013, p. 642).

[20] See Schwabe (1985), Jäger (1984, p. 26 ff.) and Heinemann (1983, p. 31 ff.).

[21] See Hunt (1958) and Schwabe (2014).

[22] See Mommsen (1989, p. 91).

[23] See, among others, Klein (1998).

states needed to convince their electorate that they had obtained considerably more than they really had; Weimar politicians equally exaggerated both to tell the German people what they wanted to hear about the horrors of Versailles and to convince world opinion that Reparations were unjust and unpayable. Thus, the orchestrations of both sides combined to heighten the distortion."

The aforementioned myths clouded German public judgement, in particular that of "stabbed-in-the-back," and not only hindered the adoption of corrective fiscal measures, but also affected the cohesion of German society and in the long run undermined the stability of the Republic. The nationalist right, having adopted these two myths, tended to accuse the SPD of accepting the Treaty and thus of betraying the country. Since the establishment of the Republic had been supported primarily by the Social Democrats, this was an implicit disavowal not only of the government's policies but, more profoundly, of the republic itself. "Already during the 'good years,' the elites were looking to challenge the political and social compromise of the 1918 settlement ... [T]he sections of society with the greatest influence on the levers of power—many business leaders, landowners, military top-brass, and some figures in prominent positions in the civil service—were increasingly determined to exploit the crisis in order to overthrow Weimar democracy ... and restore some form of authoritarian rule."[24]

Even with formal institutions in place, a democratic regime cannot survive long if it lacks a sense of general support. The latter is "... essential to overcoming the bitter class interests dividing the republic and to building a unified society to embody the Volksgemeinschaft."[25] In the absence of this, political competition between the various interest groups becomes unbridled and unregulated and, in such a context, civil society often collapses into dictatorship.[26]

2.3.2 *The Treaty as a Carthaginian Peace*

The first strong criticism of the economic implications of the draft Treaty came from the German government. In a letter to Clemenceau, the head of the German delegation, Brockdorff-Rantzau, said: "The German Peace delegation had completed its first examination of the conditions of peace which were handed to it ... [I]t was not prepared to see that the promise given expressly to the German people and to all mankind would be rendered illusory in this fashion. The draft Treaty contains

[24] See Kershaw (1990, p. 18).

[25] See Huges (2021, p. 42).

[26] The collapse of the Republic did not result, as Abraham (1981) argues, from an excessive fragmentation of the social classes. Indeed, where democratic institutions are recognized as legitimate, competition between interest groups allows for alternation and increases the possibility of exercising countervailing power (Dahl, 1971). Such competition, however, to be compatible with democracy presupposes the recognition by the competing interest groups of a general interest (Berman, 1997).

demands which are not tolerable to any people. Much of it, moreover, in the opinion of our experts, is not possible of fulfilment."[27] Despite these critical remarks by the German delegation, the final version of the Treaty remained substantially unchanged from its first draft.

The German delegation's view that the economic demands of the Treaty were unsustainable for Germany was shared by Keynes who had participated in the Paris negotiations as a member of the British delegation, and given that he did not share the approach of the negotiations he resigned in June 1919 and in December of that year published *The Economic Consequences of Peace*.[28] A book which quickly became an international best-seller.

Keynes, on the basis of Article 232 of the Treaty, calculated that the damages that might be charged to Germany would total perhaps £3000 million for physical damage and another £5000 million for pensions and allowances, or up to £8 million pounds.[29]

He estimated the upper limit of Germany's payment capacity at £2 million pounds (almost $10 billion dollars or 50 billion gold marks).[30] Therefore, "[a] capacity of £8,000,000 [about 40 billion dollars] or even of £5,000,000 [about 25 billion dollars] is not within the limits of reasonable possibility."[31] Given the difference between the Reparations required and what Germany could, in his assessment, realistically afford to pay, Keynes defined the Treaty a "Carthaginian Peace,"[32] the effort to pay the Reparations would have reduced Germany to extreme poverty.[33]

Germany's efforts to pay Reparations would have had serious economic and political consequences for the whole of Europe. According to Keynes writing in *The Economic Consequences*, a stable peace in Europe depended on the reconstruction of the international economic relations in which Germany had played a crucial role. The Treaty was, therefore, a major obstacle to economic reconstruction and would have contributed to exacerbating the monetary disorder with which the major countries of the old continent were afflicted due to the large amounts of war debt incurred. Widespread and high inflation would, according to Keynes have resulted in: "As the inflation proceeds and the real value of the currency fluctuates wildly from month to month, all permanent relations between debtors and creditors, which form the ultimate foundation of capitalism, become so utterly disordered as to

[27] See Brockdorff-Rantzau to Clemenceau, May 9, 1919, reprinted in Burnett (1940, p. 1–2).

[28] See Keynes (1919 [1920]).

[29] See Keynes (1919 [1920, p. 62–63]).

[30] See Keynes (1919 [1920, p. 53]).

[31] See Keynes (1919 [1920, p. 80]).

[32] More precisely "the Carthaginian Peace of Mr. Clemenceau." See Keynes (1919 [1920, p. 26]).

[33] "The policy of reducing Germany to servitude for a generation, of degrading the lives of millions of human beings, and of depriving a whole nation of happiness should be abhorred and detestable even if it were possible, even if it enriched ourselves, even if it did not sow the decay of the whole civilized life of Europe. Some preach it in the name of justice." Keynes (1919 [1920, p. 88]).

be almost meaningless; and the process of wealth-getting degenerates into a gamble and a lottery."[34]

To remedy this grave risk, Keynes proposed a revision of the Treaty that provided a settlement of inter-Ally indebtedness, the granting of an international loan to Germany, and a monetary reorganization of Europe, as well as measures to revitalize intra-European trade.[35]

Keynes shared, therefore, the words of Count Brockdorff-Rantzau, the head of the German delegation, who—presenting to the Peace Conference of the Allied Powers the report of the German Economic Commission charged with studying the effects of the conditions of the Treaty—said: "... after the economic depression resulting from the loss of her colonies, her merchant fleet and her foreign investments, Germany will not be in a position to import from abroad an adequate quantity of raw material. An enormous part of Germany's industry will, therefore, be condemned inevitably to destruction. The need of importing food-stuffs will increase considerably at the same time that the possibility of satisfying this demand is as greatly diminished ... [t]o put the peace conditions into execution would logically involve, therefore, the loss of several millions of persons in Germany ...".[36]

The position expressed by Keynes in *The Economic Consequences* coincided substantially with that of the German counterproposal to the Allies.[37] In particular, he shared the view of the German experts who had drafted the Supplement on Financial Questions according to which, following the imposition of Reparations on Germany, "... great deliveries of natural products can only take place if the state reimburses the producers for their value; this means issues of notes ...".[38] These implied that "the depreciation of the mark would continue. The instability of the currency would affect not only Germany, however, but all the countries engaged in export, for Germany, with her currency constantly depreciating, would be a disturbing element and would be forced to flood the world market with goods at ridiculously low prices."[39] This same conviction, in December 1919, was clearly expressed by Robert Schmidt the Minister of Economics of the Wirth government, according to whom: "... the tossing out of Germany goods abroad at slaughter price ... will compel the Entente to allow us to bring our exchange in order."[40]

It was on this reasoning, shared by Keynes, that was based the strategy of "fulfilment" adopted by Germany when it became clear that the Treaty would not be revised. There was a belief on the part of the German elite that the high depreciation of the mark attributable to Reparations and a significant increase in

[34] See Keynes (1919 [1920, p. 92]). Röpke (1931) shares the Keynes's view on Reparations.

[35] See Keynes (1919 [1920], p. 98 ff.).

[36] See Keynes (1919 [1920, p. 90]).

[37] See Ferguson (1995b, 1998).

[38] See Lukau (1941, p. 384).

[39] See Lukau (1941, p. 384).

[40] Quoted in Ferguson (1995b, p. 377).

the German inflation rate would convince the Allies that the indemnity they demanded from Germany was unsustainable.

Keynes took up the problem of Reparations after the publication of the London Schedule of Payments in *Revision of the Treaty*[41] which he considered the sequel to the *Economic Consequences of Peace*. In this book, he reiterated that the amount of Reparations imposed on Germany was unsustainable. This was mainly for two reasons. On the one hand, there was the problem of the budget. Servicing the debt was partly covered by taxes, the revenue from which was in paper marks and thus eroded by inflation, while on the other hand, German liabilities, i.e. Reparations, were in gold marks. If there was an imbalance between revenue and expenditure, the German government would have to cut expenditure or increase revenue, deciding which interest groups would bear the burden of the adjustment. In correspondence with such decisions "the struggle will be bitter and violent, for it will present itself to each of the contesting interests as an affair of life and death."[42]

Secondly, Keynes reproposed the classical "transfer problem" giving an extensive illustration of it in two contributions in the *Economic Journal* at the time of Young Plan's negotiations.[43] According to Keynes, the payment of Reparations would have meant a "secondary burden" for Germany in terms of trade deterioration in addition to the primary burden of the transfer itself. In fact, the need to achieve a trade surplus would have forced Germany to reduce the prices of exported goods. This would have resulted in a further reduction of the country's economic wellbeing. Ohlin (1929), in an article in the same Journal,[44] countered Keynes' view by arguing that, if income effects were taken into account, the payment of Reparations would have occurred without any change in the relative prices of imports and exports. In fact, an increase in taxes in Germany would have automatically led to a decrease in demand for imports. While the effect of this money in the countries receiving the Reparations would have meant an increase in their demand for German exports, hence the resulting trade surplus would have enabled Germany to pay the Reparations.

2.4 Criticism of *The Economic Consequences* and the Actual Burden of Reparations

Despite the initial extremely favorable reactions to the *Economic Consequences*, over time numerous criticisms were made of Keynes' position on German Reparations. Within these criticisms, three different threads can be distinguished.

---

[41] See Keynes (1922).

[42] See Keynes (1922, p. 79).

[43] See Keynes (1929a, b).

[44] See Ohlin (1929).

A first type of criticism concerns Keynes' claim that the amount of Reparations was unsustainable for Germany. Mantoux (1946) was the first to challenge Keynes' calculation of the incidence of Reparations annuity on the German national income. In his opinion, Keynes had underestimated the latter[45] and, as a result of this underestimation, Keynes estimated that the incidence of Reparations annuity on the national income was close to 25%. On the basis of more recent estimates, based on more accurate calculations of German national income, this ratio ranged between 5 and 10%.[46] In Mantoux's opinion, therefore, in contrast to Keynes' view, Germany could, economically, have supported the payment of Reparations. Mantoux's remarks on *The Economic Consequences* already found several supporters at the time his book was published.[47]

Mantoux's conclusions have been corroborated in recent studies.[48] Ritschl (2005, p. 89), in particular, has shown that the incidence of the total amount of Reparations and the German national debt[49] on 1913 GNP was 309%. In contrast, the incidence of the amount of the Reparations deemed unavoidable[50] in the London Schedule Payments (amounting to 50 billion gold marks) and the pre-existing national debt (amounting to 25.2 billion gold marks) on 1913 GNP was 147%. Little different from that of the victorious countries such as France (135%[51]) and England (144%[52]).[53] As Ferguson (1995b, p. 378) assesses: "The truth was that the economic consequences of peace were far less severe for Germany than Keynes had claimed."

Taking account of these reasons, the problem of Reparations payment appears eminently as a political problem rather than an economic one.[54] According to Marks (1978, 2003), if Germany had taxed its citizens as France and England did, the income of its citizens would have decreased, redirecting economic activity toward exports, the budget would have been rebalanced and the mark stabilized. Similarly, Keylor (1998, p. 502) believes that "... a relatively moderate increase in taxation and reduction in consumption in the Weimar Republic would have yielded the

[45] Even Moggridge (1992, p.372), one of Keynes' most important biographers acknowledges that the estimates of the German national income used in *A Revision of the Treaty* were wrong.

[46] See Holtfrerich (1986), Ferguson (1998) and Webb (1986).

[47] See, among others, Viner (1947), Ensor (1946) and Dalton (1946).

[48] See, among others, Marks (1978, 2003), Ritschl (2005) and Schuker (1980). For a presentation of the recent views of the Versailles Treaty and Reparations debate see Boemeke et al. (1998).

[49] 1920 national debt at gold parity

[50] The difference between Reparation debt avoidable and unavoidable is illustrated in Sect. 2.5.

[51] 1920 French national debt on 1913 GNP at gold parity.

[52] 1920 British national debt on 1913 GNP at gold parity.

[53] It should, however, be pointed out that Germany's Reparations debt differed from the public debt of other countries in two respects. Firstly, it was expressed in gold marks and, therefore, could not be eroded by inflation or other forms of financial repression, whereas that of the other countries was in their national currency. Second, unlike the debt of the Allied countries, Germany's Reparations were not only debts owed to non-residents but were to be paid by a defeated country to its victors.

[54] On this point, see, among others, Steiner (2005, p. 606).

requisite export surplus to generate the foreign exchange needed to service the Reparation debt."[55]

Why, then, was this policy not pursued? The main reason was the elite's fear that corrective fiscal measures, by increasing the economic and social hardship of workers, would encourage the emergence of greater support for the radical left and, potentially, provoke a revolutionary coup. The risk attributed to this eventuality and the measures adopted to reduce it highlight the fragmentation of German society, in which a sense of general shared interest was lacking and the spirit of national community was dormant.

A second criticism of *The Economic Consequences* concerns its consequences. The resonance of *The Economic Consequences of Peace* internationally was considerable. By 1924, the book had been translated into 11 languages[56] and its success was particularly impressive in the United States where opponents of President Wilson made good use of Keynes' fierce sarcasm[57] against him.[58] The position Keynes took on the Treaty, while reinforcing the opposition's criticism of President Wilson's conduct at the Paris Conference,[59] gave the United States arguments to justify its disengagement from European affairs and the question of the balance of power in the old continent.[60]

In England, Keynes' book was received as a confirmation of France's irrational intransigence toward Germany, Britain's most important trading partner. In the Anglo-Saxon countries, *The Economic Consequences* contributed to the "mea culpism," i.e. the feeling of guilt for the "unfair" treatment of Germany in the Treaty of Versailles, that pervaded England in the interwar period and contributed to Britain's weak resistance to Germany's increasing aggressiveness in the 1930s.[61]

As Viner writes (1947, p. 9) in his review of Mantoux's book: "But the guilt complex toward Germany and toward the Treaty of Versailles, which Keynes helped to establish in England and America; the grossly unfair caricature of the personality, the character, and the intellect of Woodrow Wilson, which is the most widely remembered part of his book on the Peace; his exaggerated account of the greed and intransigence of the French and of their obsession with a security bogey—these had long before contributed their weight to easing the path to world hegemony for a resurgent and Reparations free Nazi Germany."

[55] See Keylor (1998, p. 502).

[56] See Mantoux (1946, p. 6).

[57] He was equally harsh regarding the other heads of state, namely Lloyd George and Clemenceau who contributed to the drafting of the Treaty. In portraying these leaders Keynes was inspired by the style of "Eminent Victorians" by Lytton Strachey (1918).

[58] See Markwell (2006).

[59] See Markwell (2006).

[60] See Feldman (1993) and Ferguson (1995a).

[61] Ferguson (1998, p. 407) writes: "Keynes's attack on the Versailles Treaty without question contributed a good deal to that guilty feeling of having wronged Germany which so inhibited British diplomacy between the wars." See also Ferguson (1998, p. 399 ff.).

While it is true that Keynes contributed, as noted by Viner, a great deal to fueling the guilt complex toward Germany in the Anglo-Saxon countries, it is equally true that he cannot be blamed for the serious foreign policy mistakes of the United States and England in the interwar period.[62]

The third type of criticism concerns the theory of international relations underlying *The Economic Consequences* and the *Revision of the Treaty*. In several places in these works, Keynes emphasizes the fact that the Treaty of Versailles was inspired by the logic of power rather than the principles of cooperation between states. "The thoughts which I have expressed in the second Chapter were not present in the mind of Paris. The future life of Europe was not their concern, its means of livelihood was not their anxiety. Their preoccupations, good and bad alike, related to frontiers and nationalities, to the balance of power, to imperial aggrandizement, to the future enfeeblement of a strong and dangerous enemy ...".[63]

Clemenceau was emblematic of the policy underlying the Treaty, based on maintaining the balance of power: "His philosophy had, therefore, no place for 'sentimentality' in international relations. Nations are real things of whom you love one and feel for the rest indifference or hatred. The glory of the nation you love is a desirable end—but generally to be obtained at your neighbor's expense. The politics of power are inevitable, and there is nothing very new to learn about this war or the end it was fought for."[64]

Keynes strongly rejected an approach to international relations based on the principle of the balance of power, to which French Prime Minister Clemenceau was so firmly anchored. The rejection of this hypothesis stemmed in Keynes from the assumption that free trade would, on one hand, foster the growth of countries' income and thus their aggressiveness, but on the other, preserve peace through the growing economic interdependence of states. Thanks to the latter, according to him "... many of the boundaries between nations are being broken down and humanity was being induced to change its duties."[65] With this view he echoed a central tenet of the liberal economic orthodoxy that free trade promotes peace which was dominant among Cambridge economists in the early twentieth century.[66]

Following in this tradition, in *The Economic Consequences* Keynes shows that he believes that the main objective of a state is to maximize the income of its citizens.

---

[62] For an illustration of these errors, see Kissinger (1994).

[63] See Keynes (1919 [1920, p. 26]).

[64] See Keynes (1919 [1920, p. 17]).

[65] Paper on "Modern civilization" (dating from 1905) UA/22/1–10, KP; see also OC/5/103ff, KP.

[66] An example is Mill who writes (1848 [2004, p. 175]: "... [I]t may be said without exaggeration that the great extent and rapid increase of international trade, in being the principal guarantee of the peace of the world, is the great permanent security for the uninterrupted progress of the ideas, the institutions, and the character of the human race." Similar concepts are found in Sidgwick (1891) and Marshall (1919). As Skidelsky (1983) points out, the view that economic progress and the development of trade between countries favoured a moral improvement of mankind led Keynes to agree with much of what Angell (1909) argued, even though he disagreed with some of the extreme positions of liberal pacifism of which Angell became the promoter.

However, "... because states operate in an anarchic system, there is no night watchman to whom they can turn for help if another great power attacks them."[67] In this interpretation, economic interdependence does not prevent war; on the contrary, under certain circumstances, it can even promote it. Indeed, the gains from trade can be asymmetrical: one country gaining more from trade than another. In this case trade has a negative *security externality,*[68] where the asymmetric gains in trade can favor war via multiple paths. An example is the case where a country which has gained more from trade acquires resources and uses them in military aggression to impose its hegemony.[69]

There is no doubt that the late nineteenth century was a period of intense globalization. Between 1870 and 1913, North Atlantic transport costs fell by 45%, this substantial fall in transportation costs fostered a massive growth in international trade,[70] migration from European countries to other continents, and financial flows across countries.[71] However, interdependence created asymmetries in the independence of countries and their economic growth, inevitably affecting the balance of power.[72] Indeed, the high degree of interdependence in the decades before the First World War had mainly benefited Germany and, at a certain point, it demanded that its economic power be matched by similar power in the international arena.[73] No wonder, then, that the conventional view among most political scientists is that World War I constitutes a failure of the idea that economic integration maintains peace.[74]

Keynes in both *The Economic Consequences* and *Revision of the Treaty* systematically opposed the French Reparation policy.[75] However, in the 1970s, the opening of the French archives provided the opportunity to consult previously sealed

[67] See Mearsheimer (2001, p. 43).

[68] See Gilpin (1981, p. 130).

[69] Furthermore, trade interdependence may result from one country becoming dependent on imports of vital goods and services from another. In such a situation, the dependent country may be deprived of its independence from the other country or indeed may seek to conquer the country on which it is dependent. See Waltz (1979, p. 104).

[70] For the UK, the share of imports from and exports to Germany ranged between one fifth and one third of the total. See Mitchell and Deane (1962).

[71] See Maddison (1991) and Williamson and O'Rourke (1999).

[72] "If I depend more on you than you depend on me, you have more ways of influencing me and affecting my fate than I have of affecting yours" (See Waltz, 2000, p. 15–16). Somewhat similar considerations are made by Susan Strange (1996) with reference to recent globalization where she argues that markets have taken power away from states asymmetrically, that is to a greater extent from small states than from large ones.

[73] See Mearsheimer (2001).

[74] See, among others, Waltz (1979), Buzan (1984), Copeland (2000), Papayoanou (1999), Rowe (2005), and Mearsheimer (2001).

[75] Schuker (2014a, b) and Ferguson (1995a, b) trace Keynes' Germanophilia rather than to a scientific analysis of the facts to sentimental reasons, more precisely to his "affair" with the German financier Karl Melchior. This insinuation has been strongly contested by Moggridge and Skidelsky (2015) and in any case the motivations, whatever they were, of Keynes's viewpoint are irrelevant.

documents relating to international relations and foreign policy of the countries involved and has radically changed the debate on the Treaty of Versailles and German Reparations.[76] This information has resulted in a vast revisionist literature regarding Keynes' views and those of his contemporaries.[77] Within this new wave of studies, the changes in the balance of power that occurred after the First World War are emphasized.[78] In particular, great weight is placed on the fact that France, despite being among the victorious powers, was in a weaker position, with regard to its security, in 1919 than it had been in 1913. Indeed, as Kissinger (1994, p. 679) writes, "paradoxically, France's vulnerability and Germany's strategic advantage were both magnified by the Treaty of Versailles despite its punitive provisions. Before the war, Germany had faced strong neighbors in both the East and the West. It could not expand in either direction without encountering a major state—France, the Austro-Hungarian Empire, or Russia. But after the Treaty of Versailles, there was no longer a counterweight to Germany in the East. With France weakened, the Austro-Hungarian Empire dissolved, and Russia out of the picture for some time, there was simply no way of reconstructing the old balance of power, especially since the Anglo-Saxon powers refused to guarantee the Versailles settlement."

Being aware of his country's increased weakness, Clemenceau believed there were two possible means to guarantee its security in the years to come.[79] The first was the weakening of its former enemy through Treaty clauses that would reduce its military, economic, and territorial strength. The second consisted in strengthening the wartime alliance as a deterrent threat to Germany, whose possible aggressive intentions could be deterred by the superior military power of the Allies. The impracticability of this second alternative forced Clemenceau to focus on the first.

Therefore, a revisionist literature views French policy as rational, aimed at ensuring the country's international security, and blames English foreign policy, which considered France rather than Germany as the primary threat to the European balance of power, as entirely erroneous.[80] Thereby replacing France with Germany and England as the main obstacles to post-war stabilization.[81]

The UK's lack of consideration for France's security problems stemmed both from the need to re-establish the valuable pre-war trade with Germany and from the concern of the British elite, particularly Lloyd George, about the possible spread of

---

[76] See Feldman (1993, p. 309).

[77] A summary of this literature can be found in Jacobson (1983). As Steiner (2005, p. 606) writes: "The Versailles Treaty did not solve the German problem, but the traditional view that it was a Carthaginian peace needs to be abandoned."

[78] See, among others, Pittaluga (2022).

[79] On this aspect, see Stevenson (1998).

[80] With this in mind, Skidelsky (1983, p. 397), one of the most authoritative Keynes biographers, acknowledges that "recent scholarship based on French governmental as well as American and European banking archives is kinder to France's financial motives and logic than Keynes was. France claims for Reparations are now seen to be more modest and defensible than Britain's."

[81] See Trachtenberg (2000). The bad relations of Anglo-Saxons, in particular UK, and France were one of the main causes of the failure of the Gold Exchange Standard. See Pittaluga (2023).

Bolshevik regimes in Europe. This concern significantly influenced the Versailles negotiations, their outcome and the implementation of the Treaty.[82]

2.5 The Origin of the Early Twenties' Inflation

Despite the fact that the issue of Reparations had a major impact on Germany's international relations and domestic politics, the amount that Germany actually paid was relatively small. About 8 billion gold marks had been paid by Germany by May 1, 1921 even though the Treaty of Versailles stipulated that Germany should pay about 20 billion marks before that date. In early May 1921, the Schedule of Payments was published by the Reparations Commission, which fixed the Reparations at 132 billion gold marks. In reality, the Reparations were divided into three parts against which bonds were issued. The first portion of bonds, type "A," was intended to compensate the countries for the direct damage inflicted on them by Germany and amounted to 12 billion gold marks. The second portion, type "B," amounting to 38 billion gold marks was aimed at compensating the war debt that the Allies had incurred in World War I. Finally, the third portion, type "C" bonds, amounting to 82 billion gold marks, was to be paid to the Allies by Germany when the country had become sufficiently prosperous to bear the burden in addition to its senior debt. This last portion of the Reparations was symbolic in nature, intended more to assuage the resentment toward Germany of the Allied populations. According to Ritschl (2012, p. 945): ... "it was communicated to the Germans through diplomatic channels that the C bonds were not likely to ever be paid."[83]

Some of the Reparations were in kind, principally foreign assets. The London Schedule committed Germany to pay initially an annuity of two billion gold marks plus a variable quota of 26% of exports. As Schuker (1988, p. 17–18) writes: "If, however, one ... accepts the Reparation Commission export figures, it appears that under the London Schedule Germany would have had to pay Reparations amounting to 5.37% of 1921 national income at factor cost ... If the Allies had at length reduced the annuity to the indicated 3 milliard gold marks, the primary charge would have come down to 4.33% of national income at factor cost in 1925–29."[84]

[82]One can therefore agree with those who believe that the weakness of the Treaty of Versailles derives mainly from the fact that two conflicting objectives were pursued with it. On the one hand, it was intended to weaken Germany economically in order to contain its supposed aggressive impulses. On the other, they wanted to prevent a Bolshevik revolution similar to the Russian one from occurring in Germany due to the painful living conditions of its citizens. Extrapolating this concern, Veblen (1920), reviewing *The Economic Consequences*, considers that the Treaty of Versailles, although never mentioning it, had the containment of Bolshevism as its main objective. See Mayer (1967) and Schwabe (1985).

[83]See also Feldman (1993, p. 339).

[84]In reality, according to estimates (see Schuker, 1988, p. 307–308), between November 1918 and June 1931, Germany paid 22,891 billion Reichsmarks, 20,598 billion Reichsmarks according to

To this he adds the fact that, between 1918 and 1923, since the inflow of foreign capital, especially American, into Germany was large and the holders of these assets had substantial capital losses due to the depreciation of the mark, the German Reparations were to a large extent effectively paid for by non-residents, especially Americans.[85]

Despite this, the influence of *The Economic Consequences* on scholars regarding the economic effects of Reparations remains high and the idea that the high Reparations imposed on Germany were the decisive cause of the 1923 hyperinflation is persistent among some of them. Thus, Eichengreen (1992, p. 141) writes: "... Removing Reparations would have removed the need for monetization, inflation would have been eliminated as well. Reparations, in this sense, were ultimately responsible for the German hyperinflation." Holtfrerich even argues that the depreciation of the mark and the resulting inflation was the best way of "persuading the rest of the world of the need for a reduction of the Reparation burden."[86]

In reality, as Feldman (1993, p. 451) explains, "Reparations did not cause the German hyperinflation, and the Germans did not make the hyperinflation in order to escape Reparations, but Reparations had proven a disincentive to stabilization." As mentioned above, the elite's fears of the rise of the radical left, and the myths firmly established in the public mind by propaganda, politically hindered any measures to rebalance public finances and encouraged governments to provide monetary cover to the Reich deficits, thereby creating high inflation.

The propensity of German governments to resort to the inflation tax had already become apparent during the war years. Among the great European powers, Germany was the one that most resorted to covering military expenditure with money. In fact, between 1913 and 1918, money circulation increased by about 600% in this country compared to an increase of 110% in the United Kingdom, 370% in Italy, and 390% in France.[87]

Combined with the higher level of money financing of war expenses, Germany was also characterized by a higher cost-of-living increase of 304% between 1913 and 1918, compared to 210% in the United Kingdom and 213% in France.[88] However, it should be noted that compared to other countries, in particular the UK and France, Germany had not been able to rely on foreign, particularly American, funding.

Marks (1978) in Reparations to the Allies. Since a part of the reparations were in kind, the amount that burdened the German balance of payments was 15.986 milliard Reichsmarks according to Schuker (1988). Based on an estimate of the German national income at factor cost between 1919 and 1931 of about 842 milliard Reichsmarks, Schuker concludes that the incidence on it of the total Reparations paid by the Germans was around 2.7%; that of the Reparations in cash was around 1.9%.

[85] From 1924 until 1929, Germany, as will be seen, benefited from large capital inflows that allowed it to pay the Reparation annuities without its people being burdened with additional taxes.

[86] See Holtfrerich (1986, p. 327).

[87] See Ferguson (1998).

[88] See Maddison (1962).

Table 2.2 Inflation rate, money growth, and mark depreciation (annual changes, percentage, 1919–1922)

	Dollar/Mark exchange rate	Prices of imported goods	Wholesale prices	Domestic prices	Notes in circulation	Bank deposits
1919-Dec.	465.5	438.8	227.8	168.4	51.7	82.1
1920-Dec.	55.9	34.2	79.3	108.9	62.6	54.8
1921-Dec.	163.0	150.6	142.2	139.6	50.6	84.7
1922-Jun.	358.1	494.5	414.6	395.3	112.8	n.a.

Source: Bresciani-Turroni (1937) and Holtfrerich (1986)

After the war, Germany was faced with enormous economic problems related to demobilization, reintegration of soldiers into civilian life, and support for wounded war veterans, widows, and orphans. In this context, recourse to seigniorage exploitation was the easy choice. This choice was further encouraged by phases of depreciation of the mark that had an impact on domestic price levels. Between 1919 and June 1922 (i.e., before the onset of hyperinflation), the German year-on-year inflation rate was very high, always above 100% (Table 2.2).

In fact, as noted by Kunz (1986), among others, the hyperinflation of 1923 was part of and concluded the inflationary process that marked the early years of the Weimar Republic. Two phases of intense acceleration in price growth can be identified in this process: the first in the second part of 1919 and the other in the second part of 1921 (Fig. 2.1).

Figure 2.1 shows how both of these phases of accelerating price growth were preceded by a pronounced depreciation of the mark. The phases of pronounced depreciation of the German currency resulted from sudden stops, i.e. changes in the direction of flow of international capital.[89] Although the inflows of foreign capital into Germany became massive after the drawing up of the Dawes Plan, even in the years immediately after the First World War a certain amount of assets in marks were held by non-residents. Foreign deposits at the seven largest Berlin banks increased between 1919 and 1921 from 13.7 billion paper marks to 41.6 billion in 1921,[90] that is about 36% of the deposits of these banks.[91] Purchases of paper marks by non-residents also increased considerably during the same period.[92] Moulton and McGuire (1923) estimated that the value of German securities held by non-residents between 1919 and 1923 amounted to about 3 billion gold marks. Based on a letter from the Reichsbank-Directorium to the Foreign Minister, Holtfrerich (1986, p. 294) writes: "... estimates of the proportion of Reichsbank notes in foreign possession during 1919-20 ran at nearly fifty percent of the total circulation: fifteen billion marks out of thirty billion in 1919, and twenty-five billion in June 1920." In

[89] See Calvo (1995), Calvo and Reinhart (2000) and Bordo et al. (2007).

[90] See Webb (1986, p. 57).

[91] See Feldman (1993, p. 256).

[92] See Holtfrerich (1977) and Schuker (1988, p. 115).

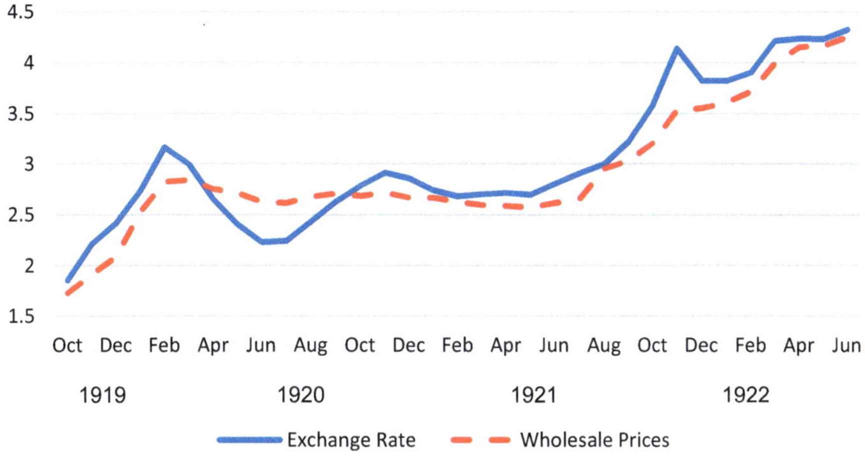

Fig. 2.1 Exchange rate vis-à-vis the US dollar and wholesale prices (Oct. 1919–June 1922). Source: For the exchange rate, see Bresciani-Turroni (1937); for the wholesale prices, see Holtfrerich (1986). Note: the variables are expressed in logarithms

December 1920, the German government estimated that short- and long-term mark securities held by non-residents amounted to at least 25 billion marks while notes and loans held by non-residents came to about 70 billion.[93] The investment in marks and mark-denominated assets by non-residents was driven, even more than by yield differentials, by the expectation of an appreciation of the mark, i.e. by high confidence in Germany's economic resilience.

Against a background of high international capital mobility, changes in the value of the mark therefore resulted from changes in the expectations of investors of "idle" money about the prospects of the German currency. This exposed Germany to sudden stops, following which accelerations in inflation occurred.[94] The latter were followed by an expansion of the quantity of money.

As Merkin (1982, p. 31) notes: "... the prices of domestic commodities rose earlier and much faster than the quantity of money in Germany between May 1921 and August 1923. For example, between May 1921 and July 1922 the quantity of money (excluding bank deposits) rose 2½ times, while the price level rose 7⅓ times. Between July 1922 and June 1923, the quantity of money increased 85 times, while the price level rose 182 times."

The changes of expectations on mark were mainly related to "news" concerning international or domestic politics such as those below. With "good" news, obviously, favoring an appreciation of the mark and "bad" news favoring its depreciation (Table 2.3).

[93] See Holtfrerich (1986, p. 294).

[94] On this aspect, see Bortkiewicz (1924) and Merkin (1982).

Table 2.3 Reichsmark's exchange rate and political news (June 1919–May 1922)

Period	"Good" or "Bad" news	Reichsmark's trend
From June 1919 to February 1920	Approval of the Treaty of Versailles	About 600% depreciation
From February to July 1920	Important successes in foreign policy. Failure of Kapp rebellion	About 60% appreciation
From July 1920 to May 1921	Election of June won by extreme parties. Breakdown of Spa Conference. Massive protests and riots in the summer of 1920 and street demonstrations	About 55% depreciation
From May to November 1921	London Ultimatum Plan of May 5. Payment of the first tranche of Reparations	About 320% depreciation
From November 1921 to May 1922	Measures to rebalance public finances	Stability of the exchange rate

The Table shows that between mid-1919 and mid-1922, there were two phases of pronounced depreciation of the mark. The first phase occurred in July 1919 immediately after the signing of the Treaty of Versailles when, between June and December, the value of the mark went from 3.34 per dollar to 11.14. The "bad" news of the terms of the Treaty encouraged an intensive sale of assets in marks by both non-residents and residents alike. With reference to the latter Bresciani-Turroni wrote (1937, p. 54): "Probably the signing of the Treaty provoked a psychological crisis in certain German circles, lack of confidence in the future of Germany dominated the German mind and was manifested—for the first time in the history of the mark—in a 'flight from the mark,' i.e. in a demand for foreign exchange."

The second phase of pronounced depreciation of the German currency took place in the middle of 1921, after the London Schedule of Payments had been drawn up (May 5, 1921). This phase intensified further in the autumn, when the Allies decided to transfer Upper Silesia, an industrial region rich in coal mines, from Germany to Poland. Between the end of May and the end of November, the exchange rate of the mark against the dollar rose from 242 to 1175. The significant depreciation of the mark led to an increase in import prices (by 271.8%), followed by an increase in domestic price levels (by 161.1%) and of the cost of living (by 65.8%).

2.6 Failure to Consolidate the Relative Stabilization of 1920

In the period between these two phases of pronounced depreciation, i.e. March 1920 to June 1921, the mark appreciated by 7.5% against the dollar. This happened for various reasons,[95] on the one hand, Germany, as an importer of commodities and

[95] See Graham (1930).

exporter of manufactured goods, benefited from an improvement in the terms of trade due to the higher relative fall in commodity prices compared to manufactured goods. On the other hand, confidence in the mark grew as the failure of the Kapp coup gave many people the impression that Germany had acquired greater political stability. This resulted in huge capital inflows from abroad.[96] In order to curb the appreciation of the mark, stabilize its value, and safeguard the competitiveness of German exports, the Reichsbank intervened heavily in foreign exchange markets.[97]

Between March 1920 and June 1921, the appreciation of the mark, the post-war slump abroad, and the worldwide fall in the prices of food and raw materials favored a significant fall in prices in Germany: with wholesale prices falling by 20% and retail prices by 22.7%, the German economy experienced relative stability during this period.

A number of scholars have viewed this period of "relative stabilization" as a lost opportunity to stabilize the German economy. Bresciani-Turroni (1937, p. 57) writes: "It would still have been possible to save the mark if the German government had taken energetic measures to re-establish a balanced budget instead of allowing Treasury bills to be discounted at the Reichsbank." Similarly, for Nurkse (1946, p. 104): "... inflation could still have been brought under control if appropriate measures had been taken at that time. But no such measures were adopted and a rapid deterioration set in ...".

According to Ferguson (1997, p. 274), cuts in government spending and increases in indirect taxes "could have effectively avoided the descent into hyperinflation ... Although such a policy would have meant a cut in living standards and an increase in unemployment, it would have been a significantly 'softer landing' than actually happened in 1923."[98]

There may be doubts about the success of the stabilization maneuver proposed by Ferguson, the fact remains that the German government made no attempt in this or, indeed, in any other direction, instead it simply remained passive: the political conditions for the stabilization of the German economy were lacking and, between the spring of 1920 and early summer of 1921, no stabilization program was initiated or even discussed.[99]

The justification given by the political class for this passivity was that it was necessary to solve the Reparations problem before stabilization measures could be taken.[100] In reality, the Republic was not strong enough to withstand the resistance,

[96] "As business conditions and opportunities deteriorated in the great post-war depression of 1920/22, however, foreign investors, particularly in the United States and Spain, looked to Germany as a place where they might employ their money profitably." See Feldman (1982, p. 185).

[97] See Feldman (1982, p. 4).

[98] See Ferguson (1997, p. 274).

[99] As Feldman (1982, p. 198) writes: "The dilemma was that neither the mechanism nor the force were available to turn these various programs and convictions into a coherent stabilization program that might have provided an alternative to what was eventually to come, while everything seemed to conspire to undermine movement in such a direction."

[100] See Feldman (1982, p. 190).

protests, and unrest that would have arisen in parts of German society by public spending cuts and tax increases. “In England and the United States, where democracy was secure, it was possible to practice the brutalities of traditional deflationary policies—at least at this time. In Germany, . . . if the very severe social conflicts and discontent . . . at the end of 1920 and beginning of 1921 demonstrated anything, it was that the distributional conflicts brought out into the open by the relative stabilization were fraught with political implication.”[101]

German society reacted negatively to the effects associated with relative stabilization. In April 1920, the Frankfurter Zeitung, the most widely read newspaper in Germany, pointed out that excessive exchange rate appreciation and tight control of the money supply could, like taking an excessive dose of a medicine, produce undesirable effects. Indeed, by the spring of 1920, prices had stabilized, but the social turmoil had increased. As a result of the pronounced increase in domestic prices between late 1919 and early 1920, real wages had fallen significantly and the living conditions of workers had, in many cases, become more precarious. It is not surprising, therefore, that in the early summer of that year there were large demonstrations by the unemployed, with scenes reminiscent of the days of the November revolution.[102] In addition to these demonstrations, the social calm was disturbed by riots and looting in which workers forcefully demanded a reduction in prices in order to put an end to the rising cost of living. The workers’ goal was to regain the purchasing power they had lost through the inflationary erosion of their real wages which occurred especially in the second half of 1919. The protests against the withholding tax on wages and salaries (introduced in mid-1920 with the entry into force of Erzberger’s fiscal reform) are to be seen in this same perspective,[103] indeed as can be seen from Table 2.4 the number of strikes reached their peak in 1920.

These expressions of social discontent fueled the rise of more radical components of the workers’ representatives and frightened the industrialists who were fearful of the possible spread to Germany of the revolutionary experience not only of Russia, but also of Hungary.[104] No wonder, then, that a large part of them adopted an accommodating policy toward demands for wage increases and, at the same time, urged the government to support industry in order to overcome the downturn and

---

[101] See Feldman (1982, p. 202–203).

[102] For a detailed description of it, see Feldman (1993, p. 222ff).

[103] See Craig Patton (1996), Feldman 1993, p. 225ff), Ferguson (1996).

[104] This concern had, moreover, often emerged in the speeches of the participants in the negotiations on the German side as a reason for the Allies to establish moderate Reparations, i.e. such that they would not destabilize Germany and encourage the Bolshevik revolution in other countries as well (See Ferguson, 1995a, p. 152). This position is found explicitly in the words of Franz Witthoeff, the President of the Hamburg Chamber of Commerce, who was later appointed member of the German delegation to the Versailles negotiations: “Bread and peace are the preconditions for order and work; otherwise we are headed for Bolshevism, and that will be the end of Germany. Yet, I detect in this very danger of Bolshevism a certain safety-valve with regard to the efforts of the Entente to checknote us absolutely. If this malaise spreads from Hungary and Germany, neither France nor England will be immune, and that means the end for all Europe” (See Staatsarchiv Hamburg, Signature A.O. Meyer I., Bd. 10, 280, Witthoeff to Dr. Niery, 24 March 1919).

Table 2.4 Labor disputes in Germany (1913–1924)

	Strikes	Persons involved in strikes	Man-days-lost in strikes
1913	2127	254,206	8,819,351
1919	4932	4,673,835	47,447,156
1920	8686	8,232,900	52,837,409
1921	4861	1,840,441	26,789,411
1922	4924	2,101,926	24,889,500
1924	1614	675,122	13,584,360

Source: Flora et al. (1987)

reduce unemployment. As a result of the demands of the trade unions, whose bargaining power had been greatly enhanced by their role in undermining the Kapp coup, there was a significant increase in monetary wages in the first part of 1920, and, between June 1920 and the same month of the previous year, they increased by about 150%, an increase not only in monetary terms but also an increase in real wages (Fig. 2.2).

As Feldman (1993, p. 216) writes: "From the standpoint of the containment of the major source of inflation, the period of relative stabilization must be viewed as a failure." This failure was clear from the acceleration of price growth that occurred in the summer of 1921 and coincided with the pronounced depreciation of the mark from July 1921.

From a strictly economic point of view, the failure to stabilize is explained by the trade-off between safeguarding real wage levels and limiting unemployment, i.e. the two main objectives pursued by the German authorities between 1919 and 1922.

Figure 2.3 shows that in Germany in the years immediately following WWI there was a direct relationship between workers' real wage and the unemployment rate: In the phases of increasing inflation and falling real wages, particularly in the latter part of 1920 and again in the second half of 1921, the unemployment rate fell. While conversely, it had increased in the early part of 1920 in concomitance with decreasing inflation and a significant increase in workers' real wages.

When real wages fell, companies increased exports and production due to improved competitiveness and, as a consequence, they hired more workers and unemployment decreased. However, Bresciani-Turroni (1929, p. 389) argues that: "Every increase in the demand for labor tended to bring about an immediate rise in nominal wages, which, however, was quickly neutralized by the rise in prices inevitably resulting from new emissions of paper money by the Government, and real wages remained at a low level."

When real wages increased and exports weakened, demand was supported by increases in government spending (Fig. 2.4). The government took measures to support certain industries (such as shipbuilding, shoes, and textiles), as well as increasing public spending on public works in various areas, from railways to postal services.[105]

[105] See Feldman (1993, p. 237).

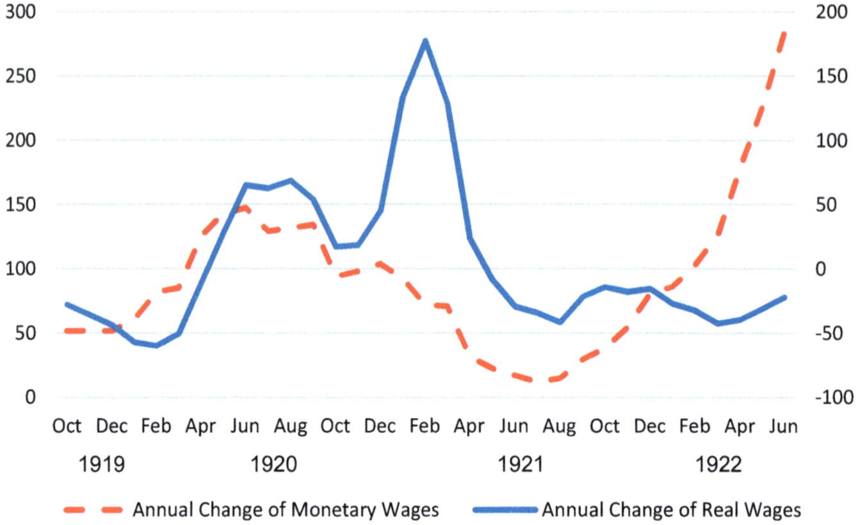

Fig. 2.2 Annual change of monetary and real wages of skilled workers (annual changes in percent; Oct. 1919–June 1922). Source: Statistisches Jahrbuch für das Deutsche Reich, several years. Note: the real wages have been deflated with consumer prices

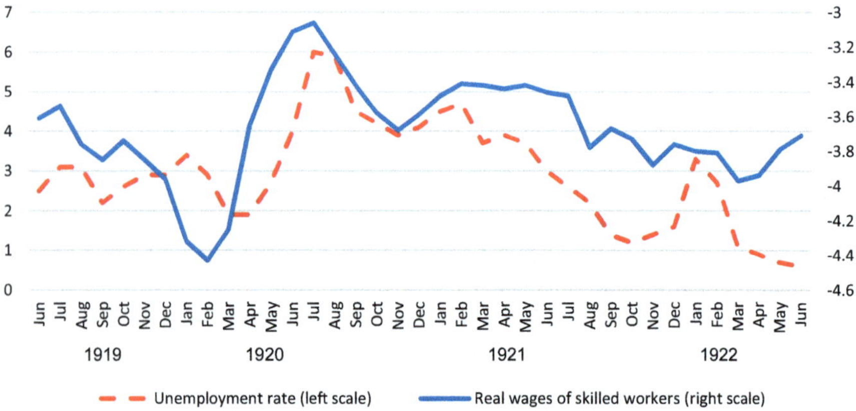

Fig. 2.3 Unemployment rate and real wages of skilled workers (June 1919–June 1922). Source: For the wages, see Statistisches Jahrbuch für das Deutsche Reich, and for the rate of unemployment, see Bry (1960). Note: the wages of skilled workers have been deflated with consumer prices; the rate of unemployment is in percent and the real wages are in logarithms

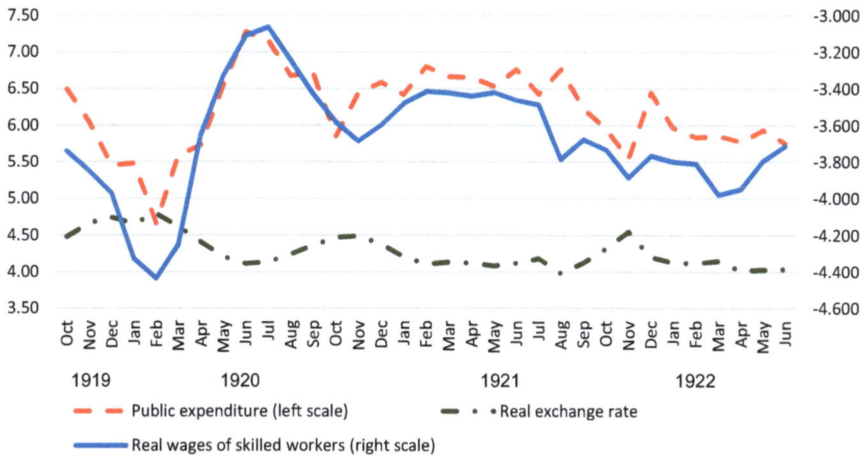

Fig. 2.4 Real exchange rate, public expenditure, and real wages of skilled workers (Oct. 1919–June 1922). Source: For wages and consumer prices, see Statistisches Jahrbuch für das Deutsche Reich; for notes in circulation and the Reich expenditure in gold mark, see Bresciani Turroni (1937). Note: Notes in circulation and wages have been deflated with consumer prices; all the variables are expressed in logarithms

As we will see in the next chapter, in the early Twenties, the Reichsbank maintained an accommodative monetary policy and increases in public spending were matched by increases in monetary and real wages. As a result, it is clear that in the years immediately following WWI, since "...[p]erspicacious managers understood ... that compromise with labor leaders was preferable to facing left-wing socialists or the enthusiasts for a government-controlled planned economy,"[106] Germany enjoyed a significant economic growth in 1920 and 1921. Agriculture was stagnant but industrial output, in particular shipbuilding and coal, showed a sharp upward.[107] Due to the remarkable growth of output in the early 1920s, Germany benefited of an unemployment rate lower than other advanced countries (Table 2.5).

This has led several scholars to believe that the inflation of the early 1920s had had beneficial effects on the German economy. Graham, for example, argued that thanks to inflation German output was higher than it would have been if the mark had been pegged to gold and, therefore, that "... the balance of material gains and losses attributable to inflation is distinctly on the side of gains."[108] This "optimistic" view was also supported by Laursen and Pedersen (1964). Comparing the deflationary policy pursued by the United Kingdom and the United States in the early 1920s with

[106] See Maier (1975, p. 58).

[107] See Hoffmann et al. (1965), Ferguson (1995a, p. 303) and Laursen and Pedersen (1964, p. 89–98).

[108] See Graham (1930, p. 321).

Table 2.5 Unemployment rate in industrial countries (in percent, 1919–1922)

	France	Germany	Sweden	United Kingdom	United States
1919	n.a.	3.7	5.5	5.2	5.0
1920	n.a.	3.8	5.4	3.2	8.6
1921	5.0	2.8	26.6	17.0	19.5
1922-June	2.0	1.5	22.9	14.3	11.4

Source: Eichengreen and Hatton (1988)

the inflationary policy of Germany in the same period, they conclude that Germany achieved higher levels of investment and growth and lower unemployment rates than the US and UK.[109] These assumptions of high economic growth, according to Laursen and Pedersen, were then undermined by the restrictive economic policy implemented by German governments in the post-1924 period.[110] Taking the same view, Holtfrerich (1986) goes so far as to argue that even hyperinflation had positive effects, declaring that it helped to cancel the real value of the Reich's debt[111] and reduce the level of inequality in income distribution.

This positive view of German inflation has been challenged by a number of scholars. Bresciani-Turroni pointed out that persistent inflation had favored a distortion in the allocation of resources, encouraging the emergence of an excessively high ratio of fixed to circulating capital.[112] While, in more recent years, Stolper (1967, p. 89) observed that inflation "... created the appearance of an industrial boom, at least as far as the volume of production and employment was concerned ...". In fact, inflation left the German economy severely weakened structurally. Lindenlaub (1985), for his part, disputes the idea that inflation had stimulated demand for investment. In his opinion, the uncertainty about the future prospects of the economy caused by high inflation adversely affected the demand for investment. Balderston (1993) showed how inflation damaged the financial market and severely weakened the German banking system, reducing its capitalization and encouraging a high maturity and currency imbalance between these institutions assets and liabilities.

---

109 See Laursen and Pedersen (1964, p. 88).

110 See Abelshauser (1981), Abelshauser and Petzina (1981), Kunz (1982) and Holtfrerich (1986).

111 Due to the pronounced depreciation of the mark, capital losses were particularly heavy on non-resident investments. They represented a form of "... free foreign aid toward the reconstruction of the German economy." Holtfrerich (1986, p. 295).

112 In this regard, he quotes the words of an industrialist at the congress of engineering industrialists held in December 1925: "We have some very extensive factories which are nothing but rubbish. Therefore, it is not sufficient, if we wish to restore our business, to close these establishments in the hope of reopening them later. Even factoring not working cost money ... Therefore, our slogan must be: Demolition! We must consider as finally lost the capital unwisely invested in those factories ... [I]t is a recognition of very grave mistakes committed during the inflation." Bresciani-Turroni (1937, p. 390).

Table 2.6 German imports and exports (billions of marks, 1919–1922)

	1919	1920	1921	1922
Imports	6.6	7.0	5.7	6.2
Exports	1.8	5.1	3.5	4.9
Deficit	4.8	1.9	2.1	2.2

Source: Young (1925)

Apart from these mainly microeconomic findings, the fact remains that the growth of the German economy was associated with high domestic absorption, which tended to reflect negatively on the balance of trade (Table 2.6).

These persistent deficits were, to a large extent, covered through trade credits and capital inflows from abroad encouraged by expectations of an appreciation of the mark.[113] The deficits and the high domestic absorption behind them would have been difficult to sustain in the long run.

In spite of the imbalances it induced, inflation, in the short term, enabled an otherwise impossible level of income and economic well-being, which granted Germany a period of relative social peace and prevented the collapse of the Republic. As Haller (1976, p. 141) writes "[inflation] secured the parliamentary form of government for the period of the Weimar Republic," and any attempt to stabilize the German economy would have led to a political crisis.

2.7 Conclusions

Socially and politically, the early 1920s were conditioned by the Reparations problem and marked by deep underlying social tension while, politically, the confrontation between the different interest groups led to a stalemate with no interest group being willing to make the economic sacrifices necessary. Underlying this behavior were two facts. Firstly, the belief that acceptance of fiscal sacrifices was tantamount to an acknowledgement of the Treaty of Versailles' content and the obligation to pay an indemnity to the Allied countries. Secondly, large sections of the population did not "recognize" themselves in the new republican regime. This fact combined with the abdication of the Kaiser had contributed to weakening the sense of national identity and the willingness of individuals to put the good of the nation ahead of their own and, in a context of heightened distributive conflict, the government's adoption of reforms and stabilization measures was problematic.

Despite this, confidence persisted in international financial markets and within the country that a solution to the Reparations problem would be found, the mark would stabilize, and that the German economy would return to pre-war growth.

From time to time, this confidence was shaken by political bad news which affected the exchange rate leading to pronounced depreciations of the German

[113] Webb (1986, p. 56–57) shows how trade mark purchases in New York increased dramatically between 1919 and 1920.

currency, this was due both to disinvestments of assets in marks by non-residents and to the purchase of assets in foreign currencies by residents. In the period leading up to the summer of 1922, Germany experienced two phases of pronounced depreciation of the mark: the first occurred after the signing of the Treaty of Versailles on 28 June 1919, and the second after the publication of the London Schedule Plan on 5 May 1921. These phases were caused by sudden outflows of capital: the declining confidence in the stability of the mark encouraged both resident and non-resident holders of mark-denominated assets to sell them in order to buy foreign assets. A significant increase in wholesale and domestic prices followed the depreciation of the mark. With some delay, under pressure from the trade unions, wages were raised in order to preserve their purchasing power.

The Reichsbank, albeit with some delay, replenished the money stock in real terms, thereby reducing the possibility of stabilization. It was not only monetary policy that was accommodating but also fiscal policy and both helped to keep domestic demand high and, consequently, the unemployment rate low, the level of which in the early 1920s was well below the average of the other leading industrial countries.

References

Abelshauser, W. (1981). Wiederaufbau vor dem Marshallplan. Westeuropas Wachstumschancen und die Wirtschaftsordnungspolitik in der zweiten Hälfte der vierziger Jahre. *Vierteljahrshefte für Zeitgeschichte, 29*, 545–578.

Abelshauser, W., & Petzina, D. (1981). Krise und rekonstruktion: zur interpretation der gesamtwirtschaftlichen entwicklung Deutschland im 20. Jahrundert. In W. Abelshauser & D. Petzina (Eds.), *Deutsche Wirtschaftsgeschichte im Industriezeitalter. Konjunktur, Krise, Wachstum*. Verlag.

Abraham, D. (1981). *The collapse of the Weimar Republic*. Princeton University Press.

Angell, N. (1909). *Europe's optical illusion*. Simpkin, Marshall, Hamilton, Kent.

Balderston T. (1993), The origins and course of the German economic crisis: November 1923 to May 1932. Haude und Spencer.

Barth, B. (2003). *Dolchstosslegenden und Politische Desintegration. Das Trauma der deutschen Niederlage im ersten Weltkrieg 1914–1933*. Droste.

Berman, S. (1997). Civil society and the collapse of the Weimar republic. *World Politics, 49*, 401–429.

Bessel, R. (1993). *Germany after the first world war*. Clarendon Press.

Bessel, R. (1997). Germany from war to dictatorship. In M. Fulbrook (Ed.), *German history since 1800*. Arnold.

Boemeke, M. F., Feldman, G. D., & Glaser, E. (1998). Introduction. In M. F. Boemeke, G. D. Feldman, & E. Glaser (Eds.), *The treaty of Versailles. A reassessment after 75 years*. Cambridge University Press.

Bordo, M. D., Cavallo, A. F., & Meissner, C. M. (2007). *Sudden stops: Determinants and output effects in the first era of globalization, 1880-1913*. NBER working paper n. 13489.

Bortkiewicz, von L. (1924). Die Ursachen der potenzierten Wirkung des vermehrten Geldumlaufs auf das Preisniveau. *Verhandlungen des Vereins für Sozialpolitik, 170*, 256–274.

Breitman, R. (1981). *German socialism and Weimar democracy*. University of North Carolina Press.

Bresciani-Turroni, C. (1929). The movement of wages in Germany during the depreciation of the mark and after stabilization. *Journal of the Royal Statistical Society, 92*, 374–427.
Bresciani-Turroni, C. (1937). *The economics of inflation: A study of currency depreciation in post-war Germany*. Allen & Unwin.
Bry, G. (1960). *Wages in Germany 1871–1945*. Princeton University Press.
Burnett, P. M. (1940). *Reparation at the Paris peace conference*. Columbia University Press.
Buzan, B. (1984). Economic structure and international security: The limits of the liberal case. *International Organization, 38*, 597–624.
Calvo, G. A. (1995). *Varieties of capital market crisis*. Inter-American Development Bank, Research Department Publication n. 4008.
Calvo, G. A., & Reinhart, C. (2000). When capital inflows come to a sudden stop: Consequences and policy options. In P. B. Kenen & A. K. Swoboda (Eds.), *Reforming the international monetary and financial system*. International Monetary Fund.
Copeland, D. C. (2000). *The origins of major war*. Cornell University Press.
Dahl, R. A. (1971). *Polyarchy, participation and opposition*. Yale University Press.
Dalton, H. (1946). *Letter to Paul Mantoux, august 9th, 1946. Jacob Viner papers box 47*. Princeton University Library.
Deist, W. (1986). Der militärische Zusammenbruch des Kaiserreichs. Zur Realität der Dolchsto*ß*legende. In U. Büttner (Ed.), *Das Unrechtsregime*. Christians.
Eichengreen, B. (1992). *Golden fetters: The gold standard and the great depression*. Oxford University Press.
Eichengreen, B., & Hatton, T. J. (1988). *Interwar unemployment in international perspective*. UC Berkeley Institute for Research on Labor and Employment working paper. Retrieved from https://escholarship.org/uc/item/7bw188gk
Ensor, R. C. K. (1946). Introduction. In P. Mantoux (Ed.), *The Carthaginian peace*. Oxford University Press.
Feldman, G. D. (1977). *Iron and steel in the German inflation, 1916–1923*. Princeton University Press.
Feldman, G. D. (1982). The political economy of Germany's relative stabilization during the 1920/21 depression. In G. D. Feldman, L. Holtfrerich, & G. A. Ritter (Eds.), *Die Deutsche inflation. Eine Zwischenbilanz – The German inflation reconsidered. A preliminary balance*. de Gruyter.
Feldman, G. D. (1993). *The great disorder: Politics, economics, and Society in the German Inflation, 1914–1924*. Oxford University Press.
Ferguson, N. (1995a). *Paper and iron: Hamburg business and German politics in the era of inflation, 1897–1927*. Cambridge University Press.
Ferguson, N. (1995b). Keynes and German inflation. *English Historical Review, 110*, 368–391.
Ferguson, N. (1996). Constraints and room for manoeuvre in the German inflation of the early 1920s. *Economic History Review, 49*, 635–666.
Ferguson, N. (1997). The German inter-war economy: Political choice versus economic determinism. In H. Fulbrook (Ed.), *Twentieth-century Germany*. Arnold.
Ferguson, N. (1998). *The pity of war*. Penguin.
Flora, P., Alber, J., Eichenberg, R., Kohl, J., Kraus, F., Pfenning, W., & Seebohm, K. (1987). *State, economy, and society in Western Europe 1815–1975*. Macmillan.
Frambach, H. A. (2019). The socialization debate of 1918: Was the socialization commission doomed to failure right from the start? In U. Backhaus, G. Chaloupek, & H. A. Frambach (Eds.), *The first socialization debate (1918) and early efforts towards socialization*. Springer.
Fulda, B. (2009). *Press and politics in the Weimar Republic*. Oxford University Press.
Geary, D. (1990). Employers, workers, and the collapse of the Weimar Republic. In I. Kershaw (Ed.), *Weimar: Why did German democracy fail*. Weidenfeld and Nicolson.
Gilpin, R. (1981). *War and change in world politics*. Cambridge University Press.
Graham, F. D. (1930). *Exchange, prices, and production in hyper-inflation: Germany, 1920–1923*. Princeton University Press.

Haller, H. (1976). Die Rolle der Staatsfinanzen für den Inflationsprozess. In Deutsche Bundesbank (Ed.), *Währung und Wirtschaft in Deutschland, 1876-1975*. Bundesbank.
Heinemann, U. (1983). *Die verdrängte Niederlage: politische Öffentlichkeit und Kriegsschuldfrage in der Weimarer Republik*. Vandenhoeck und Ruprecht.
Hiller von Gaertringen, F. F. (1963). "Dolchstob" Diskussion und "Dolchstoßlegende" in Wandel von der Jahrzchnten. In W. Besson & Hiller on Gaertringen, F.F. (Eds.), *Geschichte und Gegenwartsbewusstsein. Historische Betrachtungen und Untersuchungen. Festschrift für Hans Rothfels zum 70 Geburstag*. Vandenhoeck and Ruprecht.
Hoffmann, W. G., Grumbach, F., & Hesse, H. (1965). *Das Wachstum der deutschen Wirtschaft seit der Mitte des 19. Jahrhunderts*. Springer Verlag.
Holtfrerich, C. L. (1977). Amerikanischer Kapitalexport und Wiederaufbau der deutschen Wirtschaft 1919-1923. *Vierteljahrschrift für Sozial- und Wirtschaftsgeschichte, 64*, 497–529.
Holtfrerich, C. L. (1986). *The German inflation 1914–1923: Causes and effects in international perspective*. De Gruyter.
Huber, E. P. (1988). *Deutsche Varfassungsgeschichte seit 1789*. Kohlammer Verlag.
Huges, M. L. (2021). *Embracing democracy in modern Germany: Political citizenship and participation, 1871–2000*. Bloomsbury Academic.
Hunt, R. M. (1958). Myths, guilt and shame in pre-nazi Germany. *Virginia Quarterly Review, 34*, 355–371.
Jacobson, J. (1983). Is there a new international history of the 1920s? *American Historical Review, 88*, 617–645.
Jäger, W. (1984). *Historische forschung und politische kultur in Deutschland*. Vandenhoeck & Reprecht.
James, H. (2007). *Markets and constitutions: Lessons from Weimar Germany*. Paper prepared for EUI conference on "Constitutions and markets", June 14–15.
Kershaw, I. (1990). Perspectives of Weimar's failure. In I. Kershaw (Ed.), *Weimar: Why did German democracy fail?* Martin's Press.
Keylor, W. R. (1998). Versailles and international diplomacy. In M. F. Boemeke, G. D. Feldman, & R. Glaser (Eds.), *The Treaty of Versailles. A reassessment after 75 years*. Cambridge University Press.
Keynes, J. M. ([1919] 1920). *The economic consequences of the peace*. Harcourt, Brace & Howe.
Keynes, J. M. (1922). *A revision of the treaty, being a sequel to the economic consequences of the peace*. Macmillan.
Keynes, J. M. (1929a). The German transfer problem. *Economic Journal, 39*, 1–7.
Keynes, J. M. (1929b). Prof. Fisher discusses Reparations problems with John M. Keynes. *New York evening world*, 25 March 1929. Reprinted in E. Johnson & D. Moggridge (Eds.), *The collected writings of J.M. Keynes*. Macmillan, 1978.
Kissinger, H. (1994). *Diplomacy*. Simon & Schuster.
Klein, F. (1998). Between Compiègne and Versailles: The German and the way from a misunderstood defeat to an unwanted peace. In M. F. Boemeke, G. D. Feldman, & E. Glaeser (Eds.), *The treaty of Versailles. A reassessment after 75 years*. Cambridge University Press.
Krumeich, G. (2001). Die Dolchstosslegende. In F. Etienne & H. Schulze (Eds.), *Deutsche Erinnerungsorte*. Beck Verlag.
Kuczynski, R. (1925). *Postwar labor conditions in Germany*. Bulletin of the US Bureau of Labor Statistics n. 380.
Kunz, A. (1982). Stand versus Klasse: Beamtenschaft und Gewerkschaften im Konflict un den Personalabbau 1923/24. *Geschichte und Gesellschaft, 8*, 55–86.
Kunz, A. (1986). *Civil servants and the politics of inflation in Germany, 1914–1924*. De Gruyter.
Laursen, K., & Pedersen, J. (1964). *German inflation 1918–1923*. North-Holland.
Lindenlaub, D. (1985). *Maschinenbau-unternehmen in der deutschen Inflation, 1919–1923*. De Gruyter.
Lukau, A. (1941). *The German delegation at the Paris peace conference*. Columbia University Press.

Maddison, A. (1962). Growth and fluctuations in the world economy, 1870–1960. *Banca Nazionale del Lavoro "Quarterly Review", 15*, 127–195.
Maddison, A. (1991). *The world economy. A millennial perspective*. OECD.
Maier, C. S. (1975). *Recasting bourgeois Europe: Stabilization in France, Germany and in Italy in the decade after world war I.* Princeton University Press.
Mantoux, E. (1946). *The Carthaginian peace - or the economic consequences of Keynes*. Oxford University Press.
Marks, S. (1978). The myths of Reparations. *Central European History, 11*, 231–255.
Marks, S. (1998). Smoke and mirrors: In smoke-filled rooms and the galerie des glaces. In M. F. Boemeke, G. D. Feldman, & E. Glaser (Eds.), *The treaty of Versailles. A reassessment after 75 years*. Cambridge University Press.
Marks, S. (2003). *The Illusion of Peace: International Relations in Europe, 1918–1933*. Palgrave Macmillan.
Marks, S. (2013). Mistakes and myths: The allies, Germany, and the Versailles treaty, 1918–1921. *Journal of Modern History, 85*, 632–659.
Markwell, D. (2006). *John Maynard Keynes and international relations*. Oxford University Press.
Marshall, A. (1919). *Industry and trade*. Macmillan.
Mayer, A. J. (1967). *Politics and diplomacy at peacemaking: containment and counterrevolution at Versailles. 1918-1919*. Alfred A. Knopf.
Mearsheimer, J. (2001). *The tragedy of great power politics*. Norton.
Merkin, G. (1982). Towards a theory of the German inflation: Some preliminary observations. In G. Feldman, C. L. Holtfrerich, G. A. Ritter, & P. C. Witte (Eds.), *The German inflation reconsidered: A preliminary balance*. De Gruyter.
Mill, J. S. ([1848] 1965). *Principles of political economy, with some of their applications to social philosophy*. Reprinted in 1965 in *The collected works of J.S. Mill, vol. II*, University of Toronto Press.
Mitchell, B. R., & Deane, P. (1962). *Abstract of British historical statistics*. Cambridge University Press.
Moggridge, D. E. (1992). *Maynard Keynes, an economist's biography*. Routledge.
Moggridge, D. E., & Skidelsky, R. (2015). Critique of Schuker's 'J.M. Keynes and the personal politics of Reparations'. *Diplomacy & Statecraft, 26*, 736–744.
Mommsen, H. (1989). *The rise and fall of Weimar democracy*. University of North Carolina Press.
Moulton, H. G., & McGuire, E. C. (1923). *Germany's capacity to pay*. McGraw-Hill.
Notermans, T. (2000). *Money, markets and the state*. Cambridge University Press.
Nurkse, R. (1946). *The course and control of inflation: A review of monetary experience in Europe after World war I.* League of Nations.
Ohlin, B. (1929). The Reparation problem: A discussion. *Economic Journal, 39,* 172-178 and 400-404.
Papayoanou, P. A. (1999). *Power ties: Economic interdependence, balancing, and war*. University of Michigan Press.
Patton, C. D. (1996). Politics and labor protest in the German inflation: The tax strikes of 1920 in the chemical industry. *Central European History, 29*, 61–91.
Pittaluga, G. B. (2022). War and peace in Keynes' thought. *Economia Internazionale/International Economics, 75*, 577–600.
Pittaluga, G. B. (2023). The Genova conference of 1922: A reassessment after 100 years. *Economia Internazionale/International Economics, 76*, 567–596.
Ritschl, A. (2005). The pity of peace: Germany's economy at war, 1914-1918 and beyond. In S. Broadberry & M. Harrison (Eds.), *The economics of world war I.* Cambridge University Press.
Ritschl, A. (2012). The German transfer problem, 1920–1933: a sovereign debt perspective?, CEPR. *Discussion Paper, no. DP9062*.
Röpke, W. (1931). *Der Weg des Unheils*. Fischer Verlag.

Rowe, D. (2005). The tragedy of liberalism: How globalization caused the first world war. *Security Studies, 14*, 407–447.

Schuker, J. A. (1980). Review of E. Johnson (Ed.), *The collected writings of John Maynard Keynes, volumes 17 and 18.* Journal of Economic Literature, 19, 124–126.

Schuker, J. A. (1988). American 'reparations' to Germany, 1919-33: Implications for the Third-World debt crisis. Princeton Studies in International Finance, 61.

Schuker, J. A. (2014a). J.M. Keynes and the personal politics of Reparations, part I. *Diplomacy & Statecraft, 25*, 453–471.

Schuker, J. A. (2014b). J.M. Keynes and the personal politics of Reparations, part II. *Diplomacy & Statecraft, 25*, 579–591.

Schwabe, K. (1985). *Woodrow Wilson, revolutionary Germany, and peacemaking, 1918–1919: Missionary diplomacy and the realities of power*. University of North Carolina Press.

Schwabe, K. (2014). World War I and the rise of Hitler. *Diplomatic History, 38*, 864–879.

Sidgwick, H. (1891). *The elements of politics*. Macmillan.

Skidelsky, R. (1983). *John Maynard Keynes, I, hopes betrayed, 1883–1920.* Viking.

Steiner, Z. (2005). *The lights that failed.* Oxford University Press.

Stevenson, D. (1998). French war aims and peace planning. In M. F. Boemeke, G. D. Feldman, & E. Glaeser (Eds.), *The Treaty of Versailles. A reassessment after 75 years*. Cambridge University Press.

Stolper, G. (1967). *The German economy, 1870–1940, issues and trends*. Harcourt, Brace & World.

Strange, S. (1996). *The retreat of the state: The diffusion of power in the world economy*. Cambridge University Press.

Trachtenberg, M. (2000). Review essay: Versailles revisited. *Security Studies, 9*, 191–209.

Veblen, T. (1920). Review of John Maynard Keynes, 'The economic consequences of the peace'. *Political Science Quarterly, 35*, 467–472.

Viner, J. (1947). Review of 'The Carthaginian peace—Or the economic consequences of Mr. Keynes'. *Journal of Modern History, 19*, 69–70.

Waltz, K. (1979). *Theory of international politics*. McGraw-Hill.

Waltz, K. (2000). Structural realism after the cold war. *International security, 25*, 5–41.

Webb, S. (1986). Fiscal news and inflationary expectations in Germany after WWI. *Journal of Economic History, 46*, 769–794.

Williamson, J. G., & O'Rourke, K. H. (1999). *Globalization and history: The evolution of a nineteenth century Atlantic economy*. MIT Press.

Winkler, H. A. (1987). Die Arbeiterparteien und die Republik von Weimar. In G. Schulz (Ed.), *Weimarer Republik*. Verlag Ploetz.

Winkler, H. A. (1993). *Weimar 1918–33. Die Geschichte der ersten deutschen Demokratie*. Verlag Beck.

Young, J. P. (1925). *European currency and finance*. US Government Printing Office.

Chapter 3
The Inertial Inflation of the Early Twenties

3.1 Introduction

In the previous chapter we saw how, in a context of high distributional conflict and widespread rejection of Reparations, resistance to fiscal correction measures made recourse to inflation the easiest policy choice. This choice, however, was not so much due to the fact that it allowed the government to exploit forms of monetary "illusion," but rather that powerful organized interest groups, namely industrialists and trade unions, benefited from inflation.

The hyperinflation of 1923 was the end of the inflationary process that marked the early years of the Weimar Republic. As Kunz (1986, p. 4) writes: ". . . political and social historians alike had until recently dealt almost exclusively with the impact of the hyperinflation of 1923 and with its connection to the crisis of the Weimar state in that fateful year. By doing so, they generally failed to perceive inflation as a long-term process and, consequently, as a source of prolonged social and political conflict in the early Weimar years."

The inflationary process of the early 1920s served some basic functions.[1] First of all it was an instrument of social pacification.[2] In fact, the industrial sector believed that the risk of a Bolshevik revolution could only be averted by keeping unemployment low and ensuring an adequate welfare state. This implied maintaining public spending high and, given the widespread resistance to tax increases, large budget deficits. These deficits could only be covered by the government's exploitation of seigniorage, that is by sustained inflation. At the same time, the depreciation of the exchange rate and inflation allowed German industry to benefit from negative real

[1] On this aspect, see also Feldman (1983; p.390–391) and Hardach (2017).

[2] As Borchardt (1991, p. 135) wrote: "Whatever critical comments wise economists later made regarding this period, and however much they castigated the incomprehension of monetary theory displayed by these governments, we should admit that no theory could be useful which did not also take into account political conditions."

G. B. Pittaluga, E. Seghezza, *An Economic Historiography of Germany, 1918-1931*, Frontiers in Economic History, https://doi.org/10.1007/978-3-031-70347-8_3

interest rate in the credit market and to be competitive on international markets. This favored relatively higher growth of the German economy in those years compared to other advanced economies.

Secondly, the depreciation of the exchange rate and high inflation were an instrument of pressure on the Allies to moderate requests for Reparations. A high amount of the latter, as asserted by German scholars and politicians, would have required a pronounced depreciation of the mark and exposed the Allied economies to particularly competitive and aggressive German exports.

The unions, aware of the benefits of inflation on the unemployment rate and on the welfare state of workers, were not against it. They were, however, concerned about protecting the purchasing power of wages. Initially, they pursued this aim through wage negotiations, however, from 1920 onwards, with the publication of price level statistics by the Reich Bureau of Statistics, wages could be indexed to prices. Given the delay with which wages were adjusted to the price dynamics, in part due to the time required to collect and publish the data on price changes, real wages fell significantly during periods of accelerating inflation. To counter this, the wage indexation procedure was made more reactive by gradually reducing the time lag of wage adjustment to prices. Because of this, as is often the case in countries with forms of wage indexation, inflation became *persistent*. High inflation persistence made it more difficult for German monetary authorities to control inflation.

3.2 The Inflation Goals of the Most Influential Interest Groups

In a context where the war of attrition between various organized interest groups prevented the implementation of any fiscal adjustment measures and, at the same time, the main political objective of the elite, as mentioned above, was to maintain relative social calm, a large budget deficit was inevitable. Since the conditions to cover it with debt were lacking, there was no alternative but to resort to the exploitation of seigniorage and inflation.

In their 1964 study on German inflation, the economists Laursen and Pedersen surprisingly argue that this inflation was the result of a "lack of policy" on the part of both the government and interest groups.[3] On the contrary, the use of inflation as a government instrument to procure resources to cover budgetary imbalances was advocated by the most influential interest groups, in particular industrialists. Many of these explicitly stated that they preferred inflation to revolution, which was their greatest fear. Germany's leading industrialist, Hugo Stinnes, in a meeting he had with the American ambassador Alanson Houghton and foreign minister Walther Rathenau at the end of June 1922, declared that: "... the choice had been between

[3] On this aspect see Kunz (1986, p. 20–21).

inflation and revolution and of the two he favored inflation."[4] In his opinion it was "... politically necessary to put to work three million men coming back from the war. It was ... a question of your money or your life."[5] At the same meeting Rathenau expressed a similar view. In his opinion, "inflation was no worse economically than rent control" and maintained that inflation only took from those who had and gave to those who had not, which in a country as poor as Germany was entirely proper.[6]

This position of the industrialists was largely shared by the bankers. The Hamburg banker Melchior repeatedly emphasized that an accommodative fiscal policy and an inflationary monetary policy were necessary to maintain the country's political stability.[7] Writing to his senior partner Max Warburg in 1923, he emphasized the fact that "it was always a question of whether one wished to stop the inflation and trigger the revolution."[8]

A number of scholars have argued that alongside the explicitly stated political reasons of fearing revolution,[9] businessmen were also in favor of inflation for their own economic interests.[10] A first reason was that it favored a reduction, at least temporarily, in real wages[11] and, therefore, made it possible to render the trade unions' high wage demands compatible with higher profits. Second, inflation eroded the real value of taxable income and allowed businessmen to pay income taxes that were lower in real terms. Thirdly, since the Reichsbank tended not to change the discount rate, the cost of borrowing for businesses effectively became negative in period of high price rises. Finally, given the flexible exchange rate regime, entrepreneurs enjoyed notable competitive benefits from phases of pronounced nominal and real exchange rate depreciation, even if these phases were then followed by an acceleration of prices.

On the basis of these considerations, some scholars have come to the conclusion that inflation in Germany in the period after the First World War should be attributed mainly, if not exclusively, to industrialists and their pressure on the government for an expansive economic policy.[12] The attribution of responsibility for inflation to the

---

[4] See National Archives, Washington, RG 59, 862.00/1128, Houghton to State Dept., 25 June 1922.

[5] See National Archives, Washington, RG 59, 862.00/1199, Houghton to Secretary of State, 27 December 1922.

[6] See National Archives, Washington, RG.59, 862.00/1128. Houghon to State Dept. 25 June 1922. Quoted in Feldman (1993, p. 447 ff.).

[7] See Warburg Archive, M.M. Warburg Co., Hamburg, Politische Correspondenz 1921, Melchior to S. Japhet, 15 Jan. 1921.

[8] See Warburg Archive, M.M. Warburg Co., Hamburg, "Jahresbericht 1923" p. 43.

[9] See Maier (1975, 1987) and Feldman (1993).

[10] See Specht (1982) and Gossweiler (1971).

[11] See Bresciani-Turroni (1937, p. 104ff.) and Graham (1930, p. 313).

[12] See also Bresciani-Turroni (1937, p. 330 ff.), Graham (1930, p. 281) and Witt (1983).

entrepreneurial class and in particular to big industry often implies blaming the industrial sector for the failure of Germany's stabilization.[13]

However, while entrepreneurs clearly benefited from inflation, it cannot be said that workers were harmed by it. In fact, wages being indexed to inflation and, albeit with some delay compared to price acceleration phases, meant that their purchasing power was safeguarded. Moreover, the expansion of public expenditure which, to a large extent, was made possible by the resources that the government acquired from inflation and seigniorage, was directed mainly toward improving the living conditions of the poorer classes and workers.

The fact that both business and a large proportion of workers benefited from inflation "... involved an implicit coalition of labor and industry at the expense of rentiers, professionals, the civil service and modest entrepreneurs. Industrialists with access to credit stood to profit greatly and industry in general could benefit from heavy demand. Labor avoided post-war lay-offs and preserved relative wage protection until the final months of the monetary collapse."[14]

The erosion of income and wealth resulting from inflation was borne mainly by the interest groups not protected from inflation, in particular rentiers. Moreover, receiving a negative real return on their assets they also suffered a form of redistribution in favor not only of the state, but also of other interest groups who, like industrialists and landowners, benefited from it, or those who were protected from it, such as workers. What has just been stated makes the structural interpretation of German inflation credible.[15] In a few words this inflation can be considered the result of two factors. On the one hand, the unresolved clash between interest groups, none of whom were willing to bear the costs of paying Reparations and stabilizing German economy, thereby making the implementation of fiscal measure aimed at rebalancing the public budget impossible. And, on the other hand, the existence of a demand for inflation of the most influential interest groups that benefited from it and were worried about widespread labor unrest and the risk of revolution.

Inflation, by allowing an otherwise unsustainable level of public expenditure and domestic absorption, guaranteed Germany a period of relative social peace and prevented the collapse of the Republic. Given the weakness of the Republic it "was the least undesirable means of dealing with Germany's problems in the first post-war years,"[16] and thus contributed to the survival of that regime.

In fact, as we have seen in the previous chapter, between 1919 and 1922, Germany had particularly low unemployment rates compared to other advanced

[13]See Feldman (1977) and Maier (1987). Some scholars such as Weisbrod (1979) tended to attribute this behavior of big business to their lack of commitment to the Republic and their nostalgia for the authoritarian regime of the pre-World War I period.

[14]See Maier (1987, p. 205). A similar position is found in Borchardt ([1972] 1991, p. 135) and Ferguson (1995, p. 197).

[15]See Kindleberger (1984a, b) and Maier (1987).

[16]See Feldman (1993, p. 838).

countries, in particular the United Kingdom and the United States.[17] However, when considering the economic benefits of German inflation in the early 1920s, a distinction must be made first between the short and the long term. A distinction, moreover, already made by Bresciani-Turroni (1937, p. 404) when he wrote: "The inflation delayed the crisis for some time, but this broke out later, throwing millions out of employment. At first inflation stimulated production because of the divergence between the internal and external values of mark; but later it exercised an increasingly disadvantageous influence, disorganizing and limiting production. It annihilated thrift; it made reform of the national budget impossible for years; it obstructed the solution of the Reparations question; it destroyed incalculable moral and intellectual values."

The economic benefits of the inflation of the early 1920s were largely undermined by the hyperinflation of 1923[18] which represents the evolution of the inflationary choices of the governments of the preceding period and which, therefore, as Kunz (1986) observes, cannot be considered in isolation, as if it were an unrelated spontaneous event. These choices involved persistent Reich budget deficits and an entirely accommodating monetary policy on the part of the Reichsbank. The characteristics of these components of Germany's economic policy in the early 1920s are illustrated in the next two subsections.

3.2.1 The Way Fiscal Policy Was Accommodative

In the course of 1919, the German government, having to cope with the problems of demobilization and the economic and social impact of a lost war, increased public spending, especially current expenditure, to a pronounced extent. With the end of the war and the demobilization of the army, unemployment increased significantly, reaching 6.6% in January 1919. Employers tried to exploit this high rate of unemployment and their higher relative power to reverse the wage increases of November 1918.

However, the government, in particular the MSPD, fearing the political consequences of such high unemployment, saw the creation of new jobs as a primary political objective and hence provided substantial government subsidies to certain industries, such as ship-building.[19] At the same time, municipalities were delegated

[17] Laursen and Pedersen (1964, p. 123) write: "… a high level of employment was maintained in Germany whereas more or less severe depression prevailed in those countries that chose to combat inflation. The result was not only that total production in Germany was relatively high compared to that of other countries, but that distribution was more egalitarian."

[18] "More generally, it seems hard to deny that whatever benefits the inflation conferred in 1921 and 1922 were compensated for by the sharp falls in production and employment after hyperinflation set in." Ferguson (1996, p. 638).

[19] See Ferguson (1995, p. 182 ff.)

Table 3.1 Revenue and expenditures of German Reich (millions of gold marks, 1919–1922)

Periods	Revenue	Expenditures	Surplus (+) or deficit (−)	Increase in floating debt
April 1919 to March 1920	2559.1	8559.8	−6000.7	5999.0
April 1920 to March 1921	3178.1	9328.7	−6150.6	6053.6
April 1921 to March 1922	2927.4	6651.3	−3723.9	3675.8

Source: Bresciani-Turroni (1937)

the task of providing unemployment relief.[20] Such measures corresponded perfectly with the political and social program of the Social Democratic Party, the relative majority party at the time. These policies implied a significant increase in public spending to build houses, hospitals, schools and pay the salaries of new civil servants, but also to provide for the large number of those wounded in the war as well as for hundreds of thousands of widows and orphans.

Meeting these morally imperative commitments led to a pronounced increase in public spending in 1919, however since revenue did not increase correspondingly, a large fiscal deficit was created and the floating debt increased by almost six billions of gold marks (Table 3.1).

In an effort to make more resources available, the Erzberger-led government prepared a tax reform that came into force in August 1919. This reform pursued two different objectives. Firstly, it transferred control of taxation from the states to the federal government, providing the latter with "equalization" payments.[21] Secondly, the Erzberger reform envisaged a significant redistribution of the tax burden in favor of low- and middle-income citizens. It established progressive income taxation with rates up to 60% (compared to 8% in the years of the German empire). At the same time, it introduced a corporate income tax of 20% and a capital levy to tax capital gains, and raise the tax burden on the wealthy. The general sales tax was increased and became a general consumption tax. Furthermore, the inheritance tax was expanded.

When the reform was fully implemented, the government was expected to obtain 65% of its revenue from direct taxation and the remaining 35% from indirect taxes.

However, expectations of an increase in overall tax revenue due to Erzberger's financial reform were disappointed. The share of taxes on the government total

[20]This division of responsibility responded to the desire of the elite, in particular the Junkers, not to leave the determination of direct taxes "in the hands of a parliamentary body elected on equal suffrage." From a speech of the leader of the conservatives Heydebrand in the Reichstag on 10 July 1909. Quoted in Witt (1983).

[21]Until the end of the First World War, there was a clear separation between the Reich's taxation and that of the States and Communities. The former was responsible for expenditure on defence and war and for other less important functions, such as the country's foreign representation expenses. To cover these expenses, the Reich could only resort to indirect taxes, primarily consumption taxes and excise duties. States and cities bore the remaining expenses, particularly those of welfare, and met them, in addition to income from their property holdings in the productive sector, with direct taxes and inheritance taxes. On this aspect, see in particular Witt (1983) and Feldman (1993).

income gradually decreased from about 45% in 1921, to about 35% in 1922, to 11% in 1923. The gradual decrease in revenue from both direct and indirect taxes was due to both the Olivera–Tanzi effect[22] and inefficiencies in financial administration. Indirect taxes, in fact, were mainly based on quantity, i.e. they did not take into account price levels: it was, therefore, a system that was not very responsive to inflation.[23] A similar problem existed in the case of direct taxes. In fact, the collection of these taxes took place many months after the original assessment[24] and inflation incentivized taxpayers to exploit all available means to lengthen the time of each step of assessment, that is making the tax declaration, confirmation of the tax amount, and eventually making the payment. Workers could not, however, exploit this mechanism of delays, since a withholding tax of 10% was levied directly from their wages. The workers' complaints about the unequal tax treatment of wages compared with other sources of tax remained unresolved for many years and, in 1922, when mechanisms were finally devised to solve the problem of the lag between assessment and payment of taxes, the onset of hyperinflation had made their application unnecessary.

As a matter of fact, the effectiveness of the Erzberger reform was undermined by the war of attrition of the various interest groups, none of whom were willing to bear the tax burden necessary to cover growing public expenditure.[25] Each "blocking coalition" justified its refusal to accept new taxes with the excuse that the Allies' demands of war Reparations were unreasonable. As mentioned above, this attitude was, to a large extent, the outcome of myths originating from propaganda declaring the Treaty of Versailles a humiliation and the Reparations unjustified.

An example of the resistance of interest groups to any sacrifice can be seen in the vicissitudes of the May 1921 bill presented by the Minister of Economic Affairs, Schmidt and his secretary Hirsch and supported by the socialists, according to which industry would have to cede 20% of shares and bonds to the state.[26] This proposal was met with overwhelming opposition, within the government itself, from ministers with ties to the DNVP and DVP. In the face of this opposition, Schmidt and Hirsch revised their proposal and transformed the company tax into a capital tax, with a 4% levy on individual wealth. The industrialists' representatives reacted strongly to this new proposal and, after a debate both inside and outside parliament, it all came to nothing.[27]

---

[22] See Olivera (1967) and Tanzi (1978).

[23] See Witt (1983, p. 458).

[24] Consequently, due to inflation the real revenue of taxes was very small. See, among others, Witt (1983).

[25] As Alesina (1988, p. 43) writes with reference to the German situation in the early 1920s: "The standstill was the result of political struggle between the representatives of different constituencies which attempted to switch the tax burden away from their own group."

[26] See Maier (1975, p. 254 ff.).

[27] Toward the end of August 1921, Chancellor Wirth proposed a compromise to the industrialists: he would shelve the SPD proposals in exchange for the industrialists taking out a hard-money loan. The majority of industrialists accepted this compromise.

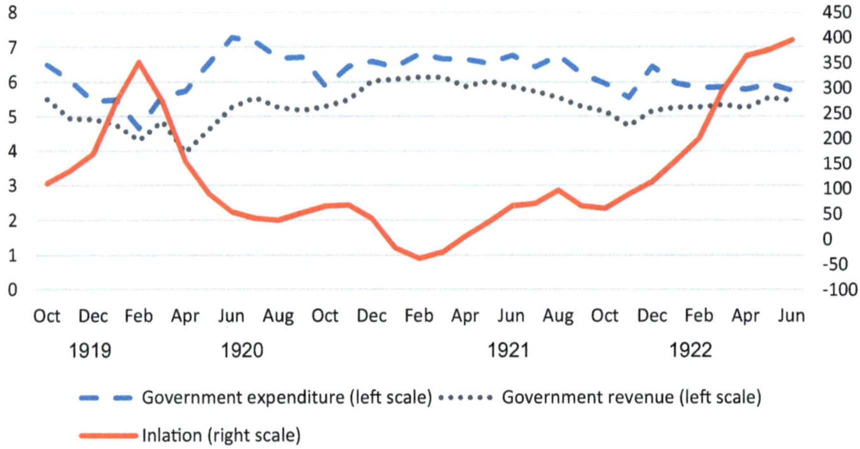

Fig. 3.1 Inflation, German government expenditure and revenue (Oct. 1919 – Jun. 1922). Source: for domestic prices, see Holtfrerich (1986), and, for the Reich's revenue and expenditure in gold mark, see Bresciani-Turroni (1937). Note: the Reich deficit is expressed in logarithm

This war of attrition between the different interest groups meant that the German state's revenue was persistently lower than its expenditure and the Reich's fiscal deficits became persistent. Their amount in real terms, however, was strongly influenced by inflation. As we have already seen, and as Fig. 3.1 shows, between 1919 and June 1922—i.e., before the onset of hyperinflation—Germany's year-on-year inflation rate was already very high, often exceeding 100%. In particular, two phases of intense acceleration of price growth can be identified: one in the second part of 1919 until the beginning of 1920 and another in the second part of 1921 until the beginning of 1922. Both of these phases of accelerating price growth were preceded by a pronounced depreciation of the mark.

The different phases of inflation just illustrated were reflected in the trend of the German government deficit in gold marks (which can be considered a good proxy for the real value of this variable). Figure 3.1 shows that in phases of accelerating inflation both the Reich's revenue and expenditure in gold marks (that is in real terms) tended to decline. They increased, however, in phases of slowing inflation and relative price stability.

The decrease in government revenue in the phases of acceleration of inflation was due to the operation of the Olivera–Tanzi effect, while that of government expenditures was due to the operation of the Patinkin effect.[28] The relevance of this last

[28] As described by Patinkin (1993, p. 115): "In a situation where ... the finance minister does not have the power to force individual ministries to make adequate reductions in their respective budgetary demands and is thus confronted with an overall budget whose planned expenditures far exceeds its expected revenues, he may seemingly accept these demands and then finance the deficit by printing money and letting the resulting inflation enforce the necessary reduction in real government expenditure."

Table 3.2 Government expenditure by economic category (as percentage of total expenditure, 1913–1925–1932)

	Goods and services			
	Current	Capital	Total	Transfers and subsidies
1913	64	19	83	17
1925	52	6	58	42
1932	49	3	52	48

Source: Andic and Veverka (1963/64)

effect was to a large extent due to the composition of the Reich's expenditure, which shifted markedly after WWI in favor of current expenditure and transfers at the expense of capital expenditure (Table 3.2). The latter was 19% of total expenditure in 1913, fell to 6% in 1925 and reached a mere 6% in 1932. During phases of accelerating inflation, the level of civil servants' salaries, pensions, transfers, subsidies, insurance benefits or items that constituted a large part of public spending fell in real terms. Similarly, the real cost of servicing public debt contracted[29]: the incidence of interest expenditure on total expenditure falls from over 12% in 1919, to 6.7 in 1920, 4.5 in 1921, and 2.5 in the first half of 1922.[30]

As shown by Fig. 3.1, in phases of accelerating inflation government expenditure in real terms contracted more pronouncedly than government revenue in gold marks in times of rising prices. Therefore, it can be said that in the years before the hyperinflation of 1923, in Germany, the Patinkin effect was greater than the Olivera–Tanzi effect (Fig. 3.1).[31]

When inflation decreased, real wages increased, the real exchange rate[32] rose, and German exports decreased with depressive effects on output (Fig. 3.2). In these phases, public spending in real terms increased more than the government revenue (Fig. 3.1): fiscal policy, therefore, was anti-cyclical.

Increases of Reich's expenditure were financed to a large extent by exploiting seigniorage (Fig. 3.3).

Taking into account the fact that, due to the prevalence of the Patinkin effect over the Olivera–Tanzi effect, the Reich's deficits tended to be higher in phases of

[29] On this aspect Bresciani-Turroni (1937, p. 69), referring to the period between 1919 and 1920, writes the following: "[T]he study of the German finances shows that in the second half of 1919 the depreciation of the mark not only produced a diminution of the real value of the receipts but also greatly reduced the expenses, calculated in gold marks. That is explained by the fact that in 1919 by far the greater part of the expenditure of the Reich was current expenditure. Therefore, the payments which were constant in paper marks, i.e. interest on the public debt, pensions and transfers, were still a substantial proportion of ordinary expenditure of the Reich."

[30] See Webb (1989, p. 37).

[31] The impact of the Patinkin effect in the years immediately post-WWI in Germany therefore calls for a reconsideration of the debate on the optimal inflation rate in phases of high price growth. This is discussed in Cardoso (1998) and Seghezza (2022).

[32] The real exchange rate is the relative price of consumption baskets across countries. It is expressed in the following way: $\varepsilon_t = \frac{e_t P_t^*}{P_t}$, where ε_t is the real exchange rate and e_t the nominal exchange rate (the mark cost of a US dollar), while P_t and P_t^* are, respectively, consumer price levels at home and abroad. See Itskhoki (2021).

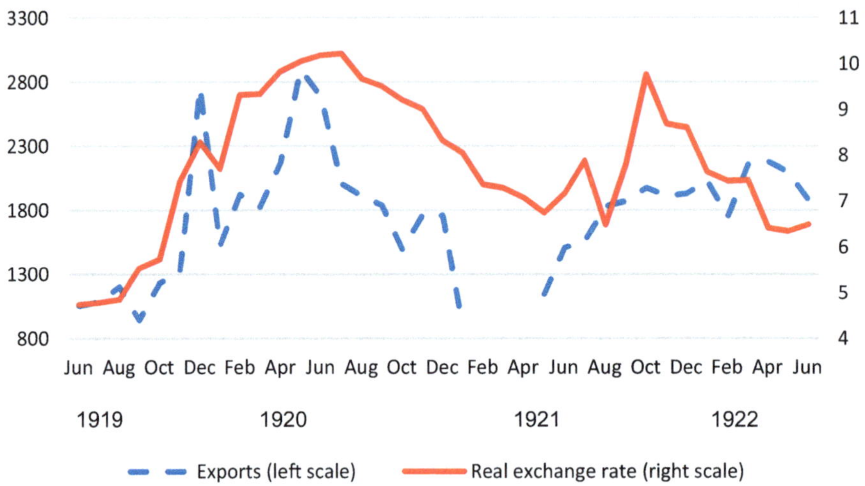

Fig. 3.2 German exports and real exchange rate of the mark (Jun. 1919 – Jun. 1922). Source: Bresciani-Turroni (1937). Notes: Export (thousands of tons). For the measurement of the real exchange rate, see footnote 32. Exports data for January–April 1921 have never been published

slowing inflation, the government's recourse to seigniorage was more consistent in these phases than in those of accelerating inflation.

In the debate on the optimal inflation rate, i.e. the inflation rate that allows the seigniorage to be maximized,[33] it is assumed that, given a certain public deficit in real terms, inflation, like any other tax, follows the trend of the Laffer curve and, therefore, the resources achieved through it increase up to a certain point (the one corresponding to the optimal inflation rate) and after this point reduce. In reality, the inflation tax not only allows the government to exploit the right of seigniorage, but also acts on the expenditure, particularly current expenditure, reducing its real value. Therefore, the plausibility of the hypothesis of a constant deficit in real terms underlying Cagan's scheme and its developments is lost.

3.2.2 The Accommodative Policy of the Reichsbank

With the war mobilization in 1914, the convertibility of the mark into gold was suspended and, in order to make government debt less costly, the discount rate was set permanently at 5%. Besides, an amendment of 9 May 1921 to the Reichsbankgesetz (the Reichsbank Act) suspended the rule that the Reichsbank

[33]See Simonsen (1970, 1983) and Pazos (1978).

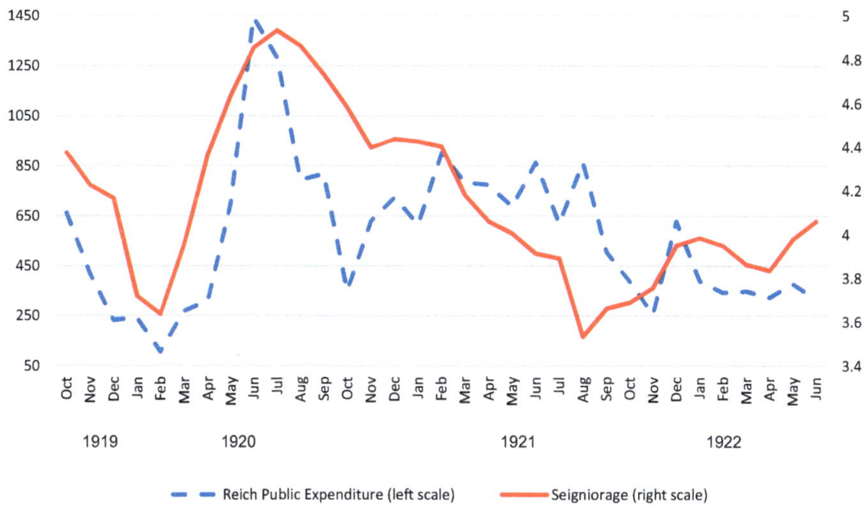

Fig. 3.3 Reich public expenditure and seigniorage (Oct. 1919 – Jun. 1922). Source: for Reich expenditure in gold marks, see Bresciani Turroni (1937). Following Obstfeld (1989), seigniorage is calculated as given by: $\frac{M_t - M_{t-12}}{M_t} = \pi_t m_{t-12} + (m_t - m_{t-12})$ where $\pi_t = (P_t - P_{t-12})/P_t$ and $m = M/P$

had to maintain gold reserves equal to at least one-third of the banknotes it issued.[34] All these measures extended the margins of discretion in the conduct of monetary policy. At the same time, until May 1922, the Reichsbank was entirely subordinate to the government. As Holtfrerich (1988, p. 115) aptly notes: "By cutting loose from the gold standard at the beginning of the war and by granting the Reich open access to the Reichsbank's credit, the legal subordination of the Bank under the Reich's Chancellor until May 1922 also became a practical reality." In this context, monetary policy was aimed primarily at covering fiscal deficits.[35] Indeed, the German government's persistent public deficits even before the hyperinflation of 1923 should have been covered primarily by issuing Treasury bills. A very large part of the public debt issued by the government was held by the Reichsbank.[36] It is therefore not surprising that there was a close relationship between the share of Treasury bills

[34]Moreover, the link between commercial banks and public finance had also become very close during the war. This close link persisted even in the years immediately following the war. A study of the balance sheets of the country's 19 largest universal banks shows that for them, between 1913 and 1920, the percentage of assets held in bills and Treasury bills had increased from 20.9% to 48.5%.

[35]See Webb (1986).

[36]Given the political tensions with the Allies and their own economic difficulties in the post-war period, it was unthinkable that Germany could obtain financing from abroad. It was also problematic for the German government to finance itself on the domestic financial market given the extreme economic and political uncertainty within the country.

Table 3.3 Treasury bills discounted by the Reichsbank and notes in circulation (billions of marks, 1919–1922)

Months	Amount of discounted bills held by the Reichsbank	Notes in circulation
1919—June	33.1	30.0
September	33.6	29.8
December	41.3	35.7
1920—March	42.7	45.2
June	45.0	54.0
September	49.6	61.7
December	57.6	68.8
1921—March	64.5	69.4
June	79.6	75.3
September	98.4	86.4
December	132.3	113.6
1922—March	146.5	131.0
June	186.1	169.0

Source: Graham (1930)

discounted by the Reichsbank and the amount of notes in circulation[37] (Table 3.3). This meant that the coverage of fiscal deficits was to a large extent achieved by issuing money.[38]

As seen in the previous section, the Reich's spending and its deficit tended to increase in phases of relative price stability. Therefore, it was in these phases that money in real terms increased (Fig. 3.4).

The President of the Reichsbank, Rudolph Havenstein, at least until 1921, in confidential reports to the government did not fail to express his dissent, both he and his staff pointing out that the root cause of inflation was to be found in the excessive growth of the money supply.[39] The latter in turn, in their view, was due to the Reichsbank's massive absorption of government bonds to cover fiscal deficits. With this, they urged the government to adopt a more virtuous financial policy. From 1921, after the London Plan, the German central bank, however, changed its position, claiming that it regarded the large German public debt as a consequence of the Reparations imposed by the Allies.[40]

In the years immediately following WWI, the Reichsbank's monetary policy was accommodative not only with respect to the expansionary fiscal policy pursued by the government, but also with respect to demand for private credit. In fact, this

---

[37] The share of Treasury bills discounted by the Reichsbank varied in relation to the propensity of commercial banks and private individuals to hold these securities and therefore depended to a large extent on the public's confidence in the stability of the mark: in phases of pronounced depreciation of the German currency, this share decreased, while that of the Reichsbank increased.

[38] See Webb (1984).

[39] See Reichsbank-Direktorium, memorandum, 1 July 1919. BArch R 2/3889; Reichsbank-Direktorium 1919. Reichsbank-Direktorium, memorandum, 29 July 1919. BArch R 2/1894.

[40] See Holtfrerich (1986).

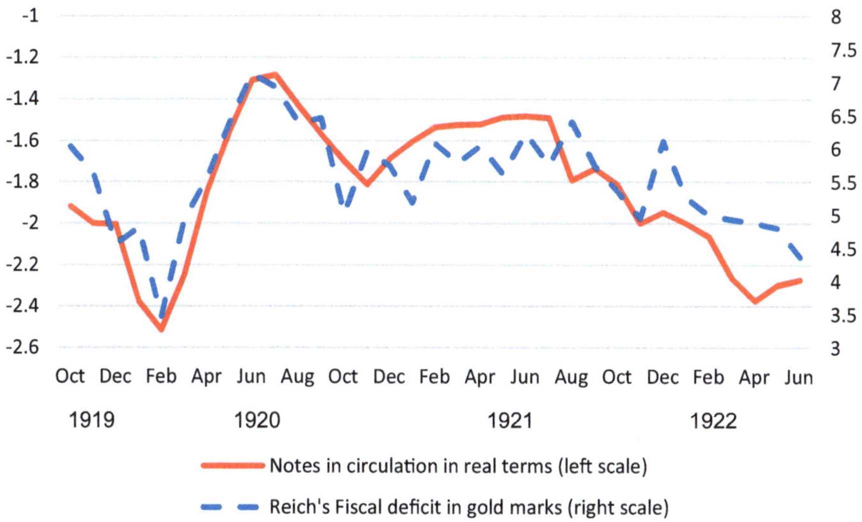

Fig. 3.4 Reich's fiscal deficit and notes in circulation in real terms (Oct. 1919 – Jun. 1922). Source: for notes in circulation in nominal terms and deficit in gold marks Bresciani-Turroni (1937); for the index of wholesale prices Holtfrerich (1986). Note: the variables are expressed in logarithms; the notes in circulation in real terms is given by the ratio of the notes in circulation in nominal terms on the index of wholesale prices

attitude of the German central bank stemmed from different factors. First of all, the President of the Reichsbank adhered in some way to the principles of the "real bills doctrine." As Nurkse writes in a study of the League of Nations: "... Havenstein, President of the Reichsbank, in so far as he had any theoretical notions at all, adhered to a form of the 'banking principle' which told him that the rise in prices created a need for money on the part of businessmen as well of the government, a need which it was the Reichsbank's duty to meet, and which it could meet without any harmful effects."[41]

Secondly, the objective of maintaining relaxed monetary conditions for businesses was shared by the government. In the early part of 1921, when temporary monetary restraint was affecting productive activity, a proposal was put forward by State Secretary, Julius Schmidt, to set up a state "Economic Bank" with the task of granting credit to enterprises of national importance.[42] This was a way of urging the Reichsbank to provide credit to industry, particularly heavy industry, i.e. to relax its stance on monetary policy.

For the reasons just mentioned monetary policy in Germany was generally absolutely accommodating toward the demand for loans of the private sector. In

[41] Quoted by Yeager (1966, p. 271). See also Humphrey (1982).

[42] See Ferguson (1996, p. 289 ff) and Feldman (1982).

particular, in the second part of 1921, when the mark depreciated significantly and inflation accelerated markedly and wholesale prices between June and December increased up to 142.2%, the German central bank, by keeping the policy rate at 5%, accepted a markedly decrease of the short-term real interest rate and in such a way encouraged an increase in demand for credit from firms.[43] Between June and December 1921, the discounted commercial bills held by Reichsbank rose from 2.6% to 32.6% of the circulating notes.

The negative real interest rate on loans added to the high amount of banking credit to firms in encouraging high production growth. The expansionary pressures on output came above all from firms with high leverage which benefited significantly from the progressive decrease in the interest expenses as a share of total expenses.[44] This process, on the one hand, contributed to reducing the production costs of a large part of German firms, increasing their level of competitiveness, and, on the other hand, relaxed their financial constraints.

The easy access to credit for firms, in addition to stimulating production, also favored distortionary phenomena. Many firms acquired real assets, in particular capital goods, thus protecting themselves from inflation, but giving rise to an over investment in their physical capital thus creating the prerequisites for the structural weakening of the German economy, which will be discussed below. However, some firms also went into debt in order to speculate against the mark, thus contributing to its further depreciation. The persistently high inflation and negative real interest rate favored also a change in the behavior of commercial banks. In the second half of 1921, following the significant depreciation of the mark that occurred after the issuing of the London Ultimatum,[45] the hope in a future appreciation of the mark faded in the minds of many German bankers. As a result, they began to take measures to safeguard their position and to regain some of the capital strength they had lost between 1913 and 1919.[46] Firstly, the big German banks took measures to protect themselves against the depreciation of the mark by holding part of their deposits in foreign currencies with foreign banks. Secondly, they used another substantial part of their deposits to buy industrial shares and real estate[47] and finally, they profited from the intense expansion of loans, the demand for which was stimulated by inflation and negative real interest rates.[48] Notwithstanding these steps, the efforts of banks to recover the capital strength which they had enjoyed

[43] See Pfleiderer (1976), Petzina et al. (1978) and Holtfrerich(1986).

[44] Brunnermeier et al. (2022), taking this aspect into account, argue that inflation stimulated Germany's economic growth via a debt-inflation channel.

[45] Occurred on 5 May 1921.

[46] These banks lost about 90% of their capital during this time. See Goldschmidt (1927).

[47] See Wixforth (2003).

[48] Despite a partial capital restoration thanks to these management choices, the German banking system lost a large part of its capital and reserves between 1913 and 1923 and was structurally weakened in the following years. See Lansburgh (1923).

before the war were only partially successful. This weakening of the banks will weigh on the German economy in the following years.

Because of its accommodative behavior toward the public and the private sector,[49] at that time the Reichsbank was blamed. It was blamed mainly for the failure to stabilize the German economy in 1920.[50] In this context, the Allied powers, particularly Britain, demanded the German government that the Reichsbank be made independent. The Autonomy Law, passed on 21 May 1922, stipulated that the Chancellor was no longer the head of the Reichsbank and that the members of the Reichsbank directorate were selected by the Reichsrat and were formally appointed by the President. However, the Reparations Commission complained that in the Autonomy Law there were no limit to the amount the Reichsbank could lend the government and, in fact, the Reichsbank's accommodating behavior did not change after the Autonomy Law came into force. Havenstein defended this behavior in a reply in *The Daily Telegraph* to an article published there that blamed the Reichsbank for Germany's high inflation[51] assessing that he was a civil servant devoted exclusively to the Reich.[52] For the same reason Havenstein always carefully avoided public criticism of the government, even if he disagreed with its budgetary policy.[53]

3.3 The Inflation of the Early Twenties: The Role of Wage Adjustment

During the war, big industry had been strengthened both economically and politically thanks to military orders, but equally the German labor movement obtained recognition from the state for the first time. In December 1916, the necessity of increasing production induced the German government to pass the Auxiliary Service Act; this recognized the unions as representative bodies, setting up employer councils in essential industries and establishing joint conciliation boards. With the "November revolution" the employers, fearing the spread of the radical left, felt the need to appeal to the socialist unionists in order to counter the tide of

[49] Due to its concern that both the state and companies might be subject to a credit restrain and that this would have a negative impact on productive activity. See Webb (1989, p. 24).

[50] At that stage, the Reichsbank should have raised the discount rate and thus stimulated capital inflows from abroad, thereby facilitating the non-monetary coverage of public deficits. In particular, the Reichsbank's monetary policy was criticized by the committee that investigated the causes of the mark's fall in the spring of 1923. See Bresciani-Turroni (1937, p. 78).

[51] Havenstein Ubersetzung aus *The Daily Telegraph* vom 6. September 1922: "Die deutsche Reichsbank," 6 Sep. 1922, Bundesarchiv, Berlin-Lichterfeide.

[52] See Kopper (2006).

[53] See Müller (1973, p. 38).

Table 3.4 German trade union members (1913–1918–1919)

Periods	Socialist	Christian	Hirsch-Dunker	Total
1913	2,574,000	343,000	107,000	3,024,000
1918	1,665,000	393,000	114,000	2,172,000
1919	5,479,000	858,000	190,000	6,527,000

Source: Correspondenzblatt der Generalkommission der Gewerkschaften Deutschlands, Statitische Beilage, no. 20, 1920

Bolshevism[54] and thus declared themselves willing to make important concessions to the unions.[55]

On 15 November 1918, an agreement was concluded between the country's leading industrialists and the labor representatives, the so-called Stinnes–Legien Agreement, which laid down the principles that would regulate the relationship between capital and labor. "These were: recognition of the trade unions as representing the working classes; determination of the conditions of work in each industry by collective agreements between employers and workers, and the establishment of workers' committees to supervise the implementation of the terms agreed upon; affirmation of the principle of the eight-hour day; reorganization, on an equal representation basis, of the employment exchanges; the setting up of conciliation committees for the various different industries (made up of equal numbers of employers and workers); and of a central Council to deal with disputes affecting more than one industrial group."[56]

In part as a result of this agreement trade unions' membership rose significantly from just over 2 million at the end of the war to over 6.5 million at the end of 1919 (Table 3.4). This contributed to a significant increase in the political pressure capacity of the unions.[57]

In the early 1920s, "political power" rather than "economic laws" led wage policy.[58] The main goal of the trade unions was to recover the purchasing power of wages lost during the war. In the months immediately following the revolution, however, workers' demands were conveyed rather than by traditional labor representatives, by workers' councils, an indication of a new found labor radicalism. This radicalism was also reflected in a resumption of industrial unrest. In June 1919, a two-week fishermen's strike was largely successful, while in August bank clerks went on strike. They, like employees in other sectors of the economy, obtained

[54] See Ham (1934).

[55] As Ferguson (1995, p. 178) writes: "The November Revolution manifested itself in the workplace as an unprecedented explosion of labor demands to which employers, suddenly deprived of military support, had no option but to accede ... workers' representatives were insistent that for the transitional period the question of wages is to be determined not according to productivity, but according to what the workers need."

[56] See Bresciani-Turroni (1929, p. 385).

[57] See Feldman (1993, p. 125).

[58] See Kunz (1986, p. 83).

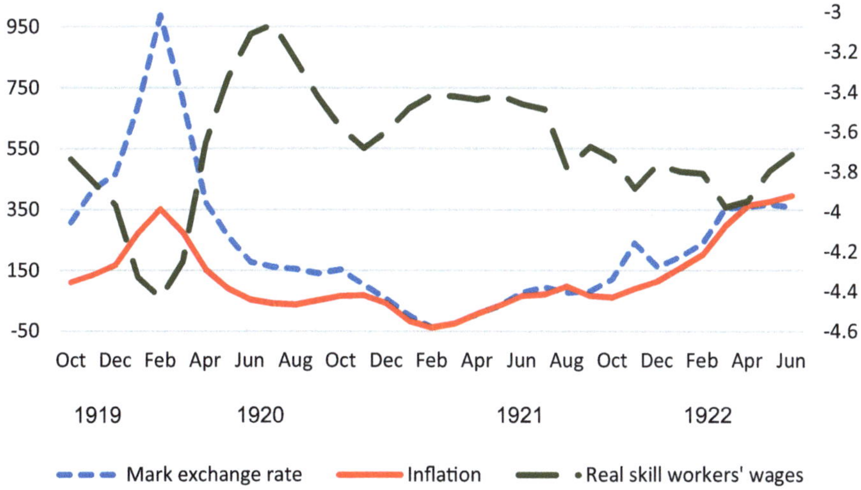

Fig. 3.5 Mark exchange rate, inflation and real skill workers' wages (Oct. 1919 – Jun. 1922). Source: for the mark's exchange rate and inflation, see Holtfrerich (1986); for skill workers' wages, see Statistisches Reichsamt (1925). Note: real wages are given by the ratio of monetary wages and consumer prices

substantial wage increases and this trend later extended to industrial workers and civil servants. In a period of extensive price controls on basic necessities and thus subject to only a moderate rise in the cost of living, the rise in nominal wages represented a significant rise in real wages.

The large increase in monetary wages in the period immediately following the November revolution was, however, eroded significantly between the latter part of 1919 and the beginning of 1920 (Fig. 3.5).

In fact, during this period, the pronounced depreciation of the mark that occurred after the German acceptance of the Treaty of Versailles and the removal of exchange controls in September 1919 by the Bauer government caused a significant increase in the price of imported and wholesale goods. These increases eventually had an impact on the workers' cost of living, reducing the purchasing power of wages. The translation process just described was relatively slow as it was, at least initially, mitigated by price controls on food and rents. It gradually became more pronounced during the early 1920s as a large part of these controls were removed. Consequently, the purchasing power of wages fell dramatically. By March 1920, their value was between 15 and 40% below pre-war levels.

However, in March, the bargaining power of the workers was significantly strengthened by the contribution made to the failure of the Kapp coup by the general strike called by the works' councils and unions. This political success of the workers and unions gave them "... an opportunity to make clear to whoever ruled in Berlin that the workers had no intention of abandoning their power and surrendering the gains of the November revolution."[59]

Thanks to their increased bargaining power, the trade unions were able to present significant economic and regulatory demands to the government.[60] And, in the immediate aftermath of the Kapp coup, significant wage increases occurred in the public sector which were enshrined in the Salary Reform Act passed by the Reichstag on 28 April 1920, an act which was estimated to involve an additional public expenditure of around 4 billion marks.[61] "... The state rail and tram workers won a 5% wage increase in April 1920, and struck again in August 1920 and January 1921; while the postal employees were said to work 'only when the mood takes them.' But even groups with little experience of collective action were drawn into the wage spiral."[62] In fact, the spiral of wage increases quickly extended from the public to the private sector.

After the London Ultimatum, the mark depreciated again in the second half of 1921: By December, it had depreciated by more than 160% compared to the same month of the previous year. Correspondingly, domestic price growth also accelerated and a phase of pronounced decline in real wages began.

A process of wage adjustment to price dynamics similar to that which occurred between the spring and summer of 1920 took place in the first part of 1922.[63] Figure 3.5 shows that during exchange rate depreciations, there was a fall in real wages.[64] This was due to the fact that the exchange rate depreciation provoked an increase in domestic prices. The level of monetary wages adjusted to the trend in prices with some delay and in this way the real wage was, in due course, restored to its previous level.

In the pre-hyperinflation period, therefore, there does not seem to have been a run-up between wages and the exchange rate: wages were adjusted to price dynamics with some delay. The latter being led by variations of the exchange rate.

However, the speed with which wages were adjusted to price dynamics changed over time, the delay with which the level of wages was revised to account for inflation being gradually reduced.

It is questionable, therefore, whether German inflation in the years following the First World War, as happened in several Latin American countries in certain periods

---

[59] See Feldman (1993, p. 213).

[60] Within the latter, they made demands such as economic equality for the blue and white collar workers, the socialization of coal and potash business, the expropriation of the properties of large agrarians who had violated the food regulations, a government reshuffle.

[61] See Kunz (1986).

[62] See Ferguson (1995, p. 301).

[63] Referring to that period, Joan Robinson writes: "With the collapse of the mark in 1921, import prices rose abruptly, dragging home prices after them. The sudden rise in the cost of living led to urgent demands for higher wages ... Wage rises had to be granted. Rising wages, increasing both home costs and home money incomes, counteracted the effects of exchange depreciation in stimulating exports and restricting imports." See Robinson (1938, p. 510).

[64] Given by the ratio of the monetary wage level to the domestic price level.

after the Second World War,[65] assumed an inertial character. When inflation takes on these characteristics, not only does stabilization become more expensive and problematic, it can, as the experience of many emerging countries shows, become explosive.

3.4 Wage Indexation and Inflation Persistence

In the years immediately following WWI, it was the goal of the German unions to try to bring workers real wages back to their pre-war level and to maintain the purchasing power of wages stable in a period of high inflation. This objective could only be pursued by means of price indexation mechanisms. These mechanisms, irrespective of the specific details, entail two types of delay in the adjustment of monetary wages. First, there is, inevitably, a time lag in collecting information on the price trend and secondly, a further delay since wage payments are not made continuously but rather at discrete points of time. When inflation is constant, workers are able to keep wages constant, but due to these lags, not their "peak wages"; conversely, when the inflation rate accelerates, the delay with which wages are adjusted leads to losses in average wages as well.

These losses can only be avoided or contained by reducing the delay with which wages are adjusted to price dynamics. This is what happened in Germany in the inflationary phase of the early 1920s. In this phase, in the immediate aftermath of the First World War, although the inflation rate was already very high in 1919, no instruments were available to measure the development of the cost of living. Therefore, employers and unions produced their own assessments based on incomplete information for the purpose of concluding wage contract negotiations each to their own advantage.[66] It was to these "indexes" that wages could be adjusted to reflect price developments.

At the beginning of 1920, the Federal Statistical Office, after long consultation with the Federal Ministry of Labor and the central organizations of employers and workers, produced an official index[67] to measure changes in the cost of living. This index was later used as a reference for adjusting wages to changes in the inflation rate. When inflation eroded real wages, trade unions demanded to renegotiate

[65] See, among others, Simonsen (1986), Novaes (1993), Durevall (1999), and Roncaglia de Carvallo (2019).

[66] See, Sitzler (1924, p. 646).

[67] For an illustration of the method by which this index was calculated, see Bresciani-Turroni (1929, p. 379–381). On the various price indices useful for the indexation of wages developed in Germany in the early Twenties, see Teupe (2021).

Table 3.5 Delays in wage adjustments to inflation (1921–1923)

Periods	Coal (Ruhr, White collar)	Metal (Ruhr, steal, white collar)
1921	2 months	2 months
1922 between January and August	1 month	1 month
1922 from September	15 days	1 month
1923 February	10 days	1 month
1923 May	10 days	15 days
1923 August	5 days	10 days
1923 September	3–4 days	5–7 days
1923 October	3–4 days	3–4 days

Source: Sitzler (1924) and Webb (1989)

contracts in order to attempt to re-establish their peak real incomes.[68] Until 1920, the adjustment of wages to price movements normally took place every 3 months.[69]

As inflation increased, the delay in the adjustment of wages became ever shorter: falling to 2 months in 1921, 1 month in 1922, fortnightly at the beginning of 1923, and becoming weekly at the middle of that year.[70] The reduction in the lag with which wages were adjusted went hand in hand with an increase in the inflation rate (Table 3.5).

In the course of 1923, in order to reduce the lag in the adjustment of wages to prices at some point, it became impossible to refer to the cost-of-living index since its calculation, even when "express" dates were used,[71] was necessarily late. At that point, the benchmark became the mark/dollar exchange rate.[72] This process is well described by Pazos (1978, p. 92–93) in his seminal study of inflation in Latin America: "When the inflation rate approaches the limit of tolerance, a growing number of trade unions ask for raises before their contracts become due. And management grants them. These wage increases give an additional push to inflation and bring about a further reduction of the adjustment interval. Probably the interval

[68]This situation has been described by Simonsen (1964, p. 17): "Besides the chronic increase in prices, an important phenomenon tends to unfold: the oscillation of real income among different individuals . . . The case of wage earners (globally the most important) is typical: as nominal wages re-adjust discontinuously, workers' purchasing power shows an oscillatory movement. But after the wage readjustment, real wages reach a peak and since workers' nominal income remains fixed, its purchasing power progressively declines until a new wage adjustment takes place. The wage rate jumps to its peak and the process goes on." See also Simonsen (1970) and Pazos (1978).

[69]See Sitzler (1924, p. 645).

[70]See Sitzler (1924) and Webb (1989).

[71]That is, when at the end of 1920, it was decided to calculate the cost-of-living index, against which wages would be measured, by reference to 70 towns of different sizes instead of 600 communes.

[72]". . . [I]n the last phase of the depreciation for the 'multiplier' represented by the index number of the cost of living there was substituted, in some industries, a multiplier deduced from the exchange rate of the dollar at Berlin on the day the wages were paid. This system was much easier than that based on the index number of prices, the calculation of which required some days. . .". Bresciani-Turroni (1937, p. 310).

is initially shortened to six months, and then, successively, to three months, one month, one week, and one day. At first the readjustment is based on the cost-of-living index; but since there is a delay of one or two months or more in the publication of this index, it must soon be replaced by another. The best-known and more up-to-date of the possible indicators in Latin America is the quotation of a foreign currency, generally the US dollar."

The indexation of wages to the inflation rate and the reduction of the lag with which they are adjusted to price changes haves two effects. First, they gave rise to an unstable equilibrium.[73] In fact, while wages are adjusted for past inflation, prices of goods are fixed by the producers taking account of expected inflation. If producers expect a future acceleration of inflation, prices rise. Because of that, the losses on wages are higher than those which workers consider acceptable. Therefore, they react demanding further increases in their wages and producers are led to anticipate this behavior. They therefore raise prices yet further hence accelerating current inflation until, at a certain point it becomes explosive.[74] This is what happened in Germany, in the second half of 1922, following the pronounced depreciation of the exchange rate, when the delay in the adjustment of wages to prices had become drastically reduced. A vicious circle between exchange rate, prices, and wages occurred according to the Simonsen–Pazos mechanism.[75]

The second implication of the indexation of wages and their progressively more frequent adjustment is that German inflation depended more and more on its own past.[76] Normally the inflation rate has some reasonable steady-state level from which it can deviate by shocks.[77] The process of adjusting the inflation rate to steady-state level measures the degree of persistent inflation. The greater (lower) the speed of adjustment the less (more) persistent inflation is.[78] An increase in the importance of backward-looking indexation will generally also increase the degree of inflation persistence, i.e. the speed at which shocks to inflation die out and the inflation rate returns to its target or its mean.

3.5 The Persistence of the German Inflation

When inflation is highly persistent, shocks to inflation exert long-lasting effects and may require a strong policy response to bring inflation under control. In the worst case, inflation may contain a unit root, which could lead to unpalatable choices for monetary policy, since inflation randomly drifts away in any direction, making it

[73] See Simonsen (1970, 1983).

[74] For example, about this process in Brazil in the 1980s, see Carvalho (1993).

[75] See Robinson (1938, p. 510).

[76] See Dornbusch (1985).

[77] See Ascari and Sbordone (2014).

[78] See among others Altissimo et al. (2006).

difficult for the monetary authorities to control inflation. A high degree of persistent inflation implies both tighter margins for a central bank to deal with temporary shocks,[79] and a higher "sacrifice ratio," i.e. a higher loss of output in correspondence with a reduction in inflation.[80] In the best case, instead, inflation may prove stationary, implying that it reverts to its initial level rapidly after a shock occurs. Therefore, it is easier for the central bank to maintain stable prices. In view of this, it is interesting to measure the degree of persistence of German inflation in the early 1920s to have a more complete understanding of the Reichsbank's behavior.

In recent times, studies on inflation persistence have mainly focused on advanced countries. Fuhrer (2010) provides an extensive review of these studies from both a theoretical and empirical perspective.[81] In the latter respect, Pivetta and Reis (2007), Stock and Watson (2007), and Cogley et al. (2010) analyzed the inflation persistence in the United States while Altissimo et al. (2006) and Meller and Nautz (2012) cover the euro area. Benati (2006) analyzes the change in inflation persistence across advanced countries and different monetary regimes.

Some papers, however, dating to the 1990s, focused on the persistence of inflation in emerging countries.[82] These latter studies deserve particular attention because they refer to countries that, like Germany in the early 1920s, were affected by phases of hyperinflation.

Various econometric methodologies can be used to assess whether the inflation rate followed a random walk pattern and thus had the characteristics of inertial inflation.[83] A methodology frequently used to this aim is the unit root test.[84] To ascertain if German inflation in early Twenties was persistent, three types of unit root tests were performed: the Augmented Dickey–Fuller test (ADF),[85] the Phillips–Perron test (PP),[86] and finally the KPSS test proposed by Kwiatkowski et al. (1992). The first two tests verify the null hypothesis of the presence of a unit root, the last, on the other hand, starts from the null hypothesis of a stationary series: Thus, the hypothesis of inflation persistence is validated in the first two tests with the acceptance of the null hypothesis, while in the KPSS test with the rejection of the null hypothesis. In the tests just illustrated, reference was made to the period 1918.10–1923.06.

As can be seen from Table 3.6, in all three tests, both in the version with intercept only and with intercept and trend, the presence of a unit root in the inflation rate

[79] See Roache (2014).

[80] See Fuhrer (1995), Ascari and Ropele (2012).

[81] See also Mishkin and Schmidt-Hebbel (2007).

[82] See Novaes (1993) and Durevall (1999).

[83] See Fuhrer (2010).

[84] Numerous contributions test for a unit root in inflation. See, among others, Barsky (1987) and Ball et al. (1990).

[85] See Dickey and Fuller (1979).

[86] See Phillips and Perron (1988).

Table 3.6 Unit root tests of variables used in the estimates of Table 3.7

	Intercept		Intercept and trend	
	Stat	Prob.	Stat.	Prob.
ADF	1.589	99.9%	0.650	100.0%
PP	1.370	99.9%	0.100	99.7%
KPSS	0.141***		0.219***	

Source: Authors' calculations. *** means reject the null hypothesis at 99%

series is validated and thus the persistence of German inflation over the period considered is confirmed.

Univariate tests support the persistent nature of inflation in Germany from 1918 to 1923. However, this type of analysis suffers from the limitation of not being able to take into account the effects of other relevant variables in determining inflation, effects that could underlie the recorded persistence in the inflation rate. For this reason, as made in other contributions,[87] in the following we have extended our analysis in a multivariate context to see whether even once the interactions with the other relevant variables have been taken into account, the dynamics of inflation remains mainly explained by past trends in inflation itself and not by movements in the other context variables. In particular, we estimated a VAR model in which, together with the domestic inflation, we consider the changes in money, in the real exchange rate and in monetary wages. The identification of the innovations of the individual variables in the model is obtained by means of the traditional Cholesky decomposition, which produces a recursive model in which the order of the variables in the model becomes relevant: in the basic model, we will first order domestic inflation, and after that changes in notes in circulation, real exchange rate, and nominal wages, but obviously the results obtained will also be tested with a different ordering.[88] The time sample considered is the same as that taken as reference in the univariate tests, i.e. from 1918.10 to 1923.06.

In Table 3.7, we show how much of the variance of the inflation forecast error is explained by inflation itself: the higher this share is, the more the hypothesis of persistence of the inflationary process is confirmed. In order to take account of the recursive nature of the model the four columns show the contribution of past inflation to explaining current inflation according to Var models in which the four variables considered in turn occupy the first place.

From Table 3.7 (column 4) it emerges that after 12 months 82% of inflation is explained by its past values. Even in models in which, instead of inflation, the other variables are ordered first, the share of self-explanation of inflation is very high,

[87] Novaes (1993) and Durevall (1999) use this methodology to test inflation persistence in Brazil in the 1980s and 1990s. Cogley et al. (2010) to estimate a trend component of inflation due to the adoption of inflation targeting by central banks.

[88] The lag length test indicates a model with 2 lags as more significant. The tests for stability show the model is stable.

Table 3.7 Inflation persistence (share of the forecast error variance of inflation due to past inflation)

	First variable in VAR			
Months in forecast	Notes in circulation	Real exchange rate	Wages	Domestic inflation
1	90.0	83.6	82.7	100.0
2	85.8	69.3	76.6	91.9
3	80.4	64.3	70.4	86.5
4	78.2	63.2	67.6	85.6
5	77.7	63.0	66.6	85.6
6	76.2	62.1	64.8	84.5
7	75.1	61.6	63.3	83.9
8	74.4	61.4	62.4	83.7
9	73.6	61.0	61.3	83.2
10	72.9	60.8	60.4	82.8
11	72.3	60.6	59.7	82.6
12	71.8	60.4	59.0	82.3

Source: Holtfrerich (1986), Bresciani-Turroni (1937) and Statistisches Reichsamt (1925). Note: for all variables we have considered the percent annual changes; the real exchange rate is given by the nominal exchange rate of mark vs US dollar multiply for the ratio of wholesale prices in U.S and in Germany; the wages are those of skilled workers

ranging from a minimum of 59%, when wages are placed first, to 72% when the dynamics of money are placed first.

In this case, therefore, the inertial inflation hypothesis is once again confirmed, with the variance decomposition showing that even when considering interactions with context variables, price dynamics in Germany between 1918 and 1923 appears to depend mainly on its own past behavior rather than on the impulses of the other relevant variables. For a persistent inflation "... to fall, there has to be a major break in the process whereby each sector, including the monetary authorities, accommodates the inflation rate of every other sector."[89]

A high degree of inflation persistence can only be lowered through a strategy that attaches primary importance to price stability.[90] Central banks in recent decades have mainly used two monetary policy strategies to reduce the degree of inflation persistence: in some cases they have resorted to inflation targeting,[91] in others, above all in emerging countries, to a constraint on the exchange rate arrangement.[92] As will be seen in Chap. 5, the German government and the Reichsbank followed this second approach.

[89] See Dornbusch and Fischer (1993, p. 11).

[90] See Gerlach and Tillmann (2012).

[91] See Siklos (1990).

[92] See Alogoskoufis and Smith (1991).

3.6 Conclusions

In the years following the First World War, particularly between 1919 and the first half of 1922, Germany was plagued by high inflation, albeit varying widely. This inflation was not the outcome, as argued by some scholars, of a lack of policy, but was rather a policy choice which, if not actively supported, was certainly not opposed by some influential interest groups. In particular, large sectors of industry believed that it would help reduce the risk of a Bolshevik revolution by keeping growth high and unemployment low. The trade unions, for their part, were not actively averse to inflation, so long as their members' purchasing power was protected (by forms of wage indexation) and the goal was to maintain expansive economic policies that would keep unemployment relatively low. In this context, a sort of implicit alliance emerged between the productive classes who benefited from the redistributive process resulting from inflation, to the detriment of the rentiers who lost conspicuously.

Phases of accelerating inflation followed phases of pronounced depreciation of the mark which were due to massive withdrawals of mark-denominated assets by non-residents provoked by a temporary loss of confidence in Germany's solvency and the stability of the mark. They were associated with two processes.

First, as the Patinkin effect prevailed over the Olivera–Tanzi effect, the real value of government expenditure contracted more than government revenue in these phases, thus creating room for future expansionary fiscal maneuver.

Secondly, during the acceleration of price growth there was a reduction in workers' real wages resulting in an increase in the competitiveness of German industry, an expansionary cycle of its exports and output, and a fall in the unemployment rate. In this context, the bargaining power of the trade unions increased and, with it, workers' wage demands. The acceptance of these demands, largely driven by politics, caused a loss of competitiveness of German exports, which was followed by a slowdown in economic growth.

This slowdown was countered by the increase of public spending and government deficit. This increase was due not only to policy choices, but also to the prevalence of the Patinkin effect over the Olivera–Tanzi effect. Keeping the unemployment rate low, German governments were able to maintain reasonable social calm and supporting a certain consensus in favor of the Republic.

The use of inflation as a policy instrument meant that it increasingly tended to take on the characteristics of persistent inflation, i.e. backward-looking inflation, which made resistance to stabilization policies increasingly strong. This trend was fostered primarily by improvements in wage indexation procedures and, in particular, by the reduction in the lag with which wages were adjusted to the price level.

In fact, initially the trade unions, to maintain the real wage level stable, periodically renegotiated employment contracts but these negotiations took place without adequate data on the real loss of purchasing power of wages and, as a result, the adjustment of wages to price dynamics was approximate and delayed.

In 1920, the government, aiming to improve the mechanism by which wages were adjusted to inflation, commissioned the Central Statistical Office to calculate a cost-of-living index to which wages could be pegged. Of course, the publication of this index was itself delayed to a certain extent, a delay which was compounded by the delay in the frequency with which wages were adjusted.

As the inflation rate rose, the need for a reduction in the delay with which monetary wages were adjusted to price growth became more acute, in 1921 the delay was 2 months, but fell to 1 month in the first part of 1922, to 15 days in the latter part of that year, and to a few days during 1923. The gradual reduction in the delay with which wages were adjusted for inflation eventually made the use of the cost-of-living index drawn up by the Reich Bureau of Statistics useless as a benchmark, since the time required to calculate this index made it obsolete. As a replacement for this index, the mark/dollar exchange rate was adopted when hyperinflation sets in, the availability of which was, of course, immediate.

Adjustment of wages in a backward-looking fashion tends to increase inflation persistence, a tendency which is all the more pronounced the smaller the lag with which wages are adjusted to price dynamics. At the same time, a decrease in the lag with which wages are adjusted to inflation can affect the forward-looking expectations of producers, leading to a rise in their expectations. If this happens, in the presence of a shock, e.g. a pronounced depreciation of the exchange rate and the consequent increase in domestic prices, a vicious circle between price and wage changes can be triggered, turning inflation explosive. As will be seen in the next chapter, this is what happened in Germany starting in the summer of 1922.

References

Alesina, A. (1988). The end of large public debt. In F. Giavazzi & L. Spaventa (Eds.), *High public debt: The Italian experience*. Cambridge University Press.

Alogoskoufis, G. S., & Smith, R. (1991). The Phillips curve, the persistence of inflation, and the Lucas critique: Evidence from exchange-rate regimes. *American Economic Review, 81*, 1254–1275.

Altissimo, F., Ehrmann, M., & Smets, F. (2006). *Inflation persistence and price-setting behaviour*. ECB Occasional Paper Series n. 46.

Andic, S., & Veverka, J. (1963/64). The growth of government expenditure in Germany since the unification. *Finanzarchiv/Public Finance Analysis, 23,* 169–278.

Ascari, G., & Ropele, T. (2012). Sacrifice ratio in a medium-scale new Keynesian model. *Journal of Money, Credit and Banking, 44*, 457–467.

Ascari, G., & Sbordone, A. M. (2014). The macroeconomics of trend inflation. *Journal of Economic Literature, 52*, 679–730.

Ball, L., Cecchetti, S. G., & Gordon, R. J. (1990). Inflation and uncertainty at short and long horizons. *Brookings Papers on Economic Activity, 1*, 215–252.

Barsky, R. B. (1987). The Fisher hypothesis and the forecastability and persistence of inflation. *Journal of Monetary Economics, 19*, 3–24.

Benati, L. (2006). *Investigating inflation persistence across monetary regimes*. Unpublished.

Borchardt, K. ([1972], 1991). Germany's experience of inflation. In K. Borchardt (Ed.), Perspectives on Modern German Economic History and Policy, Cambridge University Press. English translation from K. Borchardt (1972), Die Erfahrung mit Inflationen in Deutschland; in J. Schlemmer (Ed.), Enteignung durch Inflation? Piper. Reprinted in 1982 in K. Borchardt (Ed.), Wachstum, Krisen, und Hundlungsspielraume der Wirrschuftspolitik. Vandenhoeck and Ruprecht.

Bresciani-Turroni, C. (1929). The movement of wages in Germany during the depreciation of the mark and after stabilization. *Journal of the Royal Statistical Society, 92*, 374–427.

Bresciani-Turroni, C. (1937). *The economics of inflation: A study of currency depreciation in post-war Germany*. Allen & Unwin.

Brunnermeier, M., Correia, S., Luck, S., Verner, E., & Zimmermann T. (2022). *The debt-inflation channel of the German hyperinflation*. NBER working paper n. 31298.

Cardoso, E. (1998). Virtual deficits and the Patinkin effect. *IMF Staff Papers, 45*, 619–646.

Carvalho, F. (1993). Strato-inflation and high inflation: The Brazilian experience. *Cambridge Journal of Economics, 17*, 63–78.

Cogley, T., Primiceri, G. E., & Sargent, T. J. (2010). Inflation-gap persistence in the US *American Economic Journal: Macroeconomics, 2*, 43–69.

Dickey, D., & Fuller, W. (1979). Distribution of the estimator for autoregressive time series with a unit root. *Journal of the American Statistical Association, 74*, 427–431.

Dornbusch, R. (1985). *Inflation, exchange rates and stabilization*. NBER working paper n. 1739.

Dornbusch, R., & Fischer, S. (1993). Moderate inflation. *World Bank Economic Review, 7*, 1–44.

Durevall, D. (1999). Inertial inflation, indexation and price stickiness: Evidence from Brazil. *Journal of Development Economics, 60*, 407–421.

Feldman, G. D. (1977). *Iron and steel in the German inflation, 1916–1923*. Princeton University Press.

Feldman, G. D. (1982). The political economy of Germany's relative stabilization during the 1920/21 depression. In G. D. Feldman, L. Holtfrerich, & G. A. Ritter (Eds.), *Die Deutsche inflation. Eine Zwischenbilanz – The German inflation reconsidered. A preliminary balance*. De Gruyter.

Feldman, G. D. (1983). The historians and the German inflation. In N. Schmukler & E. Marcus (Eds.), *Inflation through the ages: Economic, social, psychological and historical aspects*. Columbia University Press.

Feldman, G. D. (1993). *The great disorder: Politics, economics, and society in the German Inflation, 1914–1924*. Oxford University Press.

Ferguson, N. (1995). Paper and iron: Hamburg business and German politics in the era of inflation, 1897–1927. Cambridge University Press.

Ferguson, N. (1996). Constraints and room for manoeuvre in the German inflation of the early 1920s. *Economic History Review, 49*, 635–666.

Fuhrer, J. C. (1995). The persistence of inflation and the cost of disinflation. *New England Economic Review*, January, 3–16.

Fuhrer, J. C. (2010). Inflation persistence. In B. Friedman & H. Woodford (Eds.), *Handbook of monetary economics*. North Holland.

Gerlach, S., & Tillmann, P. (2012). Inflation targeting and inflation persistence in Asia-Pacific. *Journal of Asian Economics, 23*, 360–373.

Goldschmidt, R. W. (1927). *Das Deutsche gross- bankkapital in seiner neueren entwicklung*. Ebering.

Gossweiler, K. (1971). *Grossbanken, Industriemonopole, und Staat*. PapyRossa Verlag.

Graham, F. D. (1930). *Exchange, prices, and production in hyper-inflation: Germany, 1920–1923*. Princeton University Press.

Ham, W. T. (1934). Labor Under the German Republic. *The Quarterly Journal of Economics, 48*, 203–228.

Hardach, G. (2017). War finance and monetary consequences: The German case revisited. *International Encyclopedia of the First World War, 1914-18 online*.

Holtfrerich, C. L. (1986). *The German inflation 1914–1923: Causes and effects in international perspective*. De Gruyter.

Holtfrerich, C. L. (1988). Relations between monetary authorities and governmental institutions: The case of Germany from the 19th century to the present. In G. Toniolo (Ed.), *Central Banks' Independence in historical perspective*. De Gruyter.
Humphrey, T. M. (1982). The real bills doctrine. Federal Reserve of Richmond. *Economic Review, 68*, 3–13.
Itskhoki, O. (2021). The story of the real exchange rate. *Annual Review of Economics, 13*, 423–455.
Kindleberger, C. (1984a). *A financial history of Western Europe*. Allen & Unwin.
Kindleberger, C. (1984b). A structural view of the German inflation. In G. D. Feldman, C. L. Holtfrerich, G. A. Ritter, & P. C. Witt (Eds.), *Die Erfahrung der inflation im internationalen Zusammenhang und Vergleich*. De Gruyter.
Kopper, C. (2006). *Hijalmar Schacht*. Carl Hanser Verlag.
Kunz, A. (1986). *Civil servants and the politics of inflation in Germany, 1914–1924*. De Gruyter.
Kwiatkowski, D., Phillips, P. C. B., Schmidt, P., & Shin, Y. (1992). Testing the null hypothesis of stationarity against the alternative of a unit root: How sure are we that economic time series have a unit root? *Journal of Econometrics, 54*, 159–178.
Lansburgh, A. (1923). *Das Wesen des Geldes*. Bank-Verlag.
Laursen, K., & Pedersen, J. (1964). *German inflation 1918–1923*. North-Holland.
Maier, C. S. (1975). *Recasting bourgeois Europe: Stabilization in France, Germany and in Italy in the decade after world war I*. Princeton University Press.
Maier, C. (1987). *In search of stability*. Cambridge University Press.
Meller, B., & Nautz, D. (2012). Inflation persistence in the euro area before and after the European Monetary Union. *Economic Modelling, 29*, 1170–1176.
Mishkin, F. S., & Schmidt-Hebbel, K. (2007). Does inflation targeting make a difference? In F. Mishkin & K. Schmidt-Hebbel (Eds.), *Monetary policy under inflation targeting*. Banco Central de Chile.
Müller H. (1973). Die Zentralbankeine Nebenregierung, Westdeutscher Verlag, Opladen.
Novaes, A. D. (1993). Revisiting the inertial inflation hypothesis for Brazil. *Journal of Development Economics, 42*, 89–110.
Obstfeld, M. (1989). *Dynamic seigniorage theory: An exploration*. NBER working paper n. 2869.
Olivera, J. H. G. (1967). Money, prices and fiscal lags: A note on the dynamics of inflation. *Banca Nazionale del Lavoro Quarterly Review, 82*, 258–268.
Patinkin, D. (1993). Israel's stabilization program of 1985, or some simple truths of monetary theory. *Journal of Economic Perspectives, 7*, 103–128.
Pazos, F. (1978). *Chronic inflation in Latin America*. Praeger.
Petzina, D., Abelshauser, W., & Faust, A. (1978). *Sozialgeschtliches Arbeitsbuch: Materialen zur Statistik des Deutsche Reiches 1914–1945*. Verlag Beck.
Pfleiderer, O. (1976). Die Reichsbank in der Zeit der grossen Inflation, die Stabilisierung der Mark und die Aufwertung von Kapitalforderungen. In Deutsche Bundesbank, *Währung und Wirtschaft in Deutschland: 1876–1975*. Deutsche Bundesbank.
Phillips, P. C. B., & Perron, P. (1988). Testing for a unit root in time series regression. *Biometrika, 75*, 335–346.
Pivetta, F., & Reis, R. (2007). The persistence of inflation in the United States. *Journal of Economic Dynamics and Control, 31*, 1326–1358.
Roache, S. K. (2014). *Inflation persistence in Brazil—A cross country comparison*. IMF working paper n. WP/14/55, 1.
Robinson, J. (1938). Review of C. Bresciani-Turroni's 'The economics of inflation'. *Economic Journal, 48*, 507–513.
Roncaglia de Carvalho, A. (2019). A second-generation structuralist transformation problem: The rise of the inertial inflation hypothesis. *Journal of the History of Economic Thought, 41*, 47–75.
Seghezza, E. (2022). The Cagan's model, its developments, and the Patinkin effect. *Economia Internazionale/International Economics, 75*, 601–622.
Siklos, P. L. (1990). Hyperinflations: Their origins, development and termination. *Journal of Economic Surveys, 4*, 225–248.

Simonsen, M. H. (1964). *A experiência inflacionária no Brasil.* IPES.
Simonsen, M. H. (1970). *Inflacao:gradualismo x tratamento de choque.* Apec Editore.
Simonsen, M. H. (1986). Indexation: Current theory and the Brazilian experience. In R. Dornbusch & M. H. Simonsen (Eds.), *Inflation, debt and indexation.* MIT Press.
Sitzler, F. (1924). The adaptation of wages to the depreciation of the currency in Germany. *International Labour Review, 9*, 643–666.
Statistisches Reichsamt. (1925). *Zahlen zur Geldenwertung in Deutschland 1914 bis 1923.*
Stock, J. H., & Watson, M. (2007). Why has US inflation become harder to forecast? *Journal of Money, Credit and Banking, 39*, 3–33.
Tanzi, V. (1978). Inflation, real tax revenue, and the case for inflationary finance: Theory with an application to Argentina. *IMF Staff Papers, 25*, 417–451.
Teupe, S. (2021). Inflation and the negotiation of wages. Comparative responses to monetary changes in Germany and in the United States during the Gold Standard Era, 1876-1926. *Labor History, 62*, 1–22.
Specht, A. von (1982). *Politische und wirtschaftliche Hintergrande der deutschen Inflation 1918–1923.* Peter Lang Verlag.
Webb, S. (1984). The supply of money and Reichsbank financing of government and corporate debt in Germany, 1919-1923. *Journal of Economic History, 44*, 499–507.
Webb, S. (1986). Fiscal news and inflationary expectations in Germany after WWI. *Journal of Economic History, 46*, 769–794.
Webb, S. (1989). *Hyperinflation and stabilization in Weimar Germany.* Oxford University Press.
Weisbrod, B. (1979). Economic power and political stability reconsidered: Heavy industry in Weimar Germany. *Social History, 4*, 241–263.
Witt, P. C. (1983). Tax policies, tax assessment and inflation: Towards a sociology of public finance in the German inflation 1914-1923. In N. Schmukler & E. Markus (Eds.), *Inflation through the ages: Economic, social, psychological and historical aspects.* Columbia University Press.
Wixforth, H. (2003). German banks and their business strategies in the Weimar Republic: New findings and preliminary results. In M. Kasuya (Ed.), *Coping with crisis.* Oxford University Press.
Yeager, L. R. (1966). International Monetary Relations: Theory, History and Policy, New York, Harper & Row

Chapter 4
Was There a Sudden Stop at the Root of German Hyperinflation?

4.1 Introduction[1]

Analysis of hyperinflation during the Weimar Republic occupies a prominent place in studies into the origin and development of episodes of hyperinflation.[2] The earliest interpretations given to German hyperinflation date to the interwar period. Of these, two interpretations stand out: the *monetary view* and the *balance of payments view*.[3] The former sees hyperinflation during the Weimar Republic as being mainly due to an excess in the money supply. Put simply, in the years immediately following the end of the war, the Weimar Republic significantly increased public spending and, as tax revenue did not increase sufficiently to cover this increased public spending, the Reichsbank sought to do so by printing money, thus causing an accelerating increase in prices.[4]

The *balance of payments* view, on the other hand, concludes that the high level of inflation that afflicted Germany in the early 1920s was due to the country's current account deficit which in turn resulted from the burden of Reparations imposed by the Treaty of Versailles.[5]

A second wave of studies on hyperinflation that take Germany as a case study was set off by Cagan's seminal 1956 paper and, although they put forward various hypotheses about the formation of expectations, almost all these accept the monetary view according to which, the acceleration and explosive price growth in Weimar Germany was the result of covering large public deficits through the creation of money.

---

[1]This chapter is largely based on Seghezza and Morelli (2020).

[2]See Siklos (1990).

[3]For a survey of the various hypotheses on German hyperinflation, see Kindleberger (1984a, b).

[4]See Bresciani-Turroni (1937).

[5]Expressions of this view can be found in, among others, Williams (1922), Helfferich (1927), and Graham (1930).

G. B. Pittaluga, E. Seghezza, *An Economic Historiography of Germany, 1918-1931*, Frontiers in Economic History, https://doi.org/10.1007/978-3-031-70347-8_4

As shown by Dornbusch et al. (1990), one problem with the monetary view is that fundamentally it refers to a closed economy and disregards the role of the exchange rate, in fact the exchange rate plays a crucial role not only in the traditional balance of payments view (with its focus on current account imbalances) but also on the financial part of the balance of payments. The importance of this last aspect of German hyperinflation has long been neglected.[6]

In fact, in the years immediately following World War I, Germany was affected by a massive influx of capital from abroad driven by expectations of the capital gains to be had from a widely anticipated appreciation of the mark. As a result of this, in the early part of 1922, a large share of the country's debt, both public and private, was held by non-residents. In this context, the country was exposed to a sudden stop,[7] and in fact, a sudden reversal of capital flow occurred after mid-June 1922, when some "bad" political news led foreign investors to withdraw their deposits from German banks and sell financial assets held in marks. The consequent marked depreciation of German mark was followed by a considerable rise in the price of imports and, with some delay, of wholesale and consumer prices. After a phase of relative stability, the mark again depreciated markedly in late 1922 and early 1923. The same happened in the late spring of 1923. These phases of marked exchange rate depreciation were followed by sharp rises in inflation. The gradual reduction in the lag with which wages were adjusted to prices encouraged the consolidation of the inflation rate at progressively higher levels, leading in the course of 1923 to the emergence of a pernicious spiral of exchange rate, prices, and wages. At this point, inflation seemed unstoppable.

4.2 The Unfolding of Hyperinflation

Figure 4.1 clearly shows that a break in the trend of German inflation occurred between June and July 1923. What had been high inflation in the previous years, with the typical characteristics of chronic inflation, became explosive, shortly afterwards taking on the characteristics of hyperinflation.[8]

The structural break in the inflation rate was due to a drastic change in inflation expectations. One indicator of this is the forward exchange rate. As Table 4.1 shows, from June 1922, the forward exchange rate of the mark against the pound was traded at a discount while, in previous months, it had traded at a premium.

Various interpretations can be offered for this reversal in expectations of the mark exchange rate, as will be seen. Irrespective of this, it should be seen in connection with two major shocks that occurred in June 1922. The first of these was the decision

[6] See Gomes (2010, p. 97).

[7] See Calvo (1995, p. 1).

[8] Here we accept Cagan's (1956) definition of hyperinflation, i.e. a price growth rate of more than 50% per month. For other definitions of hyperinflation, see Saboin-Garcia (2018).

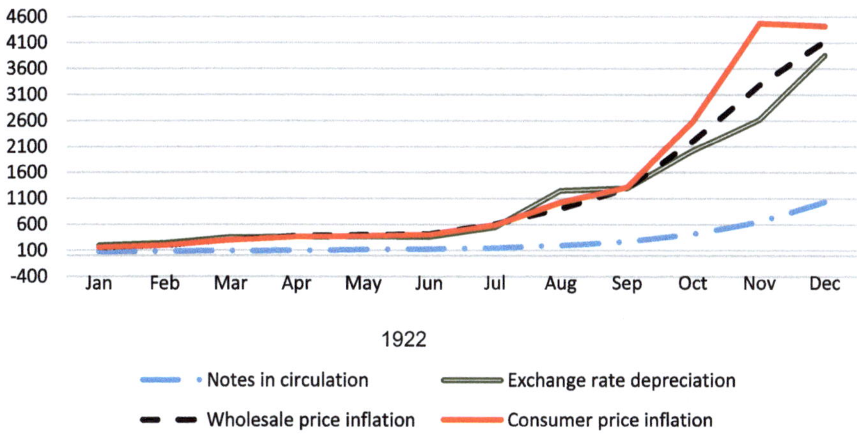

Fig. 4.1 Money, inflation, and exchange rate depreciation (annual changes percent, monthly data, 1922). Source: for wholesale prices, see Holtfrerich (1986); for notes in circulation and exchange rate, see Bresciani-Turroni (1937); for consumer prices, see Federal Reserve

Table 4.1 Spot and forward exchange rates of the German mark (weekly data, May 1922–Aug 1922)

		Forward exchange rate	
Periods	Spot exchange rate	1 month	3 months
May 6	1.231	+1/2	+1½
13	1.280	+1	+3
20	1.342	+1	+3
27	1.305	Par.	Par.
June 3	1.220	Par.	Par.
10	1.333	+1	+3
17	1.432	+1/2	+2
24	1.500	−1½	−1½
July 1	1.733	−2	−6
8	2.305	−3	−9
15	1.955	−7½	−22½
22	2.235	−8	−24
29	2.677	−10	−30
August 5	3.362	−15	−45
12	3.440	−30	−90
19	5.540	−60	−180
26	8.500	−150	−450

Source: Einzig (1937). Notes: Quotations of the spot rates and forward rates of the German mark are related to sterling. The signs (+) and (−) indicate, respectively, a premium and a discount of the German forward exchange rate in relation to sterling

Table 4.2 Exchange rate, prices, and money (index values: 1922 May = 100, monthly data May 1922–Sept. 1923)

Period	Mark/Sterling spot exchange rate	Mark/Sterling forward exchange rate[a]	Wholesale prices	Cost of living	Notes in circulation
1922 May	100.0	+ 0.625	100.0	100.0	100.0
June	109.4	+ 0.250	108.9	109.2	111.2
July	170.0	−6.1	155.8	141.8	125.0
Aug.	391.2	−63.8	297.3	204.2	156.6
Sept.	505.4	−230	444.4	350.5	208.6
Oct.	1096.5	−1200	876.4	580.8	308.6
Nov.	2461.8	−4250	1786.9	1173.9	496.1
Dec.	2616.2	−2800	2284.0	1802.9	824.1
1923 Jan.	6195.4	−7500	4309.4	2947.4	1305.3
Febr.	9623.7	−27,750	8648.2	6955.3	2311.2
March	7305.4	−6600	7568.9	7510.5	3630.3
Apr.	8431.3	−8750	8070.6	7773.7	4306.6
May	16,432.7	−25,250	12,651.0	10,042.1	5634.2
June	37,919.0	−67,600	29,862.2	20,131.6	11,375.7
July	121,832.1	−756,000	115,805.2	99,081.6	29,996.1
Aug.	159,281.0	−6.75[b]	146,181.6	154,222.4	43,618.4
Sept.	340,086.8	−20.0[b]	370,083.6	394,736.8	185,717.1

Source: Einzig (1937), Bresciani-Turroni (1937), and Holtfrerich (1986). [a] Premium (+) and discount (−). [b] in millions

taken on 10 June by the Bankers' Committee[9] that, given the Reparations schedule defined in May 1921, Germany's credit rating was insufficient to guarantee an international loan.

The second shock was the assassination on 24 June 1922 of Walter Rathenau who, in his capacity as Minister of Finance, had been working with the Allies to find a mutually acceptable solution to the Reparations problem.

The hyperinflationary process, like the inflation of previous years, was driven by phases of pronounced exchange rate depreciation, typically triggered by political "bad" news, which reduced confidence in Germany's ability to manage the economic imbalances with which it was plagued. These phases were followed by rises in the rate of increase of wholesale prices and, with some delay, in the cost of living and notes in circulation (Table 4.2).

Immediately after Rathenau's assassination, the spot exchange rate of the mark depreciated significantly, going from DM 1500 to the pound at the end of June to DM 2677 at the end of July, and DM 8500 at the end of August. The pronounced

[9]This Committee had been appointed in April 1922 by the Reparations Commission with the task of exploring the possibility of international loans for Germany.

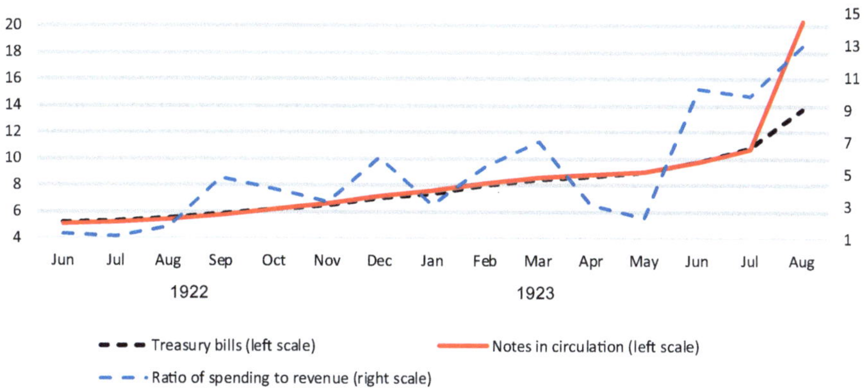

Fig. 4.2 Discounted treasury bills held by Reichsbank, notes and ratio of spending to revenue (Jun. 1922 – Aug. 1923). Source: Graham (1930) and Bresciani-Turroni (1937). Legend: the discounted Treasury bills outstanding and the notes are in logarithms

depreciation of the mark was associated with an equally pronounced increase in wholesale prices and in the amount of money in circulation (Fig. 4.1).

The increase in the latter was mainly driven by discounted Treasury bills held by the Reichsbank. However, between the end of 1922 and the first part of 1923, the Reichsbank also discounted a large quantity of commercial bills.

The high level of circulation notes issued against discounted Treasury bills was aimed at covering the Reich's deficits which, from the second half of 1922 onwards, became increasingly large (Fig. 4.2). However, it is clear from the above Figure that the rate of money creation reflected the trend of the Reich's floating debt. The growth of the latter was particularly high from the autumn of 1922 onwards when, due to the Olivera–Tanzi effect, the Reich's income in real terms contracted significantly due to the acceleration of changes in prices in the preceding months in line with the depreciation of the mark.

The hyperinflationary process was driven, like the inflation in previous years, by phases of pronounced exchange rate depreciation followed by pronounced accelerations in the growth rate of wholesale prices and subsequently in the cost of living (Table 4.2). The phases of pronounced depreciation of the mark were triggered by "bad" political news and were marked by significant increases in the forward exchange rate discount, but were followed by periods of relative stability of the mark (Table 4.2).

Although the hyperinflation, which followed the pronounced depreciation of the mark following Rathenau's assassination, slowed between August and September, the German currency depreciated significantly from October onwards when it became clear that, because of the right parties opposition to the policy of "fulfillment," the Wirth government was unable to implement a plan to stabilize the German economy and convince the Allies to grant a moratorium on Reparations' payments. Against this backdrop, Poincaré became increasingly impatient with

Germany's default and on 23 October, in a meeting with the Belgian Prime Minister, George Theunis, he explicitly threatened the occupation of the Ruhr.

In November 1922, following the failure to bring all the democratic forces, from the SPD to the DVP, into a single coalition, Joseph Wirth resigned as Chancellor. President Ebert appointed Cuno as chancellor. He formed a government composed largely of technicians (Table 4.3).

In November and December, the mark exchange rate was relatively stable. On 13 January, Franco-Belgian troops occupied the Ruhr which was followed by another substantial fall of the mark: between the end of December 1922 and January 1923, the exchange rate of the German currency against the British pound rose from 33,200 to 125,000. Between February and April, the German currency rate remained relatively stable. In addition to the absence of any political shocks, this stability was due to the Reichsbank's massive interventions in the currency market. The German central bank had been driven to this intervention by the fierce criticism of the Reich Economic Council for its passive behavior in the face of the collapse of the mark in January 1923.[10] Chancellor Cuno (who took over from Wirth in November 1922) and Finance Minister Hermes largely agreed with the criticism of the Reichsbank.

In January 1923, following Germany's failure to pay the Reparations, France and Belgium, with the support of Italy and the opposition of the United Kingdom, occupied the Ruhr, a coal mining district of primary importance for the German economy.

Because of this occupation, the German state lost tax revenue, such as coal taxes, export taxes, customs duties, etc. At the same time, as the German decided to implement passive resistance, the government was forced to provide economic support to workers and companies located in the Ruhr. This resulted in a significant increase in government expenditure, which, combined with the decrease in revenue, aggravated Germany's fiscal deficit and contributed to a further increase in the currency issued to cover it.[11]

Despite being aware that the policy of passive resistance in the Ruhr required stable prices and thus a stable exchange rate, Reichsbank president Havenstein and his vice-president Glasenapp, based on the experience of 1920 and 1921, were convinced that central bank interventions in support of the mark would be of limited effect.[12] Despite the misgivings of its leadership, the Reichsbank in February, March, and a large part of April used part of its foreign and gold reserves to buy marks in the international market and thereby support the exchange rate. This was a period of relative stability for the German currency.[13] The Reichsbank's policy of defending the mark, despite involving the loss of a substantial amount of foreign exchange reserves, had only temporary effect. Its relative failure was largely due to

[10]Hilferding, in particular, observed that there had never been such a pronounced depreciation of a currency with such a large supply of reserves held by a central bank. See Feldman (1993, p. 642).

[11]See Bresciani-Turroni (1937, p. 62 ff.).

[12]See Bergman (1927, p. 185 ff.).

[13]See Feldman (1993, p. 645–649).

Table 4.3 German governments during the hyperinflation (1921–1924)

Chancellor	Date of entry into office	USPD	SPD	Zentrum	DDP	DVP	BVP	DNVP	WP	NSDAP	Percentage of Parliament seats
Wirth	10/26/1921		R	X	R						44.7
Cuno	11/12/1922			R	R	R	R				41.2
Stresemann	8/13/1923		R	R	R	X					58.8
Stresemann	10/6/1923		R	R	R	X					58.8
Marx	11/30/1923 (until 15 December 1924)			X	R	R	R				41.2[a]

Source: Notermans (2000). Note: X: Party of Prime Minister; R: Party represented in coalition. (a): tolerated by SPD. USPD, Unabhangige Szialdemokratische Partei Deutschlands (Independent Social Democratic Party); SPD, Szialdemokratische Partei Deutschlands (Social Democratic Party); Zentrumpartei (Center Party: a Catholic party); DDP, Deutsche Democratische Partei (German Democratic Party: a liberal-socialist party); DVP, Deutsche Volkspartei (German People's Party: a center-right party supporting right-liberalism); BVP, Bayerische Volkspartei (Bavarian People's Party: a conservative party based mainly in Bavaria); DNVP, Deutschnationale Volkspartei (German National People's Party: an authoritarian and radical right party); WP, Wirtschaftspartei (Business Party: a tough conservative party; NSDAP, Nationalsozialistische Deutsche Arbeiterpartei (National Socialist German Workers' Party: the Nazi party)

Table 4.4 Short-term interest rates (in percent per annum, monthly data, May 1922-Sept. 1923)

Period	Reichsbank discount rate	Daily money rate
1922 May	5	4.34
June	5	4.91
July	5	5.40
August	6	6.50
September	7	7.40
October	8	7.75
November	10	8.22
December	10	9.21
1923 January	12	11.05
February	12	25.67
March	12	11.00
April	18	12.70
May	18	20.15
June	18	19.35
July	18	92
August	30	283
September	30	1606

Source: Federal Reserve, Bulletin, several months

its monetary policy approach, which was in conflict with the objective of exchange rate stabilization. In fact, the German central bank, on the one hand, managed the money supply, not to defend the exchange rate, but to ensure monetary coverage of the Reich's deficits, which had been made larger by the public financing of the passive resistance in the Ruhr; and on the other, adopted an accommodating attitude toward the high credit demand of private individuals. The Reichsbank's lax approach to monetary policy is confirmed not only by the rapid growth in circulating capital, but also and perhaps above all by the policy of keeping interest rates extraordinarily low, indeed below price growth (Table 4.4).

The Reichsbank's decision to keep the discount interest rate at such low levels compared to the inflation rate stemmed not only from the conviction of its directors, in particular President Havenstein, that high interest rates would contribute to an inflation of the public debt and an increase in companies' production costs, but also from the resistance of bankers and industrialists who felt that higher interest rates would lead to a rise in unemployment and social unrest. The Reichsbank's lax discount rate policy was combined with a willingness to discount commercial bills (Table 4.5).

The complacent behavior of the Reichsbank Bank meant that loans obtained by private individuals could be used not only for financing productive activity, but also in speculative operations on the mark. On the one hand, therefore, the German central bank was conducting currency market operations aimed at stabilizing the mark and, on the other hand, it was facilitating downward speculation on the mark with its policy interest rate and commercial paper discount policy.

Table 4.5 Reichsbank holdings of Treasury and commercial bills (billions of marks, monthly data, June 1922–Sept. 1923)

Period	Treasury bills discounted by the Reichsbank	Commercial bills discounted by the Reichsbank
1922 June	186	5
September	350	50
December	1185	422
1923 January	1609	697
February	2947	1829
March	4552	2372
April	6225	2986
May	8022	4015
June	18,338	6914
July	53,752	18,314
August	987,219	164,644
September	45,216,244	3660,094

Source: Statistisches Reichsamt (1925)

The rise in domestic prices encouraged by the depreciation of the mark was followed by a less pronounced growth in money circulation. High inflation expectations, in fact, as explained by Cagan (1956), discouraged private individuals from holding money. The result was an increase in the velocity of money circulation. The Treasury, attempting to cover the Reich's deficits, added to this growth in money circulation by increasing its floating debt, debt which was then discounted by the Reichsbank (Table 4.6).

The Reich's deficits gradually increased in the course of 1923 due to both the increase in public spending and the decrease in tax revenues in real terms. As mentioned above, the increase in expenditure was mainly due to the decision to financially support passive resistance in the Ruhr. The reduction in government revenue was mainly due to the Olivera–Tanzi effect. As Table 4.5 shows, the ratio of revenue to expenditure, which was 67.6% in May 1922, fell to 16.8% in December of that year and to 3.3% in September 1923.

There was a conviction amongst the German political elite, and indeed, amongst the Allies that passive resistance in the Ruhr could not last indefinitely given its cost to Germany. It was once again a question of finding a solution to the problem of Reparations. In April, the Cuno government drew up a proposal, the final version of which was similar to the one that Germany had presented at the Paris Conference.[14] Not surprisingly, it was rejected by the Allies. It was now clear that the Cuno government was unable to draw up a credible proposal for the solution of the

[14] See Maier (1975, p. 369).

Table 4.6 Income and expenditure of the Reich (in millions of gold marks, May 1922–Sept. 1923)

Period	Income	Expenditure	Increase in floating debt	Ratio of income on expenditure
1922 May	254.9	376.9	120.3	67.6
June	235.1	313.8	77.0	74.9
July	183.4	208.5	23.4	88.0
Aug.	116.4	205.1	86.9	56.8
Sept.	90.8	434.9	342.5	20.9
Oct.	66.2	269.5	201.6	24.6
Nov.	60.6	199.8	137.5	30.3
Dec.	73.4	438.6	362.9	16.7
1923 Jan.	65.9	204.6	137.0	32.2
Feb.	50.8	279.6	226.5	18.2
March	100.3	698.9	596.9	14.4
April	150.6	466.6	316.0	32.3
May	123.3	284.7	161.4	43.3
June	48.2	496.4	448.2	9.7
July	48.3	473.9	425.6	10.2
Aug.	78.1	1013.1	514.7	7.7
Sept.	55.6	1661.8	1564.1	3.3

Source: Bresciani-Turroni (1937)

Reparations problem and, given this climate of political uncertainty, a new wave of mistrust hit the mark, with expectations of depreciation between April and May increasing more than fourfold, while in the same month the spot exchange rate lost 100% of its value. A further marked deterioration of the German currency occurred in June (Table 4.2): "[T]he hesitations of May then gave way to the panic of June. The private demand for foreign exchange mounted enormously for both business and speculative purposes, and it was now more difficult than ever to tell them apart."[15]

The facts just presented lead to several questions. The first of these concerns the origin of the drift that occurred in the inflation rate: did the surge in price growth cause the depreciation of the exchange rate or did the depreciation of the exchange rate cause a surge in price growth? In the latter case, however, having adjusted the price level to the depreciated exchange rate, the inflationary process would have come to an end.

This leads to a second question, namely what factors made inflation explosive. Was this caused by unintentional errors in fiscal and monetary policy or by the attempt of interest groups to avoid the loss in their purchasing power that resulted from the depreciation of the mark and the consequent intensification of social conflict? An attempt is made to answer these two questions in the remaining part of this chapter.

[15] Feldman (1993, p. 685).

4.3 Prevailing Explanations for German Hyperinflation

Within the explanations of German hyperinflation,[16] two different "waves" can be distinguished. The first is represented by the explanations given at the time. The second wave of explanations started with Cagan's seminal essay of 1956 and its development by Sargent in the early 1980s with the introduction of the rational expectations hypothesis into the money demand function.[17]

4.3.1 The Explanations of the Period

The earliest interpretations of German hyperinflation date back to the period around or shortly after its occurrence[18] and can be divided into two strands: the monetarist view and the balance of payments view. According to the first of these views, German hyperinflation was to be explained by excessive expansion of the money supply. This view is expounded by some economists of the period,[19] in particular Bresciani-Turroni. He writes: "... German experiences show us the fundamental importance in the determination of the level of internal prices and of the currency's external value of the quantity of money issued by the government. It was only the continual increase in the issues of legal money which made possible the incessant rise in prices and the continual fall in the external value of the mark ...".[20]

In Bresciani-Turroni's view, high inflation necessarily undermined individuals' confidence in the value of money. This resulted in two distorting effects. Firstly, the loss of confidence in the value of money encouraged individuals to reduce their cash holdings, resulting in an increase in the velocity of money. As Hahn (1924, p. 295) writes: "The reason for the manifestation of a rise in velocity is well known. On the expectation of continued losses associated with every kind of money holding, everyone attempted to exchange money, that until now he had been accustomed to retaining for larger or shorter periods, as quickly as possible ... in order to transfer the loss involved onto the next recipient." Therefore, the velocity of money circulation in Germany increased significantly in the second half of 1922[21] (Fig. 4.3).

The loss of confidence in the stability of the currency had an impact not only on the speed of circulation, but also on the demand for loans and the level of the

[16]For a survey of these explanations see, among others, Hubbard (1990).

[17]See, in particular, Eulenburg (1924) Bresciani Turroni (1937).

[18]See Laidler and Stadler (1998).

[19]See, among others, Eucken (1923), Ellis (1934), Mises (1923), Hahn (1924), and Bortkiewicz (1924).

[20]See Bresciani-Turroni (1937, p. 398).

[21]Translated and quoted by Laidler and Stadler (1998). On this point, see also Bresciani-Turroni (1937, p. 166–173).

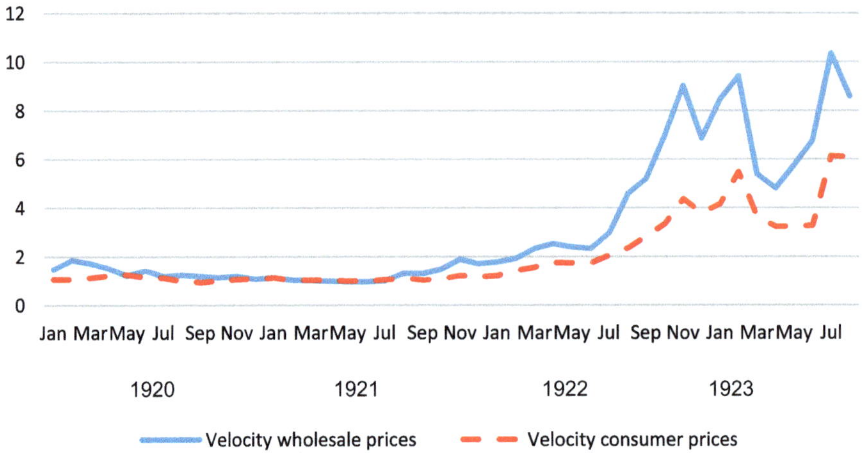

Fig. 4.3 Variations in the velocity of note in circulation in Germany (1920–1923). Source: Bresciani-Turroni (1937, p. 168). Note: By using the equation of exchange $M_tV_t = P_tQ_t$, where M is the supply of money, V the velocity of circulation, P the average price level, and Q the quantity of goods produced, and assuming constant production, Bresciani-Turroni measures variations in the velocity of circulation as $\frac{V_t}{V_{t-1}} = \frac{P_t}{P_{t-1}} / \frac{M_t}{M_{t-1}}$. He provides a measure based on wholesale prices and one based on consumer prices

exchange rate. Expectations of rising inflation encouraged companies to apply for bank loans. The Reichsbank, for its part, accommodated these demands for funds by discounting a large amount of commercial paper. Therefore, "[t]o the 'governmental' inflation, provoked by continual demands on the Reichsbank by the state, was added a second form of inflation, which Germans called 'private', that is, the creation of paper money for businessmen."[22]

The demand for loans was supported not only by companies' attempt to obtain funds at negative real interest rates, but also by speculation, more precisely by the tendency of traders to replace domestic with foreign currency.

Bresciani-Turroni argues that: "[t]he credit policy adopted by the Reichsbank reinforced the effects of the 'governmental' inflation and helped to accelerate the fall of the mark, which, indeed, had never been so rapid as it became after the summer of 1922."[23]

This process at some point gave rise to a vicious circle of a cumulative nature in which inflation, by causing distrust in the value of the currency, fostered a

[22] See Bresciani-Turroni (1937, p. 75).

[23] See Bresciani-Turroni (1937, p. 77).

depreciation of the mark, which in turn fueled inflation: the outcome of this process was hyperinflation.[24]

The monetary interpretation of German hyperinflation was used by the Allies to counter the idea that it depended on the heavy Reparations imposed on Germany in the Treaty of Versailles and the effects of these on the exchange rate.

However, these effects were also highlighted by the German authorities who maintained the opposing hypothesis, namely the "balance of payments hypothesis." According to this hypothesis, supported most notably by Helfferich in the 1923 edition of his book *Das Geld* and also by the Reichsbank, the origin of the mark's constant depreciation lay in the persistently large balance of payments deficits.[25] The collapse of the mark in the second half of 1922 had been followed by dramatic increases in prices and wages. The Reichsbank had found itself forced to increase its cash flow and discount a large amount of commercial paper in order to prevent trade and output collapsing. In the words of Helfferich (1923, [1927, p. 601]): "First came the depreciation of the German currency by the overburdening of Germany with international liabilities and by the French policy of violence. Hence followed a rise in the prices of all imported commodities. This led to a general rise in prices and wages, which in turn led to a greater demand for currency by the public and by the financial authorities of the Reich; and finally, the greater calls upon the Reichsbank from the public and the financial administration of the Reich led to an increase in the note issue." Regarding this, Hagemann (2015) explained how interest in quantitative theory remained low in Germany in the 1920s, since the representatives of the Historical School were hostile to it and Knapp's chartalist theory[26] was prevalent.[27]

In the balance of payments hypothesis, the root cause of German hyperinflation was not seen as Germany's fiscal and monetary mismanagement, but rather the Allies' imposition of excessive Reparations and until this problem was solved, it was unthinkable that the German economy could be stabilized.[28]

The balance of payments hypothesis was re-proposed and developed by Joan Robinson (1938) in her review of Bresciani-Turroni's *Economics of inflation*. After

---

[24]Bortkiewicz (1924, p. 366–367) writes: "At a certain stage of the inflation [of the note issue] it is the external value of the currency that determines the internal value, and not the other way round . . . [T]he true chain of causality is thus in my opinion: mistrust [of the internal money], resulting in a disproportionately large risk in exchange rates, consequently domestic prices and wages that have no relationship to the actual rise in the money supply."

[25]A similar view can be found in Eulenberg (1924): "A balancing of the budget is entirely impossible as the exchange varies in the proportions which we see. First stabilization of the exchange and then stabilization of the national finances. There is no sense in wishing to take the budget and its balancing as a starting-point." Quoted by Bresciani Turroni (1937, p. 43).

[26]See Knapp (1905).

[27]This led some scholars like Mises to consider Chartalism as being co-responsible for the hyperinflation and the collapse of German monetary system. See Mises (1924).

[28]The balance of payments hypothesis, perhaps exploited by Germany's political and monetary authorities to avoid the payment of Reparations or, at any rate, to reduce their amount, was shared by several economists of the time of Anglo-Saxon origin, such as Graham (1930) and Williams (1922).

objecting to the fact that this hypothesis can explain a drift in the inflation rate but not its explosive acceleration, Robinson argued that the latter can only be explained in the light of the vicious circle between the exchange rate and wages. It was from this perspective that she argued that the depreciation of the mark in 1921 increased the cost of living, this led workers to demand compensatory wage increases that (given the low level of unemployment) were generally granted. Increasing wages led to a loss of competitiveness of German industry which encouraged a further depreciation of the mark. "Each rise in wages, therefore, precipitated a further fall in the exchange rate, and each fall in the exchange rate called forth a further rise in wages. This process became automatic when wages began to be paid on a cost-of-living basis."[29]

4.3.2 Recent Versions of the Monetarist Hypothesis

Explanations of the causes of hyperinflation were, after a period of pause, given new impetus by an essay by Cagan in 1956.[30] In the essay, Cagan, analyzing the hyperinflation[31] of seven countries,[32] including that of the Weimar Republic, came to the conclusion that in all the cases considered the root cause of hyperinflation was money creation to cover explosive public deficits. This conclusion is shared by most current studies on hyperinflation.

The assumption that hyperinflation only occur in economies with large and persistent fiscal deficits financed by printing money led Cagan to clarify the conditions under which the government maximizes seigniorage. He preliminarily argues that under extreme inflationary conditions, real money holdings will largely be determined by inflationary expectations, with the components of traditional specifications of demand for money playing a relatively minor role. Because of the slope of this function of money, in Cagan steady-state seigniorage follows a Laffer curve, where, as the inflation rate increases, seigniorage first rises and then falls. In this curve (the Inflation Tax Laffer Curve—ITLC) there is an inflation rate which maximizes seigniorage, that is the "optimal" inflation rate. This rate is equal to the inverse of the semi-elasticity of money demand in real terms to expected inflation.

Using econometric estimation, Cagan estimated the optimal inflation rate for each of the hyperinflation cases considered. As Table 4.7 shows, in all cases, the

[29] See Robinson (1938, p. 310).

[30] See Cagan (1956).

[31] He defined it as a situation starting in the month that the monthly inflation rate exceeds 50% and ending when the monthly inflation drops below 50% and stays that way for at least a year.

[32] The seven examples of hyperinflation considered by Cagan (1956) are those of Austria (October 1921–August 1922), Russia (December 1921–January 1924), Germany (August 1922–November 1923), Poland (January 1923–January 1924), Hungary I (March 1923–February 1924), Greece (November 1943–November 1944), and Hungary II (August 1945–July 1946).

Table 4.7 Rates of inflation that maximizes the revenue from a tax on cash balances estimated by Cagan (1956)

Cases of hyperinflation	Period	Optimal rate of inflation (percent per month)	Actual rate of inflation (percent per month)
Austria	Jan. 1921–Aug. 1922	12	47
Germany	Sept. 1920–July 1923	20	322
Greece	Jan. 1943–Aug. 1944	28	365
Hungary I[a]	July 1922–Feb. 1924	12	46
Hungary II[b]	July 1945–Feb. 1946	32	19,800
Poland	Apr. 1922–Nov. 1923	54	81
Russia	Dec. 1921–Jan. 1924	39	57

Source: Cagan (1956, p. 81). Legend: [a]Hungarian Hyperinflation after WWI; [b]Hungarian Hyperinflation after WWII

estimated optimal inflation rate was lower than the actual average rate of inflation.[33] This is the so-called *Cagan paradox.*

Various economic explanations have been given for the fact that often in hyperinflation the actual inflation rate is on the right side (that is the "wrong" side) of ITLC. Some scholars have attributed it to the absence of a nominal anchor,[34] others to the lack of a credible commitment of the monetary authorities.[35] Frenkel (1977) and other scholars,[36] referring to the German hyperinflation, observe that in the presence of high capital mobility and flexible exchange rates, not only goods, but also foreign currencies become an important substitute for domestic currency. Hence, the need to include in the money demand equation not only the expected inflation rate, but also the expected exchange rate depreciation.

Dornbusch (1987), finding the economic explanations of Cagan's Paradox unsatisfactory, suggested giving *political economy explanations* of this paradox. Such an explanation can be given considering that inflation is not just a means to finance deficit budgets, as put forward by monetarists both old and new, but is also, as will be better seen in the next section, an instrument through which the government influences the distribution of income and wealth. It follows that, under given circumstances, it can use inflation to benefit particular interest groups and thereby gain or consolidate the support of these groups.

Given the bell-shaped form of the ITLC, except at the optimal inflation rate, two different inflation rates can be identified, one lower (π_L) and one higher (π_H), which allow the government to obtain the same degree of seigniorage. This has led to a debate about the stability of these two different equilibrium points.

[33]In Germany, as in the other six cases considered, at some point "[i]n order to compensate for the low level to which the tax base fell after many months of hyperinflation, the tax rates rose to astronomical heights." See Cagan (1956, p. 89).

[34]See Bruno and Fischer (1990).

[35]See Kiguel and Liviatan (1991).

[36]This view is shared in later studies by Abel et al. (1979) and Taylor (1991).

In Cagan (1956), given the assumption of adaptive expectations, π_L is the stable steady state and π_H is the unstable steady state. This conclusion makes it difficult to see how explosive episodes of inflation can be explained with this model.

To overcome this problem, in 1973 Sargent and Wallace proposed an alternative model in which the existence of rational expectations, in particular perfect foresight, is assumed.[37] Two differences from Cagan's model emerge, first, the price level is allowed to jump and second, in this forward-looking model of inflation, an increase in the growth rate of nominal money immediately raises both the price level and the rate of inflation. Therefore, real money decreases to a level appropriate to the higher growth rate of nominal money and prices.

Sargent and Wallace's approach, while providing an explanation of how explosive inflation is generated, nevertheless presents inconsistencies. In it, in fact, since π_L is the unstable steady state and π_H is the stable steady state, the economy falls into a "high inflation trap." This means that a small deficit can be associated with high inflation and a large deficit with hyperdeflation.

As Marcet and Nicolini (2003) show, this problem can be solved by assuming adaptive learning instead of pure adaptive expectations. Indeed, if very small departures from rationality are introduced, the dynamics of the seigniorage model à la Cagan changes in a way consistent with the facts. In this case, low inflation equilibrium is stable and hyperinflation occurs if the budget deficit is higher than the seigniorage resulting from the maximum inflation tax.[38]

A solution to the problem of high inflation traps that avoids assumptions on expectations emerges from studies that consider the inflation trap as the outcome of policy game.[39] In Zarazaga (1993), the assumption is made of the existence of a decentralized government and private information on shocks to spending opportunities. Hyperinflation occurs when too many positive expenditure shocks make the required seigniorage too high.

4.4 The Structural View of German Inflation

In the monetarist view, the social and political factors that often underlie inflation and hyperinflation are completely ignored. Appropriately, therefore, Feldman (1993, p. 11) writes: "What has been missing in the investigation of the German inflation has been a detailed analysis of the roles and interaction of business and political leaders, on the one hand, and social organizations and structures on the other." A similar thought is found in Kindleberger (1984b, p. 31) when he writes:

---

[37]This hypothesis is the basis for several subsequent studies. See, in particular, Black (1974), Sargent (1977), Salemi and Sargent (1979), and Flood and Garber (1984).

[38]This approach has been extended to the case of heterogeneous learning rules by Evans and Honkapohja (2003).

[39]See Zarazaga (1993) and Heyman and Sanguineti (1994).

"... much of the technical economic literature on the German inflation is beside the point because it fails to specify the socio-political matrix in which the economic events take place."

Indeed, both the monetary and the balance of payments hypotheses focus exclusively on the economic determinants of German hyperinflation, neglecting the social and political aspects that contributed to it. These aspects, by contrast, play a crucial role in the *structural view*. In this, unlike in the monetary and balance of payments hypotheses, society is not seen as a single entity, but rather as composed of social groups with, at least partially, conflicting economic interests. "... [I]n a society where various interests—called 'distributional coalitions'—fight for a greater share of national income in order to gain the lion's share on any increase in income, or more usually in order to avoid bearing a significant portion of a loss, inflation is a likely outcome."[40]

When a burden shock, like Reparations or the increase in the price of oil, is imposed on society, the problem arises of how to allocate it among the different interest groups. In some cases, no agreement is reached between these interest groups (and their associated political parties) and a war of attrition ensues which delays the moment when the measures necessary to absorb the shock are adopted,[41] thereby setting the conditions for the conflict to be played out through inflation.

In other cases, inflation (and the associated redistribution of income) represents a "deliberate" choice supported by interest groups who benefit from, or are not harmed by, the increase in the prices of goods and services.

From its very beginnings, as Feldman (1993, p. 193) notes, the Weimar Republic was plagued by a high level of conflict between different interest groups each of which felt disadvantaged. The conflict was wide-ranging, in particular between capital and labor, social classes and also between creditors and debtors. The iron and steel producers attributed their troubles to the coal industry. The industrialists of the Ruhr and Rhineland disagreed with those in Berlin. Manufacturers were accused by the wholesalers of profiteering, the retailers who had to cope with consumers blamed the wholesalers for the high prices of goods.[42]

Even in such a fragmented society, political coalitions emerged between interest groups with the aim of passing on to others the burden of Reparations and the costs of failure to adjust imbalances. Before hyperinflation a more or less explicit coalition existed between capital and labor. "When stabilization came under consideration in the fall of 1922, leading industrialists such as Hugo Stinnes raised the specter of serious recession. Stabilization would indeed impose transitional costs, which might involve unemployment for the working class and real taxes for industry and personal

---

[40] See Kindleberger (1984b, p. 14). The structural view, based on the contributions of Olson (1965, 1982), has significant elements in common with the sociological inflation theory of Hirsch and Goldthorpe (1978).

[41] See Alesina and Drazen (1991). A similar situation to the war of attrition is the tug of war considered by Hirshman (1985) to be at the root of the persistent inflation in Latin American countries during the 1960s and 1980s.

[42] See Kindleberger (1994).

income."[43] In the situation just outlined, as seen in the previous chapter, inflation was pursued by a coalition of workers and industrialists at the expense of the middle classes, i.e. rentiers, professionals, and civil servants.[44] At a political level, this coalition found expression in center-left governments, of which the SPD was a stable part and held the premiership until 1920 (Table 2.1).

The structural view is particularly useful in explaining why, in certain contexts like that of early Twenties Germany, politically or externally induced exchange rate depreciation can lead to an escalation of social conflict, since no interest group, in particular interest groups which support government, is willing to bear the costs of exchange rate losses. In such an environment, inflation can become explosive, as is typical of inertial inflation when wage adjustment becomes more frequent and inflation expectations are backward-looking, while price adjustment by producers is based on expectations of further exchange rate depreciation and accelerating inflation.

4.5 Was There a Sudden Stop at the Root of German Hyperinflation?

As observed in the previous section, traditional interpretations of episodes of hyperinflation are based on money demand functions in which the repercussions of capital movements on the exchange rate are disregarded. However, the cases of hyperinflation that have occurred in many emerging countries, especially in Latin America in the 1980s and 1990s, have shown that under certain circumstances inflation can degenerate into hyperinflation because of an initial sudden stop.[45]

Significant analogies with these cases can be found in what happened in Germany in the early 1920s. Between 1919 and 1921, enormous amounts of foreign capital flowed into Germany.[46] As Keynes (1922b) wrote at the time: "Everyone in Europe and America has bought mark notes. They have been hawked by itinerant Jews in the streets of the capitals, and handled by barbers' assistants in the remotes townships of Spain and South America." This capital inflow allowed Germany to cover the substantial current account deficit it had accumulated during the period.[47]

Given that official data is unavailable, the estimates of capital inflow into Germany in the years immediately following the First World War are based on the accumulated total of current account deficits. Although the estimates thus obtained

[43] See Maier (1987, p. 203).

[44] See Maier (1987, p. 205).

[45] See Montiel (1989), Dornbusch et al. (1990), and Fischer et al. (2002).

[46] On this point, see, among others, Holtfrerich (1986, p. 285 ff.) and Ferguson (1998, p. 422).

[47] See Bonn (1922, p. 29).

diverge considerably,[48] it is unanimously recognized that the inflow of capital to Germany before mid-1922 was enormous. Non-residents,[49] mainly Americans,[50] bought marks in the form of shares and securities, but above all deposited money in German banks, in the expectation of an appreciation of the German currency.[51]

According to the statistics of the *Deutsche Oekonomist* reported in League of Nations (1931), at the end of 1921, non-residents held three-fifths of the sight deposits of the major Berlin banks and around a third of their total deposits—approx. 41.6 billion (paper) marks, corresponding to one billion gold marks. During this period there was also a significant growth in investment in German securities, shares and even real estate by non-residents.[52] By mid-1922, total assets in marks held by non-residents and invested in Germany were indeed substantial.

This flow of capital to Germany was encouraged by the widespread belief, in financial circles, that the German currency would appreciate over time.[53] This conviction is evidenced by the fact that the three-month forward exchange rate showed a premium on the spot exchange rate until the spring of 1922 and a discount only after July of that year.[54]

However, as shown in Table 4.8, in June 1922 "bad" news occurred that produced a change in expectations regarding the prospects for the mark:[55] the decision of the Morgan Commission not to grant credit to Germany (11 June 1922) and the assassination of the Minister of Finance Rathenau (24 June 1922). The changed expectations regarding the mark's prospects were not caused by economic factors but by largely unpredictable political events.[56] This political "bad" news of mid-1922, destroyed all hope of the domestic and international conditions that would enable the stabilization of the German economy.

Because of these setbacks, the confidence of individuals that, over time, the mark would appreciate faded.[57] This change in expectations was followed by a sudden stop,[58] in fact the share of foreign deposits on total deposits in German banks fell

---

[48] Graham (1930) estimated 15 billion gold marks, the McKenna committee between 7.3 and 7.8 billion, and Keynes (1922b) 1–3 billion. On this point, see, among others, Schuker (1988) and Ferguson (1998; footnote 112 at p. 422).

[49] See Schuker (1988).

[50] See Fourgeaud (1926, p. 92–4).

[51] See Holtfrerich (1982).

[52] See Holtfrerich (1986, p. 285–96), Ferguson (1996) and Ferguson and Granville (2000, p. 1062).

[53] On this aspect, see Warburg (1921), Keynes (1922a), Hawtrey (1923, p. 275), and Holtfrerich (1986, p. 293–297).

[54] See Einzig (1937).

[55] See Holtfrerich (1986) and Kindelberger (1984a, p. 301).

[56] See Holtfrerich (1983, p. 410). Lopez and Mitchener (2018) rightly emphasize the role of political instability in post-WWI hyperinflation episodes.

[57] See Frère (1922).

[58] See in particular Seghezza and Morelli (2020).

Table 4.8 "Good" and "bad" news (March 1921–Dec. 1922)

Favorable events	
March 21, 1921	Favorable result in Upper Silesia's plebiscite
January 6, 1922	Start of Cannes Conference
February 9, 1922	End of railroad strike
April 4, 1922	Optimism regarding the Genoa Conference
April 17, 1922	Positive reaction to Rapallo Treaty
September 2, 1922	Positive reports from Reparations Commission on moratorium
October 10, 1922	Allied agreement with the Turks
November 15, 1922	Response to Cuno appointment
December 15, 1922	Reports that the United States favored new Reparations arrangements
Unfavorable events	
April 26, 1921	Reparations Commission announced the total amount of Reparations (132 billion gold marks)
May 5, 1921	London schedule of Reparations payment
August 24, 1921	Murder of Erzberger
October 22, 1921	Resignation of Wirth's Cabinet
February 1, 1922	Railway workers' strike
February 18, 1922	Postponement of Genoa Conference
June 11, 1922	Decision of Morgan Commission not to grant credit to Germany
June 24, 1922	Assassination of the Minister of finance Rathenau
June, 1922	Sudden stop
August 23, 1922	Poincaré's Bar-le-Duc speech
November 25, 1922	Rumors that the French planned to occupy the Ruhr
December 28, 1922	Renewed rumors of French intransigence

from 36% in 1921 to 11% by the end of 1922.[59] On the basis of estimates,[60] between the end of 1921 and the end of 1922, deposits held by foreigners in German banks fell from 1.3 billion to 140 million gold marks.[61]

In 1922, even large German banks' deposits in foreign financial institutions began to increase significantly.[62] Between 1920 and 1923, the share of such deposits in relation to the assets of these banks rose from 7.3 to 30.9%.[63]

This data gives us an indication of the dimensions of the capital flight that occurred in 1922 but fails to tell us about the precise moment it began. An indication

[59] See League of Nations (1931). The decrease in these deposits was about two standard deviations below their mean in the period from 1919 to 1922, the index generally taken as a means of identifying a sudden stop. See, among others, Calvo et al. (2003) and Hutchison et al. (2010).

[60] See Holtfrerich (1986, p. 287).

[61] This estimate is based on the trend of such deposits with the large Berlin banks (where they fell in the period under consideration from 0.9 billion to 100 million gold marks) and on the fact that, according to Whale (1930), the market share of these banks was then 72%.

[62] See Cassis (2006, p. 174).

[63] See Wixforth (2003).

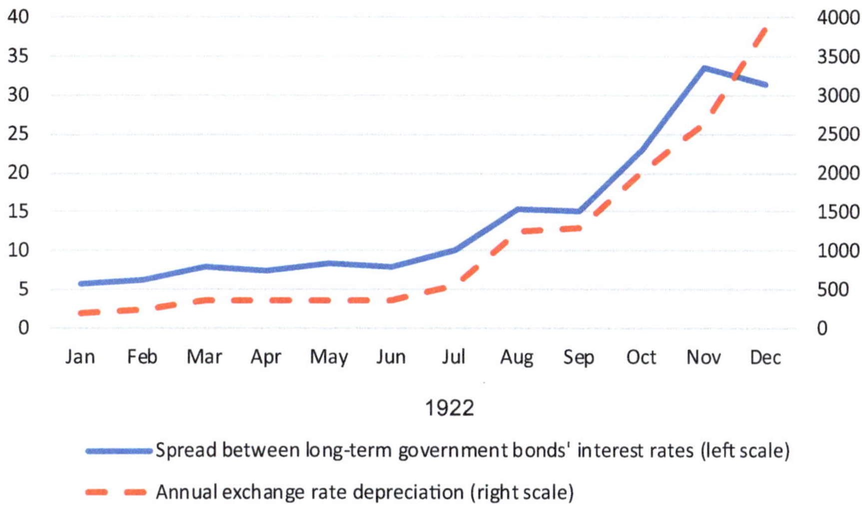

Fig. 4.4 Spread between long-term interest rates and exchange rate depreciation (monthly data, 1922). Legend: The interest rate spread between German and US long-term government bonds is measured in percentage points. The annual exchange rate depreciation of the mark vs. the US dollar is measured in percent. Source: Federal Reserve, Bulletin, several months

can, however, be obtained from the spread between the market interest rates on German and US long-term government bonds.[64] At the end of June, the spread between these interest rates was at 8.5 percentage points, at the end of July it rose to 10.9 percentage points, and by the end of August it had reached 20.6% (Fig. 4.4).

The widening of this spread suggests that investors engaged in significant sales of German government bonds.

Capital outflow from Germany from July 1922 onwards bore all the hallmarks of a sudden stop provoked by a sudden change in expectations.[65] This change in expectations led foreign investors to withdraw their deposits from German banks and sell their mark securities.

The behavior of the residents also contributed to the large outflow of gold and foreign currency from the Reichsbank. The generosity with which German banks provided loans to the private sector, in particular to large industrial groups, gave them the opportunity for speculation and thus contributed to the pronounced depreciation of the mark.[66]

---

[64]For the German securities we used the 3% Imperial bond and for the American titles the 3.5% Victory Bond 1932–1947. The data relating to these rates are taken from the Historical Archive of *The Times*.

[65]This view of the origin of German hyperinflation was first put forward by Calvo (2012, p. 10) and by Kiguel and Liviatan (1995, p. 47).

[66]See Guttmann and Meehan (1975, p. 104).

As happens in cases of sudden stop, the flight of capital was accompanied by a significant depreciation of the mark. This can be seen from the fact that the mark rose from 272 to the dollar on June 1 to 318 on June 12, when the Morgan Report came out, and to 355 on the day of the assassination of Rathenau on June 24. By July 31, it was at 670 and by the end of August it had reached 1725.[67] As seen in Sect. 4.2 and illustrated in Fig. 4.1, the significant depreciation in the exchange rate that occurred in mid-1922 led to a considerable rise in both wholesale and retail prices.[68]

As in most other cases,[69] also in Germany, the sudden stop led to a fall in output and disposable income.[70] This was followed by an exacerbation of the distributive conflict, as the various interest groups sought to maintain their purchasing power, shifting onto others the burden of diminished income. The accommodating policy pursued by the Reichsbank drove this process, thus fueling the inflationary spiral. With the acceleration of the rate of inflation output fell markedly. Consequently, between June and September 1923, the percentage of unemployed trade union workers rose from 4.1to 9.9%.[71] In October 1923, this percentage rose to 19.1%. The disintegration of the German economy was halted by the process of stabilization that began in the autumn of 1923.

4.6 The Empirical Evidence of the Sudden Stop

In order to corroborate the sudden stop hypothesis we carried out some causality tests.[72] Initially we ran a VAR Granger causality test in order to compare the monetary hypothesis and the sudden stop hypothesis. To this end we considered a VAR consisting of three variables: the consumer price index, the real exchange rate of the mark with respect to the dollar,[73] and the real monetary base.[74] The data is monthly and the sample period used is between January 1921 and June 1923, that is to say, the period when inflation first started to accelerate and then became explosive. As suggested by the various tests of lag-length criteria, three lags were used.

---

[67] As observed by Kindleberger (1984b, p. 28): "... Speculation in favor of the mark by foreigners (and some Germans) had been completely reversed."

[68] For the consumer price index, we used the workers' cost-of-living index.

[69] See, among others, Calvo and Reinhart (2000) and Bordo et al. (2007).

[70] Among these factors, the reduction in foreign funding, in particular, made the re-balancing of current accounts chiefly through a reduction in domestic absorption inevitable.

[71] See Holtfrerich (1986, p. 198) and Feldman (1993, p. 603–605).

[72] For a more detailed illustration of these tests, see Seghezza and Morelli (2020).

[73] The sources are the following: the wholesale price index and the workers' cost-of-living index are taken from Holtfrerich (1986); the nominal exchange rate of the German mark against the US dollar and the US price index from the Federal Bank Reserve of Saint Louis. The real exchange rate was calculated by multiplying the nominal exchange rate of the mark against the US dollar by the ratio between the level of prices in the USA and in Germany.

[74] Nominal narrow money divided by the consumer price index.

Table 4.9 Monetary or exchange rate induced hyperinflation (Granger Causality/Block exogeneity Wald test, Jan. 1921–Jun. 1923)

		Dependent variables		
		Inflation	Real exchange rate	Real monetary base
Excluded variables	Real monetary base	1.35	0.19	–
	Real exchange rate	20.99***	–	17.27***
	Inflation	–	0.39	1.74
	All	21.80***	2.78	20.25***

Legend: Monthly change of variables. ***reject at 1%, **reject at 5%, *reject at 10%

The variables used are logarithmic and expressed in first differences. Before proceeding to the causality tests, we test the hypothesis of stationarity of the variables in first differences using the ADF and the Dickey–Fuller (GLS) tests, both with the constant and with the constant and the trend.

The results of these tests, shown in Table 4.19 of Appendix 1, show that the first differences in real exchange rate (RER) and the real monetary base (RMB) are stationary. Inflation (INFL) proves to be stationary in three out of four tests.[75]

After establishing the stationarity of the variables, we proceeded to the estimate of the VAR Granger causality test. The results are given in Table 4.9.

The results in col. (1) show that the null hypothesis—the interest variable does not cause inflation—is rejected in the case of the real exchange rate, while it is accepted in the case of real monetary base. As evidenced by the last column in Table 4.9, real exchange rate changes seem to have had notable effects not only on price growth but also on changes in real monetary base. Furthermore, neither money nor prices seem to prove significant in explaining the variation in the exchange rate.

These results confirm that the sudden stop hypothesis is able to explain the origin of German hyperinflation better than the monetary view. In this latter view, a distinction is conventionally made between two different approaches: the monetary view in the narrow sense of the term and the monetary-fiscal view put forward by Sargent (1982), which regards episodes of hyperinflation as always originating from fiscal imbalances. Conversely, according to the monetary view in the narrow sense of the term, these episodes can also result from an excessive growth in bank credit and thus from the behavior of private individuals.[76] The results of the tests in Appendix 2 confirm the plausibility of the sudden stop hypothesis, namely that German hyperinflation originated in an exchange rate crisis caused by a sudden stop.

In order to measure its intensity we used a forecast error variance decomposition (FEVD), a methodology first used by Montiel (1989) and later by Dornbusch et al.

[75]Full confirmation of the stationarity of inflation is obtained using the Hodrick–Prescott filtered variable.

[76]For this distinction, see Bresciani-Turroni (1937, p. 75). In ascribing episodes of hyperinflation solely to fiscal imbalances financed through money, the fiscal view holds that the stabilization of an economy afflicted by hyperinflation presupposes fiscal re-equilibrium. Conversely, the monetary view assumes more simply a drastic reduction in the money supply.

Table 4.10 Monetary or exchange-rate induce hyperinflation (composition of forecast error variance of variables in the Var system, forecast at 24 months, Jan. 1921–Jun. 1923)

	Variance decomposition of		
	Inflation (INFL)	Real exchange rate (RER)	Real monetary base (RMB)
Due to	A—Var Ordering: RER—RMB – INFL		
INFL	18.4	4.0	15.5
RER	60.0	84.0	46.7
RMB	21.5	12.0	37.8
	B—Var Ordering: RMB—RER – INFL		
INFL	21.5	3.9	15.5
RER	39.6	74.5	30.1
RMB	38.9	21.6	54.4
	C—Var Ordering: INFL—RER – RMB		
INFL	67.7	26.9	58.4
RER	27.4	70.5	24.3
RMB	5.0	2.6	17.3
	D—Var Ordering: Average		
INFL	35.9	11.6	29.8
RER	42.3	76.3	33.7
RMB	21.8	12.1	36.5

(1990) and Fischer et al. (2002) to analyze the origin of episodes of hyperinflation. The results of the FEVD relative to the standard VAR Granger test estimated in Table 4.9 are given in Table 4.10.

Panels A-B-C present three different orderings of the variables, while Panel D summarizes the average values of the three previous orderings. Table 4.10 provides further evidence that the dynamics of the exchange rate significantly influence the other three system variables, in particular the dynamics of the rate of inflation. Conversely, the influence on this latter variable of changes in real monetary base is always lower than that of changes in the real exchange rate, irrespective of the order of the variables in the VAR.[77] The next section seeks to explain *when* and *why* this sudden stop occurred.

[77] It is common knowledge that in a standard VAR the result of the FEVD can be influenced by the order of the variables. As robustness test we estimated a structural VAR (SVAR) which modifies the Cholesky decomposition, on which the FEVD in the standard VAR is based, in order to make the order of real exchange rate and real monetary base irrelevant. It results that both in the short and the long term, the inflation dynamic is explained by shocks to the real exchange rate with percentages that are always above 50% and with a slight tendency toward growth, while the contribution of the real monetary base is slightly above 30% in the first 6 months and then falls to under 20% after 2 years. The basic exogeneity of the real exchange rate is also confirmed. This is explained with percentages consistently slightly below 90%.

4.7 When Did the Initial Sudden Stop Occur?

It was pointed out in the Introduction to this chapter that the balance of payments hypothesis assumes that German hyperinflation had its origin in an exchange rate crisis. That hypothesis maintained, however, that this crisis resulted from Germany's efforts to meet its Reparations obligations, while this is not the place to debate this question once again[78] there is a substantial literature that shows that in fact the effective burden of the Reparations which the Weimar republic had to pay was, in fact, sustainable.[79]

The assumption we make here, unlike the position underlying the balance of payments hypothesis, is that the crisis of the German mark resulted from a precipitous reversal of capital flows, in other words, a sudden stop. This hypothesis makes it crucial to determine the moment when this process occurred. In order to clarify this, we tested if some important pieces of political news had a significant influence on the behavior of investors and on the exchange rate of the mark.[80]

To this end we followed the "narrative approach,"[81] which takes as its point of reference events recognized as important by public opinion. Following Feldman (1993, p. 418), we assume that good news fuels hopes that a solution to the Reparations problem will be found and the German economy will be stabilized; the opposite applies in the case of bad news. It is from this perspective that we verify how the events listed in Table 4.8 influenced individual expectations and, as a consequence, the exchange rate. Since we do not have daily data for the forward exchange rate of the mark in the 1920s,[82] we attempted to determine the short-term equilibrium exchange rate using the uncovered interest parity condition.

The estimate uses the daily data of the mark-dollar exchange rate, s_t the interest rate on the 3% German Imperial bond, i_t, the interest rate on the 3.5% Victory Bond 1932–47, i_t^*[83] and the variable "news," with a value of 1 for the unfavorable events and −1 for the favorable events listed in Table 4.8, and a value of 0 during the other periods.

Prior to the estimate we tested the stationarity of the variables. As shown in Table 4.20 of Appendix 1, both the first difference of the exchange rate and the first difference of the spread between long-term interest rates are stationary, whichever test is used.

We then went on to estimate an equation specified as follows:

[78] An illustration of this can be found in Feldman (1993).

[79] See, among others, Schuker (1988) and Ritschl (2014).

[80] This hypothesis is based on the idea that markets are efficient and that accordingly each significant piece of information is incorporated into the current exchange rate.

[81] See Romer and Romer (1989) and Ramey (2011).

[82] The data for this variable is only available on a weekly basis and are provided in Einzig (1937).

[83] The mark-dollar exchange rate data and the long-term interest rate data come from the historical digital archives of *The Times*.

Table 4.11 Estimates of the beginning of hyperinflation (OLS estimates of the change in the exchange rate, Jan. 1921- Jun. 1923)

Variable	(1)	(2)	(3)	(4)
Constant	0.006996***	0.006902***	0.006857***	0.00668***
	(0.0021)	(0.0020)	(0.0022)	(0.0021)
$\Delta\left(i_{t-1} - i^*_{t-1}\right)$	0.009705***	0.008449***	0.008453***	0.007743***
	(0.0021)	(0.0021)	(0.0021)	(0.0021)
News		0.022007***		
		(0.0065)		
*News*ante*				0.015055**
				(0.0077)
Bad news			0.02242***	
			(0.0091)	
Good news			−0.021543**	
			(0.0097)	
*Bad news*post*				0.055892***
				(0.0184)
*Good news*post*				−0.027013*
				(0.0151)
Adj R-squared	0.03	0.05	0.05	0.05
S.E.R.	0.05	0.05	0.05	0.05
D.W.	1.87	1.87	1.87	1.87
Bad news+Good news = 0 Wald test t-stat			0.06	1.22
Prob			0.95	0.222

$$s_t - s_{t-1} = b_0 + b_1\Delta\left(i_{t-1} - i^*_{t-1}\right) + b_2 news_t + \varepsilon_t \tag{4.1}$$

The estimate was made by OLS for the period 1.1.1921–31.12.1922 and its results are shown in Table 4.11. In column (1), we show the basic equation, where the change in the Reichsmark-US dollar exchange rate was set as a function of the change in the spread between the long-term interest rates. In the estimate this spread is significant and, as expected, positive. In column (2), we incorporated into the basic equation the variable *news.* Also this variable is significant and has the expected sign.

In column (3), the variable *news* has been divided into *bad news* and *good news.* The results of the estimate show that both these variables are significant and have the expected signs. What is more, the Wald test provides no evidence of a significant statistical difference between the coefficients of the different types of news. A robustness test of these results according to Ramey and Shapiro's (1998) approach is shown in Appendix 3.

We have now to establish whether and at what point the importance of these effects became more pronounced. To this end we consider the recursive coefficients of the estimates in Table 4.11. This analysis shows that, starting from the summer of

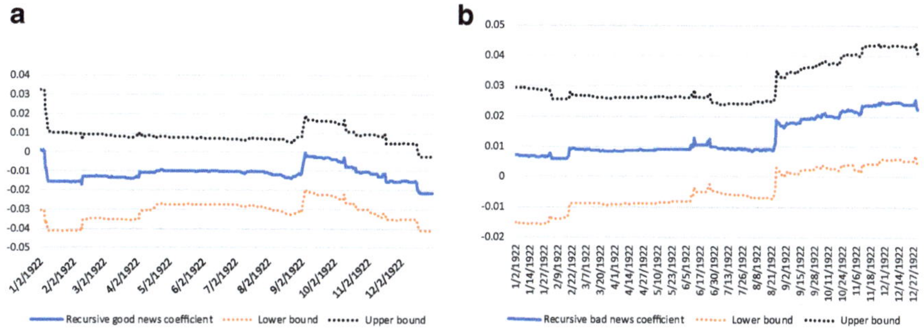

Fig. 4.5 (**a**) Recursive bad news coefficients. (**b**) Recursive good news coefficients (monthly data, 1922)

1922, the coefficients of *bad news* and *good news* followed diverging trends (Fig. 4.5a, b). While the *good news* coefficient has a tendency to fall, in the case of *bad news* it tends to rise. This increase seems to suggest a widespread conviction that stabilization in Germany had become unattainable. The consolidation of this conviction led to a dramatic depreciation of the mark.

From late August, albeit with some delay with respect to the actual exchange rate depreciation,[84] similarly the three-month forward exchange rate started to show a significant discount: between the end of July and the end of August, it rose from 10 to 150%. Given this evidence we can conclude that the months between July and August 1922 represented a benchmark for expectations about Germany's economic prospects. Accordingly, Fig. 4.5a, b show that from August of that year onwards the influence of bad news on the exchange rate became considerably more pronounced.

This is confirmed in the estimates in col. (4) in Table 4.11, which gives the values of the coefficients of news after 24 August 1922. A comparison of the results in this column with those in column (3) in the same Table shows that after late August the bad news coefficient rose from 0.022 to 0.056, while the good news coefficient tended to lose significance.

It would seem, therefore, that starting from the end of August expectations of a growing depreciation of the mark were gaining credence. Confirmation of the worsening of expectations about the mark comes from the marked widening of the spread between the interest rates of German and American long-term government bonds: between the middle and the end of August this grew from 13.8 to 20.6%.

Some scholars, following Sargent and Wallace (1987), argue that the change in expectations that occurred in the summer of 1922 concerned Germany's public finances rather than the prospects of the mark. Starting from the assumption that

---

[84]The size of the forward exchange rate discount, used by Frenkel (1977, 1980) as a proxy for expectations regarding inflation, proved in July to be considerably lower than the actual depreciation in the exchange rate and wholesale and consumer prices growth. This fact allows us to exclude the possibility that the origin of German hyperinflation can be seen as a process of self-fulfilling expectations.

Table 4.12 Prices indices in second half of 1922 (June = 100, June - Dec. 1922)

1922	Import prices	Wholesale prices	Consumer prices[a]
June	100	100	100
July	146	143	134
August	342	273	191
September	454	408	300
October	953	805	520
November	2258	1641	1073
December	2567	2098	1575

Source: Bresciani Turroni (1937) and Holtfrerich (1986). [a] Workers cost-of-living

expected inflation depends on expected deficits, Webb (1986) shows how a person, if she expects an increase in the public deficit "... [s]he would then wish to hold less of her wealth in government debt and more in real assets—stocks, steel, sausages. To try to fulfil this wish, she would discount some of her T-bills at the Reichsbank, take the cash, and go out to buy goods ...".[85] On an aggregate level, this behavior, if it spreads, leads to an increasing monetization of public debt. This corresponds to an increase in the demand for goods and services, which is inevitably followed by an increase in the price of real assets and a decrease in the real value of cash.

Emblematic, in Webb's opinion, is what happened in early summer 1922. On 11 June of that year, a committee of American and British bankers, headed by J.P. Morgan, announced that no further loans to Germany would be issued. The expectations of higher prospective deficits led to a pronounced rise in expectations of inflation and then in actual inflation.

This hypothesis, however, seems to be at odds with the evidence of the different dynamics of retail prices and wholesale prices. As shown by Table 4.12, in the second half of 1922, in particular from July onwards, the wholesale price index followed that of imports and the spread between wholesale and retail price indices widened markedly.

The more dynamic trend of wholesale prices compared to retail prices seems to confirm the existence of a causal link that goes from the depreciation of the exchange rate to import prices and to wholesale prices, and from these to retail prices, rather than vice versa, as Webb's (1989) version of the fiscal view would have it, from consumer prices to wholesale prices and from these to the exchange rate.[86]

[85] See Webb (1986, p. 772).

[86] This criticism derives mainly from the fact that in Webb (1986), as indeed in Cagan (1956) and its developments, money can only be replaced with goods and services and not with foreign currency or assets denominated in it. See Reghezza et al. (2020).

4.8 How and Why the Inflation Induced by the Sudden Stop Became Hyperinflation

The previous sections have shown how the origin of German hyperinflation can be found in a sudden stop and the consequent exchange rate crisis. However, as observed by Dornbusch (1985), the acceleration in inflation brought about by the depreciation in the exchange rate would not have transformed into explosive inflation in the absence of an accommodating monetary policy.

The accommodating monetary policy of the central bank was a response to the worsening of the social conflict caused by the fall in output and income following the sudden stop. As in other cases of sudden stops,[87] the worsening social conflict took the form of a clash between the productive classes, workers and industrialists,[88] on the one hand, and rentiers, on the other.[89]

At a time when the country's income was falling, the unions called for real wages to be maintained through rises in wages.[90] Rather than opposing such demands, industrialists adopted an accommodating attitude.[91] This attitude sprang from their concern about the possible outbreak of a Bolshevik style revolution and fear of union strength.[92] They therefore urged the government to adopt expansive fiscal and monetary policies so as to maintain GDP growth high and unemployment at minimum levels.[93] Given that this was the prime goal, it is not surprising that the leading representative of the industrialists, Hugo Stinnes,[94] argued that inflation was a "political necessity."[95] In this context, a tacit alliance grew up between the industrial lobby and the workers' unions. These two interest groups were not hostile to inflation because it enabled them to shift onto rentiers much of the fall in national income.[96]

After a currency crisis generally two mechanisms determine a further inflation rate acceleration. The first mechanism follows from the Olivera–Tanzi effect, in

[87] See, among others, Liviatan and Piterman (1986) and Montiel (1989).

[88] Some scholars, like Helmstadter (1985), stress the distribution of income and wealth mainly between capital and labor.

[89] See Kindleberger (1984b), Maier (1978), and Pittaluga and Seghezza (2012).

[90] As Fergusson (1975, p. 86) writes: "Because of the excessive rise in the cost of living in these weeks [of July], ever more pressing demand for higher wages flowed in from all classes with any leverage on their paymasters. Strikes accompanied those demands . . .".

[91] This helps explain the sharp growth in monetary wages between August 1922 and June 1923.

[92] See Feldman (1983, p.390) and Holtfrerich (1983, p. 407).

[93] See Feldman (1993, p. 447).

[94] As Widdig (2001, p. 134) claims, Stinnes ". . . personifies like no other the nexus between inflation, industrial concentration, and wealth."

[95] See Houghton Account, NA, 862.00/1199.

[96] As Maier (1978, p. 52) writes: "Hyperinflation thus involved an implicit coalition of labor and industry at the expense of rentiers. . . Inflation represented a second-best or perhaps maxmin strategy of curtailing predictable losses in a situation where the preferred policy of stabilization at full employment appeared unavailable."

Table 4.13 Government revenue, floating debt, and discounted commercial bills in the second half of 1922

Months	Ratio of taxes to total expenditures	Floating debt (millions of gold marks)	Commercial bills discounted by the Reichsbank (trillions of paper marks)
June	74.8	100	6.9
July	66.8	129	18.3
August	56.7	171	164.6
September	20.8	552	3660.1
October	24.5	388	1,058,129.9
November	30.2	290	347,301,037.7
December	16.8	588	322,724,949.0

Source: Graham (1930)

other words, from the fact that as inflation increases, the real value of tax revenue tends to fall,[97] thus leading to fiscal deficits which, when they cannot be covered by debt, are "resolved" by increasing the money supply.[98]

The second mechanism results from the fact that in phases of inflation acceleration and negative real interest rates, the demand for credit rises significantly. When this demand is satisfied, bank loans and the monetary multiplier increase,[99] resulting in a notable increase in the monetary base.

In Germany in the latter half of 1922, both of these mechanisms were at work. On the one hand, mounting reductions in real government revenue began in August 1922.[100] However, the government sought to maintain a high level of spending in real terms. In contrast to the previous years, the Patinkin effect significantly diminished. This implied a significant increase in fiscal deficit, in the floating debt held by the Reichsbank and in the money base created by the Treasury (Table 4.13).

In order to maintain workers' purchasing power, re-negotiations of wages between unions and industrialists became increasingly frequent.[101] As wage increases affected production costs, this inevitably led to price increases, which, in turn, had an effect on production cycles. Firms were unable to pay wages and buy capital goods, raw materials, and intermediate goods using the cash flow coming from the previous period's production, since their purchasing power was eroded due to rising inflation. Especially after the sharp depreciation of the mark between 1921 and 1922, businessmen had to resort to bank credit to keep up production cycles. This helps explain the considerable growth of bank loans in 1921 and 1922.[102]

[97] As this is based on the nominal revenue of the previous year.

[98] See Dornbusch (1985, p. 24–25).

[99] See Tullio (1985, p. 353).

[100] According to Graham (1930), between June and December 1922, government revenue decreased from 305 to 119 billion gold marks.

[101] See Colles (1922, p. 464).

[102] See Prion (1924, p. 172).

Table 4.14 Money and money multiplier in Germany (1920–1924)

	1920	1921	1922	1923	1924
Deposits in all commercial banks (a)	83,891	154,989	2,216,067	1,481,019,370	4977
Saving deposits (b)	43,100	46,500	136,180	–	–
Total money in circulation (c)	81,388	122,500	1,295,231	2,274,000,000	3891
a/c	1.03	1.27	1.71	0.65	1.28

Source: Graham (1930)

When, in mid-1922, the banks had insufficient liquidity to meet the demand for loans, the Reichsbank decided to address this situation by introducing liquidity into the system and considerably increasing the discount of commercial bills (Table 4.13).[103] Between June and December 1922, the monetary base created by refinancing operations increased by 1416 billion (paper) marks, that is to say, more than that created via the Treasury, which rose in the same period by 1111 billion paper marks. At the same time, given the high level of bank loans, the significant growth of the monetary base was accompanied, between 1920 and 1922, by a particularly sharp increase in the money multiplier (Table 4.14).

The acceleration of inflation prompted trade unions to make the adjustment of wages to price movements more rapidly. To this end, as Table 3.5 of Chap. 3 shows not only was the lag with which wages were adjusted gradually reduced, but during 1923 the dollar exchange rate in Berlin on the day of the wage payment was used instead of the cost-of-living index to calculate the loss of purchasing power of wages.[104]

The gradual reduction in the lag with which wages were adjusted for inflation led to the emergence of a vicious circle between exchange rate, prices, and wages. As Fig. 4.6 shows, in some moments of 1923 wage increases exceeded price increases and price increases exceeded exchange rate increases, in other periods the opposite occurred.

This is also evident from the development of the real wage. In spite of the accelerated pace of inflation, the real wage increased in some months during 1923, outpacing that of prices (Table 4.15).

The process just illustrated appears entirely similar to those of extreme inflation and hyperinflation which occurred in the 1980s in Latin America and illustrated as follows by Elena Cardoso: "Current inflation depends on past inflation via indexation of wages, the exchange rate, and public-sector prices . . . Shocks such as an oil price increase, a real currency depreciation, increases in indirect taxes, elimination of public-sector subsidies, and increases in the real price of agricultural goods raise the current rate of inflation. These are transmitted via indexation into increased inflation

[103] See Graham (1930) and Webb (1984).

[104] See Bresciani-Turroni (1937, p. 310).

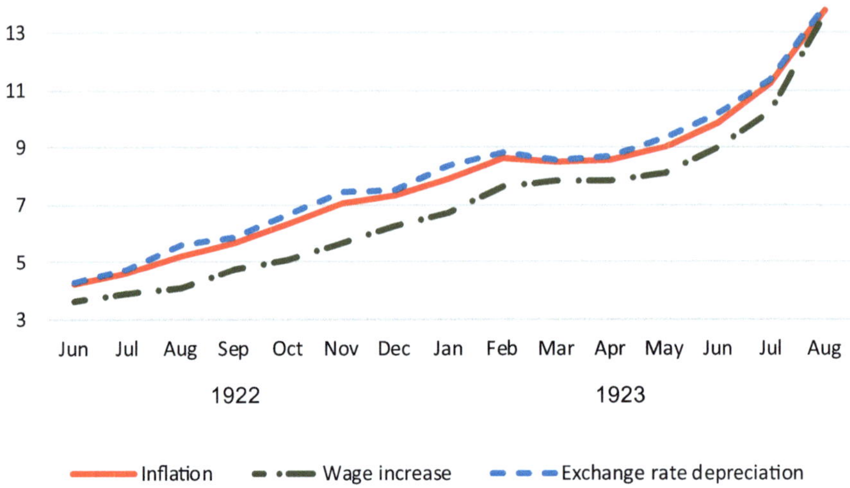

Fig. 4.6 Wage increase, inflation, and exchange rate depreciation (Jun 1922–Aug.1923). Source: for wages, see Bry (1960); for exchange rate, see Bresciani-Turroni (1937); and for wholesale prices, see Holtfrerich (1986). Note: all the variables are in logarithms

Table 4.15 Real wages of workers (1913 = 100, April 1922–Sept. 1923)

		Total workers	Coal mine workers in the Ruhr District
1922	April	71.9	73.8
	July	71.6	69.5
	October	54.8	51.6
	December	61.6	62.2
1923	January	48.7	47.7
	February	63.5	75.6
	March	78.7	86.2
	April	74.1	79.9
	May	65.1	69.6
	June	65.1	70.8
	July	48.0	47.6
	August	67.2	78.5
	September	61.2	74.7

Source: For total workers Statistiches Reichsamt (1925). For Coal mine workers Bresciani-Turroni (1937)

Table 4.16 Indices of German public debt and amount of interests on public debt in real terms (1919-IV = 100, Quarterly data, 1920-I–1923-II)

	Index of real public debt	Index of real interests on public debt
1920-I	47.6	44.7
1920-II	57.1	48.6
1920-III	71.4	56.6
1920-IV	81.0	59.2
1921-I	95.2	67.1
1921-II	107.9	69.7
1921-III	93.6	51.3
1921-IV	60.3	28.9
1922-I	49.2	22.4
1922-II	34.9	13.2
1922-III	15.9	3.9
1922-IV	7.9	1.3
1923-I	7.9	1.3
1923-II	11.1	1.3

Source: Alesina (1988) and Webb (1986)

in the subsequent periods. In the vicious circle created by indexation, inflationary shocks, like a devaluation or an increase in public-sector prices, are perpetuated."[105]

Over time, inflation eroded the public debt. This erosion was particularly pronounced in the hyperinflation phase when the real value of the Reich's debt essentially fell to zero (Table 4.16).

Like the Reich's debt, inflation erodes the public debt of industrialists and landowners. How Guttmann and Meehan (1975, p. 110) writes: "German agricultural property before the war was mortgaged to the tune of a total of about 15 milliard gold marks, a burden of which they rid themselves. But in the meantime the payment of interest, which constituted a constant drain on their incomes, dwindled rapidly and became insignificant, while their incomes themselves remained more or less stable, the real prices for agricultural produce, with certain interruptions, remaining almost at world price level."

The erosion of the real value of private and public debt in the national currency was associated with significant capital losses on rentiers.[106] As Table 4.17 shows, between the end of 1913 and 1923, the net financial wealth of the German population fell on average by 61.2% with reductions affecting the wealthiest exceeding 85%.[107]

[105] See Cardoso (1989, p. 15).

[106] See, among others, Huges (1982).

[107] Thus, German inflation and hyperinflation significantly lowered distributional inequality in Germany. See Piketty (2014).

Table 4.17 Distribution of wealth by individuals according to the wealth tax statistics (percent of the total; Germany, Dec. 1913 and Dec. 1923)

	31 December 1913	31 December 1923
From 10,000 to 20,000	7.38	14.87
20,000 to 30,000	7.36	10.45
30,000 to 50,000	11.03	13.30
50,000 to 100,000	14.88	16.09
100,000 to 500,000	9.78	25.61
500,000 to 1000,000	0.94	7.40
1000,000 to 3000,000	0.48	7.29
3000,000 to 10,000,000	0.09	3.46
Over 10,000,000	0.01	1.53
Total	100.00	100.00

Source: Stistisches Reichsamt, Die Deutsche vermögensbesteuerung vor und nach dem kriege. Statistik des Deutschen Reichs, Berlin, 1927

Table 4.18 Distribution of taxpayers (1913–1928)

Tax band	1913	1926	1928
1	47.6	62.2	54.5
2	42.6	28.6	34.2
3	5.2	5.0	6.8
4	2.4		2.6
5	0.9	2.4	0.8
6	0.2	0.4	0.3
7	0.3	0.2	0.2
8	0.2		0.1
9	0.1	0.13	0.04
10	0.05	0.01	0.01

Source: McElligott (2013). Note: For the meanings of "band," see Appendix 4

Without any doubt the holders of financial assets were extremely affected by inflation. However, other members of the middle class, such as small holding farmers, at least initially, benefited from inflation. In fact, the real value of their debt exposures fell dramatically. More questionable were the effects of inflation on the income and wealth of home-owners. On the one hand, the latter benefited from the decreased real value of their debt exposures. On the other hand, they, however, saw their real income decrease given the government control of rental market.[108] Overall, however, the middle class was certainly weakened by hyperinflation. Evidence of this can be seen from the increased incidence of taxpayers in the lower income groups (Table 4.18).

[108] See Geyer (1986).

Some scholars tend to believe that hyperinflation paved Hitler's way to power. Robbins, for example, writes: "... It [hyperinflation] destroyed the wealth of the more solid elements in German society: and it left behind a moral and economic disequilibrium, apt breeding ground for the disasters which have followed. Hitler is the foster-child of the inflation."[109] This view is shared by Guttmann and Meehan (1975), when they write: "The traumatic experience of the inflation, the impoverishment, the proletarianization, the loss of status and influence, all had lasting effect on the middle classes and especially on their sons and daughters. Their material, political and spiritual values were destroyed ... The Nazi party was waiting for them, offering a safe haven, a promise of stability."[110] A similar opinion is found more recently in Ferguson and Granville (2000) and Acemoglu et al. (2019).

Other scholars, such as Krugman (2013), Feldman (1993) and Fazio (2022) tend to downplay the importance of hyperinflation in Hitler's rise to power, favored in their opinion by the deep economic crisis of the early 1930s. This last view was recently corroborated by a contribution by Galofré-Vilà (2023),[111] in which it is shown that the areas of Germany in which inflation was highest in 1923 were not those in which the Nazi party obtained at the end of 1932 and at the beginning 1933 the highest electoral consensus.

As McElligott (2013, p. 77): writes "... [I]n spite of the perceived and real travails of the early inflationary period, Mittelstand voters were not radicalized to the extent that they would later be. Indeed, we could argue that the two elections of 1924 and the presidential election of 1925 reveal a desire for stability based on a conservative and traditionalist authority."

However, if hyperinflation was not the determining factor in Hitler's rise to power, the fact remains that the proletarianization of the middle class weakened the democratic regime. In fact, it not only undermined the confidence in it of large sections of the middle class, but reduced the weight of the latter in German society. As political scientists tirelessly remind us, there is no democracy without a bourgeoisie.[112]

Extreme inflation resulted in a redistribution of wealth and income not only within Germany, but also between this country and foreigners. In fact, foreigners, mostly American banks, who had invested in marks or assets held in this currency, were significantly affected by it. Different quantifications have been given of the

---

[109] See Robbins (1937, p. 6).

[110] See Guttmann and Meehan (1975, p. 239). A similar point of view can be found in Hill et al. (1977).

[111] See also Galofré-Vilà et al. (2021).

[112] See, among others, Moore (1966). In the same vein, Aristotle (1984, p. 210) writes: "The political community that depends on the middling sort is best as well, and that those cities are capable of being well governed in which the middling element is numerous, most particularly if it is superior to both of the other parts, but if not, superior to either of them; for when added to one it will tip the scale and prevent the opposing excesses from arising."

losses of foreign investors due to hyperinflation and the depreciation of the mark.[113] These quantifications amount, in any case, despite the differences, to several billion gold marks.[114] The destruction of the value of credits in marcs held by foreigners is similar to the benefits that a country can derive from non-repayable foreign credits.

4.9 The Modest Revaluation of Rentiers' Claims

As shown in the previous paragraph, the redistributive effects of hyperinflation on rentiers were devastating. It is inevitable to ask firstly why this interest group accepted so passively the process of impoverishment that inflation and finally hyperinflation forced upon them and secondly because the request for a revaluation of rentiers to revalue their assets after stabilization was accepted only minimally.

The first reason for this passive attitude probably was that while industrialists and workers were organized interest groups, thus capable of exerting concerted political pressure, the rentiers were an unorganized interest group with little ability to exercise pressure.[115]

The second reason for the passivity of the middle class, with respect to the despoliation process that affected them, lay in the fact that the rentiers, because of propaganda, had for some time remained convinced that the erosion of the value of their wealth was due to the effects on mark of the financial burdens imposed on Germany by the Treaty of Versailles. When they realized that certain interest groups had benefited from inflation, indeed had grown rich at their expense, they tried to fight back and demanded compensation. They then began lobbying the nationalist parties, in which most of them recognized themselves, for compensation.[116] However, by the end of 1922, the judiciary had reaffirmed the principle: "mark equals mark." The center-right parties, fearing that they would lose the consent of this component of the electorate, put forward bills in the course of 1923 that foresaw a revaluation of mortgage credit. Not coincidentally in March 1923, however, the judiciary changed its view: the Court of Appeal at Darmstadt ruled that according to the Civil Code a debt had to be paid according to equity and good faith. Repayment of a debt with depreciated money was contrary to good faith. Initially, the government was against the revaluation of credit. However, after the judgement of the Supreme Tribunal of Leipzig in November 1923, the government, which was in favor of the revaluation of debts, realized that a legislative solution to the problem

[113] See Moulton and McGuire (1923).

[114] According to Holtfrerich about 15 billion of gold marks.

[115] See Morelli and Seghezza (2014).

[116] On the revaluation of claims expressed in paper marks, see Bresciani-Turroni (1937, p. 320–326), Jones (1979), and De Broeck and James (2019).

was needed and issued a decree in February 1924, which provided for the revaluation of some private debts by about 15% and postponed a possible revaluation of debts owed to the state until the solution of the Reparations problem.[117] The decree made no provision for debts which had already been paid off. Moreover, the sums due under the law did not become payable before January 1 of 1932.

The dissatisfaction of the rentiers with this decree resulted in protests putting great pressure on the government of the German National People's Party (Deutschnationale Volkspartei, DNVP). In July 1925, despite the vehement opposition of Reichsbank President Schacht, the government (based on a coalition of the Center Party, DNVP, DVP, and BVP and chaired by Luther) enacted two laws: the Revaluation Law, which dealt with private loans and which raised their revaluation rate from 15% foreseen in the decree of February 1924 to 25%, and the Public Loan Discharge Law, according to which war-loans and other (paper mark denominated) debts of the Reich, lander, and local authorities were converted into new Reich loan stock at a ratio of 40:1, i.e. 1000 paper marks of Reich, lander, and local authorities debt were converted into 25 Reichsmark of "new" loan stock. Given the revaluation amounts, it is clear that the two laws represented an "... epitaph written to middle-class hopes for recovering claims on wealth that had long since been expropriated by other social groups or squandered in the war."[118] The interests of big industry and agrarian landowners had prevailed, but even more so the concern, voiced several times by Luther, first as Minister of Finance and later as Chancellor, to safeguard the monetary stability acquired in late 1923 and early 1924.

4.10 Conclusions

The monetarist interpretation of German hyperinflation—in the version given by Cagan (1956) and its developments—over time has become prevalent. According to this interpretation, the origin of this hyperinflation is to be traced back to the need of governments to obtain adequate resources through seigniorage to cover large budget deficits. From this view, therefore, inflation is equated to a tax; it does so, however, ignoring the fact that inflation also has an impact on the distribution of private income and wealth. In inflationary processes there are, therefore, interest groups that benefit from price increases and others that are harmed by them. This implies that in the political arena there is a "demand" for inflation (or deflation) and a "supply" of inflation (or deflation).

We have seen in the previous chapter how, in the immediate post-war Germany, an implicit coalition of interest groups (mainly industrialists and workers), for

[117] For a detailed discussion of the problem of revaluation, see Bresciani-Turroni (1937, p. 320–325) and Southern (1979).

[118] See Maier (1975, p. 493).

various reasons including that they would benefit from inflation, successfully lobbied the government for lax fiscal and monetary policies. Taking this into account, it is not difficult to see a line of continuity between the high inflation of the immediate post-WWI years and the hyperinflation of 1923. Indeed, the latter represents the inevitable outcome of the high level of persistence of the former.

The likening of inflation to a tax in the monetarist view implies that, as for any other tax, a Laffer curve can be drawn. Problematic, however, within the monetarist approach is to explain why in almost all cases of hyperinflation, certainly in the case of German hyperinflation, the inflation rate is higher than the optimal inflation rate (i.e., the rate at which seigniorage is maximized) and is on the downward side of the Laffer curve. This fact can be explained from a political economy approach,[119] i.e. by taking into account social and political aspects that conditioned the choices of the Weimar Republic governments. Using this approach, a distinction can be made between the causes that led to a pronounced acceleration in price growth in the second half of 1922 and those that made inflation explosive.

The acceleration in price growth that occurred between June and July 1922 seems to be attributable rather to a sudden stop triggered by "bad" news of a political nature, in particular the announcement by the Bankers' Committee that they would not grant any further credit to Germany and the assassination of Finance Minister Rathenau, rather than to a sudden worsening of the government budget or expectations of such a worsening. This "bad" news undermined the confidence of foreign investors in their expectations of an appreciation of the mark. These investors had until then invested in German currency driven by this belief and Germany benefited from a massive inflow of foreign capital. The change in expectations induced by the forementioned "bad" news was followed by an initial sudden stop in mid-1922. Subsequently on other occasions "bad" news provoked outflows of capital from Germany. Both in the summer of 1922 and on these other occasions, the reversal of flows of capital led to a significant depreciation of the mark and then to an acceleration in inflation. The gradual reduction in the lag with which wages were adjusted to prices consolidated the rate of inflation at progressively higher levels, at a certain point a vicious circle between wages, prices, and the exchange rate emerged.

[119] Gutierrez and Vasquez (2004) give another explanation of this fact showing that in a money-in-the-utility-function model the ITLC is ruled out and an explosive hyperinflation can occur.

Appendix 1 Unit Root Tests

Table 4.19 Unit Root Test for the variables used in the estimates of Table 4.10

	Augmented Dickey–Fuller		Dickey–Fuller GLS	
Augmented Dickey–Fuller	Intercept	Trend and Intercept	Intercept	Trend and Intercept
Real exchange rate	−5.85***	−5.76***	−5.81***	−5.92***
Consumer prices	−2.70*	−3.67**	−2.11**	−3.80***
Notes in circulation in real value Real government revenue Real fiscal deficit	−4.84*** −6.44*** −5.27***	−4.75*** −6.66*** −5.16***	−4.76*** −3.35*** −3.44***	−4.90*** −4.80*** −6.09***

Note: The number of lags has been chosen according to the Schwarz Information Criterion. The null hypothesis is that the variable has a unit root. ***reject at 1%, **reject at 5%, *reject at 10%

Table 4.20 Unit root tests for the variables used in the estimates of Table 4.11

	Augmented Dickey–Fuller		Dickey–Fuller GLS	
	Intercept	Trend and Intercept	Intercept	Trend and Intercept
Mark-Dollar exchange rate	−18.94***	−19.27***	−13.34***	−19.22***
Spread long-term interest rates	−25.56***	−25.56***	−25.56***	−25.60***

Note: The number of lags has been chosen according to the Schawarz Information Criterion. The null hypothesis is that the variable has a unit root. ***reject at 1%, **reject at 5%, *reject at 10%

Appendix 2 VAR Granger Causality/Block Exogeneity Wald Test in the Case of Sargent's Monetary-Fiscal View

In order to compare the sudden stop view with Sargent's monetary-fiscal view we repeated the estimate of the VAR Granger test in Table 4.9, replacing the monthly variations of the monetary base in real terms (RMB) with those of government revenue in real terms (RGR).[120] The results of this test are provided in Table 4.21.

These show that, as in the case of the monetary view in the narrow sense (referred to in Table 4.9), the null hypothesis—the variable of interest has no influence on inflation—is rejected in the case of the real exchange rate, while it is accepted in the case of real government revenue. This corroborates the sudden stop view as opposed to the monetary-fiscal view.[121]

[120] As is clear from Table 4.19, also this variable is stationary.

[121] Similar results are obtained if the real fiscal deficit and not the real government revenue is used in the estimate of the VAR Granger test.

Table 4.21 VAR Granger Causality/Block exogeneity Wald Test in the case of Sargent's monetary-fiscal view (Sept. 1921- Jun. 1923)

		Dependent variables		
		Inflation	Real exchange rate	Real government revenue
Excluded variables	Real government revenue	4.04	2.16	
	Real exchange rate	24.01***		13.10***
	Consumer prices		4.77	2.45
	All	27.08***	5.01	26.19***

Legend: Monthly change of variable. *** rejected at 1%; ** rejected at 5%; * rejected at 10%

Appendix 3 Impulse Response of Exchange Rate to Political News in a VAR Model

In order to test the robustness of the results of the estimates just described we used an extended version of the Ramey and Shapiro (1998) approach, specifically the approach proposed by Edelberg et al. (1998) and further refined by Romer and Romer (2010). As in that paper we used a VAR with an exogenous variable: political news. Two reasons prompted the use of this type of model. Firstly, it helps overcome possible problems of endogeneity in the OLS estimates and in particular those between changes in the real exchange rate and changes in the spread. Secondly, the use of the VAR methodology makes it possible to show the impulse response function (IRF) of the exchange rate to political news.

The VAR includes the following three variables: the first difference in the mark-dollar exchange rate, the first difference in the spread between the German and the US long-term interest rates, and the variable *news*. In order to identify the innovations in the three variables under consideration we used the Cholesky decomposition, first ordering the variable *news* in the VAR system. As for the OLS estimates, the VAR system was estimated on daily data from 1 January 1921 to 31 December 1922. For each variable 5 lags were considered, in line with the results of the various tests of lag-length criteria.[122] The VAR estimated in this way proves to be stable in that all the roots lie within the unit circle.

The Cholesky decomposition renders the various impulses in a VAR system orthogonal by imposing order on the variables. For our purposes, having first ordered the variable *news,* this means that while the change in the exchange rate or in the interest rate spread reacts immediately to impulses in the variable *news*, this last variable reacts only with lags to shocks to the first two variables.

The estimate thus obtained enables us to evaluate the response of the exchange rate to a standard impulse of political news. Figure 4.7 shows the dynamic response

[122] In particular, five lags are indicated by the Akaike information criterion (AIC), the Schwarz information criterion (SC), and the Hannan–Quinn information criterion (HQ).

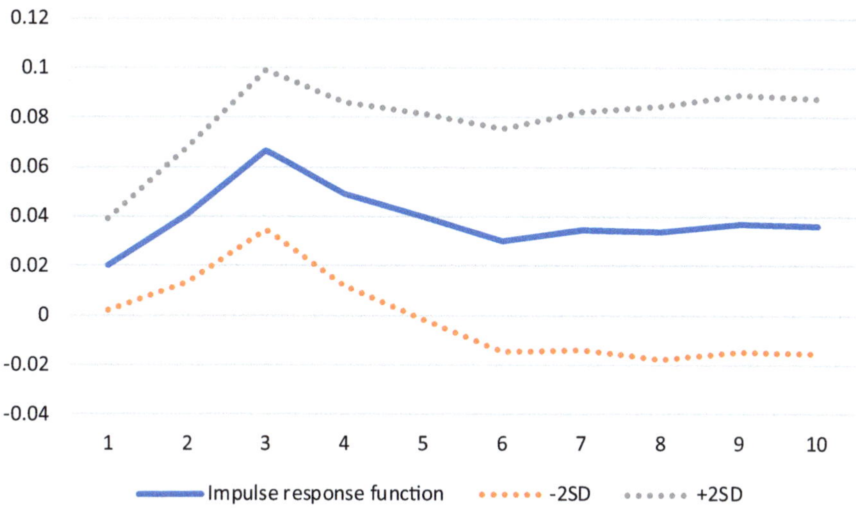

Fig. 4.7 Impulse response of exchange rate to political news (VAR model)

of the change in the real exchange rate to political news over a span of 10 working days.

As can be seen from Fig. 4.7, the dollar-mark exchange rate reacts significantly to political news at the moment it is announced. In the first 3 days it accumulates an elasticity value close to 8%. Subsequently, the effect of political news on the change of the real exchange rate tends to decrease and becomes insignificant after the sixth day. However, because we are referring to the first difference in the real exchange rate, the increases accumulated in subsequent periods have permanent effects.

Appendix 4 Tax Bands by Income Groups

Tax bands were based on the following income groups (1913–1928)

Bands	1913 Marks	1926 Reich Marks	1928 Reich Marks
1	0 > 900	0 > 1200	0 > 1200
2	900 > 2100	1200 > 3000	1200 > 3000
3	2100 > 3300	3000 > 5000	3000 > 5000
4	3300–5500	5000 > 9000	5000 > 9000
5	5500 > 8500	9000 > 12,000	9000 > 12,000
6	8500 > 10,500	12,000 > 16,000	12,000 > 16,000
7	10,500 > 16,500	16,000 > 25,000	16,000 > 25,000
8	16,500 > 30,500	25,000 > 100,000	25,000 > 50,000
9	30,500 > 70,000	100,000+	50,000 > 100,000
10	70,000 +		100,000+

References

Abel, A., Dornbusch, R., Huizinga, J., & Marcus, A. (1979). Money demand during hyperinflation. *Journal of Monetary Economics, 5*, 97–104.

Acemoglu, D., Laibson, D., & List, J. A. (2019). *Economics*. Pearson.

Alesina, A. (1988). The end of large public debt. In F. Giavazzi & L. Spaventa (Eds.), *High public debt: The Italian experience*. Cambridge University Press.

Alesina, A., & Drazen, A. (1991). Why are stabilizations delayed? *American Economic Review, 81*, 1170–1188.

Aristotle. (1984). *Politics*. Translated by C. Lord. Chicago University Press.

Bergman, C. (1927). *A history of reparations*. Ernest Benn.

Black, F. (1974). Uniqueness of the price level in monetary growth models with rational expectations. *Journal of Economic Theory, 7*, 53–65.

Bonn, M. J. (1922). Die Stabilisierung der Mark. Verlag. English transl. *The Stabilization of the Mark,* First National Bank of Chicago.

Bordo, M. D., Cavallo, A. F., & Meissner, C. M. (2007). *Sudden stops: Determinants and output effects in the first era of globalization, 1880-1913*. NBER working paper n. 13489.

Bortkiewicz, L. von (1924). Die Ursachen der potenzierten Wirkung des vermehrten Geldumlaufs auf das Preisniveau. *Verhandlungen des Vereins für Sozialpolitik, 170*, 256–274.

Bresciani-Turroni, C. (1937). *The economics of inflation: A study of currency depreciation in post-war Germany*. Allen & Unwin.

Bruno, M., & Fischer, S. (1990). Seigniorage, operating rules, and the high inflation trap. *Quarterly Journal of Economics, 105*, 353–374.

Bry, G. (1960). *Wages in Germany 1871–1945*. Princeton University Press.

Cagan, P. (1956). The monetary dynamics of hyperinflation. In M. Friedman (Ed.), *Studies in the quantity theory of money*. Chicago University Press.

Calvo, G. A. (1995). *Varieties of capital market crisis*. Inter-American Development Bank, Research Department Publication n. 4008.

Calvo, G. A. (2012). *The price theory of money, Prospero's liquidity trap, and sudden stop: Back to basics and back.* NBER working paper n. 18285.

Calvo, G. A., & Reinhart, C. (2000). When capital inflows come to a sudden stop: Consequences and policy options. In P. B. Kenen & A. K. Swoboda (Eds.), *Reforming the international monetary and financial system*. International Monetary Fund.

Calvo, G. A., Izquierdo, A., & Talvi, E. (2003). *Sudden stops, the real exchange rate and fiscal sustainability: Argentina's lessons*. NBER working paper n. 9829.

Cardoso, E. (1989). Hyperinflation in Latin America. *Challenge, 32*, 11–19.

Cassis, Y. (2006). *Capitals of capital. A history of international financial centres, 1780–2005.* Cambridge University Press.

Colles, W. M. (1922). Wage movements at home and abroad: The high water mark. *Manchester Guardian Commercial*, 6 April.

De Broeck, M., & James, H. (2019). Germany in the interbellum: Camouflaging sovereign debt. In E. Dabla-Norris (Ed.), *Debt and entanglements between the wars*. International Monetary Fund.

Dornbusch, R. (1985). *Inflation, exchange rates and stabilization*. NBER working paper n. 1739.

Dornbusch, R. (1987). Lessons from the German inflation experience of the 1920s. In R. Dornbusch, S. Fischer, & J. Bossons (Eds.), *Macroeconomics and finance: Essays in honor of Franco Modigliani*. MIT Press.

Dornbusch, R., Sturzenegger, F., & Wolf, H. (1990). Extreme inflation: Dynamics and stabilization. *Brookings Papers on Economic Activity, 2*, 1–64.

Edelberg, W., Eichenbaum, M., & Fisher, J. D. M. (1998). *Understanding the effects of a shock to government purchases*. Federal Reserve Bank of Chicago working paper n. WP-98-7.

Einzig, P. (1937). *The theory of forward exchange rate*. Macmillan.

Ellis, H. S. (1934). *German monetary theory, 1905–1933*. Harvard University Press.

Eucken, W. (1923). *Kritische Betrachtungen zum deutschen Geldproblem*. Fischer.

Eulenburg, F. (1924). Die sozialen Wirkungen der Wahrungs-Verhältnisse. *Jahrbücher für Nationalökonomie und Statistik, 122*, 748–754.

Evans, J., & Honkapohja, S. (2003). Adaptive learning and monetary policy design. *Journal of Money, Credit and Banking, 35*, 1045–1072.

Fazio, A. L. F. (2022). *L'inflazione in Germania 1918–1929 e la crisi mondiale del 1929*. Treves.

Feldman, G. D. (1983). The historians and the German inflation. In N. Schmukler & E. Marcus (Eds.), *Inflation through the ages: Economic, social, psychological and historical aspects*. Columbia University Press.

Feldman, G. D. (1993). *The great disorder: Politics, economics, and society in the German Inflation, 1914–1924*. Oxford University Press.

Ferguson, N. (1996). Constraints and room for manoeuvre in the German inflation of the early 1920s. *Economic History Review, 49*, 635–666.

Ferguson, N. (1998). The balance of payments question: Versailles and after. In M. F. Boemeke, G. D. Feldman, & E. Glaser (Eds.), *The Treaty of Versailles. A reassessment after 75 years*. Cambridge University Press.

Ferguson, N., & Granville, B. (2000). Weimar on the Volga: Causes and consequences of inflation in 1990s Russia compared with 1920s Germany. *Journal of Economic History, 60*, 1061–1087.

Fergusson, A. (1975). *When money dies: The nightmare of the Weimar collapse*. William Kimber.

Fischer, S., Sahay, R., & Végh, C. (2002). Modern hyper- and high inflations. *Journal of Economic Literature, 40*, 837–880.

Flood, R. P., & Garber, P. M. (1984). Collapsing exchange rate regimes: Some linear examples. *Journal of International Economics, 17*, 1–13.

Fourgeaud, A. (1926). *La dépréciation et la revalorization du mark allemande*. Payot.

Frenkel, J. A. (1977). The forward exchange rate, expectations, and the demand for money: The German hyperinflation. *American Economic Review, 67*, 653–670.

Frère, M. (1922). Report by the intelligence service on the balance of Germany accounts, Paris, Oct. 19, 1922. PRO, Fo 371/7486/311/166-93.

Galofré-Vilà, G. (2023). Spoils of war: The political legacy of the German hyperinflation. *Explorations in Economic History, 88*, 1–17.

Galofré-Vilà, G., Meissner, C. M., McKee, M., & Stuckler, D. (2021). Austerity and the rise of the Nazi Party. *Journal of Economic History, 81*, 81–113.

Geyer, M. H. (1986). Wohnungsnot und Wohnungswangswirtschaft in München 1917 bis 1924. In G. D. Feldman, C. L. Holtfrerich, G. A. Ritter, & P. C. Witt (Eds.), *Die Anpassung an die inflation – The adaptation to inflation*. De Gruyter.

Gomes, L. (2010). *German reparations, 1919–1932: A historical survey*. Palgrave Macmillan.

Graham, F. D. (1930). *Exchange, prices, and production in hyper-inflation: Germany, 1920–1923*. Princeton University Press.

Gutierrez, M. J., & Vasquez, J. (2004). Explosive hyperinflation, inflation-tax Laffer curve, and modeling the use of money. *Journal of Institutional and Theoretical Economics, 160*, 311–326.

Guttmann, W., & Meehan, P. (1975). *The great inflation. Germany 1919–23*. Saxon House.

Hagemann, H. (2015). The German economy and German economics in crisis during the Weimar Republic 1918-33. In H. Peukert (Ed.), *Taking up the challenge!* Festschrift für Jurgen Backaus, Metropolis.

Hahn, L. A. (1924). Zur Frage des sogenannten 'Vertrauens in die Währung'. *Archiv für Sozialwissenschaft und Sozialpolitik, 52*, 289–316.

Hawtrey, R. G. (1923). *Currency and credit*. Longmans.

Helffrerich, K. (1927). *Money*. Adelphi. English translation from K. Helffrerich (1923), Das Geld, Verlag.

Helmstadter, E. (1985). Die Wirtschaftliche Lage am Jahresbeginn 1984 im Urteil des Sachverständigenrats. In H. Hanusch, K. W. Roskamp, & J. Wiseman (Eds.), *Staat und Politische Ökonomie heute: Horst Claus Recktenwald zum 65*. Gustav Fischer Verlag.

Heyman, D., & Sanguineti, P. (1994). Fiscal inconsistencies and high inflation. *Journal of Development Economics, 43*, 85–104.

Hill, L. E., Butler, C. E., & Lorenzen, S. A. (1977). Inflation and the destruction of democracy: the case of the Weimar Republic. *Journal of Economic Issues, 11*, 299–313.
Hirsch, F., & Goldthorpe, J. (1978). *The political economy of inflation*. Martin Robertson.
Hirshman, A. D. (1985). Reflections on the Latin American experience. In L. N. Lindberg & C. S. Maier (Eds.), *The politics of inflation and economic stagnation*. The Brookings Institution.
Holtfrerich, C. L. (1982). Domestic and foreign expectations and the demand for money during the German hyperinflation. In C. P. Kindleberger & J. P. Laffargue (Eds.), *Financial crises: Theory, history and policy*. Cambridge University Press.
Holtfrerich, C. L. (1983). Political factors of the German inflation 1914-23. In N. Schmukler & E. Marcus (Eds.), *Inflation through the ages: Economic, social, psychological and historical aspects*. Columbia University Press.
Holtfrerich, C. L. (1986). *The German inflation 1914–1923: Causes and effects in international perspective*. De Gruyter.
Hubbard, W. H. (1990). The new inflation history. *Journal of Modern History, 62*, 552–569.
Huges, M. L. (1982). Economic interest, social attitudes, and creditor ideology: Popular responses to inflation. In G. Feldman, G. A. Ritter, & P. C. Witt (Eds.), *The German inflation: A preliminary balance*. De Gruyter.
Hutchison, M., Noy, I., & Wang, L. (2010). Fiscal and monetary policies and the cost of sudden stops. *Journal of International Money and Finance, 29*, 973–987.
Jones, L. E. (1979). Inflation, revaluation, and the crisis of middle-class politics: A study in the dissolution of the German party system, 1923-28. *Central European History, 12*, 143–168.
Keynes, J. M. (1922a). *A revision of the treaty, being a sequel to the economic consequences of the peace*. Macmillan.
Keynes, J. M. (1922b). Speculation in the mark and Germany's balances abroad. *Reconstruction in Europe. Manchester Guardian commercial supplement*, 28 September 1922, 480–482. Reprinted in E. Johnson & D. Moggridge (Eds.), *The collected writings of J.M.* Keynes, XVIII, Cambridge University Press.
Kiguel M. A. & Liviatan, N. (1991). The inflation-stabilization cycles in Argentina and Brazil, In M. Bruno, S. Fischer, E. Helpman, & N. Liviatan (Eds.), "Lessons of Economic Stabilization and its Aftermath", Cambridge, MIT Press.
Kiguel, M. A., & Liviatan, N. (1995). Stopping three big inflations: Argentina, Brazil and Peru. In R. Dornbusch & S. Edwards (Eds.), *Reform, recovery and growth: Latin America and the Middle East*. University of Chicago Press.
Kindleberger, C. (1984a). *A financial history of Western Europe*. Allen & Unwin.
Kindleberger, C. (1984b). A structural view of the German inflation. In G. D. Feldman, C. L. Holtfrerich, G. A. Ritter, & P. C. Witt (Eds.), *Die Erfahrung der inflation im internationalen Zusammenhang und Vergleich*. De Gruyter.
Kindleberger, C. P. (1994). Review of the great disorder by G.D. Feldman. *Journal of Economic Literature, 32*, 1216–1225.
Knapp, G. F. ([1905] 1924). *The state theory of money*. Macmillan. English translation from Knapp G.F. (1905), Staathiche theorie des geldes. Verlag Duncker & Humblot.
Krugman, P. (2013). It's always 1923. *The New York Times*, 12 February 2013.
Laidler, D. E. W., & Stadler, G. W. (1998). Monetary explanations of the Weimar Republic's hyperinflation: Some neglected contributions in contemporary German literature. *Journal of Money, Credit, and Banking, 30*, 816–831.
League of Nations. (1931). *Memorandum on commercial banks, 1919–1929*. League of Nations.
Liviatan, N., & Piterman, S. (1986). Accelerating inflation and balance of payments crises, 1973-1984. In Y. Ben-Porath (Ed.), *The Israeli economy*. Harvard University Press.
Lopez, J. A., & Mitchener, K. J. (2018). *Uncertainty and hyperinflation: European inflation dynamics after World War I*. NBER working paper n. 24624.
Maier, C. S. (1975). *Recasting bourgeois Europe: Stabilization in France, Germany and in Italy in the decade after world war I*. Princeton University Press.

Maier, C. (1978). The politics of inflation in the twentieth century. In F. Hirsch & J. Goldthorpe (Eds.), *The political economy of inflation*. Martin Robertson.
Maier, C. (1987). *In search of stability*. Cambridge University Press.
Marcet, A., & Nicolini, J. P. (2003). Recurrent hyperinflations and learning. *American Economic Review, 93*, 1476–1498.
McElligott, A. (2013). *Rethinking the Weimar Republic. Authority and authoritarianism, 1916-1936*. Bloomsbury.
Mises L. von (1923). Die geldtheoretische Seite des Stabilisierungsproblems, in "Schriften des Vereins fiir Sozialpolitik", 164, pp. 1–37.
Montiel, P. J. (1989). Empirical analysis of high-inflation episodes in Argentina, Brazil and Israel. *IMF Staff Papers, 36*, 527–549.
Moore, B. (1966). *Social origins of dictatorship and democracy: Lord and peasant in the making of the modern world*. Beacon Press.
Morelli, P., & Seghezza, E. (2014). Conflict inflation and delayed stabilization. *Journal of Macroeconomics, 39*, 171–184.
Moulton, H. G., & McGuire, C. E. (Eds.). (1923). *Germany's capacity to pay: A study of the reparation problem*. MacGraw Hill.
Notermans, T. (2000). *Money, markets and the state*. Cambridge University Press.
Olson, M. (1965). *The logic of collective action*. Harvard University Press.
Olson, M. (1982). *The rise and decline of nations economic growth, stagflation and social rigidities*. Yale University Press.
Piketty, T. (2014). *Capital in the Twenty-first century*. Harvard University Press.
Pittaluga, G. B., & Seghezza, E. (2012). The role of rentiers in the stabilization processes of the twenties. *European Review of Economic History, 16*, 188–210.
Prion, W. (1924). Deutsche Kreditpolitik 1919-1922. *Schmollers Jahrbuch, 49*, 381–405.
Ramey, V. (2011). Identifying government spending shocks: it's all in the timing. *Quarterly Journal of Economics, 126*, 1–50.
Ramey, V., & Shapiro, M. D. (1998). Costly capital reallocation and the effects of government spending. *Carnegie-Rochester Conference Series on Public Policy, 48*, 145–184.
Reghezza, A., Seghezza, E., & Thornton, J. (2020). Expectations in an open economy hyperinflation: Evidence from Germany 1921-23. *Economics Letters, 192*, 1–3.
Ritschl, A. (2014). The German transfer problem, 1920-1933: A sovereign debt perspective? In A. Nutzenadel & C. Torp (Eds.), *Economic crises and global politics in the 20th century*. Routledge.
Robbins, L. (1937). Foreword. In C. Bresciani-Turroni. *The economics of inflation*. Allen & Unwin.
Robinson, J. (1938). Review of C. Bresciani-Turroni's 'The economics of inflation'. *Economic Journal, 48*, 507–513.
Romer, C. D., & Romer, D. H. (1989). Does monetary policy matter? A new test in the spirit of Friedman and Schwartz. *NBER Macroeconomic Annual, 4*, 121–184.
Romer, C. D., & Romer, D. H. (2010). The macroeconomic effect of tax changes: Estimates based on a new measure of fiscal shocks. *American Economic Review, 100*, 763–801.
Saboin-Garcia, J. L. (2018). *The modern hyperinflation cycle: Some new empirical regularities*. IMF working paper n. WP/18/266.
Salemi, M. K., & Sargent, T. J. (1979). The demand for money during hyperinflation under rational expectations: II. *International Economic Review, 20*, 741–758.
Sargent, T. J. (1977). The demand for money during hyperinflations under rational expectations. *International Economics Review, 18*, 59–82.
Sargent, T. J. (1982). The ends of four big hyperinflations. In R. E. Hall (Ed.), *Inflation: Causes and effects*. University of Chicago Press.
Sargent, T. J., & Wallace, N. (1987). Inflation and the government budget constraint. In A. Razin & E. Sadka (Eds.), *Economic policy in theory and practice*. Palgrave Macmillan.
Schuker, J. A. (1988). American 'reparations' to Germany, 1919-33: Implications for the Third-World debt crisis. Princeton Studies in International Finance, 61.

Seghezza, E., & Morelli, P. (2020). Was there a sudden stop at the origin of German hyperinflation? *Financial History Review, 27*, 161–186.

Siklos, P. L. (1990). Hyperinflations: Their origins, development and termination. *Journal of Economic Surveys, 4*, 225–248.

Southern, B. D. (1979). The revaluation question in the Weimar Republic. *Journal of Modern History, 51*, D1029–D1054.

Statistisches Reichsamt. (1925). *Zahlen zur Geldenwertung in Deutschland 1914 bis 1923.*

Taylor, M. P. (1991). The hyperinflation model of money demand revisited. *Journal of Money, Credit and Banking, 23*, 327–351.

Tullio, G. (1985). Inflation and currency depreciation in Germany, 1920-1923: A dynamic model of prices. *Journal of Money, Credit and Banking, 27*, 350–362.

Warburg, M. (1921). Speech before RWM Scholz, 12.12.20. *Warburg Papers, Pol. Corr. 1921.*

Webb, S. (1984). The supply of money and Reichsbank financing of government and corporate debt in Germany, 1919-1923. *Journal of Economic History, 44*, 499–507.

Webb, S. (1986). Fiscal news and inflationary expectations in Germany after WWI. *Journal of Economic History, 46*, 769–794.

Webb, S. (1989). *Hyperinflation and stabilization in Weimar Germany.* Oxford University Press.

Whale, P. B. (1930). *Joint stock banking in Germany. A study of the German credit banks before and after the war.* Macmillan.

Widdig, B. (2001). *Culture and inflation in Weimar Germany.* University of California Press.

Williams, J. G. (1922). German foreign trade and the reparation payments. *Quarterly Journal of Economics, 36*, 482–503.

Wixforth, H. (2003). German banks and their business strategies in the Weimar Republic: New findings and preliminary results. In M. Kasuya (Ed.), *Coping with crisis.* Oxford University Press.

Zarazaga, C. (1993). *Hyperinflations and moral hazard in the appropriation of seigniorage.* Federal Reserve Bank of Philadelphia working paper n. 93-26.

Chapter 5
The End of Inflation

5.1 Introduction

As seen in the previous chapter, German inflation reached astronomical levels during 1923. Despite this, for several months no agreement could be reached at the political level on what stabilization measures to take. This was due to a "war of attrition" between the various interest groups, each of which was unwilling to bear additional fiscal burdens, which delayed the government's adoption of stabilization measures.

Only when the economic and social situation reached extreme levels, that is, when, in addition to work, there was a lack of food, and riots and violations of property rights became widespread, a form of resignation prevailed in the face of the need to implement radical reforms. This situation is well described in a memorandum sent in July 1923 by the German Ambassador in London to Lord Curzon, the British Foreign Secretary: "It is an ominous sign that the mark following its latest tremendous collapse ... is now beginning to lose its purchasing power in internal trade also ... Distrust of the depreciating currency is driving goods from the market, while the late harvest has produced an exceptionally alarming scarcity of foodstuffs in the towns, especially Berlin. The desperation of masses is being exploited by radical agitators from both Left and Right ...."[1]

Workers' standards of living were aggravated by the burgeoning urban food supply shortage: farmers refused to deliver crops in exchange for a currency that was depreciating day by day.

The workers' malaise found expression in severe communist-led unrest and in a radicalization of the Left.[2] The German inflation process was completed in such a way. Its development was summarized by Hermann Bücher, managing director of

[1]Quotation from Fergusson (1975, p. 88).

[2]Graham (1930, p. 12) writes: "The masses of the urban population were living from hand to mouth, they had nothing in their hands but worthless bits of paper which the farmer would no longer accept in exchange for grain. Food riots were general. Political dissolution was in imminent prospect and

G. B. Pittaluga, E. Seghezza, *An Economic Historiography of Germany, 1918-1931*, Frontiers in Economic History, https://doi.org/10.1007/978-3-031-70347-8_5

the National Association of German Industry, as follows: "If you attempt to bring the total depreciation which we have in Germany ... into one formula, then it is that, first, there was the depreciation of pensions and liquid capital wealth while, at the same time, you had very good conditions in industry and a relatively favorable living standard for the producing groups in comparison to the others; the second stage was a complete depreciation of the so called 'Mittelstand' alongside only relatively good conditions in industry and the productive sectors; the third stage is the depreciation of operating capital; the fourth is unemployment and the complete collapse of our economy."[3]

Given its inability to cope with the situation, the Cuno cabinet was forced to resign in August and was replaced by a "Great Coalition" government led by the Deutsche Volkspartei (the DVP: a center-right liberal party) leader Gustav Stresemann. In addition to the DVP, the Great Coalition included the Zentrumpartei (a centrist catholic party), the Deutsche Demokratische Partei (the DDP: a liberal middle-class party), and the Social Democratic Party (the SPD).

The formation of a national coalition government reflected the fact that the situation was now detrimental to virtually all parts of society and in the autumn of 1923, economic and social unrest in Germany reached such a level that it "threatened the very existence of civil society itself as well as the political order and the integrity of the German state.[4] The survival of the Republic was, therefore, at risk."[5]

It became therefore the shared goal of the various interest groups to put an end to inflation and stabilize the German economy and, in this context of widespread economic and social malaise, there was little resistance to monetary and fiscal adjustment measures.

On September 26, this government put an end to passive resistance in the Ruhr and, with this, to the increase in public spending that it entailed.

In correspondence with an increase in any type of disorder, Stresemann requested and obtained emergency power from the President of the Republic to deal with the dramatic crisis. The German constitution, in fact, in its article 48, provided that in emergency situations the government could legislate by decree of the President of the Republic.[6]

It was also on the basis of the emergency powers obtained that Stresemann was able to issue a decree on October 15,1923, which contemplated a monetary reform and the introduction of a new currency, the Rentenmark. This currency was indexed to the price of gold, but not convertible into it. The currency reform was followed by fiscal measures to reduce the government deficit. As a result of these measures,

armed revolt had already raised its head. Affairs were indeed so black that it is clear, in retrospect, that they actually facilitated the reform by imbuing the people with the resolution of despair."

[3]See RWR Finance Committee meeting, Dec. 7, 1922, BAP, no. 552, Bd. 7, Bl. 245 f.

[4]See Feldman (1993, p. 699).

[5]See Bessel (1997, p.247).

[6]As Weitz (2007, p. 142) writes: "Given the crisis situation, it was probably necessary, but it was a dangerous precedent and a sad sign of the state of the Republic."

between November and December of 1923, German inflation decelerated, and the mark and price levels stabilized. The sudden success of the October monetary reform was completely unexpected, indeed, not only most contemporary scholars and practitioners but even the Finance Minister, Hans Luther, who had proposed and implemented the reform described the effects of the currency reform as "miraculous."

The price and exchange rate stabilization achieved in this way was consolidated in 1924 with Germany's acceptance of the Dawes Plan. This Plan, in addition to fixing the annual Reparations Germany had to pay over the 5-year period, forbade the Reichsbank from providing monetary coverage to the Reich's fiscal deficits, gave the German central bank effective independence and imposed gold convertibility on the German currency, the Reichsmark.

Thanks to the Dawes Plan, Germany was reintegrated into the international financial markets and, in the period following its acceptance by Germany in April 1924, the inflow of capital was so large that it gave rise over time to a form of over-borrowing and its associated problems, issues which will be discussed in Chap. 6.

The particular characteristics of the stabilization of the German economy between 1923 and 1924 raise a series of questions. An attempt is made to answer them in this chapter. A first question concerns the delay with which stabilization measures were taken: why were these measures not taken more promptly so as to end the economic and social devastation caused by hyperinflation?

An answer to this question, as will be seen in Sect. 5.2, can be given from a Political Economy perspective. In particular, it is hypothesized here that the reforms aimed at disinflating the German economy were adopted when the war of attrition ceased because businessmen strengthened their bargaining power with respect to other interest groups. Given their increased bargaining power, they induced the government to approve adjustment measures that shifted a large part of the burden of stabilization onto labor.

A second question concerns the reasons for the almost instant success of the October 1923 monetary reform. Various explanations have been given and are reviewed later in Sect. 5.4. According to Sargent (1982), the stabilization of the German economy resulted from a "regime change" and its impact on individuals' expectations. According to other scholars,[7] instead, it was the result of exchange rate stabilization and is therefore comparable to the Exchange Rate Based Stabilization (ERBS) adopted in the 1980s and 1990s by many emerging countries.

A third question relates to the costs of price stabilization in Weimar Germany. Sargent (1982) argued that the immediate adjustment of inflation expectations induced by the regime change made the costs of stabilization very modest. An assessment of this hypothesis involves an examination of both the timing of the adjustment of expectations and the impact of disinflation measures on resource

[7] See among others Franco (1989) and Block (2002). According to Dornbusch (1986), in addition to the stabilization of the exchange rate, the monetary tightening initiated by Schacht with his rise to the presidency of the Reichsbank contributed to the end of the German hyperinflation.

allocation. In this regard, a comparison between the stabilization of Germany and those undertaken by the League of Nations in the early 1920s in countries affected by hyperinflation, such as Austria and Hungary, seems appropriate.

5.2 Why So Much Delay in German Economy Stabilization?

As will be seen in detail in the next section, the stabilization process of the German economy began only in October 1923, more than a year after the start of hyperinflation. The question therefore arises as to why stabilization measures for the German economy were not taken earlier.

As Maier (1975, p. 376) writes: "The delay was due to the rivalry of several stabilization schemes and interests, the inertia of Reichsbank President Havenstein, whose death alone cut short his resistance, and finally perhaps to the failings of the Socialist Finance Minister Hilferding as an effective administrator."[8] Therefore, as argued by Alesina (1988), the delay in the stabilization of the German economy cannot be explained by economic models based on the assumption of the "representative agent" and the "social planner." It is necessary, in fact, to take into account the fact that adjustment measures entail redistributive effects between the various interest groups and therefore generate resistance on the part of the latter, each of which attempts to pass on the costs of stabilization to others. Adjustment measures are adopted when a political majority capable of imposing them on the minority prevails.

These aspects can only be taken into account in a political economy approach. The best-known approach in this type of literature is the war of attrition hypothesis put forward by Alesina and Drazen (1991). According to this model, the conflict between different interest groups arises from the attempt by the individual interest groups to shift the cost of realignment onto other interest groups. The deadlock is due to the existence of information asymmetries in the ability of rival interest groups to bear the effects of inflation caused by the adjustment delay. Stabilization takes place when it becomes clear which interest group is least capable of withstanding inflation. This group is the one bound to bear most of the burden resulting from adjustment.

When applied to the stabilization of Weimar Germany the Alesina and Drazen's hypothesis presents some critical issues. Firstly, Alesina and Drazen make the assumption that interest groups are unable to establish ex-ante, which of them will suffer the greatest losses from inflation. Nonetheless, these interest groups, if they are heterogeneous in terms of forms of income and in terms of their financial assets and liabilities, will necessarily know in advance who will gain and who will lose by inflation.

[8] Maier (1975, p. 376).

Secondly, in their model they see inflation as the result of an unresolved conflict between interest groups, none of which in principle wants inflation. In actual fact, in an economy with a large financial system and fixed-interest-rate bonds, inflation will damage some interest groups, creditors, while benefiting others, debtors. Therefore, some interest groups demand for inflation. This is what we have seen in previous chapters as having happened in the Weimar Republic between 1919 and 1922, when an implicit alliance between businessmen and workers, i.e., between the productive classes, prevailed. This is, however, a process that also affected some advanced countries after the first oil shock, primarily Italy.[9]

Third, since one of the causes of high inflation is that some interest groups benefit from the redistributive effects of inflation, these groups' demand for inflation is exhausted when these redistributive effects fade, in particular as the financial wealth of rentiers dwindles or they learn to protect themselves from inflation. When this occurs, for the productive classes the costs of inflation become higher than the redistributive advantages they derive from it: consequently, their resistance to stabilization measures weakens until it disappears. At this point, however, the problem arises of what measures to take to stabilize the economy. To clarify this aspect, we used a model where the aim of the government is to consolidate a large domestic public debt.[10] At this aim the government can resort to three types of taxes: inflation, direct taxes, and indirect taxes. In the economy, there are three economic groups that have different forms of income: The rentiers who hold long-term non-indexed financial assets and short-term financial assets; businessmen who hold physical capital and earn profits from their entrepreneurial activity; and workers who earn wages.

These three economic groups have different preferences regarding the measures to be taken to reabsorb the debt. Rentiers opposed inflation and preferred indirect taxes to direct ones. Businessmen favor inflation and subordinately indirect taxes. In fact, they opposed taxes on profits and capital. Workers, finally, opposed indirect taxes and favored direct taxes and subordinately inflation (since their wages are indexed).

In the first period, businessmen and workers band together and favor high inflation, which erodes the real value of the public debt. Therefore, here we maintain that high inflation, at least in some circumstances, is not the unintentional consequence of deadlock but rather the outcome of a political entente between some interest groups and political parties. With this choice, the interest groups that benefit from inflation or are not affected by it avoid fiscal measures, which would be burdensome for them. There is, therefore, a demand for inflation on the part of some interest groups.[11] If these groups have political bargaining power, the government tends to meet their demands in exchange for their support. Therefore, the type

---

[9] See among others Pittaluga and Seghezza (2012a).

[10] An analytical presentation of this model can be found in Morelli and Seghezza (2014).

[11] See Gordon (1975) and Olson (1975).

of tax chosen by the government to reabsorb the debt is the outcome of a bargaining process between the political class and interest groups.

In the model, as long as the redistributive process induced by inflation and the coalition of businessmen and workers lasts, there is no reason for the government to take stabilization measures. However, in the second period, rentiers restructure their residual portfolio so as not to be exposed to its inflationary erosion by holding index-linked or short-term assets. In this context, inflation is no longer an effective tax to absorb the remaining part of the public debt; to stabilize the economy, it is necessary to resort to different resources, in particular, increases in explicit taxes.[12] The conditions are created for a new political equilibrium and, therefore, a change in alliances between interest groups compared to the first period. In this context, an alliance emerges between industrialists and rentiers which shifts the burden of stabilization onto workers.

The theoretical scheme just described helps to explain the conditions for the stabilization of the German economy at the end of 1923. In fact, in the early 1920s the implicit alliance between producers favored the adoption by governments of inflationary policies. The coalition of *producers* achieved advantages from inflation through several channels. In particular, businessmen derived benefits from the persistently negative real interest rates on their debts and workers from welfare measures adopted by the governments. At the same time, the exploitation of seigniorage allowed the government to increase public spending, in particular to increase transfers and social spending. Furthermore, the flexible exchange rate allowed businessmen to accommodate salary demands without repercussions on the competitiveness of their companies thanks to the depreciation of the mark.

Even in the first months of 1923, productive interest groups, in particular industrialists, benefited from the government's use of the inflation tax as a tool to cover public deficits. The absence of widespread consensus among all interest groups toward disinflation measures explains the failure of the first stabilization attempt made by the government between February and April 1923. In this short period of time, the government tried to stabilize the exchange rate using the foreign exchange reserves of the Reichsbank.[13] The attempt to stabilize the mark failed. In June the German currency, also due to the tax burdens imposed by the passive resistance in the Ruhr, began to depreciate significantly again.

However, in the next months, as inflation progressed, government and producers, who had previously benefited from the redistributive process driven by inflation, no longer benefitted from this process. On the one hand, in fact, as shown in Table 4.17, the extreme levels reached by inflation after July 1922 led to the destruction of a large part of rentiers' wealth. On the other hand, the rentiers, in order to protect themselves from inflation, between 1920 and 1922 adjusted gradually the structure of their portfolios in favor of short-term assets. This is indirectly confirmed by the

[12] See Pittaluga and Seghezza (2012b).

[13] See Dornbusch and Fischer (1986, p. 6–7). The amount of the latter between January and May decreased by over 150 million gold marks.

Table 5.1 Short-term public debt (percentage of total public debt, 1920–1929)

Year	Belgium	France	Germany	Great Britain	Italy
1920	62.0	38.8	51.8	19.7	29.8
1921	59.5	36.0	65.5	19.6	36.4
1922	57.0	35.7	77.7	15.4	38.0
1923	55.2	32.1	99.6	12.2	37.1
1924	49.0	30.7	24.8	II.8	35.1
1925	46.0	31.9	7.3	11.3	30.4
1926	18.6	32.2	0.8	10.8	30.5
1927	16.1	26.7	2.2	10.9	25.1
1928	14.1	15.5	2.5	10.5	1.9
1929	10.6	12.3	11.6	11.3	2.9

Source: Confalonieri and Gatti (1986)

Table 5.2 Income and expenditure of the Reich (millions of gold marks, Apr. 1923–Oct. 1923)

1923	Income	Expenditure	Increase in floating debt
April	150.6	466.6	316.0
May	123.3	284.7	161.4
June	48.2	496.4	448.2
July	49.3	473.9	425.6
August	78.1	1013.1	914.7
September	55.6	1661.8	1564.1
October	14.5	881.8	860.1

Source: Bresciani-Turroni (1937, p. 438)

change in the maturity structure of German public debt in that period of time (Table 5.1).

The adjustment of the rentiers' portfolio in favor of liquid assets also affected bank deposits. The share of time deposits of big Berlin banks,[14] which according to the statistics of the Deutsche Oekonomist was equal to 41% in 1913, had fallen to 24% in 1920 and at the end of 1922 was equal to 7%.[15]

Due to the loss of wealth of rentiers and the adjustment of their financial portfolios in favor of short-term assets, the government was obliged to increase its resort to seigniorage. However, as the inflation rate increased, the real value of ordinary revenue decreased (Table 5.2), and that required massive increases in inflation rates to keep the level of seigniorage constant in real terms.

The export premium provided by inflation ended in the summer of 1923 when the growth of domestic prices assumed a higher dynamic than that of the depreciation of

[14]That is Deutsche Bank, Danat Bank, Dresdner Bank, Commerzbank, and the two non-branch banks Reichs Kredit Gesellschaft and Berlinen Handels Gesellschaft.

[15]See League of Nations (1931, p. 154–155).

the exchange rate. This led to a trend of real appreciation of the mark. The latter had a negative impact on the cost of imports and the competitiveness of German exports. In quantitative terms, foreign trade decreased significantly.[16]

At the same time, business activity was conditioned by growing financial constraints. For them, on the one hand, it was impossible to raise finance by issuing securities in marks because the domestic financial market had been destroyed by extreme inflation, and, on the other hand, access to banking loans had become more difficult as bank capital was eroded by inflation. In fact, by the end of 1923, the value of the share capital of the large German banks was about one-fifth what it had been in 1913.[17] In this contest it became difficult for companies to obtain credit.[18] The financial constraints that weighed on businesses translated into a shortage of working capital in a phase in which, due to the depreciation of the mark and the increased price of imports, the need for it for industrialists and merchants increased.[19] The scarcity of working capital favored a drastic reduction in company inventories[20] and put an end to the construction boom that had started in the autumn of 1921.[21]

Due to both supply and demand factors, between 1922 and 1923, industrial production plummeted by 34.3%.[22] The collapse of the economy weighed heavily on workers: in the second half of 1923 the level of real wages fell considerably for both skilled and unskilled workers, with a pronounced narrowing of the wage gap.[23] At the same time, the unemployment rate had risen progressively coming close to 20% in October (Table 5.3).

By the end of August 1923, the need to implement stabilization measures was now shared in German society. In the late summer of 1923, businessmen, in particular industrialists, also became convinced of this: the social crisis, in fact, threatened the foundations of the capitalist economy. Widespread centrifugal tendencies—such as the growing communist influence in Saxony, the Bavarian government's challenge to the central government, the separatist tendencies of the

---

[16] See Bresciani-Turroni (1937, p. 448).

[17] See Bresciani-Turroni (1937, p. 280).

[18] See Dornbusch and Fischer (1986), Graham (1930), and Feldman (1993). The significant rise in the market rate for call money in the second half of 1923 was due to the scarcity of credit compared to demand.

[19] See Bresciani-Turroni (1937, p. 266–267) and Feldman (1993, p. 603).

[20] See Feldman (1993, p. 603).

[21] See Feldman (1993, p. 605).

[22] See Wagenführ (1933).

[23] This gap had already significantly reduced in the previous period. Indeed, as Kuczynski (1925, p. 143) notes: "Before the war there had been in Germany quite a difference between the wages of skilled and unskilled workers, a skilled worker receiving, in general, from 20 to 50% more than an unskilled worker. With the outbreak of the revolution the self-consciousness of the unskilled laborers was, of course, considerably intensified and the tendency to level wages became very strong."

Table 5.3 Unemployed members of trade unions and real wages (Jun. 1922–Nov. 1923)

Period	Unemployed members of trade unions (percent)	Real wages in the Ruhr area (1913 = 100)	
		Skilled	Unskilled
1922—II[a]	0.7	71.8	97.8
—III[a]	0.7	73.5	100.6
—IV[a]	2.1	52.3	72.2
1923—I[a]	5.0	50.6	70.0
—II[a]	5.8	54.2	75.0
July	3.5	42.9	59.4
August	6.3	53.7	74.3
September	9.9	51.8	71.5
October	19.1	44.1	60.8
November	23.4	46.4	62.0

Sources: For real wages Statistisches Reichsamt (1925). For the unemployment rate Bresciani-Turroni (1937)
[a] Average of the quarter

Rhineland—and social unrest undermined the power of the Reich and its ability to protect property rights.

High inflation had, in fact, changed the balance of power between the various interest groups. In particular, it had weakened, in addition to the rentiers, the working class. The bargaining power of the latter was significantly reduced both due to growing unemployment and the deteriorated living conditions of workers and because inflation had thoroughly eroded "... the trade-union treasuries that allowed strikes that enforced political as well as wage bargains ... ."[24]

In this context, the war of attrition that had hindered any form of stabilization between the spring of 1920 and 1921 came to an end.[25] Faced with the weakness of the rentiers and workers, the industrialists emerged as the politically dominant interest group. They called for stabilization measures from the government, the burden of which fell mainly on the workers.[26] As Maier (1975, p. 364) writes: "Industrial managers imposed massive wage cuts... In addition, they reintroduced the ten-hour day and thus succeeded once again in passing much of their new taxation and Reparation burden on to labor."

[24] See Maier (1975, p. 364).

[25] On preconditions for stabilization see, among others, Maier (1987).

[26] See Eulenburg (1924, p. 782–783) and Maier (1975, p. 364–365).

5.3 The 1923 Monetary Reform and Other Adjustment Measures

The decree of the monetary reform was passed by the Stresemann government on October 15, 1923. The definition of it was preceded, starting in the summer, by a broad debate. Its terms were influenced not a little by the spontaneous evolution of the German monetary system in the period of extreme inflation.

As invariably occurs in these cases, private individuals in Weimar Germany sought to replace paper marks not only with real goods but also with other means of exchange. As we have seen, the process of replacing the German currency with foreign currencies was intense. However, the depreciation of the domestic currency also favored the introduction of monetary innovations.[27]

Already in the latter part of 1922 private institutions had issued emergency currencies (notgeld) in the form of small loans indexed to commodities. By 1923, several public bodies (cities, states, and public utilities' companies) had also started to issue loans denominated in commodities such as rye and coal.[28]

These "loans" were issued in small denominations and so could circulate as a medium of exchange. The stable value of these loans, or "currencies," depended on the fact that their value was indexed to the price of commodities, into which, however, they were not convertible.[29] In March 1923, the Reich, in order to finance the passive resistance in the Ruhr, issued an indexed loan, but in large denominations, while in August of the same year it issued a further loan in both large and small denominations. Banks were authorized through the Notgeld law to issue "emergency monies with stable value" (wertbeständiges Notgeld) against this type of loan. Later, "stable value" private currencies backed by stable value loans of the railway system were added to those backed by government loans. Following the replacement of the paper mark by other means of exchange in the latter part of 1923, a wide variety of currencies circulated in Germany.[30]

The use of such monetary instruments eroded the Reich's monopoly on the issuance of money but also the presence of a plurality of currencies undermined the efficiency of the payment system. All this made monetary reform urgent.

---

[27] On this aspect, see Franco (1990).

[28] Schacht (1967, p. 68) notes with regard to Notgeld: "While before the war the presses of the Reichsbank had printed all banknotes, in 1923 133 additional printing firms with 1783 machines were needed to supply the demand. More than 30 paper manufacturers worked at full capacity solely to provide paper for the Reichsbank notes. Yet even with this immense output the Reichsbank was unable to deliver enough banknotes to satisfy the demand. It often had to ask the provinces, municipalities and individual large concerns to print and put into circulation their own emergency money. In such cases it gave an assurance that it would redeem these emergency notes exactly as if they were its own banknotes. By the end of 1922 the amount of emergency money in circulation already amounted to one tenth of the Reichsbank notes, and by the end of 1923 there was as much emergency money as Reichsbank money."

[29] See Schacht (1927).

[30] See Franco (1990).

Within the debate regarding the monetary reform to be undertaken to stabilize price levels and rebuild an efficient payment system, two proposals emerged as the most widely supported.[31] The first, put forward by Hilferding and Schacht, was to stabilize the mark by returning it to gold convertibility. This proposal was supported by, amongst others, the Federation of Industries, but was undermined by the fact that the German authorities considered Germany's gold reserves insufficient to support gold convertibility.

An alternative proposal, reminiscent in several respects to the emergency currencies mentioned previously, was put forward by Hellferich. This envisaged the establishment of a new bank of issue and a new currency. More specifically, according to this proposal, certain business sectors—industry, trade, banking, and agriculture—were to (compulsorily) purchase mortgages representing the capital of the new bank to the extent of 5% of their 1913 fixed capital.[32] These securities, the Roggenrentenbriefe (rye bonds) charged 6% interest and were denominated in rye, i.e., they were indexed to the price of this commodity. Against this, the new bank would issue notes (the Roggenmark) that were convertible into Roggenrentenbriefe.

Given the concerns and doubts as to whether the Reichsbank could support the convertibility of the mark into gold, Hellferich's proposal gained broad support despite some aspects raising criticism. One aspect subject to criticism was the form of indexation of the new currency. In fact, the indexation to rye was intended to allow the landowners (the "Junkers") to receive loans in a currency whose value fluctuated with the price of this agricultural commodity. In this way, Hellferich believed he could gain the Junkers' acceptance of his proposed monetary reform. The industrial interest groups, however, believed that Hellferich's plan would favor agriculture and that if the price of the rye increased more at home than abroad, the cost of labor per unit of product would rise. This would affect the competitiveness of exports. Despite these criticisms, industrialists were acutely aware of the need for monetary reform, i.e., a stable currency that would reduce the transaction costs of trade. The banking sector, on the other hand, was skeptical about the desirability of bypassing the Reichsbank by establishing another central bank.

In October 1923, after Stresemann the previous month had put an end to the passive resistance in the Ruhr, Finance Minister Hans Luther put forward a proposal for monetary reform based to a large extent on Hellferich's draft, in which, however, it was envisaged that the new currency, called the Rentenmark, would be indexed to the price of gold instead of the price of rye, but not convertible into this precious metal. The problem of the supposed insufficiency of gold reserves to defend the new currency was thus overcome. The Rentenmarks were to be issued by a new issuing institution, the Rentenbank, alongside the Reichsbank, whose role as central bank was, however, preserved by the fact that precise quantitative limits were set on the amount of credit that the Rentenbank could issue to the private and public sectors.

[31] An illustration of these proposals can be found in Holtfrerich (1986).

[32] Half of the capital was to be raised from the agricultural sector, the other half from other sectors.

Thus, two central banks coexisted. Just as the two issuing banks coexisted, so did the new and the old currency: the Rentenmark and the papermark.

The issuing of Rentenmark, which began on November 15, 1923, was linked to the government's definition of two exchange rates. On the one hand, by indexing the Rentenmark to gold, it ensured that this currency maintained a fixed exchange rate with the US dollar, set at a ratio of 4.2 marks to one dollar.[33] On the other hand, the government fixed the exchange rate of the Rentenmark against the papermark at a rate of a trillion to one. This implied that it took 4.2 trillion paper marks to buy one dollar. In short, even the old mark came to be valued on the basis of a fixed exchange rate.

On November 13, 1923, following Havenstein's illness and sudden death, Schacht took over as president of the Reichsbank. In this way, the accommodative monetary policy of the German central bank followed by Havenstein came to an end. Schacht adopted two measures that proved effective in stabilizing the exchange rate and prices.

The first measure consisted of a Reichsbank decree issued on November 17, whereby it would not accept notgeld money after November 22. In this way, the German central bank regained control over the quantity of money in the system. The Reichsbank's decision to eliminate the government's ability to obtain resources from central bank credits operated in the same direction.

The second measure consisted of preventing lending to be used for speculative purposes on the mark. To this end, the Reichsbank ruled that the Rentenmark could not be used to settle debts abroad.

These measures contributed to the stabilization of the exchange rate and a re-establishment of confidence in the domestic currency. Referring to the speculation on the mark in the period preceding his Presidency of the Reichsbank, Schacht (1967, p. 69–70) writes: "In previous years such speculation had been carried on either with loans which the Reichsbank granted lavishly, or with emergency money which one printed oneself, and then exchanged for Reichsmarks. Now, however, three things had happened. The emergency money had lost its value. It was no longer possible to exchange it for Reichsmarks. The loans formerly easily obtainable from the Reichsbank were no longer granted, and the Rentenmark could not be used abroad. For amongst the stipulations governing the issue of the Rentenmark, there was one which forbade the surrender of Rentenmarks to foreigners. For these reasons the speculators were unable to pay for the dollars they had bought when payment became due."

In late November, the exchange rate of the mark against the dollar stopped depreciating and, in the first week of December, stabilized definitively (Table 5.4).

[33] As Schacht (1967, p. 69) notes: "This rate was chosen essentially for accounting reasons. The peacetime exchange rate had been 4.2 Marks for the Dollar. Thus it was now only necessary to remove the noughts from the 4.2 billion in order to achieve a simple conversion to the old gold Mark basis."

Table 5.4 Mark's exchange rate and prices (1913 = 1; in thousands, 1923)

Year 1923	Wholesale prices	Cost of living	Exchange rate mark/US dollar[a]
October 30	18.7	3.0	72
November 06	129.0	13.7	420
November 13	265.0	98.5	840
November 20	1413.4	218.5	4200
November 27	1422.9	792.8	4200
December 04	1337.4	1535.0	4200
December 11	1274.5	1515.0	4200
December 18	1244.6	1244.0	4200
December 27	1200.4	1200.0	4200

Source: Graham (1930), Bresciani-Turroni (1937) and Holtfrerich (1986)
[a] Milliards of US dollar

Wholesale prices stabilized in the first week of December; the cost of living the following week. While the latter increased by 51.4% between November 27 and December 27, in the same period of time wholesale prices decreased by 18.6%.

The October monetary reform did not merely introduce a new currency and stabilize the mark, but placed constraints on the creation of money to cover public deficits. In fact, the decree of 15 October set the maximum amount of Rentenmarks at 2.2 billion marks. Of these 1.2 billion marks could be issued to cover the Reich's expenditure needs. At the same time, the possibility for the government to obtain resources by rediscounting Treasury bills at the Reichsbank was eliminated. Compliance with this last provision was facilitated by the fact that first the slowdown and then the stabilization of prices was associated with a marked improvement in the states' budget. This was helped by expenditure reductions and tax increases, but above all by the Olivera-Tanzi effect on tax revenues. Between the end of November and December 1923, the Reich's revenue rose from 11.1 to 164.5 million gold marks. In the same period, government expenditure increased from 421.4 to 499.4 million gold marks, while the ratio of revenue to expenditure rose from 2.6 to 32.9%[34] (Table 5.5).

Although the contribution of the Tanzi-Olivera effect to the improvement of the Reich's public accounts was decisive, some of the government's fiscal policy measures cannot be overlooked. In order to reduce public spending, by a decree of October 27, 1923, government employees were reduced by 25%, civil servants with temporary contracts were discharged and those over the age of 65 years were forcibly retired. A further 10% of civil servants had to be discharged by January 1925. Also, railways discharged about 120,000 employees in 1923, while the postal administration reduced its staff by 65,000 units.

Only after these spending cuts were announced did the government proceed to approve the revenue part of the budget maneuver. In December 1923, a 10% tax on corporate profits was decided upon, income tax rates were redefined, raising the

[34] See Thelwell (1924).

Table 5.5 Revenue and expenditure (millions of gold marks, Sept. 1923–Jan. 1924)

	Period	Expenditure	Revenue	Revenue/Expenditure
1923	September	689.2	14.4	2.1
	October	235.8	1.2	0.5
	November 1–10	134.2	0.1	0.1
	November 10–20	88.5	0.4	1.5
	November 20–30	258.7	10.6	4.1
	November Total	421.4	11.1	2.6
	December 1–10	179.9	32.8	18.2
	December 10–20	165.7	42.9	25.9
	December 20–30	153.8	88.8	57.8
	December Total	499.4	164.5	32.9
1924	January 1–10	63.9	98.4	154.0
	January 10–20	180.4	153.6	85.1
	January 20–30	199.1	185.9	93.3
	January Total	443.4	437.9	99.0

Source: Thelwell (1924)

maximum rate to 40%, and a wealth tax ranging between 0.5 and 5% was introduced.[35] Finally, in December, the government sought to place the existing tax system on a gold basis.[36]

These fiscal measures were aimed at recovering part of the revenue eroded by inflation. Given the high bargaining power achieved, the industrialists tried to pass on the cost of these fiscal measures to the workers. A large part of them, in particular the heavy industry, claims to claw back some of the workers' gain from the "November revolution," in particular, the length of the working day.[37] In fact, there was a firm conviction in large part of them, that the Reparation burden and the stabilization of the mark could only be borne by an extension of the working day.[38]

The Stresemann government yielded to this pressure by stipulating that the 8-hour day referred only to heavy work, for others the working day could be extended through collective bargaining agreements.[39]

The monetary reform and fiscal measures of October 1923 were accompanied by a highly restrictive monetary policy by the Reichsbank: as a result of this in November and December money market rates rose significantly: in the third week of November the daily money interest rate exceeded 3200%; in December it still remained above 300% although continuing to fall (Table 5.6).

35 See Kunz (1982) and James (1986, p. 42).

36 See Republic of Germany (1924) and Robert (1926).

37 See Maier (1987, p. 204).

38 See Feldman (1993).

39 See, among others, Mommsen (1989, p. 143).

Table 5.6 Weekly interest rates (percentage per year, Nov. 1923–Jan. 1924)

Period		Daily money	14 day loans	Monthly loans
1923	Nov. 3rd week	3230	4338	4740
	Nov. 4th week	765	3276	3636
	Dec. 1st week	578	1248	1512
	Dec. 2nd week	360	641	695
	Dec. 3rd week	328	391	522
	Dec. 4th week	360	459	488
1924	Jan. 1st week	81	255	300
	Jan. 2nd week	56	159	198
	Jan. 3rd week	36	75	149
	Jan. 4th week	15	36	36

Source: Franco (1989)

The credit restriction discouraged speculation on the German currency and, combined with the introduction of the Rentenmark, encouraged the return of capital and thus the stabilization of the mark.

However, there were concerns in the government that the restrictive monetary policy and fiscal austerity measures would create the conditions for deflation and, therefore, at the beginning of 1924, the monetary policy stance became accommodative again. Money market interest rates fell sharply and discounting of commercial bills increased significantly. "Short-term credits allowed by the Reichsbank amounted to—on November 30th, 1923—364 million gold marks; December 31st, 1923, 600 million; January 31st (1924) 1,102 million; February 29th, 1,482 million; and March 31st, 1,915 million . . . ."[40] The change in the monetary policy approach from the last months of 1923 was due to the Reichsbank's fear that the continuation of that policy could lead to a severe recession but, nonetheless, threatened the stability of the mark. In fact, the German central bank's significant credit expansion not only contributed to a high currency growth but also fuelled speculation on the mark and promoted its depreciation in the free market. On April 07, the Reichsbank, fearing that the mark would fall again and inflation would rise, chose to restrict its lending, limiting it to the level of the end of March. With this measure, Germany's monetary stabilization was finally complete.

5.4 Explanations for the Success of Monetary Stabilization

Scholars of German stabilization are still astonished by the short time span in which it was achieved for which various explanations have been given. These can be traced back to three different hypotheses: (1) the *psychological hypothesis*, (2) the

[40]See Bresciani-Turroni (1937, p. 351).

monetary-fiscal hypothesis, and (3) the *exchange rate-based stabilization* (ERBS) *hypothesis*.

Among contemporaries, the idea was widespread that the introduction of the Rentenmark had had a positive psychological impact on private individuals, leading to a change in their behavior in setting prices and wages. Bresciani-Turroni (1937, p. 344) writes, for example: "It is unnecessary to state that the guarantee of the so-called 'money with a stable value' was purely fictitious ... The public allowed itself to be hypnotized by the word 'wertbeständing' (stable value) written on the new paper money. And the public accordingly accepted and hoarded these notes." A similar view can be found in Graham (1930, p. 12), according to whom the Rentenmark was "nothing more than a new tenor of inconvertible paper" and, despite this, "... has been hailed as a miracle." Angell (1932, p. 24) referred to the Rentenmark as a "confidence trick" and more recently Stolper (1967) as a "psychological device." Hardach (1980) believes that even if the backing of Rentenmark was fictitious, it was enough to generate the desired psychological effect.

The psychological hypothesis explains the stabilization of prices by arguing that the increased confidence in the stability of the value of money caused a slowdown in the velocity of circulation of money and consequently price growth. Hahn writes (1924, p. 310–311): "Because of the spontaneous reduction in the velocity of money from a maximum ... money remained incredibly short. First of all the cash boxes and cash registers filled themselves. Only when the cash registers and pocket book balances had acquired a normal level did money again take on the form of deposits with the banks, whereupon a quite extraordinarily strong relief of the situation in the money market certainly occurred, compared to the time before the introduction of the Rentenmark."

The psychological hypothesis, while emphasizing the effects of a change in confidence in the stability of the value of money, tends to overlook changes of an objective nature due to policy choices.[41]

In the monetary-fiscal hypothesis, the factor underlying German stabilization is identified as the government's renunciation of seigniorage as a means to obtain resources to cover public expenditure and fiscal deficits. This view already belongs to Bresciani-Turroni who writes: "The best empirical demonstration of the influence of the financial and banking policy as a fundamental cause of the depreciation of the mark was given by the German government itself, when it found at last, in November 1923, the necessary energy to proceed with a monetary reform. As soon as the government issues had been stopped the exchange and prices were stabilized ... ."[42]

Bresciani-Turroni, however, does not explain why the government decided to stop issues or to give up on obtaining resources by resorting to the inflation tax. An explanation for this is given by Cagan (1956), according to whom at very high

[41] As Sargent (1982, p. 82–83) writes: "While great psychological significance has sometimes been assigned to this unit change [the introduction of Rentenmark], it is difficult to attribute any substantial effects to what was in itself only a cosmetic measure."

[42] See Bresciani-Turroni (1937, p. 399).

inflation, seigniorage income becomes increasingly scarce as the amount of money held by individuals diminishes in real terms. Thus, in his view, in Weimar Germany as in other central European countries plagued by hyperinflation in the early 1920s, "[i]n order to compensate for the low level to which the tax base fell after many months of hyperinflation, the [inflation] tax rates rose to astronomical rates. This explosion of the rates in the final months completely disrupted the economy and forced the government to substitute a traditional tax program for a policy of printing money."[43]

However, as we have seen in the previous section, at least with reference to Germany, this explanation does not hold up. In fact, as will be seen later, between November 1923 and January 1924 the increase in government revenue was due rather to the Olivera-Tanzi effect than to taxation increases: it was price stabilization that favored the absorption of the fiscal deficit and not vice versa.

Partially different from Cagan's is Sargent's (1982) explanation of the stabilization of the German economy following the monetary reform. Assuming rational expectations in place of the adaptive expectations underlying Cagan's approach, Sargent believes that extreme inflation can be stopped quickly and at a low cost through a regime change that causes individuals to revise their inflation expectations downwards. Indeed, according to Sargent to stop hyperinflation "... would require far more than a few temporary restrictive fiscal and monetary actions. It would require a change in the policy *regime*: there must be an abrupt change in the continuing government policy, or strategy, for setting deficits now and in the future that is sufficiently binding as to be widely believed."[44] In the case of Germany, the regime change consisted of the monetary reform of October 1923 that placed limits on state financing through the issuance of Rentenmark and prohibiting the Reichsbank from discounting public debt. Associated with this reform were fiscal measures that included cuts in public spending and tax increases. The regime change associated with these reforms led to a drastic change in inflation expectations, which was followed by a sudden halt in price growth.

At least three observations can be made regarding Sargent's hypothesis. The first concerns the reasons for the credibility of regime change. As Dornbusch (1987, p. 352) writes: "How does a government that plans to do all the right things and, indeed, puts them on paper, secure the credibility that then makes it possible to live with the policies?" Sargent, in fact, assumes that the institutional framework is given and that policy choices take place within this framework. However, the regime change might be seen by the public as temporary or the political costs of a breach of commitments under the regime change might be small. All this would undermine the credibility of the new institutional framework and its constraints. Evidence of the relative fragility of regime change comes from the fact that, as seen above, the Reichsbank's accommodative approach in early 1924 began to threaten the stability of the mark and the success of stabilization.

---

[43] See Cagan (1956, p. 89).

[44] See Sargent (1982, p. 42).

A second observation on Sargent's hypothesis concerns the assumption that inflation expectations immediately adjust downward following the announcement of the regime change. As far as Weimar Germany is concerned, it is noted that although the parity of the paper mark had been established, albeit indirectly, at 4.20 billion marks/1 US dollar, at the end of November 1923, when the official exchange rate was by then stable, the level of the free market exchange rate was still significantly lower.[45] Only in mid-December did these two exchange rates equalize.[46] Similarly, as Table 5.6 shows market interest rates were still extremely high in early 1924.

The most critical observation that can be made of Sargent's hypothesis, however, concerns the causal link between price stabilization and budget rebalancing. Table 5.5 shows that between November and December 1923, the public deficit was drastically reduced. The same table also shows that this rebalancing was due to a significant increase in government revenue rather than to decreases in government expenditure. The latter was mainly due to the Olivera-Tanzi effect and only to a negligible extent to rate increases or new taxes.[47]

The fiscal adjustment would thus have resulted from a pronounced slowdown in price growth. The latter in turn would have been induced by the stabilization of the exchange rate.[48] Evidence of this is to be found in the fact that, as Table 5.4 shows, first the depreciation of the mark comes to a pronounced halt, almost immediately after the wholesale prices halted, while the cost of living dynamic slows before coming to a halt.

The definition of a stable exchange rate of the mark against the dollar (directly for the Rentenmark and indirectly for the paper mark) made it possible to manage inflation expectations and at the same time to favor a downward adjustment. "... [The exchange rate stabilization] appears invariably as the key step in a program. It is not sufficient by itself... to stabilize, but it is the critical step that coordinates expectations, at least temporarily, around a new trend of prices and thus gives a chance to fiscal stabilization via the revenue effects."[49] In a context in which the exchange rate trend had become the benchmark for setting wages and prices, its

[45] While the official exchange rate was 4.20 billion paper marks for 1 US dollar, in the free market in Cologne the same exchange rate was 7.20 billion paper marks for 1 US dollar. See Schacht (1927, p. 70).

[46] See Dornbusch (1987). A similar view is found in Bresciani-Turroni (1937, p. 362), according to whom: "In December 1923 complete confidence in German money was not yet re-established and the premium for the risk of depreciation remained, although it was lower. In the same month ... one day-to-day loan in paper marks ... an interest not lower than 3–5% per day was paid on the average."

[47] According to Bresciani-Turroni (1937, p. 357): "... [T]he increase in income was mainly due to the higher yield of existing taxes. In February 1924 extraordinary taxes yielded only 8.2% of the total sum."

[48] See Franco (1990).

[49] See Dornbusch (1987, p. 355).

Table 5.7 Ordinary revenues and expenditures of the federal government (millions of gold marks, 1924-I–1924-III)

	Ordinary revenue	Total of which taxes yielded	Ordinary expenditures	Excess of revenue (+) or of expenditures (–)
1924-I	1598.0	1516.8	1358.0	+240.0
1924-II	1675.9	1514.8	1487.1	+188.8
1924-III	1896.0	1784.3	1714.4	+191.6

Source: Young (1925)

stabilization was the prerequisite for putting an end to hyperinflation, which had been fed by this form of indexation.

From the perspective just outlined, therefore, the causal link underlying the German stabilization would proceed in the opposite direction from that suggested by the different versions of the monetary-fiscal hypothesis: exchange rate stabilization would have favored price stabilization and the latter would have contributed (through the Olivera-Tanzi effect) to the reabsorption of the fiscal imbalance.[50] German stabilization of 1923, therefore, seems to be a classic case of *exchange rate-based stabilization* (ERBS).[51]

Even more recent historical experience shows that this type of stabilization is generally more effective than money-based stabilization (MBS) for at least three reasons.[52] Firstly, the exchange rate, being the price to which the prices of tradable goods are linked, constitutes a more direct anchor for inflation than money. Secondly, as a nominal target, the exchange rate is more transparent than money. Lastly, the experience of the Gold Standard has shown that the fixed exchange rate is a useful tool for avoiding inflation.

However, for a successful stabilization fixing the exchange rate does not exclude the need for budget correction and a strict monetary policy.[53] Such policies were indispensable also in Weimar Germany to keep the exchange rate stable over time. In particular, the restrictive monetary policy initiated by Schacht in November 1923 and adopted definitively in early April 1924 tended to discourage downward speculation on the mark, such as had occurred earlier in the year, while encouraging capital inflows from abroad so as to strengthen the exchange rate of German currency.

However, the stability of the mark could only be maintained if the balance between public revenue and expenditure was consolidated. This happened in 1924 (Table 5.7).

[50] See Franco (1990).

[51] About the characteristics of this kind of stabilization see Aisen (2004).

[52] On this aspect see, among others, Bordo and Rockoff (1996).

[53] Kiguel and Liviatan (1994) have shown that the sustainability of fiscal balance is a necessary condition for the stabilization and that most ERBS failed for the lack of respect of this condition.

Table 5.8 Industrial production, rate of unemployment, and number of bankruptcies (averages of the period, 1924-I–1925-IV)

Periods	Index of industrial production (1928 = 100)	Percentage rate of union members fully unemployed	Number of bankruptcies
1924—I	57.8	22.7	47
1924—II	68.6	9.8	346
1924—III	70.1	11.8	948
1924—IV	79.7	7.9	564
1924—year average	77.0	13.1	476
1925—I	85.0	7.1	735
1925—II	86.3	3.8	708
1925—III	82.6	4.2	801
1925—IV	79.1	12.0	1352
1925—year average	83.2	6.8	899

Source: For the index of industrial production and the unemployment rate Vierteljahreshefte zur konjunkturforschung 1927, 1928, 1929; for the number of bankruptcies Flink (1930)

5.5 The Costs of Stabilization

In his analysis of the disinflation of the German economy between 1923 and 1924 Sargent (1982) comes to the conclusion that "... the stabilization of the German mark was accompanied by increases in output and employment and decreases in unemployment."[54] Indeed, as Table 5.8 shows, in the course of 1924 industrial output gradually rose and the unemployment rate fell, from 26.3 to 8.6% between January and May 1924.

The high growth of German output in the period following price stabilization was mainly due to a pronounced recovery in consumer demand. "The statistics of consumers' cooperatives, which included in round figures 1,700,000 members, showed a continual increase in sales. The weekly average purchase of each member rose to 2.74 marks in January 1924; 3.22 in July of the same year; 3.65 in January 1925, and 4.14 in July 1925. The consumption of meat, which before the war had reached 52 kg per person, was reduced to 22 kg in 1923, and rose again to 41 kg in 1924. Immediately after the monetary stabilization the consumption of beer, tobacco, sugar, and coffee also increased... ."[55] The consumption levels of the great mass of citizens were sustained, not only by the increase in the propensity to consume but also by the significant increase in the real income of workers: the latter for unskilled workers had increased by more than 45% between January 1924 and January 1925.

[54] See Sargent (1982, p. 93).

[55] See Bresciani-Turroni (1937, p. 379–380), Coyner (1977) and Feldman (1993, p. 850).

Table 5.9 Dividends of German industries (financial year 1924)

Production of consumer goods and services		Production of instrumental goods	
Brewing	7.16	Chemicals	5.52
Gas, water, and electricity	6.27	Electricals	4.91
Textile	5.66	Engineering	3.02
Rubber	5.44	Metallurgical industries	1.93
Games and musical instruments	5.31	Coal	1.16
Theatrical and sports	5.20	Mixed coal and iron and steel	0.53
Paper manufacturing	5.14	Lignite	7.51
Leather manufacturing	5.10		
Banking	6.49		
Insurance companies	6.05		

Source: Statistical Annual for Germany (1925). Dividends were calculated on a sample of 7666 companies

In the post-stabilization period, while the demand for consumption increased significantly, demand for capital goods stagnated. The latter was affected by various factors, primarily over-investment during the inflationary period, the high level of the real interest rates, which highlighted the low availability of financial capital in the country, and the relatively low profits in heavy industry. Taking the year 1924 as a reference, it can be seen that the dividends paid by firms producing consumer goods were much higher than those producing capital goods and raw materials[56] (Table 5.9).

The high demand for consumption, while, on the one hand, supported output, on the other, favored a high domestic absorption, evidenced by the pronounced increase in 1924 in the demand for imported goods. Since this increase was not offset by a similar increase in exports, the trade balance was, if we exclude the third quarter, persistently negative for the year[57] (Table 5.10).

In Germany, as today in many emerging countries, above all after the acceptance of the Dawes Plan (discussed in the next section), the persistent external account deficits (Table 5.10) were covered thanks to large capital inflows from abroad: in fact, between the beginning of 1924 and the end of 1925, 6 billion Reichsmarks flowed into Germany.[58]

[56]According to Bresciani-Turroni (1937, p. 339): "...[M]any facts show that the first effect of the stabilization of the currency was an increase in consumption by many classes of society, i.e. by those classes—salary and wage earners—whose purchasing power had formerly been reduced by the rapid depreciation of the sums received as salaries or wages."

[57]"Owing to the rise in the home demand, some industries—especially the textile industry—entered on a new phase of prosperity. Imports increased considerably: especially those of luxury goods. The unfavorable balance of trade was in January 1924, 136 million gold marks; in February 1924, 232; in March, 236; April, 312; and in May, 354. . . ." Bresciani Turroni (1937, p. 339).

[58]See Harris (1935, p. 7).

Table 5.10 German imports and exports (millions of marks, 1924-I–1925-IV)

Periods	Exports (a)	Imports (b)	(a)-(b)
1924—I	1351	1995	−644
1924—II	1469	2463	−994
1924—III	1722	1589	+133
1924—IV	2006	3070	−1064
1925—I	2035	3363	−1328
1925—II	2086	2957	−871
1925—III	2246	3356	−1110
1925—IV	2430	2686	−256

Source: NBER, Macrohistory Database

The dynamics of macroeconomic variables just illustrated seem congruent with the real effects of an ERBS.[59] An extensive literature, referring to ERBS in emerging countries, in particular in the Southern Cone of Latin America (Argentina, Chile, and Uruguay) in the late 1970s,[60] has shown that this type of stabilization in countries afflicted by high inflation or hyperinflation presents a common pattern:[61] Countries that use ERBS immediately experience a boom in economic activity (high growth in consumption and GDP), increase in real wages, appreciation of the real exchange rate and deterioration of foreign accounts. Subsequently, however, in many cases these effects are reversed and the economy contracts. Various theoretical explanations have been given for this pattern[62]—such as inflation inertia (due to which real interest rate is negative at the start of disinflation),[63] lack of credibility (agents expect that the inflation stabilization will be reversed in the future and consumers tilt their consumption),[64] or efficiency gains (because low inflation may result in the rise in investment and labor supply).[65]

Alongside the various hypotheses advanced in these theories, it should be highlighted that in an ERBS the money supply increases automatically when domestic wealth holders convert foreign currencies into domestic currencies. This process determines an increase in the quantity of money in real terms which stimulates domestic demand and output growth.[66] This also occurred in Germany. As Bresciani-Turroni (1937, p. 349) writes: "The increase in the circulation of legal money which occurred after the introduction of the Rentenmark can be explained, up to the amount of 1,100–1,200 million marks, by the substitution of Rentenmarks and

[59] See Block (2002).

[60] See among others Kiguel and Liviatan (1992), Vegh (1992), Reinhart and Vegh (1995), De Gregorio et al. (1998), Easterly (1996), and Fischer et al. (2002).

[61] See Kiguel and Liviatan (1992, 1994), Vègh (1992).

[62] For a survey of these theories see Rebelo and Vègh (1995).

[63] See Dornbusch (1982).

[64] See Calvo (1986) and Calvo and Vègh (1993).

[65] See Roldos (1995) and Uribe (1997).

[66] As Sachs (1995, p. 182) observes, this does not happen in money-based stabilizations, where the quantity of money in nominal and real terms initially does not change or is reduced.

Table 5.11 Gold value of total Reichsbank's note circulation (Dec. 1923–Dec. 1924)

	Note circulation[a]	Gold value of circulation on basis of exchange rates[b]	Gold value of circulation on basis of purchasing power parities[b]
1923			
December	496,507,425,000,000	112,700	141,600
1924			
January	483,675,000,000,000	109,300	148,300
February	587,875,000,000,000	128,200	183,200
March	689,864,000,000,000	151,800	204,300
April	776,949,000,000,000	170,900	220,800
May	926,874,000,000,000	206,700	265,000
June	1,097,309,000,000,000	256,800	326,900
July	1,211,038,000,000,000	289,400	369,000
August	1,391,895,000,000,000	331,300	413,100
September	1,520,511,000,000,000	361,900	425,300
October	1,780,913[c]	423,900	491,500
November	1,863,200[c]	443,400	528,400
December	1,941,440[c]	462,100	552,942

Source: Young (1925). Notes: [a]000.000 omitted, [b]000 omitted, [c]In thousands of Reichsmarks (1 Reichsmark = 1000,000,000,000 former paper marks)

paper marks for the various kinds of auxiliary monies." Due to this process of substitution, during 1924 the notes in circulation in nominal and real terms increased significantly (Table 5.11).

The significant increase in the monetary base corresponded to an equally significant increase in bank deposits. Between the end of 1923 and 1924, the deposits of the large Berlin banks increased by more than 175%. This increase in deposits corresponded in the same period of time to an increase in loans and advances of these same banks of approximately 191%.[67]

German inflation stabilization confirms the cliché according to which ERBS is "boom first, bust later," while MBS is "burst first, boom later." Actually, the expansionary cycle of the German economy ended in the second part of 1925. Industrial production peaked in May, then began to decline; correspondingly, in the final part of 1925, the unemployment rate began to increase again (Table 5.12).

The recessionary phase that began in late 1925 derived not only from the effects of restrictive monetary and fiscal policies, but also from the structural adjustments of the economy that accompanied the stabilization. Indeed, the high post-war inflation had a profound structural impact on the German economy. First of all, easy access to credit favored industrial concentration and speculative activities which led certain activities, like banking, to grow abnormally. After stabilization, many small banks sprang up but between 1924 and 1925 more than 100,000 banking employees were

[67] See League of Nations (1931, p. 340–341).

Table 5.12 Index of industrial production (1913 = 100) and rate of unemployment (Jan. 1924–Dec. 1925)

	Index of industrial production	Union members' rate of unemployment		Index of industrial production	Union members' rate of unemployment
1924			1925		
January	51.2	26.5	January	83.1	8.1
February	58.3	25.1	February	85.4	7.3
March	64.0	16.6	March	86.5	5.8
April	76.0	10.4	April	86.8	4.3
May	59.1	8.6	May	86.9	3.6
June	70.6	10.5	June	85.3	3.5
July	69.3	12.5	July	83.4	3.7
August	68.2	12.4	August	81.6	4.3
September	72.7	10.5	September	82.7	4.5
October	76.1	8.4	October	80.4	5.8
November	81.0	7.3	November	81.4	10.7
December	82.0	8.1	December	75.6	19.4

Source: Vierteljahrshefte zur konjunkturforschung, 1926

made redundant.[68] At the same time, many relatively unproductive businesses founded and developed during the period of high inflation ceased trading: the number of registered business enterprises fell by more than 14,000 during this period.[69]

High inflation had also transformed the way entrepreneurs operated,[70] some becoming "brasseurs d'affairs" who bought companies and businesses in the most diverse sectors. A typical example of this behavior was Stinnes an industrial group that came to operate in an extremely wide variety of sectors, from coal, to cellulose, paper manufacturing, banking, and so on.

Other entrepreneurs had made capital investments that would later prove to be unproductive.[71] In fact, given the Reichsbank's accommodative policy, high inflation had given rise to a form of "forced saving" channelled from rentiers, whose wealth and consumption had shrunk, to entrepreneurs who borrowed at interest rates that were heavily negative in real terms. Some firm's owners, thanks to easy access to bank credit, had accumulated large shareholdings by buying them from small savers. The result was a high concentration of capital and ownership of many industrial enterprises. In many cases, this process favored forms of vertical business integration that later proved to be inefficient.

[68] See Frankfurter Zeitung, September 12th, 1925.

[69] See Bresciani-Turroni (1937, p. 392).

[70] See Garber (1982).

[71] See Bresciani-Turroni (1937) and Garber (1982).

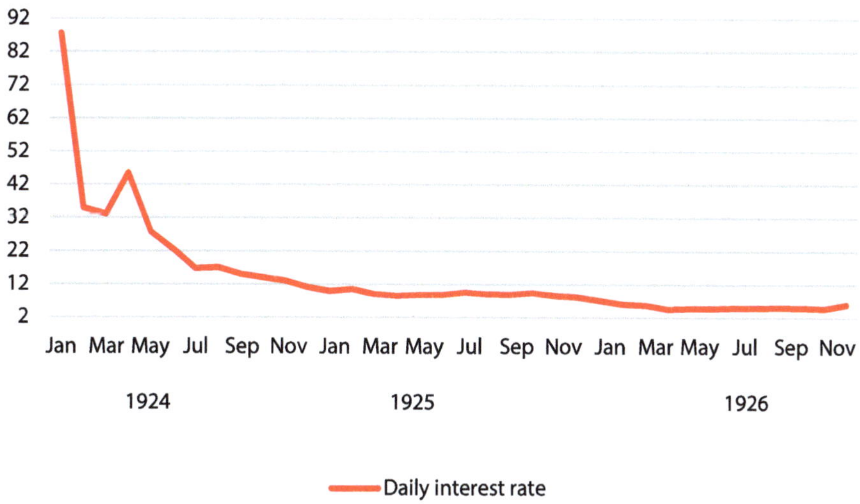

Fig. 5.1 Short-term interest rates in Germany (Jan.1924–Dec.1926). Source: NBER History database

The adjustment of Germany's production structure inevitably entailed high transition costs, evident from the persistently high unemployment rates (even as late as 1925) and the high number of bankruptcies[72] (Table 5.8).

This process was made more difficult by the scarcity of capital. The propensity of private individuals to save was low, as was the credit capacity of German banks, whose capitalization had been eroded by the war and post-war inflation. At the same time, Germany remained isolated from international financial markets.

This combination of factors helps to explain why in 1925 the real interest rate remained very high in Germany, at around 8%, just as the differential between the German and British short-term interest rates was high, by approximately 500 basis points. Only in the spring of 1926 did the German short-term interest rate reach the level of the English one, just above 4% (Fig. 5.1).

Tensions in the capital market gave rise to a shortage of working capital that hampered the recovery of production. These tensions eased with the approval of the Dawes Plan and the massive inflow of capital from abroad that followed it. However, the distortions in the German economic structure were not resolved by stabilizing prices and continued to affect the growth of the German economy in the remaining part of the 1920s.

[72]These costs are similar to those associated with the stabilizations of emerging countries, as found, for example, in the stabilizations of some Latin American countries in the 1980s. See Solimano (1990).

5.6 The Dawes Plan

As we have seen, the problem of the German Reparations remained unresolved even after the Franco-Belgian occupation of the Ruhr. The failure to solve this problem contributed to European instability, which was of particular concern to the Americans, who were convinced that stabilizing Europe was essential to the health of their economy.[73] Hence, the need to provide a solution to the Reparations problem that would contribute to Germany's economic recovery and, with it, facilitate American exports. This concern, shared by the British, was further reinforced by the fear that in an economically and politically unstable Germany bolshevism could establish itself and spread more easily. Following a proposal by the United States at the end of November the Allied governments agreed on the formation of two expert committees whose main task was to examine Germany's ability to pay the Reparations defined in the London ultimatum of 1921. Of the two committees, the main one was chaired by the American banker Charles G. Dawes.[74] In addition to the United States, the Committee included representatives from England, France, Belgium, and Italy. The Committee sent its findings in a written report to the Reparations Commission on April 9, 1924, and, on the basis of this report, the Dawes Plan was approved on August 16, 1924. This Plan, apart from providing for the withdrawal of France and Belgium from the Ruhr, made no reference to the total amount of Reparations that Germany would have to pay, but merely set out the first five annuities of the Reparations that Germany undertook to pay. These annuities were defined as follows: 1 billion marks were to be paid in the financial year 1924–1925; this amount would gradually increase until it reached 2.5 billion marks in 1928–1929. Only half of the sum was to come from the German budget with the remainder coming from the interest on mortgage bonds issued on the capital assets of German industry and railways.

The values of the annuities had been set based on Germany's (estimated) ability to bear the financial burden without compromising the stability of its currency and on the principle that the real value of the payments should not, in the long run, exceed Germany's export surplus. In short, the Committee had adhered to the "classical transfer problem," which, as seen in Chap. 2, was the subject of a dispute in the *Economic Journal* between Keynes and Ohlin in 1929.

The Dawes Committee envisaged the implementation of policy measures that would enable Germany to meet its payment commitments,[75] and to make it easier for Germany to pay the first annuity, a loan of 800 million marks was granted.

The main institutional reforms that Germany was to implement on the basis of the Plan were of a monetary nature. They included the establishment of a new currency,

---

[73] On this aspect see Costigliola (1976).

[74] He was the Chairman of the Board of the Central Trust Company of Illinois.

[75] See Costigliola (1976) and Schuker (1976).

Table 5.13 Sums to be raised within Germany according to the Dawes Plan (in millions of Reichsmarks, 1924–1929)

Year period	1924–25	1925–26	1926–27	1927–28	1928–29
Budget surplus	–	–	110	500	1250
Transport tax	–	250	290	290	290
Railroad securities	200	845	550	600	600
Industrial bonds	–	125	250	300	300
Total	1000	1220	1000	1750	2500

Source: Moulton (1929)

the Reichsmark, pegged to gold, and a reorganization of the Reichsbank. The latter is to be based on these main points:[76]

(i) The Reichsbank had the exclusive right to issue paper money. The money issued by the Reichsbank was to be protected by a legal reserve of $33^{1/3}\%$ and other liquid assets.
(ii) A new gold-convertible currency, the Reichsmark, would replace the old non-convertible mark. At the same time the Rentenmark would be taken out of circulation altogether.
(iii) The Reichsbank would operate as a bankers' bank, establishing the official rate of rediscounting short-term bills. It would also deal with the public, granting loans, and receiving deposits.
(iv) The Reichsbank would retain complete independence from the government and would have strict limits on advances to the German federal government.
(v) The German central bank would act as a depository for Reparations payments.
(vi) Finally, the Reichsbank was to be administered by a German president and managing board. In addition to this board, there was a second board, the General Board, which had wide organizational and management powers and consisted of seven German and seven foreign members. One of the latter exercised the role of Commissioner, whose task was to ensure compliance with the provisions of the Plan regarding reserves and convertibility of the Reichsmark.

As can be seen, the Dawes Plan limited Germany's monetary sovereignty by subjecting it to a double constraint: that on the convertibility of the Reichsmark and that on the governance of the Reichsbank. These constraints were intended to reassure potential foreign investors, primarily American banks, about the prospective stability of the Reichsmark.[77]

In the fiscal arena, on the other hand, the Plan provided for a schedule of resources to be raised within Germany. Part of these resources were from budget surpluses (Table 5.13).

[76] See the text of the Dawes Plan reported in the Federal Reserve Bulletin (1924).

[77] See Morgan (1931).

This schedule was purely indicative and had no binding character. In fact, the schedule merely required the German government to make fiscal policy choices congruent with maintaining stable prices and exchange rates with the government having sole discretion for these choices. The Agent General was, however, tasked with periodically presenting a report on the German state budget.

Finally, the Plan distinguished between the "payment" of Reparation funds by Germany and the transfer of these funds to the receiving countries. The responsibility for this transfer lay with the Reparations Commission, which was under an obligation to verify whether such a transfer could take place "... without threatening the stability of German currency." This was intended to instil confidence in foreign investors wishing to invest in Germany.

The Dawes Plan had undoubted beneficial effects in the immediate term. Firstly, it limited the demand for Reparations to amounts that Germany was able to pay without destabilizing the exchange rate. Moreover, it helped to ease the political dispute over Reparations by treating them "like an ordinary commercial debt."[78]

However, alongside these beneficial effects, the Dawes Plan also had serious flaws. Among these was the fact that the transfer protection clause gave de facto higher seniority to commercial loans than to Reparations. Contributing to the Plan being "... followed by an orgy of German borrowing."[79] The large inflow of capital from abroad and the absence of conditions in the Plan regarding policy choices meant that the strict fiscal policy it envisaged was short-lived.

Initially, the indications of the Dawes Plan in fiscal matters prompted the German government, headed at the time by the conservative Luther, to implement a restrictive fiscal maneuver and, during the course of 1925, it was clear that the budget would show a large surplus at the end of the year.[80] However, there was widespread public opinion that this result had been achieved through a fiscal burden "... which was generally held to be out of proportion to the contributive capacity of the German people."[81] In particular, industrialists believed that the level of taxation, combined with the restrictive credit policy, was severely damaging the level of productive activity by significantly reducing prospective profits.

The RDI (Reichsverband der Deutcher Industrie, that is, the Reich Association of German Industry), therefore, demanded a reduction of public spending and of taxes affecting the industry. In August 1925, income, inheritance, and wealth taxes were reduced. These measures were suggested to the government not only by pressure from industrialists but also by the deepening recession. These and other measures to counter the latter proved, at least in the short term, to be ineffective in counteracting the fall in productive activity.[82]

[78]See Carr (1946, p. 84).

[79]See Carr (1946, p. 85).

[80]See Clingan (2000).

[81]See Bresciani-Turroni (1937, p. 357).

[82]See James (1986, p. 43).

Table 5.14 Revenue and expenditure of the German Reich (millions of gold marks, 1924/25–1929/30)

Financial year	Revenues	Expenditures	Balance
1924–1925	7757	7220	+536
1925–1926	7334	7444	−110
1926–1927	7690	8543	−853
1927–1928	8961	9316	−355
1928–1929	9751	10,888	−1237
1929–1930	10,061	10,846	−785

Source: Agent General for Reparation Payments, Report, May 21st, 1930

At the beginning of 1926, the new Minister of Finance, Peter Reinhold, in contrast to his predecessor, argued that in order to stimulate the German economy, the planned budget surplus had to be absorbed and, if necessary, budget deficits incurred.[83] Reinhold's position was shared by Chancellor Luther and Foreign Minister Stresemann, who were concerned that a possible budget surplus might lead the Allies to believe that Germany was able to pay Reparations.

In early February 1926, when outlining his proposal to the Council of Ministers for the financial year 1926–1927, Reinhold proposed cutting a set of taxes, in particular, the turnover tax. The Reichstag approved the tax package proposed by the Minister of Finance but went yet further: the fusion tax was repealed entirely, capital tax was reduced, and tax payment periods were extended.[84]

Further tax reductions called for by the Social Democrats, and related to foodstuffs such as salt and wine, were also passed by the German parliament while, at the same time, it approved spending increases, primarily the extension of unemployment support to 52 weeks.[85]

With these concessions to both right and left-wing parties Luther hoped to strengthen political support for his government. However, they impacted negatively on the state's budget, in stark contrast to the commitment made by the German political authorities when they had signed the Dawes Plan to keep the state budget in balance. The Reich budget of 1926–1927 has been aptly defined as a "kind of revolution"[86] as it broke from the previous fiscal policy and brought German public finance back to a structural imbalance between revenue and expenditure that, according to Reinhold, was to have been covered by debt, in particular, by issuing securities to be placed on the market. This imbalance consolidated and worsened in the following years (Table 5.14).

As can be seen, the fiscal adjustment measures adopted in 1924 and the first part of 1925 were short-lived. Two factors in particular contributed to a renewed propensity for an accommodating fiscal policy in the political class. On the one hand,

[83] See Reinhold speech in Reichstad February 10, 1926, Verhandlungen des Reichstages, III, Wahlperiode 1924, Bd. 388, 5402–13.

[84] See Clingan (2000).

[85] See Hertz-Eichenrode (1982).

[86] See Upmeier (1973).

such a policy made it possible to manage the conflict between the various interest groups, in particular, between capital and labor, which had been dormant in the period of hyperinflation but re-emerged after the stabilization of the Reichsmark and intensified due to the recession of 1925–1926. The renewed propensity for fiscal laxity led the Reichstad to pass the Tax Reduction Act of 31 March 1926.

On the other hand, the return to deficit fiscal policies, even if they entailed high domestic absorption and current account deficits, was made possible by foreign financing from which Germany benefited after the Dawes Plan. In fact, in the period following the signing of the Plan a set of factors such as the high liquidity of international markets[87] and the greater seniority to commercial loans than to Reparations[88] foreseen by the Plan favored a vast inflow of capital into Germany. This enormous influx of capital, although in the short term it allowed Germany to enjoy relative social peace, exposed the country to the risk of a sudden stop. A risk that took on a particularly dramatic form, as will be seen in Chap. 7 , in 1931. The inflow of capital from abroad disincentivized the German authorities from adopting measures to consolidate the public finances which would have finally stabilized the German economy. This was possible because the Dawes Plan facilitated Germany's access to international financial markets and imposed monetary conditions on Germany (independence of the Reichsbank and convertibility of the Reichsmark), but failed to establish any fiscal conditions, such as the pursuit of a balanced budget.

In this respect, the Dawes Plan differed substantially from the measures imposed by the League of Nations on countries of the former Habsburg empire, primarily Austria and Hungary, in return for the financial support offered to mitigate the costs of stabilization.

5.7 The Stabilization Programs of the League of Nations in Austria and Hungary

Some scholars have assimilated the German stabilization of 1923 to the cases of stabilization of hyperinflations that occurred in emerging states after the collapse of the Habsburg Empire. Sargent (1982), in particular, brings these cases under the common denominator of the effects on the expectations of drastic regime changes. Franco (1989, 1990) considers the stabilizations that occurred in these states as forms of ERBS like the German one.

In reality, the stabilization of Germany has somewhat different characteristics from the stabilization plans implemented by the League of Nations in central European countries plagued by hyperinflation after the First World war.[89] These

[87] See Accominotti and Eichengreen (2016).

[88] See Ritschl (1999, 2002, 2014).

[89] See Heilperin (1931).

plans, in fact, have very similar characteristics to those adopted today by the International Monetary Fund (IMF) to stabilize the economies of emerging or developing countries. This similarity emerges clearly from the words of Arthur Salter, at that time head of the Economic and Financial Section of the League of Nations: "By [the late 1920s] the very fame of the League's action entailed disadvantages. It led to the belief that the appropriate clients for the League were countries who were completely down and out and who both needed, and would be required to accept, the same onerous and rather humiliating form of control for a period. Other countries therefore . . ., while profiting from the technical experience gained in the League's experiments, preferred to make direct arrangements with foreign issuing houses and to carry reforms through without any impairment of national responsibility beyond what might be imposed by the lenders."[90]

Like the IMF today, so in the 1920s the League, on the one hand, gave financial support to the countries to be stabilized, but, on the other hand, demanded from them the adoption of fiscal measures aimed at reabsorbing budget imbalances. These measures implied a loss of sovereignty both due to the fact that they were dictated by the League and due to the fact that the latter monitored their implementation.

The plans adopted for the stabilization of Austria and Hungary are emblematic in this sense.[91] The examination of them and their implementation allows us to pick up the differences between the stabilizations in these countries and in Germany.

In Austria, inflation had assumed an explosive character from late 1921 and peaked in August 1922[92] (Fig. 5.2).

The consequences of hyperinflation were dramatic. Hunger was widespread, Austrian society and the state were on the brink of dissolution. The situation is described thus by Zweig (1943, [1964, p. 292]): "A man who had been saving for forty years and who, furthermore, had patriotically invested his all in war bonds, became a beggar. A man who had debts became free of them. A man who respected the food rationing system starved; only one who disregarded it brazenly could eat his fill. A man schooled in bribery got ahead, if he speculated he profited. If a man sold at cost price, he was robbed, if he made careful calculation he yet cheated. Standards and values disappeared during this melting and evaporation of money. . . ."

Toward the end of August, the Council of the League of Nations started negotiations for the stabilization of Austria and its financial reconstruction. These negotiations ended on October 2, 1922, with the signing of a plan for the financial reconstruction of Austria, which was approved by the Austrian Parliament on November 28, 1922. Although the Austrian Socialist Party (SDAP) was radically

[90] Salter (1961, p. 182). Very appropriately Pauly (1996, p.18) writes: "Substitute 'IMF' for 'League', and few would be surprised to see Salter's words applied to the contemporary period."

[91] See League of Nations (1926a, 1926b).

[92] See Salter (1961), Dornbusch (1994) and Garber and Spencer (1994).

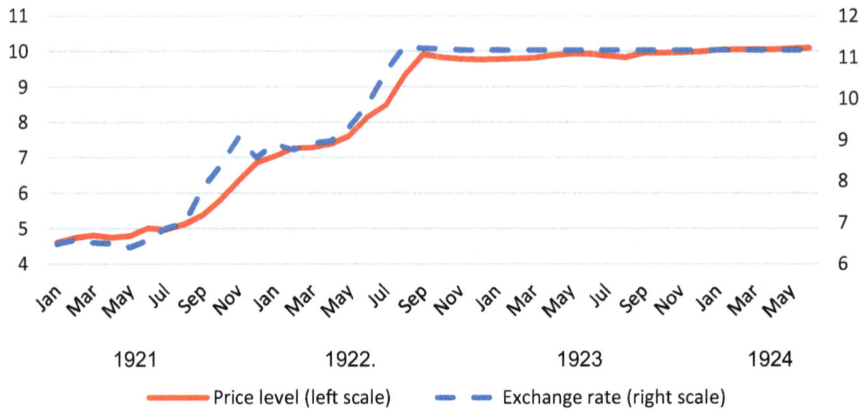

Fig. 5.2 Austria exchange rate and price level (logarithmic scale; Jan. 1921–May 1924). Source: Young (1925). Legend: Kronen per dollar exchange rate as quoted in New York; the price level refers to retail prices

opposed to the League's stabilization scheme in public, in practice it did not oppose its approval.[93]

The Austrian Reconstruction Plan drawn up by the League of Nations and signed in Geneva on October 4, 1922, represented an unprecedented intervention by an international institution in the affairs of a sovereign state.[94] As such it was a landmark in international monetary relations.[95]

Austria's reconstruction plan consisted of three protocols:[96] In Protocol No. 1, the governments of Great Britain, France, Italy, and Czechoslovakia recognized Austria's territorial integrity and sovereignty. For its part, Austria undertook not to

[93]The SDAP's "responsible" behavior was helped by the persuasive work of the League delegation. The latter encouraged a compromise between the Christian Social Chancellor Seifel and the SDAP, on the basis of which the latter would abstain in parliament on those parts of the scheme it disagreed with in exchange for increased government funding for Vienna's socialist city authorities (see Marcus, 2012, p. 111–112). According to Young (1925), the socialists behaved 'responsibly' not only because of this, but also because they were "alarmed at the prospect of disorder" (See G.M. Young to Charles Whigham of Morgan Grenfell, 15 June 1922, RAL 111/189, Special Correspondence from Austria).

[94]See Berger (2003).

[95]There were several reasons why the victorious powers, first and foremost England and France, called for an intervention by the League of Nations to support the reconstruction of Austria. The first being the concern of these powers to ensure the stability of Europe. They were worried that if Austria collapsed, conditions would be created for its takeover by Italy or, more likely, for an Anschluss (on this point see, among others, Mazower, 2012, and Marcus, 2012). A second reason the European powers were keen to avoid the collapse of Austria was to prevent a chaotic situation in Eastern Central Europe, which was seen as a bastion against the wild and barbarian east. See Meinl J., The reconstruction of Europe, February 1920, PA L4/F/198/21 and Lindley to Earl Curzon, 3 November 1920, TNA T160/57, 14/10/20–23/10/20.

[96]See League of Nations (1922) and de Bordes (1924).

seek to give up its independence or to engage in negotiations, including economic and financial negotiations, that would undermine it.

Protocol No. 2 dealt with the loan that was to be granted to Austria and determined the means of supervision of the administration of the loan.

Finally, Protocol No. 3, signed only by Austria, contained the "conditions," i.e., the obligations that the Austrian government undertook to fulfil. Among which two were principal. Firstly, the Austrian government undertook to accept a Commissioner General appointed by the Council of the League of Nations. The Commissioner had the power to veto any measure by the government that would damage the value of the revenues placed as collateral for the foreign loan received by Austria and the power to demand additional reserves as collateral for this loan. Secondly, the Austrian government, in return for the loan received from the League of Nations, also undertook to implement fiscal and monetary reforms that would enable it to respect the principle of fiscal equilibrium, defined at the International Financial Conference held in Brussels in 1920 as the basic precondition for monetary stability. In order to rebalance the budget, the Austrian government was required to increase tax and non-tax revenues, to eliminate most subsidies, to reduce the size of its bureaucracy, to cut other types of expenditure, and to carry out a reform of public administration that would allow the central government to control and monitor public finance. In the monetary sphere, the Austrian government was obliged to create a bank of issues whose task was to facilitate Austria's reconstruction process. In order to guarantee its independence from politics, the bank's capital was held by private individuals. This bank of issue was prohibited from purchasing public securities or financing the government in any way and the money that the bank issued had to be covered, in the first 5 years of its existence, by at least 20% metal reserves. This coverage ratio was to be gradually increased to $33^{1/3}$%. Also in the monetary sphere, the government was to proceed with the introduction of a new currency, convertible into gold. This took place at the end of 1924 with the first issuing of the Austrian schilling, the value of which was set at 0.21172086 g of pure gold or 0.142 dollars.

Austria's Stabilization and Reconstruction Plan was successful:[97] with the price level stabilizing in the latter part of 1922 (Fig. 5.2) and the exchange rate finally stabilized in April 1923.[98] The stabilization of prices and the exchange rate was associated with the rebalancing of the public budget. The balance of the latter improved significantly as early as 1923, with the ratio of state revenue and expenditure rising from 47.8% the previous year to 81.1%. In 1924, this ratio rose to 98.7% and the following year reached 109.2%. In absolute terms, the budget deficit was gradually absorbed and, in 1925, it became a surplus (Table 5.15).

---

[97] As evidenced by Stiefel (2008), Austrian bankers and financial institutions strongly supported the League project.

[98] On the stabilization of Austria see Gaertner (1923), de Bordes (1924), Heilperin (1931), Pasvolsky (1928), League of Nations (1926a), and Kerschagl (1929).

Table 5.15 Austrian budgets (millions of schillings, 1922–1925)

Period	Revenue	Expenditure	Deficit (−)	Ratio of income to expenditure (in percent)
1922	209.8	437.5	−137.8	47.9
1923	697.4	859.6	−162.2	81.1
1924	900.6	913.6	−13.6	98.7
1925	908.5	832.0	+76.5	109.2

Source: Pasvolsky (1928)

Table 5.16 Unemployed in receipt of benefits in Austria (in thousands, 1922–1926)

Quarters	1922	1923	1924	1925	1926
I	39.7	160.3	117.7	184.0	220.7
II	38.7	111.0	72.0	132.3	159.7
III	33.3	83.3	72.7	117.3	150.3
IV	86.0	84.3	112.0	166.0	175.0
Year average	49.4	109.7	93.6	149.9	176.4

Source: Statistsche Handbook fur die Republic Ostereich (1927)

Unlike German stabilization, therefore, in Austria the balanced budget was not a short-lived event, but rather persisted and was consolidated over time. This path was guided by the League of Nations in terms of the conditions imposed in return for its financial support and also through its mediation which helped to ease resistance to reforms and strengthened the position of Chancellor Seifel and his government.

Sargent (1982), as he also argues was the case in Weimar Germany, claims that stabilization following hyperinflation had only moderate economic and social costs in Austria. In particular, he writes: "The available figures indicate that the stabilization of the crown was attended by a substantial increase in the unemployment rate, though unemployment had begun to climb well before stabilization was achieved."[99] Thus, according to Sargent, the increase in unemployment should rather be blamed on hyperinflation than stabilization.

However, it appears from Table 5.16 that the unemployed in Austria rose above all from the autumn of 1922 and remained high in the years immediately afterward.

It, thus, seems to be an effect of the restrictive fiscal measures put in place to balance the budget and the fact that monetary policy was no longer conditioned by the need to cover public deficits. As Wicker (1986, p. 355) writes: "The increases in unemployment during the winters of 1924–25 and 1925–26 can be attributed largely, though not entirely, to the earlier measures of monetary reform. Taking average unemployment to be at least 3% in 1931, the currency stabilization policies resulted in at least a 4% point increase in the unemployment percentage, a not insignificant increase assignable to currency reform."

Despite the social costs just highlighted, the austerity fiscal policy undertaken in 1922 was not abandoned but rather it continued, as Table 5.15 shows, in the years following the stabilization.

[99] See Sargent (1982, p. 55).

Hungary's experience of hyperinflation and subsequent stabilization in the first half of the 1920s was similar to that of Austria in several respects. Indeed, starting in the summer of 1921, after Finance Minister Hegedius's[100] attempt at monetary stabilization had failed, inflation became a policy choice aimed at appeasing the distributional conflict and stimulating the economy.[101] The benefits of inflation were short-lived: industrial production only increased in 1922 and then declined in the following years, despite a significant increase in public spending: "subsidies to government employees and railway deficits were chiefly responsible."[102] This increase was not matched by an adequate growth in revenue: in 1922 the ratio of revenue to expenditure was 75.8%, falling to 65.5% in 1924. The resulting public deficits of that period were covered to a large extent with money.

Severe macroeconomic imbalances and the failure of attempts to stabilize the economy encouraged a "flight from the crown" and, starting in mid-1923, the exchange rate of the Hungarian krona plummeted. As a result, price increases took on the explosive characteristics of hyperinflation (Fig. 5.3).[103]

After an attempt to stem the dramatic situation by resorting to a loan from Switzerland failed,[104] the government decided, as Austria had done before, to ask the League of Nations for help.[105] Subsequent negotiations were complex,[106] but in the end reached a positive outcome:[107] the Hungarian government's request for financial assistance from the League of Nations was accepted by the latter on October 17, 1923.

As in the case of Austria, the League of Nations drew up a reconstruction plan. The Plan, against which a loan of 250 million gold krone was granted to Hungary, was based on two Protocols.

Protocol No. 1 was signed by the representatives of Great Britain, France, Italy, Czechoslovakia, Romania, Yugoslavia, and Hungary. In it, the first six powers recognized the political independence, the territorial integrity, and the sovereignty of Hungary. For its part, Hungary undertook to fulfil the obligations contained in the Treaty of Trianon.[108]

---

[100] See Pasvolsky (1928).

[101] See Berend and Ranki (1974).

[102] See Pasvolsky (1928, p. 298).

[103] See Pasvolsky (1928), Sargent (1982) and Siklos (1994).

[104] See Orde (1990).

[105] See Zimmermann (1927).

[106] This was mainly due to the neighboring countries' fears of Hungarian irredentism. See Salter (1926).

[107] This success was mainly due to the role played by England. In a note to the Foreign Office the governor of the Bank of England, Montagu Norman, wrote: "We are decided to prevent the Czechs and the Romanians from obtaining money from London until Hungary's position is ensured. This is not a political, but rather a financial issue, and I do not hesitate to ask for your support for this political line I have adopted ... in the interest of Eastern Europe." See Orde (1990, p. 270).

[108] See Borossi (1994).

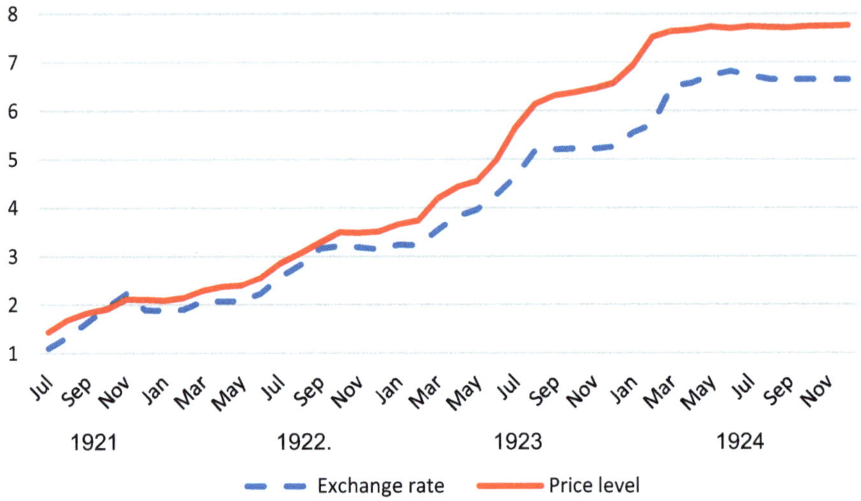

Fig. 5.3 Hungary exchange rate and price level (logarithmic scale; Jan. 1921–June 1924). Source: Young (1925). Legend: Krone per US dollar exchange rate as quoted in New York; the price level refers to retail prices

Protocol No. 2, signed by Hungary alone, expressed Hungary's commitment to fiscal and monetary reforms aimed at balancing the budget and stabilizing the exchange rate and prices. A necessary prerequisite for monetary stabilization was the establishment of a new bank of issue. The implementation of these reforms was to be supervised by a League Commissioner General.

In 1924, the Hungarian government implemented a large part of the planned reforms and in April of that year, the Hungarian National Bank was established and began operations in June. However, the bank's operations were hampered by the shortage of foreign exchange reserves. The Hungarian government solved this by taking out a loan from the Bank of England for 4 million pounds sterling. Against this loan, the Hungarian government pledged to stabilize the Hungarian currency against sterling rather than gold.

When sterling became convertible into gold again in 1925, the Hungarian currency appreciated and there were large inflows of capital from abroad. In this favorable situation, the government decided to introduce a new currency, known as pengö, whose value in gold was fixed: 1 pengö was worth 0.263157789 g of pure gold.

The stability of the pengö was guaranteed by the autonomy of the central bank from the government, to which, by statute, it was forbidden to grant advances to the public sector. Like the Austrian central bank, the Hungarian central bank was a private corporation and had a monopoly on issuing notes. Like the Austrian central bank, it had to hold a minimum amount of foreign exchange reserves: 20% in the first 5 years rising progressively in the following years to $33^{1/3}$%.

Table 5.17 Hungarian budgets (1924/25–1928/29)

Periods	Fiscal balance[a]	Ratio of revenue on expenditure[b]
1924–1925	+99.2	107.2
1925–1926	+88.4	107.7
1926–1927	+151.1	112.1
1927–1928	+97.1	107.1
1928–1929	+2.5	100.2

Source: League of Nations (1929, 1930). Legend: [a] in millions of pengö; [b] In percentage

Table 5.18 Unemployment and ratio of demand for jobs on employment offers (in percentage; 1923–1926)

Period	Union members who are fully unemployed	Ratio of demand for jobs to employment offers
1923	15,432	131
1924	34,864	135
1925	27,984	181
1926	22,332	170

Source: Revue Hongroise de Statistique (1927)

The objective of balancing the budget was achieved both by eliminating part of the expenditure, keeping the amount of expenditure within the threshold reached in the first half of 1925, and by increasing taxes, in particular direct taxes. With these measures, the Hungarian government brought the budget into balance in the financial year 1924–1925 (Table 5.17), in part, thanks to the effective supervision by the Commissioner General, Jeremiah Smith.

The rebalancing of budgets corresponded with a pronounced slowdown in the growth of money. Until the end of the 1920s, both the wholesale and the retail price levels remained broadly stable, as did the exchange rate (Fig. 5.3).[109]

Also in Hungary, stabilization and the associated fiscal austerity were not without economic and social costs.[110] Evidence of this is provided by the significant increase in unemployment in 1924 and the subsequent 2 years (Table 5.18).

However, the slowdown in economic growth and rise in unemployment provoked by the restrictive measures of 1924–1925 did not provoke resistance to fiscal austerity sufficient to undermine reaching a balanced budget.

---

[109] See Siklos (1994) and Seton-Watson (1962).

[110] See Salter (1926) and Wicker (1986).

5.8 The Dawes Plan and the League of Nations' Programs: A Comparison

It is clear from the above section that the stabilization process and their associated social costs, unlike in Germany, did not lead to an interruption in the public finance rebalancing process in either Austria or Hungary in the years following stabilization. This was largely due to the fact that the financial support of the League of Nations after the First World War[111] was conditional on the implementation of reforms aimed at eliminating budget deficits.[112] The conditions imposed by the League of Nations on governments, on the one hand, represented guarantees as to the ability of these countries to repay the loan received and, on the other, helped to overcome resistance to the adoption of reforms within the country and, thus, to temper the war of attrition that had previously prevented their implementation. In the majority of other cases, the intervention of the League of Nations was successful in achieving an adjustment of public accounts.[113]

The Dawes Plan, although providing, as we have seen in Sect. 5.6, that the resources for Reparations were to be derived in part from fiscal resources and that the tax burden of German citizens was to be commensurate with that of the citizens of the Allied countries, did not make these prescriptions binding. The Plan specifically ruled out any form of Allied control over the German public budget: "We do not hesitate to reject as undesirable, for the purpose which all have in view, save in certain extreme events, any system which would involve directly or indirectly the virtual control of all Germany's revenue or expenditure."[114] But further stipulated that as a matter of principle, a "minimum" level of domestic public expenditure would have precedence over other commitments, including Reparations. "The amount that can safely be fixed for Reparation purposes tends therefore to be the difference between the maximum revenue and minimum expenditure for Germany's own needs."[115] In the absence of conditions, it is not surprising that between 1925 and 1929 the German fiscal budget was persistently in deficit and that Germany's foreign debt increased disproportionately. As Carr (1947, p. 84) writes: the Dawes Plan "... had serious flaws. It provided for annual payments, but it failed to prescribe their duration or to make any pronouncement on Germany's total indebtedness."

The contrasting outcome of the Dawes Plan and the almost contemporaneous stabilization programs conducted by the League of Nations highlights the importance of conditions in foreign financing in support of stabilization processes. The

[111] Precisely for six countries of Central Europe: Austria, Hungary, Greece, Bulgaria, Estonia, and Danzig.

[112] These reforms and measures were aimed at increasing tax and non-tax revenues, reducing the number of public employees, the elimination of subsidies and other types of public spending. See Santaella (1993).

[113] In particular, budget balances improved significantly in Austria and Hungary.

[114] Dawes Plan, Part. I, no. XIV.

[115] Dawes Plan, Part. I, no. VIII.

literature on the role of such conditions is very extensive[116] and most highlights the fact that these conditions represent a guarantee of the debtor country's ability to repay the debt incurred. In this context, the analysis generally assumes that the government of a country receiving financial support is a single actor. From this perspective, conditionality has the function of binding the government to carry out reforms without changing the policy guidelines over time. Thanks to the implementation of the reforms to which the government has committed, the country can escape the risk of debt overhangs and repay the loans received. Following this logic, Sachs (1989) showed that a government, when it receives external support and has to decide how to use these resources, is faced with the alternative of whether to spend on consumption or investment. If its discount rate exceeds the return on investment, it will choose to spend the resources it has obtained on consumption. Conversely, it will use the resources in investment if the return of the latter exceeds its discount rate. Only in the latter case will it be able to repay the loan received.[117]

If you remove Sachs' hypothesis that the government is not a single actor and instead assume that there is opposition to reforms or, indeed, a war of attrition between various interest groups none of whom are willing to bear the burden of reform, the conditions imposed for international financial aid take on another function in addition to guaranteeing the repayment of the loan received. In fact, they are posed as an external imposition on the implementation of the adjustment measures and act as a support to the government or interest groups who favor them. The way in which such conditions can alter the internal political equilibrium so that reforms are implemented has been illustrated in various papers on political economy.[118]

The Dawes Plan, by favoring a large inflow of capital into Germany and failing to place fiscal conditions, removed the incentive for the German political elite to adopt reform and hence did not affect the internal political equilibrium of Germany. Various explanations have been given as to why fiscal conditions were not set in the Plan. According to some scholars, the Plan in question was designed to meet the need of the US banking community to re-open the German financial market to foreign investors.[119] A second hypothesis is that the experts, writing the Dawes Plan, did not fully realize its implications.[120]

Whatever the correct explanation, the fact remains that two important lessons can be learned from the unintended effects of the Dawes Plan. The first is that, in the absence of conditions that provide for measures to adjust the macroeconomic imbalances of a country, in particular its fiscal imbalances, the latter may easily

[116] For a survey of this literature see among others Dreher (2009).

[117] Similar considerations to Sachs are found in Diwan and Rodrik (1992) and Fefchamps (1996).

[118] See, in particular, Vreeland (1999) and Drazen (2002).

[119] See Link (1970), Schuker (1988) and McNeil (1986).

[120] See Kindleberger (1984).

fall into a situation of overborrowing.[121] The second lesson is that the effectiveness of external financial support by two or more countries as opposed to by an international institution that has the task of guaranteeing international monetary and financial stability is quite different. In the case of two or more countries, in fact, the decision to impose conditions, the nature of these, and compliance with them, are inevitably influenced by the relationships between these countries. If these relationships are conflictual or not always satisfactory, as was the case between France and England in the 1920s, compliance with the conditions imposed may be more easily disregarded by the debtor country.

5.9 Conclusions

As we have seen, in the monetary-fiscal approach that started with Cagan's (1956) paper, hyperinflation arises from public finance imbalances. The decision to finance these imbalances by exploiting seigniorage leads to a vicious circle: faced with the diminishing demand for money in real terms by individuals (who in this way seek to minimize the costs of the expected inflationary erosion of their monetary holdings) the government, if it wants to keep seigniorage revenues stable, must continually expand the money supply: an explosive inflationary process ensues. With this in mind, Sargent (1982) comes to the conclusion that monetary and fiscal measures which indicate regime change lower inflation expectations and stabilize the economy with low social and economic costs. Examination of the data, however, shows that, at least in the case of Germany, price stabilization did not so much result from spending cuts and tax increases as from the Olivera-Tanzi effect on the Reich's tax revenues. The increase in the latter, in fact, instead of preceding price stabilization, as Sargent's hypothesis would have it, followed it. In turn, the stabilization of prices rather than the effect on expectations of regime change seems to be attributable to the stabilization of the mark that occurred between November and December 1923. Evidence of this is to be found among other things in the fact that between the end of October and December 1923, the exchange rate of mark with respect to the US dollar rose by 166.7 times, wholesale prices by 177.7 times, and the cost of living by 325.4 times.

Price stabilization in Germany appears to be a case of ERBS. As is generally the case with this type of mechanism, in the periods immediately following stabilization, the German economy was characterized by an increase in consumer demand, output growth, the re-emergence of public finance imbalances, and large capital inflows from abroad. However, in the second part of 1925, the German economy started to

[121] In the debate on the transfer problem, Keynes (1929a, b) and Ohlin (1929) focused exclusively on the real effects of transfers for the payment of Reparations, neglecting the financial aspects of the problem.

slow down, as usually occurs in ERBS. This slowdown was due not only to the restrictive monetary and fiscal policies, but also to a restructuring of the economy.

In fact, hyperinflation had brought about structural changes in this economy, the reabsorption of which took time and entailed non-negligible adjustment costs. For example, between 1924 and 1925 the number of companies included in the national companies register fell by 14,000, or similarly the fact that 100,000 banking employees lost their jobs in the same period. Even in 1925, the number of bankruptcies remained high, as did the unemployment rate. Hyperinflation affected not only the aggregate structure of the German economy, but also the internal choices of enterprises and the behavior of individuals. The latter's propensity to save decreased significantly and the ability of the financial market to mobilize capital was profoundly affected. A compensatory function for these deficiencies was exercised by the particularly large capital inflows after the acceptance of the Dawes Plan. Thanks to these resources, the German government was able to increase public spending considerably, despite the absence of the Olivera-Tanzi effect on revenue and from 1925 to 1926 the Reich's budget balance turned negative again. The budget balance that had been associated with price stabilization was therefore short-lived in Germany, especially compared with countries where stabilization was managed by the League of Nations, such as Austria and Hungary.

Comparing the outcomes over time of these two types of stabilization leads to an appreciation of the role of the conditions applied to international lending. The Dawes Plan placed conditions on the management of monetary policy, but did not place them on the management of fiscal policy. It thereby gave foreign investors guarantees on the stability of the Reichsmark, but at the same time favored a form of overborrowing that allowed Germany to maintain public finance and current account imbalances.

References

Accominotti, O., & Eichengreen, B. (2016). The mother of all sudden stops: Capital flows and reversals in Europe, 1919-32. *Economic History Review, 69*, 469–492.

Aisen, A. (2004). *Money-based versus exchange-rate-based stabilization: Is there space for political opportunism?* IMF working paper n. WP/04/94.

Alesina, A. (1988). The end of large public debt. In F. Giavazzi & L. Spaventa (Eds.), *High public debt: The Italian experience*. Cambridge University Press.

Alesina, A., & Drazen, A. (1991). Why are stabilizations delayed? *American Economic Review, 81*, 1170–1188.

Berend, I. T., & Ranki, G. (1974). *Hungary: A century of economic development*. Barnes & Noble Books.

Berger, P. (2003). The league of nations and interwar Austria: Critical assessment of a partnership in economic reconstruction. In G. Bischof, A. Pelinka, & A. Lassner (Eds.), *The Dollfuss-Schuschnigg era in Austria: A reassessment*. Routledge.

Bessel, R. (1997). Germany from war to dictatorship. In M. Fulbrook (Ed.), *German history since 1800*. Arnold.

Block, T. H. (2002). Economic stagnation in Weimar Germany: A structuralist perspective. *Structural Change and Economic Dynamics, 13*, 127–150.
Bordo, M., & Rockoff, H. (1996). The gold standard as a 'good housekeeping seal of approval'. *Journal of Economic History, 56*, 389–428.
Borossi, E. A. (1994). *Inflation and industry in Hungary, 1918–1929*. Hande und Spener.
Bresciani-Turroni, C. (1937). *The economics of inflation: A study of currency depreciation in post-war Germany*. Allen & Unwin.
Cagan, P. (1956). The monetary dynamics of hyperinflation. In M. Friedman (Ed.), *Studies in the quantity theory of money*. Chicago University Press.
Calvo, G. A. (1986). Temporary stabilization: Predetermined exchange rates. *Journal of Political Economy, 94*, 1319–1329.
Calvo, G. A., & Végh, C. A. (1993). Exchange rate-based stabilization under imperfect credibility. In H. Frasch & A. Worgotter (Eds.), *Open economy macroeconomics*. Macmillan.
Carr, E. H. (1946). *The twenty years' crisis 1919–1939*. Macmillan.
Carr, E. H. (1947). *International relations between the two world wars 1919–1939*. Macmillan.
Clingan, C. E. (2000). The budget debate of 1926: A case study in Weimar democracy. *European History Quarterly, 30*, 33–48.
Confalonieri, A., & Gatti, F. (1986). La politica del debito pubblico in Italia (1919–1943). Laterza.
Costigliola, F. (1976). The United States and the reconstruction of Germany in 1920s. *Business History Review, 50*, 477–502.
Coyner, S. J. (1977). Class consciousness and consumption: The new middle class in the Weimar Republic. *Journal of Social History, 10*, 310–331.
De Bordes, J. (1924). *The Austrian crown*. P.S. King & Son.
De Gregorio, J., Guidotti, P. E., & Végh, C. A. (1998). Inflation stabilization and the consumption of durable goods. *Economic Journal, 108*, 105–131.
Diwan, I., & Rodrik, D. (1992). *External debt, adjustment, and burden sharing: A unified framework*. Princeton Studies in International Finance n. 73, November.
Dornbusch, R. (1982). Stabilization policies in developing countries. What have we learned? *World Development, 10*, 701–708.
Dornbusch, R. (1986). Inflation, exchange rates, and stabilization, Essays in International Finance, n. 165, Department of Economics, Princeton University, Princeton, NJ.
Dornbusch, R. (1987). Lessons from the German inflation experience of the 1920s. In R. Dornbusch, S. Fischer, & J. Bossons (Eds.), *Macroeconomics and finance: Essays in honor of Franco Modigliani*. MIT Press.
Dornbusch, R. (1994). *Post-communist monetary problems: Lessons from the end of the Austro-Hungarian empire*. ICS.
Dornbusch, R., & Fischer, S. (1986). Stopping hyperinflation past and present. *Weltwirtschaftliches Archiv., 122*, 1–47.
Drazen, A. (2002). Conditionality and ownership in IMF lending: A political economy approach. *IMF Staff Papers, 49*, 36–67.
Dreher, A. (2009). IMF conditionality: Theory and evidence. *Public Choice, 141*, 233–262.
Easterly, W. (1996). When is stabilization expansionary? Evidence from high inflation. *Economic Policy, 11*, 65–107.
Eulenburg, F. (1924). Die sozialen Wirkungen der Wahrungs-Verhältnisse. *Jahrbücher für Nationalökonomie und Statistik, 122*, 748–754.
Fefchamps, M. (1996). Sovereign debt, structural adjustment, and conditionality. *Journal of Development Economics, 50*, 313–335.
Feldman, G. D. (1993). *The great disorder: Politics, economics, and society in the German Inflation, 1914–1924*. Oxford University Press.
Fergusson, A. (1975). *When money dies: The nightmare of the Weimar collapse*. William Kimber.
Fischer, S., Sahay, R., & Végh, C. (2002). Modern hyper- and high inflations. *Journal of Economic Literature, 40*, 837–880.
Flink, S. (1930). *The German Reichsbank and economic Germany*. Harper & Brothers.

Franco, G. (1989). *Hyperinflations. The experience of the 1920s reconsidered*. Ph.D. Dissertation, Pontifical Catholic University of Rio de Janeiro.

Franco, G. (1990). Fiscal reforms and stabilization: Four hyperinflation cases examined. *Economic Journal, 100*, 176–187.

Gaertner, F. (1923). Die Stabilisierung der Österreichischen Krone. In M. Palyi (Ed.), *Geschichte der Stabilisierungsversuche*. Schriften des Vereins für Socialpolitik, vol. 165.

Garber, P. M. (1982). *Transition from inflation to price stability*. In "Carnegie-Rochester Conference on Public Policy", 16, p. 11–42.

Garber, P. M. & Spencer, M. G. (1994). The dissolution of the Austro-Hungarian Empire: Lessons for currency reforms, Essays in International Finance, n. 191, Department of Economics, Princeton University, Princeton, NJ.

Gordon, R. J. (1975). The demand for and supply of inflation. *Journal of Law and Economics, 18*, 807–836.

Graham, F. D. (1930). *Exchange, prices, and production in hyper-inflation: Germany, 1920–1923*. Princeton University Press.

Hahn, L. A. (1924). Zur Frage des sogenannten 'Vertrauens in die Währung'. *Archiv für Sozialwissenschaft und Sozialpolitik, 52*, 289–316.

Hardach, K. (1980). *The political economy of Germany in the 20th century*. University of California Press.

Harris, C. R. S. (1935). *Germany's foreign indebtedness*. Oxford University Press.

Heilperin, M.A. (1931). Le problème monétaire d'aprés-guerre et sa solution en Pologne, Autriche et en Tchécoslovaquie. .

Hertz-Eichenrode, D. (1982). *Wirtschaftskrise und Arbeitsbeschaffung: Konjunkturpolitik 1925/26 und die Grundlagen der Krisenpolitik Brünings*. Campus Verlag.

Holtfrerich, C. L. (1986). *The German inflation 1914–1923: Causes and effects in international perspective*. De Gruyter.

James, H. (1986). *The German slump, politics and economics, 1924–36*. Clarendon Press.

Kerschagl, R. (1929). *Die mitteleuropäischen Währungen und Notenbanken*. Spaeth and Linde.

Keynes, J. M. (1929a). The German transfer problem. *Economic Journal, 39*, 1–7.

Keynes, J. M. (1929b). Prof. Fisher discusses Reparations problems with John M. Keynes. *New York evening world*, 25 March 1929. Reprinted in E. Johnson & D. Moggridge (Eds.), *The collected writings of J.M. Keynes*. Macmillan, 1978.

Kiguel, M. A., & Liviatan, N. (1992). The business cycle associated with exchange-rate-based stabilization. *World Bank Economic Review, 6*, 279–305.

Kiguel, M. A., & Liviatan, N. (1994). Exchange-rate-based stabilizations in Argentina and Chile: A fresh look. In C. Cottarelli & T. J. T. Balino (Eds.), *Frameworks for monetary policy*. IMF.

Kindleberger, C. (1984). *A financial history of Western Europe*. Allen & Unwin.

Kuczynski, R. (1925). *Postwar labor conditions in Germany*. Bulletin of the US Bureau of Labor Statistics n. 380.

Kunz, A. (1982). Stand versus Klasse: Beamtenschaft und Gewerkschaften im Konflict un den Personalabbau 1923/24. *Geschichte und Gesellschaft, 8*, 55–86.

League of Nations (1922). *The reconstruction of Austria: Agreements signed at Geneva on October 4*. League of Nations.

League of Nations (1926a). *The financial reconstruction of Austria*. League of Nations.

League of Nations (1926b). *The financial reconstruction of Hungary*. League of Nations.

League of Nations (1929). *International statistical yearbook 1928*. League of Nations.

League of Nations (1930). *International statistical yearbook 1929*. League of Nations.

League of Nations (1931). *Memorandum on commercial banks, 1919–1929*. League of Nations.

Link, W. (1970). *Die amerikanische Stabilizierungspolitik in Deutschland, 1921–1932*. Verlag Droste.

Maier, C. S. (1975). *Recasting bourgeois Europe: Stabilization in France, Germany and in Italy in the decade after world war I*. Princeton University Press.

Maier, C. (1987). *In search of stability*. Cambridge University Press.

Marcus, N. (2012). *Credibility, confidence and capital: Austrian reconstruction and the collapse of global finance*. New York University Press.
Mazower, M. (2012). *Governing the world. The history of an idea*. Penguin.
McNeil, W. C. (1986). *American money and the Weimar Republic: Economics and politics on the eve of the great depression*. Columbia University Press.
Mommsen, H. (1989). *The rise and fall of Weimar democracy*. University of North Carolina Press.
Morelli, P., & Seghezza, E. (2014). Conflict inflation and delayed stabilization. *Journal of Macroeconomics, 39*, 171–184.
Morgan, S. (1931). Conditioning precedent to the settlement. *Proceedings of the Academy of Political Science, 14*, 5–16.
Moulton, H. G. (1929). Differences in Dawes and Young reparation plans, in "Current History", 30, p. 854–860.
Ohlin, B. (1929). The reparation problem: A discussion. *Economic Journal, 39,* 172-178 and 400-404.
Olson, M. (1975). Comment on R.J. Gordon's 'The demand for and supply of inflation'. *Journal of Law and Economics, 18*, 859–869.
Orde, A. (1990). *British policy and European reconstruction after the First World war*. Cambridge University Press.
Pasvolsky, L. (1928). *Economic nationalism of the Danubian states*. Macmillan.
Pauly, L. W. (1996). *The league of nations and the foreshadowing of the International Monetary Fund*. Princeton studies in International Finance n. 201.
Pittaluga, G. B., & Seghezza, E. (2012a). The role of rentiers in the stabilization processes of the twenties. *European Review of Economic History, 16*, 188–210.
Pittaluga, G. B., & Seghezza, E. (2012b). *La Grande Inflazione in Italia*. ECIG.
Rebelo, S., & Végh, C. A. (1995). Real effects of exchange rate-based stabilization. An analysis of competing theories. *NBER Macroeconomics Annual, 10*, 125–174.
Reinhart, C. M., & Vegh, C. A. (1995). Nominal interest rates, consumption booms, and lack of credibility: A quantitative examination. *Journal of Economic Development, 46*, 357–378.
Republic of Germany (1924). *Germany's economy, currency and finance*. Kriegslasten Kommission.
Ritschl, A. (1999). Les réparations Allemandes, 1920-1933. Une controverse revue par la théorie de jeux. *Economie Internationale, 78*, 129–154.
Ritschl, A. (2002). *Deutschlands Krise und Konjunktur, 1924–1934: Binnenkonjunktur, Auslandsverschuldung und Reparationsproblem zwischen Dawes-Plan und Transfersperre*. Akademie Verlag.
Ritschl, A. (2014). The German transfer problem, 1920-1933: A sovereign debt perspective? In A. Nutzenadel & C. Torp (Eds.), *Economic crises and global politics in the 20th century*. Routledge.
Robert, J. M. (1926). *Dépréciation de la monnaie et equilibre budgétaire: étude sur les finances allemandes, 1922–1923*. Les Presses Universitaires de France.
Roldos, J. E. (1995). Supply-side effects of disinflation. *IMF Staff Papers, 42*, 158–183.
Sachs, J. D. (1989). Conditionality, debt relief, and the developing country debt crisis. In J. Sachs (Ed.), *Developing country debt and economic performance*. University of Chicago Press.
Sachs, J. D. (1995). Comment on S. Rebelo & C.A. Vegh, real effects of exchange-rate-based stabilization: An analysis of competing theories. *NBER Macroeconomics Annual, 10*, 180–185.
Salter, J. A. (1926). The reconstruction of Hungary. *Foreign Affairs, 5*, 91–102.
Salter, J. A. (1961). *Memoirs of a public servant*. Faber & Faber.
Santaella, J. A. (1993). Stabilization programs and external enforcement: Experience from the 1920s. *IMF Staff Papers, 40*, 584–621.
Sargent, T. J. (1982). The ends of four big hyperinflations. In R. E. Hall (Ed.), *Inflation: Causes and effects*. University of Chicago Press.
Schacht, H. (1927). *The stabilization of the mark*. Allen and Unwin.
Schacht, H. (1967). *The magic of money*. Oldbourne.

Schuker, J. A. (1976). *The end of French predominance in Europe: The financial crisis and the adoption of the Dawes plan*. University of North Carolina.
Schuker, J. A. (1988). American 'reparations' to Germany, 1919-33: Implications for the Third-World debt crisis. Princeton Studies in International Finance, 61.
Seton-Watson, H. (1962). *Eastern Europe between the wars, 1918–1941*. Cambridge University Press.
Siklos, P. L. (1994). Interpreting a change in monetary regimes: A reappraisal of the first Hungarian hyperinflation and stabilization: 1921-28. In M. Bordo & F. Capie (Eds.), *Monetary regimes in transition*. Cambridge University Press.
Solimano, A. (1990). Inflation and the costs of stabilization: Historical and recent experiences and policy lessons. *The World Bank Research Observer, 5*, 167–185.
Statistisches Reichsamt. (1925). *Zahlen zur Geldenwertung in Deutschland 1914 bis 1923*.
Stiefel, D. (2008). The bankers' view: Austria's economic and political development and the role of banks. In G. D. Feldman & P. Hertner (Eds.), *Finance and modernization: A transnational and transcontinental perspective for the nineteenth and twentieth centuries*. Ashgate.
Stolper, G. (1967). *The German economy, 1870–1940, issues and trends*. Harcourt, Brace & World.
Thelwell, J. W. F. (1924). *Report on the economic and financial conditions of Germany, revised up to April I924*. U.K. Department of Overseas Trade.
Upmeier, G. (1973). Die Versuche einer 'endgültigen' Regelung des Finanzausgleichs. In K. H. Hansmeyer (Ed.), *Kommunale Finanzpolitik in der Weimarer Republik*. Verlag Kohlhammer.
Uribe, M. (1997). Exchange rate-based inflation stabilization. The initial real effects of credible plans. *Journal of Monetary Economics, 39*, 197–221.
Vegh, C. A. (1992). Stopping high inflation: An analytical overview. *IMF Staff Papers, 39*, 626–695.
Vreeland, J. R. (1999). *The IMF: Lender of last resort or scapegoat?* Yale University, Dept. of Political Science, Leitner working paper n. 1999-03.
Wagenführ, R. (1933). *Die Industriewirtschaft: Entwicklungstendenzen der deutschen und internationalen Industrieproduktion 1860 bis 1932*. Verlag Hobbing.
Weitz, E. (2007). *Weimar Germany: Promise and tragedy*. Princeton University Press.
Wicker, E. R. (1986). Terminating hyperinflation in the dismembered Hasburg monarchy. *American Economic Review, 76*, 350–364.
Young, J. P. (1925). *European currency and finance*. US Government Printing Office.
Zimmermann, C. (1927). La Société des Nations et l'assainissement financier de l'Autriche. *Arhiva Pentru Stiinta si Reforma Sociala, 6*, 241–254.
Zweig, S. ([1943], 1964). *The world of yesterday: An autobiography*. Viking Press. Reprinted in 1964 by University of Nebraska Press.

Chapter 6
Foreign Capital Inflows and Economic Stagnation in Weimar Germany

6.1 Introduction

In the period after its hyper-inflationary phase was stabilized, Weimar Germany was characterized by low output growth[1] and a high rate of unemployment.[2] This quasi-stagnation, which some have called "a crisis before the crisis,"[3] has largely been explained in terms that are almost exclusively economic and has been seen as due to a lack of investment.

The reasons why, in the second half of the 1920s, German industry was little inclined to invest has been the focus of the so-called "Borchardt debate," within which two opposing views can be identified.[4] Prior to this debate, the traditional Keynesian view had dominated, this attributed the low growth of the German economy in the 1920s to a lack of domestic demand. In particular, arguing that the demand for investment was low due to high domestic interest rates—these high rates being the result of the Reichsbank's need to defend the stability of the German currency and its convertibility into gold.[5]

This view started to be challenged from the 1970s onward, initially by Borchardt ([1979] 1991a)[6] and later by other scholars,[7] who saw the low German demand for industrial investment between 1925 and 1929 as being caused by wage increases that exceeded the growth in productivity, caused by the growth in the contractual power of the trade unions and political interference in the wage-setting process. They argue that this excessive growth of wages and the consequent fall in profits was what lay

[1] See among others Balderston (1993).

[2] See among others Dimsdale et al. (2006).

[3] See Petzina (1990).

[4] For a summary of this debate see Holtfrerich (1990a, b) and Borchardt (1990).

[5] See mainly Temin (1976), Falkus (1975), Holtfrerich (1986) and Hagemann (1984).

[6] See also Borchardt (1983, [1980] 1991b).

[7] See James (1986) Kruedener (1990) and Ritschl (1990).

G. B. Pittaluga, E. Seghezza, *An Economic Historiography of Germany, 1918-1931*, Frontiers in Economic History, https://doi.org/10.1007/978-3-031-70347-8_6

behind the unwillingness of industrial entrepreneurs to invest. This has given rise to some debate on the extent of the difference between productivity and wages of workers.[8]

The supply view supported by Borchardt and others has been the subject of a number of critical observations. Petzina (1990), for example, has objected that the contemporaries did not consider the second half of the Twenties as a period of crisis. Walter (1995) in a textbook of German economic history has denoted the years 1924–1929 as the "Golden Twenties." Voth (1995), instead, has argued that in Germany in the second half of the 1920s employment increased more than in the United Kingdom and the United States. On the basis of this evidence, he argues that the growth of German wages in that period was determined by demand for labor rather than by pressure from trade unions or the government's compliant economic policy, that the German industrial investment in the half of the 1920s was satisfactory and that the Borchardt debate was "much ado about nothing." Voth's thesis has been criticized, among others, by Spoerer (1994), who however shares with him the view on the dynamics of German investment between 1924 and 1929. In fact, Spoerer (1997), using data compiled by Gehrig (1961), calculated a time series for fixed investment that differs from Hoffmann et al. (1965), taken as a reference in the Borchardt debate. Recalculated in this way German investment in the second half of the 1920s as a percentage of GNP[9] seems in line with that of other advanced countries even if the growth of output in Germany was lower than in these countries.

In Spoerer's view, therefore, it was not low investment, but low productivity that held back Germany's growth between 1925 and 1929. This evidence shifts some terms of the Borchardt debate. The question to be asked, therefore, is not why the demand for investment in Germany in the second half of the 1920s was low, but why productivity was low.

In this chapter, we advance the hypothesis that the huge inflow of foreign capital into Germany after the Dawes Plan had negative effects on Germany's economic structure and growth. This plan, thanks in part to the greater seniority given to commercial loans than Reparations,[10] marked a renewed interest of American financial investors in Germany,[11] indeed, various studies have highlighted the fact that capital inflows from abroad determined the cycles of the German economy between 1925 and 1929.[12] Here, we intend to show that the availability of these financial resources coming from abroad allowed the political elite to maintain support for the regime by expanding public spending. However, it had effects on the German economy similar to a financial Dutch disease. In fact, the huge capital inflow made it possible to sustain high public spending and high domestic demand. This provoked an increase in prices of non-tradable goods more marked than those

---

[8] See Ritschl (1990, p. 398) and Balderston (1993, p. 55).

[9] Calculated by Hoffman and Muller (1959) instead of the more widely used Hoffmann et al. (1965).

[10] See Ritschl (2014).

[11] See Kindleberger (1984, p. 258).

[12] See among others Ritschl (1996, 1998, 2012) and Accominotti and Eichengreen (2016).

of tradable goods. Hence, between 1925 and 1929, there was a shift of capital and labor away from the sector exposed to international competition toward that of non-tradables. In this context, labor productivity growth in German industry and in the economy as a whole proved to be less marked than before the war and compared unfavorably with most other advanced countries.

If it is true that the Weimar Republic was able to survive so long thanks to the substantial foreign loans it enjoyed after the Dawes Plan, it is equally true that, as shown in the previous Chapter, because the Plan did not lay down conditions for the adoption of reforms, it neither incentivized nor supported the political elite in their efforts to adopt measures designed to stabilize the German economy. In short, it did not contribute in any way to solving the social conflict that afflicted the Weimar Republic and which threatened its survival.

6.2 Stabilization and Stagnation in the Weimar Republic

The years between 1924 and 1929 have been called by some the "golden years" of the Weimar Republic. These years, in fact, were characterized by satisfactory political stability, relative social peace, and a lively cultural life. From 1924 to 1928, Germany was governed by a succession of coalition cabinets based on the three bourgeois parties, the Center, the Democrats, and the People's Party, and in some cases tolerated by the SPD (Table 6.1).

In this same period, the number of strikes and lockouts was relatively low, especially when compared to that of the early 1920s: between 1920 and 1923 there were 20,506 strikes, while between 1924 and 1929 their number had fallen to 5375.[13]

However, when one considers Germany's economic growth in 1924 and compares it to its pre-war situation and to that of other industrialized countries at that time, one finds that it was, in fact, relatively weak[14] (Table 6.2).

Many academics have attributed the slow revival of the German economy in the period after World War One to poor growth in private investment.[15] According to the data from Hoffmann et al. (1965), between 1925 and 1929 the average ratio of net investment to GNP (Gross National Product) in Germany was only about 10–11% compared with about 13–16% in the period from 1910 to 1913.

For a long time, scholars, taking a Keynesian perspective, attributed the weak investment growth highlighted by Hofmann et al. primarily to the interest rate gap

---

[13] See Flora et al. (1987).

[14] Borchardt ([1980] 1991b).

[15] See, among others, Kroll (1958) and Temin (2008).

Table 6.1 German governments in the so-called "golden years" of the Weimar Republic (1924–1928)

Chancellor	Date of entry into office	USPD	SPD	Zentrum	DDP	DVP	BVP	DNVP	WP	NSDAP	% of Parliament seats
Marx	6/3/1924			X	R	R					29.2
Luther	1/15/1925			R	R	R	R	R			55.6
Luther	1/20/1926			R	R	R	R				34.7[a]
Marx	5/16/1926			X	R	R	R				34.7
Marx	1/29/1927			X		R	R	R			49.1
Müller	6/28/1928		X	R	R	R	R				61.3

Source: Notermans (2000). Note: X: Party of Prime Minister; R: Party represented in coalition. [a] Tolerated by SPD. Legenda: USPD, Unabhangige Szialdemokratische Partei Deutschlands (Independent Social Democratic Party); SPD, Szialdemokratische Partei Deutschlands (Social Democratic Party); Zentrumpartei (Center Party: a Catholic party); DDP, Deutsche Democratische Partei (German Democratic Party: a liberal-socialist party); DVP, Deutsche Volkspartei (German People's Party: a center-right party supporting right-liberalism); BVP, Bayerische Volkspartei (Bavarian People's Party: a conservative party based mainly in Bavaria); DNVP, Deutschnationale Volkspartei (German National People's Party: an authoritarian and radical right party); WP, Wirtschaftspartei (Business Party: a tough conservative party; NSDAP, Nationalsozialistische Deutsche Arbeiterpartei (National Socialist German Workers'Party: the Nazi party)

Table 6.2 An international comparison of the development of GNP (1913 = 100, 1913–1932)

	France	Germany	United Kingdom	United States
1913	100.0	100.0	100.0	100.0
1925	110.6	90.3	108.5	142.6
1929	130.6	106.2	122.8	164.5
1932	115.3	89.5	123.4	120.4

Source: Maddison (1962)

between Germany and other advanced countries:[16] in the second half of the 1920s, long-term interest rates were higher in Germany than in Britain and the United States.[17] In 1925, the spread of German long-term rates over British and American long-term rates was about 4% points. Although it decreased in the following years, it was still about 2.7% points in 1929.[18]

The high level of German interest rates led various scholars to believe that the ultimate reason for the low growth of the German economy was to be viewed in their negative effects on investment demand.[19] In turn, the low demand for investment negatively affected aggregate demand, leading to low growth in the economy.

Placing himself in this perspective, Holtfrerich (1990b, p. 80) writes: "... the primary cause of the Weimar economy's partly unsatisfactory performance even before the Great Depression was the high price of capital, with interest rates double the level of pre-war Germany."[20] With this in mind, Holtfrerich (1990b, p. 84) argues that the economic and social system of the Weimar Republic could have survived and, indeed, consolidated if the collective bargaining partners and government instead of quarrelling over the level of wages had reached an agreement for promoting capital formation. As Feldman (1992) notes, such an arrangement would have been wonderful. But there was not. Therefore, "... it is hard to see how Borchardt is refuted."[21]

[16]See Netzband and Widmaier (1964), Blaich (1977), Hertz-Eichenrode (1982) and Holtfrerich (1984).

[17]Several factors contributed to the high level of long-term interest rates in Germany after hyperinflation. One of these factors was the decline in the supply of domestic savings, which was largely due to the process of income redistribution to the detriment of rentiers, whose financial wealth in the years of high inflation was almost entirely destroyed. As Feldman (1993, p. 850) writes: "... inflationary memories and expectations served as a natural disincentive to saving" (see, also, James, 1990, p. 34; Feldman, 1993, p. 351–352). A second factor that contributed to keeping the German long-term interest rate high in the period was the fact that the memory of inflation led investors to demand a substantial risk-premium on German bond yields (see Ferguson, 2002).

[18]See Homer and Sylla (2005).

[19]This aspect is also highlighted by Schumpeter ([1927] 1985), Hagemann (1984) and Balderston (1983). However, James (1986) argues that the effects of tightening interest rates on the real sector are difficult to isolate.

[20]See also Diehl (1932).

[21]See also Balderston (1982, p. 490) and Schuker (1988, p. 31).

Starting in the late 1970s, the Keynesian explanation of Germany's low economic growth in the second half of the 1920s was challenged by Borchardt in a large series of writings.[22] According to Borchardt, the weakness of the German economy in those years was mainly due to two factors: real wages higher than labor productivity[23] and, therefore, a reduction in firms' profits. In this perspective, the low investment demand did not derive, as the Keynesians maintained, from a lack of aggregate demand, but from a recomposition of the latter in favor of consumption. Indeed, in the second half of the 1920s, while the investment ratio had remained substantially below the pre-war level, in 1928 private consumption exceeded the pre-war level by 16% and government consumption by 35%.

Between 1925 and 1929, the average export share on the net national product (at market prices) was of 14.9%; it was of 17.5% between 1910 and 1913.[24] In the second half of the 1920s exports no longer played the role they had done before the war and occasionally before hyperinflation.

Regarding the relative decline of exports, Keynes (1929a, b) writes: "For after all, what is the reason why Germany's exports are no larger than they are at the moment? It is certainly not that her export industries cannot get the necessary labor, for there is a surplus of labor in nearly all the leading export industries. Undoubtedly, the reason why she has no more exports is because her costs of production do not enable her manufacturers to compete on international markets on a large scale. She can only export more if she cuts down her costs of production, and it is roughly true to say that she can only cut down her costs of production materially if her wages are reduced."[25]

Therefore, in the second half of the 1920s economic growth in Germany was led by domestic demand. The high level of the latter implied a high domestic absorption and large and persistent trade balance and current account deficits (Table 6.3).

The recomposition of aggregate demand in favor of consumption, according to Borchardt, was due to a growth in real wages higher than that of labor productivity. Consequently, in the period 1925–1929 the unit labor cost in industry increased notably, undermining the international competitiveness of German products, causing a reduction in profit margins and a fall in investment.[26]

At the origin of the low growth of the German economy in the second half of the 1920s there was, therefore, the fact that the determination of wages had become a highly political issue. In fact, as in support of Borchardt's thesis, Kruedener (1990, p. XXIV) writes in those years: "... collective bargaining conflicts were more and more frequently solved by using the new institution of compulsory arbitration by the

[22] See, in particular, Borchardt ([1979] 1991a).

[23] This view is contested by Voth (1995) according to whom lower wages would have lowered investment still further.

[24] See Borchardt ([1983] 1991c, p. 123).

[25] See Keynes ([1929b], 1978, p. 316).

[26] Other scholars have given different explanations regarding the trend of investments in Germany in the second half of the 1920s. Balderston (1993), for example, believes that the demand for investment only declined from 1928 onward and that this was due to a correction by entrepreneurs of their overoptimistic expectations of the growth of the German economy.

Table 6.3 Germany's current account balance of payments, 1925–1929 (in millions of Reichsmarks, 1925–1931)

	Trade balance	Reparations	Interest and dividends	Other services	Current account balance	Net foreign capital inflows	Reichsbank's gold reserves and foreign exchange
1925	−2444	−1057	−6	462	−3045	3135	−90
1926	793	−1191	−173	532	−39	607	−568
1927	−2.96	−1584	−345	645	−4244	3792	452
1928	−1.311	−1990	−563	672	−3192	4123	−931
1929	−44	−2337	−800	712	−2469	2304	165
1930	1558	−1706	−1000	538	−601	490	120
1931	2778	−988	−1200	450	1040	−2693	1653

Source: Harris (1935). Legend: Outflows (−)

government. This was a disastrous development, because it transferred the determination of wages to the government and undermined important fundaments of the Weimar Republic."[27]

The gap between productivity and monetary wage growth highlighted by Borchardt and other scholars has, subsequently, been contested by other scholars, among them Holtfrerich (1984), who claimed that Borchardt understated productivity growth and overstated wages, by failing to consider that in 1918 the working day had been reduced from 10 to 8 h.

Ritschl (1990) showed some inconsistencies in the data used by Holtfrerich in his calculations, ultimately reiterating the existence of a gap between wage growth and productivity growth.

Borchardt's point of view was subsequently shared by other scholars. Kruedener (1985) observed that social insurance must be taken into account in calculating labor costs, as well as wages. The incidence of the latter on the gross wage payments rose from 2.5% in 1913 to 7.4% in 1925 and 10% in 1932.

James (1990) has underlined the fact that during Weimar's years of relative stability, investments were not only too few, but were also of bad quality: most of them were directed toward unproductive sectors, such as the food industry and textiles.

The Borchardt debate developed in the belief that the amount of investment in Germany in the second half of the 1920s was low compared to the pre-war period and to what happened in other countries. In a 1994 contribution, Voth (1994b) showed that using an appropriate measure for the expansion of the capital stock, no significant differences were found between the performance of investments during the Empire and the years 1925–1929.

Subsequently, Spoerer (1997), considering the investment data of Hoffmann et al. (1965)—used in the Borchardt debate—unreliable, carried out a recalculation of the

[27] See Borchardt ([1980] 1991b, p. 183). This argument was later taken up by Voth (1994a).

Table 6.4 Growth of real per capita output and gross fixed investment/output ratio of advanced countries (percentage values, respectively 1913–1928 and 1921–1930)

Variable	Germany	France	Japan	United Kingdom	United States
Growth of real per capita output:					
1928 vs. 1913	+7.7	+27.2	+43.7	+1.6	+23.9
Investment/output ratio:					
1901–1910	n.a.	10.4	11.0	7.4	15.7
1921–1930	11.5	12.1	13.9	6.4	12.7

Source: Spoerer (1997, Table 4)

investment data. On the basis of the economic series reported by Gehrig (1961) and Wagenführ (1933), he calculates that the ratio of investment on GNP in Germany in the 1920s was substantially in line with that of other industrialized countries, however, the growth of German output in the period was not (Table 6.4).[28]

From the recalculation of the investment data made by Spoerer, it emerges that in the 1920s the investment ratio is similar to other advanced countries. However, because the German output growth in this period was low, this evidence leads to the conclusion that in this period the productivity of investment in Weimar Germany was relatively low. Therefore, it was not the low investments that held back the German economy in the 1920s, but their low productivity.

This view does not imply that the Borchardt debate was, as Voth (1994b) argues, "much ado about nothing," but rather forces a shift in its focus, leading one to question the reasons for the low total factor productivity of the Weimar Republic economy.[29]

One explanation for this can be found in Bresciani-Turroni's (1937) observations on the tendency of many entrepreneurs in the inflationary phase to make investments that later turned out not to be very productive.[30] The "rationalization" process itself was, in many cases, an irrational pursuit of size. In many cases "... [r]ather than a general wave of technical advances and improvements there was simply a sectoral maldistribution of investment that created overcapacity in some basic heavy industry and in textiles."[31]

A second explanation for the low total factor productivity of the Weimar economy points, in particular, to the pronounced expansion of public investment characterized by low productivity.[32] However, a large share of public investment does not represent necessarily an indicator of low capital productivity.[33]

A third explanation highlights the misallocation of credit by German banks, who were (allegedly) induced by excessive domestic and foreign competition to lend to

[28] Similar conclusions are reached by Schremmer (1987) and Fremdling (1988).

[29] For a deep criticism of this point of view, see Spoerer (1994).

[30] On this aspect see also James (1986, p. 127–129).

[31] James (1986, p. 149). See also Lederer ([1932] 1979).

[32] See Spoerer (1997).

[33] Nevertheless, Borchardt (1990) believes this to be the case in the Weimar Republic in 1924–1929.

marginal and risky enterprises to the detriment of the efficient allocation of resources.[34] James (1990), instead, has argued that only a small fraction of German business investment came from profits, while most of it was financed by banks. This led these companies to prefer conservative investments.

More recently, Collet and Postel-Vinay (2021), taking up the hypothesis that the global financial cycle amplifies bank risk-taking[35] showed that German banks in the second half of the 1920s were encouraged to adopt risky lending policy by the large inflow of capital from abroad that occurred at the time.

Here, an alternative hypothesis to those just mentioned is put forward. In particular, it is hypothesized that the huge inflow of foreign capital into Germany after the approval of the Dawes Plan caused a form of Dutch disease. The German economy saw an appreciation of the Reichsmark in real terms and an increase in the ratio between the prices of non-tradables and tradables and in the ratio between the profits of companies in these two sectors, resulting in a reallocation of capital in favor of non-tradables. This reallocation was matched by a relative increase in labor productivity in non-tradables relative to tradables. Since labor productivity in non-tradables is normally lower than in tradables, the increased weight of the former in the German economy in the second half of the 1920s led to lower overall labor productivity growth.

6.3 The German Economy's Overborrowing After the Dawes Plan

The most notable effect of the Dawes Plan was the temporary withdrawal of Reparations from the battleground of politics, by linking the annuities to be paid to Germany's (supposed) ability to pay. The plan encouraged the restoration of confidence in the country and opened access to the international financial market.[36] Therefore, in the period following the signing of the Dawes Plan a series of factors, such as the high liquidity of international markets[37] and the higher seniority of commercial loans to Reparations,[38] led to a vast inflow of capital into Germany.[39] This huge inflow of capital had two beneficial effects on the German economy: on the one hand, it provided the resources for the country's economic recovery, and on the other hand, it allowed the government to finance the trade deficits that were

[34] See James (1986) and Wixforth (2003).

[35] On this aspect, see among others Borio (2012).

[36] See among others Morgan (1931, p. 7) and Carr (1947, p. 84).

[37] See Accominotti and Eichengreen (2016).

[38] See Ritschl (1999, 2002, 2014).

[39] In addition, with the aim of starting off the payment of the first annuity of the Reparations, a German External Loan was issued on the New York stock exchange for a total of 800 million gold marks or 190.4 million dollars.

Table 6.5 Weimar Germany balance of capital movements (millions of Reichsmarks, 1925–1929)

Instruments	1925	1926	1927	1928	1929
Long-term loans and bonds repurchased	+1124	+1376	+1210	+1268	+229
Short-term capital movements	+107	+147	+1779	+1335	+765
Indefinable capital movements	+1704	−916	+310	+1000	+879
Others	+200	–	+617	+606	+451
Balance of capital movements	+3135	+607	+3792	+4123	+2304

Source: Harris (1935)

associated with this recovery and the due Reparations without using domestic resources.[40] Thus, the large inflow of capital, at least in the short term, allowed Germany to enjoy relative social peace and temporarily consolidated the Republic.

Between 1924 and 1929, the net flow of resources from abroad from which Germany benefited amounted to 17,088 million marks, thus exceeding the sum of Reparations and interest accrued during the period by a total of 6586 million marks.[41] Initially, it consisted mainly of long-term financing. From 1927 onward, however, short-term financing became predominant (Table 6.5).

Both the private and the public sectors contributed to the issuance of a vast sum of long-term bonds on foreign markets[42] (Table 6.6). Within the public sector, the main contributors to the issuance of long-term bonds were central government and municipal authorities.

Most foreign loans to Germany came from American banks,[43] enticed by Germany's higher rates of interest and the perceived stability of the exchange rate of the Reichsmark. As Schuker (1988, p. 37) writes: "... on Wall Street and in financial centers across the land everyone wanted a piece of the action in German bonds. In particular, they wanted to hold assets in Reichsmark new entrants who, unlike long-standing houses like J.P. Morgan & Co., had little international experience and little reputation to protect."[44]

Seymour Parker Gilbert, the Agent General in charge of monitoring the implementation of the Dawes Plan, realized that Germany was not going to make any

[40] Tooze (2006, p. 6) writes: "Between October 1925 and the end of 1928 the inflow of foreign capital was so large that Germany could meet its Reparations payments without even having to earn a surplus on its trade account. This was convenient for the British and French since it enabled them to insist on German payments without having to open their markets to billions of goldmarks worth of goods."

[41] According to Feinstein and Watson (1995) between 1924 and 1929, the inflow of capital from abroad to Germany amounted to over 17 billion marks, or 4190 billion US dollars.

[42] The composition of foreign loans changed over time. In particular, from 1927 the share of short-term loans increased significantly. Corresponding to the fall in long-term issuing was a progressive increase in the short-term provision, especially by banks that in this way expanded their credit activity in currency. See Feldman (1993, p. 848).

[43] In May 1932, these banks accounted for more than 40% of foreign loans: to be precise, some 31% of short-term loans and 49% of long-term loans.

[44] On incentives of lenders to invest in German securities see Accominotti and Eichengreen (2016).

Table 6.6 German foreign long-term indebtedness by type of credit granted (in millions of Reichsmarks, February, 1932)

Type of debt	Reich, states, municipalities, and other public bodies	Credit banks and other German debtors	Industry, commerce, communications, agriculture, etc.	Total
Foreign currency bonds issued abroad	3484	1238	3202	7924
Mortgages	12	176	345	533
Long-term advances	29	322	1229	1580
Other long-term debt	–	279	164	443
Total	3525	2015	4940	10,480

Source: US State Department, NA RG59 862.51/3636, Memorandum from the Office of the Economic Advisor, May 1933

corrections to its fiscal imbalances by paying Reparations with foreign debt. Debts which, in the future would have prevented it from fulfilling its payment of Reparations. Aware of this, he sought to oppose the German government's massive recourse to large foreign loans proposing limits on these forms of financing of the German public sector.[45] Even the President of the Reichsbank Schacht was extremely concerned about the massive influx of capital from abroad. According to McNeil (1986), however, Schacht wanted to demonstrate that Germany was not able to deal with the Reparations by putting an end to foreign debt.

The pressure coming from Gilbert on the German authorities to exercise some control and impose limits on foreign loans to the public sector was ineffective for several reasons. First, the Reichsbank could not prevent non-residents from buying German securities. Second, a possible ban on public institutions issuing securities on the international market would have put more competition for domestic loans thereby crowding out private domestic borrowers. Last but not least, the government's imposition of a ban on peripheral institutions from financing themselves abroad would have altered the constitutionally prescribed equilibrium of power.

Gilbert's call to the US authorities to place limits on the purchase of German securities by American banks also proved ineffective. In fact, the American State Department and the President of the Federal Reserve Bank, Strong, after initially adopting a favorable response to Gilbert's requests, that took concrete form in 1927 with a ban on the banker Harris Forbes granting a loan to the state of Prussia, subsequently decided that, in the words of Strong, "... if dollar loans to Germany were to be stopped or checked it was only in Berlin."[46] This behavior was prompted not only by the American administration's concern not to interfere in Germany's

[45] See the Agent General's October 1927 Report.

[46] Quoted in McNeil (1986, p. 179).

Table 6.7 Government expenditure (in millions of Reichsmarks, current values, 1925–1929)

	Government expenditure and transfer			Surplus/deficit	
	Central Government	Public sector	Reparations	Central Government	Public sector
1925	5380	16,920	1080	−290	−520
1926	6120	19,130	1300	−780	−1910
1927	6550	21,930	1710	+10	−930
1928	6870	23,770	2160	+150	−640
1929	7790	26,050	1960	−770	−2230

Source: Ritschl (2014)

affairs, but also by pressure from many American banks, attracted by the large profits to be earned by purchasing German securities.[47]

6.4 Foreign Debt and High Domestic Absorption

The large capital inflows in the second half of the 1920s enabled Germany to keep domestic absorption high, even at times of large and persistent current account deficits.[48] In 1929, the demand for private consumption, expressed in real terms, was over 10% above its 1913 level, while national income was much lower than its pre-war level.

What contributed to the demand for private consumption was firstly workers' higher disposable income, due to the increase in their real wages, combined with the increase in their propensity to spend (or reluctance to save). The significant increase in domestic absorption was not only due to the dynamics of private consumption but also to the pronounced increase in public spending. Having access to large amounts of foreign finance enabled the Reich, the states and the municipalities to adopt a particularly accommodating fiscal policy. In this context, the growth of public expenditure, financed through foreign loans, was associated with substantial and persistent fiscal deficits (Table 6.7).

Within this expenditure, the German government privileged above all transfers and subsidies. Spending on this item, as a percentage of GNP, rose from 2.6 to 10.4 and 14.5 from 1913 to 1925 and 1929, respectively, and, in the same period, current expenditure on goods and services also registered a noticeable increase rising from 9.5 to 13.1 and to 13.9%.

[47] See Manzano and Rigobon (2007).

[48] As Harris (1935, p. 14) writes: "... Germany's foreign borrowings did much more than merely enable her to pay Reparations; they contributed directly to an enormous increase in the standard of living of her people." For an analysis of the effects of the inflow of foreign capital on the German business cycle, see Schmidt (1934).

What contributed most to the significant increase in public spending (on GNP) were central government and the municipalities. Social spending by the central government was not only designed to alleviate the deep-seated social wounds of the war by the provision of pensions to widows, orphans, and invalids but also, through a range of measures, to improve workers' standard of living. This was the goal of various laws passed immediately after the stabilization of the mark which sought to reconstruct and broaden the social insurance system with pension reforms and the introduction of unemployment insurance in 1927.[49]

A significant contribution to the increase in current spending came about thanks to the increased numbers of civil servants and the considerable increase in their salaries.

Regarding the municipalities, the loans obtained—not only on the domestic market but also on foreign ones—were used to improve transport, the supply of utilities, and housing but also to provide some "luxury" goods.[50] Indeed, "[t]he basic problem concerning the [German public] debts was that the loans were, to a great extent, not invested in productive facilities that could have produced the goods and increased the profits necessary to pay back the debt. They were used to enlarge the welfare state and boost public expenditure. They built sport arenas, parks or other recreational infrastructure, etc."[51]

While the high level of domestic demand created by this combination of public spending and private consumption encouraged a satisfactory level of production it also led to higher import than export growth. This resulted in persistent current account deficits in the second half of the 1920s, deficits which could be covered thanks to the large capital inflows from abroad. This even allowed the Reichsbank to increase its gold reserves despite large and persistent external account imbalances (Table 6.3).

Thanks to this accommodative fiscal policy, the government's efforts to maintain workers' income and improve their standard of living combined with the contractual weight of the trade unions, the share of labor in the total German national income between 1913 and 1929 rose from 45.3 to 56.6%.[52]

It was largely thanks to high government expenditure and high domestic demand that the intensity of social conflict, in the second part of the 1920s, was contained.[53]

However, maintaining a level of domestic absorption that was incompatible with a satisfactory balance of payments was only possible thanks to the country's large inflow of foreign capital and thus its increasing level of foreign debt. This

---

[49] Inflation led to a change in the coverage methods of the German social security system, the burden of which increasingly fell on the Reich budget. See Feldman (1986).

[50] See Bingham (2016). Lieberman (1998) criticizes the arguments used against municipal expenditures considering these arguments a confirmation of Peukert's (1987) thesis of Weimar's fate as a "crisis of classical modernity."

[51] See Bagus (2015, p. 167).

[52] See Holtfrerich (1986).

[53] See Herbert (2019, p. 181).

indebtedness not only exposed Germany to the risk of sudden stops, which would occur between 1929 and 1931,[54] but also had structural effects on the economy that are typical of overborrowing.[55]

6.5 Overborrowing and the Dutch Disease

The overborrowing that affected Germany in the second half of the 1920s can be likened to the processes of large capital inflows from abroad that often characterize emerging countries today[56] and tend to lead to changes in the economic structure of these countries through the so-called Dutch disease. The latter occurs when a resource boom reduces domestic incentives to produce tradable manufactured goods. The Dutch disease has been a widely accepted explanation of the deindustrialization process that occurred in several resource-rich developed countries in the 1970s and 1980s. In the 1990s, it was progressively supplanted by the "Resource Curse" theory[57] to explain the reasons why many resource-rich countries are characterized by weak economic growth.

In the literature on the resource curse and its causes, the Dutch disease is considered one of the various channels of the curse, together with other channels, such as high levels of corruption or the deterioration of the quality of institutions, which result in a low growth of the economy.[58] In reality, the Dutch disease view does not focus so much on the weak growth that characterizes some emerging and developing resource-rich countries, but rather on the structural changes that derive from a huge influx of resources from abroad. In this sense, it is more suitable than the resource curse for analyzing what happened in already industrialized countries following a resource boom.[59]

The term "Dutch disease" was first used by *The Economist* in 1977 to explain industrial decline after oil reserves discovery in the Netherlands in the 1960s, then in the United Kingdom, in Australia, and in many other countries.

---

[54] See among others Ho and Yeh (2019).

[55] For a comparison of two cases of over borrowing, that of Germany in the 1920s and Brazil in the 1980s, see Fraga (1986).

[56] See, among others, Calvo et al. (1996).

[57] See Auty (1993) and Sachs and Warner (1995).

[58] See Frankel (2010), Van der Ploeg (2011) and Sala-i-Martin and Subramanian (2012).

[59] For a survey of the literature on Dutch disease, see Mien and Gouion (2022).

The most relevant theoretical explanation of Dutch disease is represented by the model of Corden and Neary (1982).[60] This scheme has become the basis of numerous theoretical[61] and empirical works.[62]

The Corden and Neary model refers to a three-sector economy, namely a resource sector, a tradable manufacturing sector, and a non-tradable service sector. While the tradable sector is exposed to international competition and the price of goods in this sector is determined worldwide, the price of non-tradable goods and services is not exposed to international competition and depends on internal supply and demand.[63] The model shows that a resource boom affects the rest of the economy through two channels: the *spending effect* and the *resource movement effect.*

The *spending effect* is due to the fact that a resource boom leads to an increase in domestic income for the country as a result of which the demand for both tradable and non-tradable goods increases. Since the prices of tradables are set internationally and those of non-tradables are flexible, the price ratio (given by the ratio of non-tradable price to tradable price) rises. This results in an appreciation of the real exchange rate.[64]

The appreciation of the real exchange rate makes tradables less competitive, encouraging a shift of labor and capital from tradables to the non-tradable sector, where wages and profits are higher. This is the *resource movement effect.*

The Dutch disease effects illustrated above are typical of countries rich in raw materials, but are found in all cases where there are foreign inflows, whether they are due to resource booms, emigrant remittances, foreign aid, or simply investments by foreign financial institutions.

Taking into account what has been said so far, it seems plausible that the huge inflows of capital into Germany between 1924 and 1929 led to a form of Dutch disease in this country. This would explain the low productivity of investment and low output growth, despite a degree of accumulation similar to that of other advanced countries.

In order to test that the "crisis before the crisis" of the Weimar Republic was largely the result of a form of a financial Dutch disease we conducted a two-step empirical test. In the first step, we show the existence of the *spending effect*, in other words the effect that the inflow of capital brought about an appreciation of the Reichsmark in real terms. In the second step, we show that the real appreciation of the exchange rate caused a process of restructuring of the economy in favor of

[60] This model was the most important development in the Dutch disease literature of the early 1980s. In the context of this literature see Bruno and Sachs (1982), Corden (1984), Van Wijenbergen (1984), Aoki and Edwards (1983), and Paldam (1997).

[61] With reference to the most recent years see, among others, Behzadan et al. (2017) and Bahar and Santos (2018).

[62] For a survey on empirical contributions on Dutch disease see Magud and Sosa (2013).

[63] Furthermore, the model assumes that: (1) Labor and capital are perfectly mobile between sectors; (2) All goods are for consumption; (3) The trade balance is always in equilibrium; and (4) Factors are internationally immobile and their prices are flexible.

[64] See among others Agenor (1998).

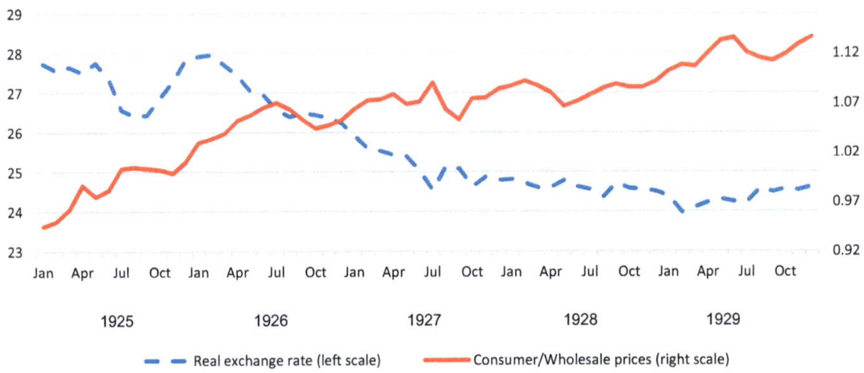

Fig. 6.1 Ratio of consumer prices to wholesale prices and real exchange rate of the Reichsmark (Jan.1925–Dec.1929) Source: Federal Reserve Bulletin, various months, and Holtfrerich (1986). Note: For the definition of the real exchange rate see footnote 32 of Chap. 3

non-tradable goods and to the disadvantage of tradables due to the *resource movement effect*, which helps explain the low investments' productivity in Germany in the second half of the 1920s.

In the next section, therefore, we proceed to the empirical verification of this hypothesis.

6.5.1 *The Spending Effect*

It has been said previously that in the case of Dutch disease the price ratio (i.e. the ratio of consumer prices to wholesale prices) increases. Between 1924 and 1929 in Germany, there was a higher increase in the prices of non-tradables than tradables. As shown by Fig. 6.1, this led to an increase in the price ratio of this country, associated with a real appreciation of the Reichsmark.

The different development of the relationship between the prices of non-tradables and tradables makes it possible to hypothesize that the overborrowing that occurred in Weimar Germany in the second half of the Twenties led to effects typical of Dutch disease in that country's economy.[65]

To verify the extent to which the vast inflow of capital from abroad, induced a rise in domestic absorption and contributed in this way to the appreciation of the real exchange rate, following the major empirical works on Dutch disease, we estimated the following equation:

[65] The literature on this hypothesis is extensive. The first contributions dating back to the first half of the 1980s (Corden & Neary, 1982; Van Wijenbergen, 1984; Aoki & Edwards, 1983). Developments of these studies can be found in subsequent papers, like Arellano et al. (2005).

$$RER = a_1 + a_2 INFLOW + a_3 MONEY + a_4 G\_SPENDING + u \qquad (6.1)$$

where RER is the logarithm of the Reichsmark/US dollar exchange rate in real terms.[66] All variables are considered in terms of their quarterly average in order to reduce their variability. In the initial estimate, the independent variables reported in Eq. (6.1) were considered in logarithms. Since INFLOW indicates the quantity of capital flows, it is to be expected that when inflows increase the real exchange rate appreciates, as a large empirical literature has shown with reference to developing countries.[67] An inflow of capital from abroad leads to an increase in available liquidity in the system, which drives an increase in domestic prices: the expected sign of this variable is thus negative. MONEY is the quantity of circulating notes and captures the monetary policy stance. Corresponding to an expansionary monetary policy we would expect to see an increase in domestic consumer prices: the expected value for this variable is negative. Also, an increase in G_SPENDING, which indicates the amount of public spending, implies an increase in domestic demand and thus an increase in the level of domestic prices; therefore, its expected sign is negative.

The data on the exchange rate Reichsmark/US dollar, consumer prices in the United States and Germany, Inflow, and on German money in circulation are taken from the Federal Reserve's Monthly Bulletin, while the data regarding public spending are taken from the Statistische Jahrbuch für das Deutsche Reich. The statistical characteristics of the variables are given in Table 6.17 of the Appendix. The time sample considered goes from January 1925 to December 1929.

Before proceeding to the econometric estimation of Eq. (6.1), the degree of integration of the variables was verified. Since, as emerges from Table 6.18 in the Appendix, there is a mixture of I(0) and I(1) variables, the ARDL methodology appears to be most suitable for estimating the determinants of the Reichsmark's real exchange rate. This model, put forward by Pesaran and Shin (1999) and later improved by Pesaran et al. (2001), has various advantages when carrying out the test we wish to conduct. Firstly, the ARDL model allows for an investigation of both short- and long-run relationships between variables at the same time. In addition, it makes it possible to analyze the relationship between variables that do not have the same degree of integration. This methodology makes it possible to mix variables I(0) and I(1) as regressors. Care need only be taken not to use I(2) variables in the estimates. Secondly, with ARDL the problem of the endogeneity of the variables is overcome since there is no residual correlation. Thirdly, compared to other methods, ARDL reduces the problem of sample size[68] and omitted variables. The results of the estimates of Eq. (6.1) for the period 1924.12–1929.12 with the model described above are shown in Table 6.8.

[66] Calculated as illustrated in footnote 32 of Chap. 3.

[67] Within this literature see among others Calvo et al. (1994) and Combes et al. (2011).

[68] See, among others, Nkoro and Uko (2016).

Table 6.8 Estimates of the Spending effect (Dec. 1924–Dec. 1929)

Variables	(1)	(2)
INFLOW	−0.071***	−0.054***
	(0.017)	(0.011)
MONEY	−0.223***	−0.142***
	(0.016)	(0.026)
G_SPENDING		−0.144***
		(0.044)
Constant	5.741***	6.019***
	(0.141)	(0.119)
Sample period: 1925.01–1929.12		
No. obs.	42	42
Bond test	5.563***	8.713***
ARDL lags	(1,6,6)	(2,6,4,6)

Legend: *** means rejection at 99%, ** rejection at 95%, * rejection at 10%. Stars in the bound test mean that the variables are co-integrated

From column (1), it emerges that MONEY is significant and has the expected sign. Equally, the variable G_SPENDING, in column (2), has the expected sign. From these estimates, it emerges that the real appreciation of the Reichsmark depended not only on expansionary monetary and fiscal policies, but also on the large inflows of capital (INFLOW) that occurred in Germany after the acceptance of the Dawes Plan.

In order to obtain confirmation of the results of Table 6.8 two different kinds of robustness checks were carried out. In the first of these tests, we considered the ratio of the independent variables of Eq. (6.1) on the Nominal National Product (NNP) instead of their logarithms.[69] The results of the estimates using these variables are shown in Table 6.9. Both Column (1) and Column (2) show that the variable INFLOW/NNP is significant and has a negative sign as expected.

A further robustness test was performed using the VAR methodology in order to ascertain which of the three variables used as independent variables in the estimates in columns (1) and (2) of Table 6.8 (therefore, considered in logarithms) has the greatest influence on the real exchange rate of the Reichsmark.

To this end, we first performed a Var Granger causality test on the first differences of the variables in Table 6.8. The result of this test, reported in Table 6.10, seems to indicate that the variables INFLOW and MONEY have a higher degree of exogeneity than the others. The real exchange rate, on the other hand, is the most endogenous variable of the system, significantly influenced by both MONEY and INFLOW, while G_SPENDING is significantly influenced only by INFLOW.

To determine the order of influence of the three independent variables on the Reichsmark's real exchange rate Table 6.11 presents breakdowns of the forecast error variance at one-quarter intervals for the period 1925.01–1929.12. Panels A–C

[69]The data on the National Nominal Product is taken from Ritschl's historical dataset.

Table 6.9 Estimates of the spending effect - Robustness check (Dec. 1924–Dec. 1929)

Variables	(1)	(2)
INFLOW/NNP	−1.966***	−2.731***
	(0.568)	(0.308)
MONEY/NNP	−1.794***	−1.656***
	(0.117)	(0.102)
G_SPENDING/NNP		−4.248***
		(1.098)
Constant	4.264***	4.424***
	(0.027)	(0.031)
Sample period: 1925.01–1929.12		
N. obs.	50	50
Bound test	5.400***	5.547***
ARDL order	(6,6,2)	(6,5,6,6))

Legend:*** means rejection at 99%, ** rejection at 95%, * rejection at 10%. Stars in the bound test mean that the variables are co-integrated

Table 6.10 Estimates of the Spending effect - VAR Granger Causality/Block Exogeneity Wald tests (Robustness check, Dec. 1924–Dec. 1929)

		Dependent variables			
Excluded variables		INFLOW	MONEY	G_SPENDING	RER
	INFLOW		2.498	7.864**	8.969**
	MONEY	0.184		1.850	8.747**
	G_SPENDING	0.468	3.094		1.339
	RER	2.219	2.037	4.332	
	ALL	3.161	7.038	13.568	17.774**

Legend: ***reject at 1%, **reject at 5%, *reject at 10%

present three orderings of the variables expressed in logarithms. When a variable is placed at the top of the variable ordering, a shock in this variable is expected to explain a larger part of real exchange rate forecast errors. In the panels, the capital inflow—INFLOW—corresponds to a larger proportion of the forecast error than the other two variables, MONEY and G_SPENDING. This is also confirmed by the average values of forecast error variance reported in panel D of the same Table.

From panels A–D shown in Table 6.11, it emerges that the variable that had most influence on the real exchange rate of the Reichsmark (in the period considered) was the inflow of foreign capital. This confirms the results presented in Table 6.8.

The appreciation in real terms of the Reichsmark, to which the inflow of capital from abroad contributed significantly, inevitably had negative effects on the competitiveness of German exports. The share of the latter in the national product at market prices, which had averaged 17.5% in the period 1910–1913, fell to an average of 14.9% in the period 1925–1929.[70]

[70] See Borchardt ([1983] 1991c, p. 123 and p. 175).

Table 6.11 Estimates of the Spending effect - Composition of forecast error variance for the Reichsmark's real exchange rate (Robustness check, Dec. 1924–Dec. 1929)

	Variance decomposition of			
Period	INFLOW	MONEY	G_SPENDING	RER
A—Var Ordering: INFLOW—MONEY -G_SPENDING-RER				
3	24.7	1.7	1.4	72.2
6	27.3	10.0	1.4	61.3
9	29.4	10.1	1.6	58.8
12	30.1	10.2	1.6	58.0
B—Var Ordering: MONEY—INFLOW -G_SPENDING-RER				
3	23.7	2.7	1.4	72.2
6	27.3	10.0	1.4	61.3
9	29.4	10.2	1.6	58.8
12	30.0	10.3	1.6	58.0
C—Var Ordering: G_SPENDING—INFLOW—MONEY—RER				
3	25.0	1.6	1.2	72.2
6	27.5	9.9	1.2	61.3
9	29.6	10.1	1.4	58.8
12	30.3	10.2	1.5	58.0
D—Var Ordering: Average				
3	24.4	2.0	1.4	72.2
6	27.4	10.0	1.3	61.3
9	29.5	10.1	1.6	58.8
12	30.2	10.2	1.6	58.0

6.5.2 The Resource Movement Effect

As already clarified, the increase in the ratio of consumer prices to wholesale prices shown in Fig. 6.1 indicates a stronger dynamic of prices of "non-tradables" to those of "tradables." This different price trend means that the demand for non-tradables has been particularly high.

Given this trend of the demand for non-tradables it is no wonder that in the period under consideration it was the companies operating in this latter sector that registered the highest profits between 1927 and 1929. Evidence of this, based on James (1986, p. 286–287), can be found in Table 6.12.[71]

Since, according to Balderston (1982), in 1925–1929, high-quality 10-year bonds had an average expected yield of 8.24%, German corporate profits were discouraging low. Only non-tradable companies, such as those operating in trade, finance, and construction, guaranteed returns close to those expected on high-quality 10-year bonds.

[71] Similar evidence is obtained from Sweezy's (1940) estimates according to which in the period between 1927 and 1929, the sectors that enjoyed significantly higher than average profits for all industries were those of "building, trades and materials," "water, gas, and electricity" and "banks, insurance companies and financial houses," that is the typically non-tradable sectors.

Table 6.12 Economic sectors net profit/loss as a proportion of capital (1927–1929)

	1927	1928	1929	Average 1927–1929
Tradables:				
Extractive industry	6.7	6.9	7.0	6.9
Manufacturing industry	8.1	7.0	4.0	6.4
Non-tradables:				
Water, gas, and electricity	7.1	7.2	6.5	6.9
Trade	8.3	8.8	8.0	8.1
Banks, insurance companies, and financial houses	8.7	8.8	8.0	8.5
Building	8.5	8.8	9.5	8.9
Total industry	7.5	7.1	6.8	7.1

Source: James (1986)

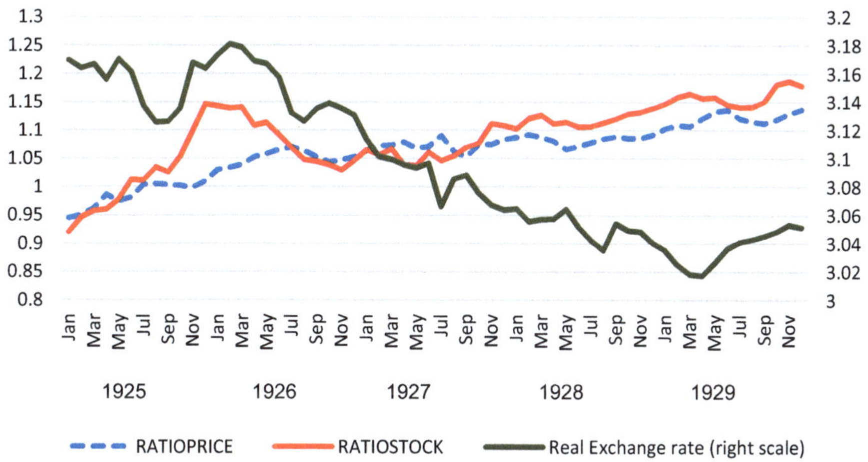

Fig. 6.2 Ratio of consumer prices to wholesale prices ($RATIO_{PRICE}$), ratio of stock price index of non-tradables on the general stock index ($RATIO_{STOCK}$), and real exchange rate of the Reichsmark (Jan 1925–Nov. 1929). Source: Federal Reserve Bulletin, various months, Holtfrerich (1986) and Statistisches Jahrbuch für das Deutsche Reich, several years. Note: For the definition of the real exchange rate see footnote 32 of Chap. 3

Similar indications can be obtained from the data on the profits of German companies in the late 1920s found in Sweezy (1940). They show that only four of the 26 sectors considered offered shareholders returns above 8.24% in 1926–1929. Essentially, all of these sectors produced non-tradable goods.

The higher profits of companies in non-tradable sectors were reflected in the price of their shares, whose index between 1925 and 1929 had a more pronounced dynamics than the general stock index, as shown by the ratio of the two indices in Fig. 6.2.

Taking this evidence into account, in order to verify if the appreciation of the real exchange rate was accompanied by a resource movement effect, we have estimated an equation in which the ratio between the index of non-tradable stock prices and the general stock price index ($RATIO_{STOCK}$) is regressed on the real exchange rate RER and control variables:

$$RATIO_{STOCK} = \alpha_0 + \alpha_1 RER + \alpha_2 controlvariables + z \quad (6.2)$$

where z is a random error normally distributed with zero mean and constant variance. We expect an appreciation (depreciation) of the real exchange rate to correspond to an increase (decrease) in $RATIO_{STOCK}$, i.e., to an increase in the ratio between the stock price index of non-tradables and the general stock price index.

Some control variables were then introduced. Among these variables, FAILURES, the logarithm of the number of bankruptcies of industrial companies, captures the degree of risk of purchasing and holding shares of companies in the tradable sector. It is plausible that an increase in these bankruptcies contributes to depressing the share price of tradable firms and favors, in this way, an increase in $RATIO_{STOCK}$. The variable $RATIO_{PRICE}$ is the ratio between the level of consumer prices and the level of producer prices. As stated above, we expect the sign of this variable in Eq. (6.2) to be positive. The descriptive statistics of the variables used are in Table 6.17 in the Appendix, while in Table 6.19 is shown the degree of integration of the variables.

As in the estimates of Eq. (6.1), the regression covers the period between January 1925 and December 1929. On the basis of the unit root tests all the variables are I(0) or I(1) and therefore, also in this case, the preferred methodology is the ARDL. The results are shown in Table 6.13.

Table 6.13 Estimates of the Resource movement effect (Jan. 1925–Dec. 1929)

Variables	(1)	(2)	(3)
RER	−0.173*** (0.044)	−0.178*** (0.054)	−0.230*** (0.041)
FAILURES	0.131*** (0.020)	0.084*** (0.021)	0.096*** (0.015)
$RATIO_{PRICE}$	0.803*** (0.109)		
G_SPENDING		0.181*** (0.021)	
GOLD			0.169*** (0.015)
Sample period: 1925.01–1929.12			
No. obs.	55	53	55
Bond test	7.507***	8.292***	8.424***
ARDL lags	(1,0,2,5)	(1,5,4,5)	(1,2,0,5)

Legend: *** means rejection at 99%, ** rejection at 95%, * rejection at 10%. Stars in the bound test mean that the variables are co-integrated

Table 6.14 Gross investment by sectors at current prices (millions of Reichsmarks, 1925–1929)

	1925	1926	1927	1928	1929
Agriculture	763	772	845	945	921
Industry	2183	1778	2248	2615	2013
Total tradables (a)	2946	2550	3093	3560	2934
Public utilities	757	855	727	1023	1083
Transport	1650	1709	2167	1931	1800
Construction	1712	1940	2622	2825	2877
Public sector	1859	2285	2690	2658	2670
Other	1388	1337	1667	1679	1422
Total non-tradable (b)	7366	8126	9873	10,116	9852
(a)/(b)	40.0	31.4	31.3	35.2	29.8

Source: Statistisches Jahrbuch fur das Deutsche Reich 1941/42, p. 610

Column (1) of this table shows that real exchange rate appreciations lead to an increase in $RATIO_{STOCK}$, that is, a positive change in the variation of the stock price index of non-tradables compared to the general stock index. The variables FAILURES and $RATIO_{PRICE}$ are also significant and have the expected sign.

In the robustness tests, the $RATIO_{PRICE}$ variable was initially replaced with G_SPENDING, the logarithm of the government expenditure, based on the assumption that its increase, being mainly due to the current account component, favors a higher domestic absorption and, therefore, an increase in expected profits and share prices of non-tradable sectors. Subsequently, G_SPENDING was replaced with GOLD, the logarithm of gold reserves, expressed in millions of Reichsmarks. An increase in gold reserves due to capital inflows—since they were used in large part to support public expenditure, which, given its composition, had a positive effect on the relative prices of non-tradables—leads to an increase of $RATIO_{STOCK}$.

The significance and negative sign of RER are confirmed in the robustness tests conducted in columns (2) and (3). The results in these columns also confirm the significance, in addition to FAILURES, of the variables used to replace $RATIO_{PRICE}$: all these variables have the expected sign.

The appreciation of the exchange rate in real terms in the years following 1926 favored an increase in stock prices of non-tradable firms and in their expected profits, hence discouraging industrial firms from investing.

In this context, the ratio of gross investment in tradable sectors (given by Agriculture and Industry) on that in non-tradable sectors decreased markedly, falling from 40.0% in 1925 to 29.8% in 1929 (Table 6.14).

A shift of invested capital from tradables to non-tradables simultaneously leads to an increase in labor productivity in the non-tradable sector. This favors an increase in wages in this sector. Between 1925 and 1929 in Germany wages increased by about 90% in non-tradable sectors, such as "Building" and "Woodworking" while wage

Table 6.15 Hourly wage rates (yearly average, 1924–1929)

	Building	Woodworking	Metal products	Textiles	Chemicals	Brewing	Hard coal
1924	100	100	100	100	100	100	100
1925	145	146	129	127	132	133	124
1926	160	159	140	134	141	144	134
1927	166	168	146	146	150	154	144
1928	178	186	160	161	163	171	150
1929	189	196	171	167	173	180	156

Source: Bry (1960)

increases were much less pronounced in the main tradable sectors, such as "Metal products," "Chemicals" and "Hard coal" (Table 6.15).

The different trends in wages in different sectors, particularly in the construction sector and in some tradable sectors, such as hard coal mining, show that they largely reflected the trend in demand. This is in partial contrast to the thesis supported by Borchardt ([1980] 1991b)[72] according to which wages were determined not on the basis of labor supply and demand, but on the basis of political reasons and, therefore, without any reference to labor productivity.[73]

Conveniently, Köhler (1983) argues that Borchardt overestimated the role of the Central Labor Council (Zentralarbeitsgemeinschaft) and the government in wage determination.[74] As argued by Weisbrod (1985), the influence of government compulsory arbitration only increased from mid-1927. In that year, the leading role of wages in non-tradables was reinforced by government policies. In fact, the Finance Minister Kohler proposed an increase of 33% of the salaries of civil servants of the Reich, a measure which was approved by the German parliament at the end of that year.[75] Similar requests for salary increases also came from employees of states and cities; demands for wage adjustments also came from employees in the private sector, in particular, those in the mining industry. The result was a reverse Balassa-Samuelson effect in which wage increases in non-tradables were translated into

[72] See also Petzina (1886, p. 43) and James (1986, p. 191 and ff). The latter, in particular, refers to the thesis supported by Hilferding in the SPD's Heidelberg Congress in 1925 according to which there was a "political wage."

[73] The importance of these reasons in determining wages in Germany in the second half of the 1920s is econometrically demonstrated by Dimsdale et al. (2006).

[74] See also Kruedener (1990).

[75] This measure, adopted in order to gain support for the Deutsche Volkspartei (the Minister's party) from the government's civil servants, had a knock-on effect.

increases in tradables, where the productivity of labor, because of the low industrial investments, had increased more slowly.[76]

The discrepancy in industry between wage growth and productivity growth is here traced, rather than to an intensification of the political conflict between industrialists and unions, to structural changes in the German economy due to Dutch disease. The social and political conflict between capital and labor intensified after wages in the industry were adjusted to those of non-tradables following government mediation.

Over the course of 1928, the industrialists of the Ruhr reacted to these requests with a series of lockouts. The social conflict that had been held in check in previous years regained intensity. In particular, industrialists, or at least those working in traditional sectors, showed that they no longer regarded the government as a third party in the distributive conflict which had always set them in opposition to the workers.[77]

The temporary wage gap between non-tradable and tradable sectors favored, as in the case of capital, a reallocation of labor in favor of the former[78] (Table 6.16).

The reallocation of capital and labor toward non-tradables, i.e., in the sector where productivity is structurally lower, explains why in the 1920s, despite investment being not far behind the other advanced countries, Germany had significantly lower output growth.[79]

[76] Evidence of this can be found in recent times in the case of emerging commodity exporting countries or in the Southern European countries joining the euro in the start-up phase of the EMU. See Belke et al. (2018) and Kyrkilis and Hazakis (2014).

[77] See Kershaw (1990, p. 21).

[78] Broadberry shows econometrically, against the Balderston's (1993) view, that between 1925 and 1929, the rise in employment was fastest in non-tradable sectors.

[79] The productivity trend in industrial investment seems to have been little affected by the "rationalization" process emphasized by industrialists in the mid-1920s. The rationalization processes, in fact, remained confined to certain industrial sectors (Homburg, 1991; Shearer, 1989, 1995), primarily mining and automotive. According to James (1986, p. 149): "Rationalization in retrospect turned out to be simply a vogue-word used to describe the mistaken investments made in the 1920s and should not lead to a conclusion that there was too much capital investment or too much investment in Weimar." A similar view can be found in Maier (1975). This is also why the effects of rationalization on the productivity of German industry as a whole were modest, as pointed out by Maier (1975) and James (1986). The best overview on rationalization of German industry is still Brady (1933).

Table 6.16 Employees for economic sectors (percentage share of the total, 1925–1929)

Year	Non-tradable sectors				Tradable sectors			Total
	Transports	Services	Housebuilding and public utilities	Sub-Total	Agriculture, fishing, and forest	Manufacturing and mining	Sub-total	
1925	4.7	23.6	5.6	34.0	31.5	34.5	66.0	100.0
1927	4.7	24.7	6.7	35.9	30.0	34.0	64.0	100.0
1929	4.8	25.7	6.8	37.4	29.2	33.4	62.6	100.0

Source: Hoffmann et al. (1965, Table 20)

6.6 Conclusions

Between 1925 and 1929, the German economy was characterized by relatively low output growth. This development was for a long time attributed to the modest demand for investment, explained from a Keynesian perspective by the high level of German interest rates.

This explanation was challenged in the late 1970s by Borchardt, who argued that the low investment in Germany in the second half of the 1920s was attributable to significantly higher wage growth than labor productivity growth and, thus, a consequent compression of profits due to both trade union pressure and the government's accommodative attitude. From this clash of views a broad debate, the so-called Borchardt debate, ensued.

Toward the end of the 1990s, however, Spoerer (1997) showed that, using a different time series from those taken as reference in the Borchardt debate, between 1925 and 1929, while the trend of German output was relatively weak compared to those of most advanced countries, the trend of German investment was broadly in line with those countries. In light of this, the question arises of why German investment was less productive than investment in the other advanced countries.

Several explanations have been put forward. While some scholars have asserted that in the phase of inflation and hyperinflation, industrialists made unfruitful investments, which then affected the efficiency of enterprises in the following years, others have emphasized the fact that between 1925 and 1929 public investment, often not very productive, was very high.

Here, the hypothesis was put forward that the large inflow of foreign capital that occurred after the Dawes Plan, while enabling Germany to keep domestic demand high, also had effects on the economy similar to those characterizing the Dutch disease. In fact, the increase in public spending and domestic demand led to a significant increase in consumer prices relative to wholesale prices. This increase implied more rapid changes in the prices of non-tradables compared to tradables, and it determined a real appreciation of the Reichsmark. The different dynamic of consumer and wholesale prices was reflected in companies' profits, higher in non-tradable sectors than in tradable ones. This encouraged a shift of capital from the tradables to the non-tradables.

This reallocation of capital led to an increase in labor productivity and wages in the non-tradable sectors, giving rise to a reallocation of workers in favor of this sector and to a reverse Balassa-Samuelson effect: in fact, the wages increase in non-tradables was followed by wages increase in tradables.

Two effects arose from the process just described. On the one hand, since the process of reallocation of labor was slower than that of capital, increases in wages exceeded those in productivity. On the other hand, the reallocation of labor in favor of non-tradables (i.e., sectors structurally characterized by lower labor productivity than tradables) caused a slowdown in the growth of labor productivity in Germany and, therefore, in the economy of this country.

Appendix Statistical Tables

Table 6.17 Descriptive statistics of the variables used in the estimates of Tables 6.8 and 6.9

	Mean	Median	Maximum	Minimum	Std. Dev.
RER (in log)	3.887	3.877	3.972	3.817	0.050
INFLOW (in log)	0.190	0.212	0.529	−0.134	0.179
MONEY (in log)	8.229	8.282	8.503	7.806	0.225
G-SPENDING (in log)	6.572	6.563	6.852	6.280	0.149
INFLOW/NNP	0.011	0.013	0.033	−0.037	0.012
MONEY/NNP	0.202	0.201	0.256	0.135	0.033
G-SPENDING/NNP	0.038	0.037	0.049	0.033	0.004
RATIO PRICE	1.062	1.071	1.136	0.945	0.047
RATIO STOCK	1.088	1.106	1.187	0.920	0.062

Table 6.18 Unit Root Tests of the variables used in the estimates of Tables 6.8 and 6.9

Augmented Dickey-Fuller	Intercept		Trend and Intercept	
	Level	First difference	Level	First difference
RER (in log)	−1.35	−4.72***	−2.94	−4.76***
INFLOW (in log)	−2.81*	−5.55***	−2.82	−5.52***
MONEY (in log)	−4.00***	−6.07***	−2.29	−6.43***
G-SPENDING (in log)	−0.98	−5.22***	−4.17***	−5.16***
INFLOW/NNP	−3.92***	−10.19***	−4.15***	−10.09***
MONEY/NNP	−1.59	−5.79***	−2.43	−5.79***
G-SPENDING/NNP	−2.65*	−4.29***	−4.57***	−6.66***

Legend: The number of lags has been chosen according to the Schwarz Information Criterion. The null hypothesis is that the variable has a unit root. ***reject at 1%, **reject at 5%, *reject at 10%

Table 6.19 Unit Root Tests of the variables used in the estimates of Table 6.13

Augmented Dickey-Fuller	Intercept		Trend and Intercept	
	Level	First difference	Level	First difference
$RATIO_{STOCK}$	−1.34	−7.55***	−2.62	−7.52***
GOLD (in log)	−3.06**	−4.93***	−2.82	−3.69**
FAILURES (in log)	−3.08**	−3.80***	−3.77**	−2.38
$RATIO_{PRICE}$	−2.14	−5.23***	−2.92	−5.36***

Legend: The number of lags has been chosen according to the Schwarz Information Criterion. The null hypothesis is that the variable has a unit root. ***reject at 1%, **reject at 5%, *reject at 10%

References

Accominotti, O., & Eichengreen, B. (2016). The mother of all sudden stops: Capital flows and reversals in Europe, 1919-32. *Economic History Review, 69*, 469–492.

Agenor, P. R. (1998). Capital inflows external shocks, and the real exchange rate. *Journal of International Money and Finance, 17*, 713–740.

Aoki, M., & Edwards, S. (1983). Oil export boom and Dutch disease: A dynamic analysis. *Resources and Energy, 5*, 219–242.

Arellano, C., Bulir, A., Lane, T., & Lipschitz, L. (2005). *The dynamic implications of foreign aid and its variability*. IMF working paper n. WP/05/119.

Auty, R. (1993). *Sustaining development in mineral economies: The resource curse thesis*. Routledge.

Bagus, P. (2015). *In defense of deflation*. Springer.

Bahar, D., & Santos, M. (2018). One more resource curse: Dutch disease and export concentration. *Journal of Development Economics, 132*, 102–114.

Balderston, T. (1982). The origins of economic instability in Germany 1924-30: Market forces versus economic policy. *Vierteljahrschrif für Sozial-und Wirtschaftsgeschichte, 69*, 488–514.

Balderston, T. (1983). The beginning of the depression in Germany 1924-30: Investment and the capital market. *Economic History Review, 36*, 395–415.

Balderston, T. (1993). *The origins and course of the German economic crisis: November 1923 to May 1932*. Haude & Spener.

Behzadan, N., Chisik, R., Onder, H., & Battaile, B. (2017). Does inequality drive the Dutch disease? Theory and evidence. *Journal of International Economics, 106*, 104–118.

Belke, A., Haskamp, U., & Schnabl, G. (2018). Beyond Balassa and Samuelson: Real convergence, capital flows, and competitiveness in Greece. *Empirica, 45*, 409–424.

Bingham, J. (2016). *Weimar cities: The challenge of urban modernity in Germany, 1913–1933*. Routledge.

Blaich, F. (1977). Die Wirtschaftscise 1925/26 und die Reichsregierung. *Von der Erwerblosenfürsorge zur Konjunkurpolitik*. Lassleben.

Borchardt, K. (1983). Die deutsche Katastrophe, Wirtschaftshistorische Anmerkungen zum 30 Januar 1933. *Frankfurter Allgemeine Zeitung*, January, 29.

Borchardt, K. (1990). A decade of debate about Brüning's economic policy. In J. B. von Kruedener (Ed.), *Economic crisis and political collapse. The Weimar Republic 1924–1933*. St. Martin's Press.

Borchardt, K. ([1979], 1991a). Constraints and room for manoeuvre in the Great Depression of the early Thirties: towards a revision of the received historical picture. In K. Borchardt (Ed.), *Perspectives on Modern German Economic History and Policy*, Cambridge University Press. English translation from K. Borchardt (1979), Zwanglagen un Handlungsspielr*ä*ume in der *großen* Wirtschaftskrise der frühen drei*ß*iger Jahre: zur Revision des *ü*berlieferten Geschichtsbildes. *Jahrbuch der Bayerischen Akademie der Wissenschaften, 72*, 85–132. Reprinted in 1982 in K. Borchardt (Ed.), *Wachstum, Krisen, und Hundlungsspielräume der Wirrschuftspolitik*". Vandenhoeck & Ruprecht.

Borchardt, K. ([1980], 1991b). The economic causes of the collapse of the Weimar Republic. In K. Borchardt (Ed.), *Perspectives on Modern German Economic History and Policy*, Cambridge University Press. English translation from K. Borchardt (1980), Wirtschaftliche Ursachen des Scheiterns der Weimarer Republik, in K.D. Erdmann, & H. Schulze (Eds.), *Weimar, Selbstpreisgabe eimer Demokratie. Eine Bilanz heute*, Droste. Reprinted in 1982 in K. Borchardt (Ed.), *Wachstum, Krisen, und Hundlungsspielräume der Wirtschaftspolitik*. Vandenhoeck & Ruprecht.

Borchardt, K. ([1983], 1991c). The Federal Republic of Germany in the secular trend of economic development. In K. Borchardt (Ed.), *Perspectives on Modern German Economic History and Policy*. Cambridge University Press. English translation from K. Borchardt (1983), Die Bundesrepublik Deutschland in den Säkularen Trends der wirtschaftlichen Entwicklung, in

W. Conze & M.R. Lepsius (Eds.), *Sozialgeschichte der Bundesrepublik Deutschland*, Kiett-Cotta. Printed in 1982 in K. Borchardt, (Ed.), *Wachstum, Krisen, und Handlungsspielräume der Wirrschuftspolitik*, Vandenhoeck and Ruprecht.

Borio, C. (2012). *The financial cycle and macroeconomics: What have we learnt?* Bank of International Settlements working paper n. 395.

Brady, R. A. (1933). *The rationalization movement in German industry: A study in the evolution of economic planning*. University of California Press.

Bresciani-Turroni, C. (1937). *The economics of inflation: A study of currency depreciation in post-war Germany*. Allen & Unwin.

Broadberry, S. N., & Ritschl, A. (1994). The iron twenties: Real wages, productivity in Britain and Germany before the great depression. In C. Buchheim, M. Hutter, & H. James (Eds.), *Zerrissene Zwischenkriedszeit: wirtschaftshistorische Beiträge. Knut Borchardt zum 65 Geburstag*. Nomos Verlag.

Bruno, M., & Sachs, J. (1982). Energy and resource allocation: A dynamic model of the 'Dutch disease'. *Review of Economic Studies, 49*, 845–859.

Bry, G. (1960). *Wages in Germany 1871–1945*. Princeton University Press.

Calvo, G. A., Leiderman, L., & Reinhart, C. M. (1994). Capital inflows and real exchange rate appreciation in Latin America: The role of external factors. *Contemporary Economic Policy, 12*, 54–66.

Calvo, G. A., Leiderman, L., & Reinhart, C. M. (1996). Inflows of capital in developing countries in the 1990s. *Journal of Economic Perspectives, 10*, 123–139.

Carr, E. H. (1947). *International relations between the two world wars 1919–1939*. Macmillan.

Collet, S., & Postel-Vinay, N. (2021). *Hot money inflows and bank risk-taking: Germany from the 1920s to the great depression*. CEPR Discussion paper n. 16606.

Combes, J. L., Kinda, T., & Plane, P. (2011). *Capital flows, exchange rate flexibility, and the real exchange rate*. IMF working paper n. WP/11/9.

Corden, W. M. (1984). Booming sector and Dutch disease economics: Survey and consolidation. *Oxford Economic Papers, 36*, 359–380.

Corden, W. M., & Neary, J. P. (1982). Booming sector and de-industrialization in a small open economy. *Economic Journal, 92*, 825–848.

Diehl, K. (1932). *Wirkungen und Ursachen des Hohen Zinfusses in Deutschland*. Fischer.

Dimsdale, N. H., Horsewood, N., & van Riel, A. (2006). Unemployment in interwar Germany: An analysis of the labor market, 1927-1936. *Journal of Economic History, 66*, 778–808.

Falkus, M. E. (1975). The German business cycle in the 1920s. *Economic History Review, 28*, 451–465.

Feinstein, C. H., & Watson, K. (1995). Private international capital flows in Europe in the inter-war. In C. H. Feinstein (Ed.), *Banking, currency, and finance in Europe between the wars*. Clarendon Press.

Feldman, G. D. (1986). The fate of the social insurance system in the German inflation, 1914-1923. In G. D. Feldman, C. L. Holtfrerich, G. A. Ritter, & P. C. Witt (Eds.), *The adaptation to inflation*. De Gruyter.

Feldman, G. D. (1992). Industrialists, bankers, and the problem of unemployment in the Weimar Republic. *Central European History, 25*, 76–96.

Feldman, G. D. (1993). *The great disorder: Politics, economics, and society in the German Inflation, 1914–1924*. Oxford University Press.

Ferguson, N. (2002). Public debt as a postwar problem: The German experience after 1918 in comparative perspective. In C. Levy & M. Roseman (Eds.), *Three postwar eras in comparison*. Palgrave.

Flora, P., Alber, J., Eichenberg, R., Kohl, J., Kraus, F., Pfenning, W., & Seebohm, K. (1987). *State, economy, and society in Western Europe 1815–1975*. Macmillan.

Fraga, A. (1986). *German Reparations and Brazilian debt: A comparative study*. Princeton University Dept. of Economics, International Finance Section, Essays in International Finance, n. 163.

Frankel, J. (2010). *The natural resource curse: A survey*. NBER working paper n. 15836.
Fremdling, R. (1988). German national accounts for the 19th and early 20th century. A critical assessment. *Vierteljahr Schrift für Sozial-und Wirtschaftsgeschichte, 75*, 339–357.
Gehrig, G. (1961). Eine Zeitreihe für den Sachkapitalbestand (1925 bis 1938 und 1950 bis 1957). *Ifo-Studien, 7*, 7–60.
Hagemann, H. (1984). Lohnsenkungen als Mittel der Krisenbekämpfung? Überlegungen zum Beitrag der 'Kieler Schule' in der beschäftigungspolitischen Diskussion am Ende der Weimarer Republic. In H. Hagemann & H. D. Kurz (Eds.), *Beschäftigung, Verteilung und Konjunktur*. Fetschrift Adolph Lowe.
Harris, C. R. S. (1935). *Germany's foreign indebtedness*. Oxford University Press.
Herbert, U. (2019). *A history of the twentieth-century Germany*. Oxford University Press.
Hertz-Eichenrode, D. (1982). *Wirtschaftskrise und Arbeitsbeschaffung: Konjunkturpolitik 1925/26 und die Grundlagen der Krisenpolitik Brünings*. Campus Verlag.
Ho, T., & Yeh, K. (2019). Were capital flows the culprit in the Weimar economic crisis? *Explorations in Economic History, 74*, 17–29.
Hoffman, W. G., & Müller, J. H. (1959). *Das deutsche Volkseinkommen 1851–1957*. Mohr Verlag.
Hoffmann, W. G., Grumbach, F., & Hesse, H. (1965). *Das Wachstum der deutschen Wirtschaft seit der Mitte des 19. Jahrhunderts*. Springer Verlag.
Holtfrerich, C. L. (1984). Zu hohe Löhne in der Weimarer Republik? *Geschichte und Gesellschaft, 10*, 122–141.
Holtfrerich, C. L. (1986). *The German inflation 1914–1923: Causes and effects in international perspective*. De Gruyter.
Holtfrerich, C. L. (1990a). Was the policy of deflation in Germany unavoidable? In J. V. von Kruedener (Ed.), *Economic crisis and the political collapse. The Weimar Republic 1924–33*. Berg Publishers.
Holtfrerich, C. L. (1990b). Economic policy options and the end of the Weimar Republic. In I. Kershaw (Ed.), *Weimar: Why did German democracy fail?* St. Martin's Press.
Homburg, H. (1991). *Rationalisierung und Industriearbeit: Arbeiterschaft in Siemens-Konzern Berlin, 1900–1939*. Haude & Spener.
Homer, S., & Sylla, R. (2005). *A history of interest rates*. Wiley.
James, H. (1986). *The German slump, politics and economics, 1924–36*. Clarendon Press.
James, H. (1990). Economic reasons for the collapse of the Weimar republic. In I. Kershaw (Ed.), *Weimar: Why did German democracy fail?* St. Martin's Press.
Kershaw, I. (1990). Perspectives of Weimar's failure. In I. Kershaw (Ed.), *Weimar: Why did German democracy fail?* Martin's Press.
Keynes, J. M. (1929a). The German transfer problem. *Economic Journal, 39*, 1–7.
Keynes, J. M. (1929b). Prof. Fisher discusses Reparations problems with John M. Keynes. *New York evening world*, 25 March 1929. Reprinted in E. Johnson & D. Moggridge (Eds.), *The collected writings of J.M. Keynes*. Macmillan, 1978.
Kindleberger, C. (1984). *A financial history of Western Europe*. Allen & Unwin.
Köhler, H. (1983). Knut Borchardts 'Revision des überlieferten Geschichtsbildes' der Wirtschaftspolitik in der Grossen Krise – eine Zwangsvorstellung? *Internationale Wissenschaftliche Korrespondenz zur Gschichte der deutschen Arbeiterbewegung, 19*, 164–180.
Kroll, G. (1958). *Von der Weltwirtschaftskrise zur Staatskonjunktur*. Verlag Duncker & Humblot.
Kyrkilis, D., & Hazakis, K. (2014). *The impact of economic adjustment programs on Greek competitiveness*. Paper presented at the conference "Greek economy: From crisis to development", University of Thessaly, Volos, 4-5 April.
Lederer, E. (1979). Die Weltwirtschaftskrise - Eine Krise des Kapitalismus: Ursachen und Auswege (1932). In E. Lederer (Ed.), *Kapitalismus, Klassenstruktur und Probleme der Demokratie in Deutschland 1910–1940*. Vandenhoeck & Ruprecht.
Lieberman, B. (1998). *From recovery to catastrophe: Municipal stabilization and political crisis in Weimar Germany*. Berghahn Books.

Maddison, A. (1962). Growth and fluctuation in the world economy, 1870-1960. *Banca Nazionale del Lavoro Quarterly Review, 15*, 127–195.
Magud, N., & Sosa, S. (2013). When and why worry about real exchange rate appreciation? *Journal of International Commerce, Economics and Policy, 4*, 1–27.
Maier, C. S. (1975). *Recasting bourgeois Europe: Stabilization in France, Germany and in Italy in the decade after world war I*. Princeton University Press.
Manzano, O., & Rigobon, R. (2007). Resource curse or debt overhang. In D. Lederman & W. F. Maloney (Eds.), *Natural resources: Neither curse nor destiny*. Stanford University Press.
McNeil, W. C. (1986). *American money and the Weimar Republic: Economics and politics on the eve of the great depression*. Columbia University Press.
Mien, E., & Gouion, M. (2022). 40 years of Dutch disease literature: Lessons for developing countries. *Comparative Economic Studies, 64*, 351–383.
Morgan, S. (1931). Conditioning precedent to the settlement. *Proceedings of the Academy of Political Science, 14*, 5–16.
Netzband, K. B., & Widmaier, H. P. (1964). *Währungs – und Finanzpolitik der Ära Luther 1923–25*. Verlag Kyklos-Mohr.
Nkoro, E., & Uko, A. K. (2016). Autoregressive distributed lag (ARDL) cointegration technique: Application and interpretation. *Journal of Statistical and Econometric Methods, 5*, 63–91.
Notermans, T. (2000). *Money, markets and the state*. Cambridge University Press.
Paldam, M. (1997). Dutch disease and rent seeking: The Greenland model. *European Journal of Political Economy, 13*, 591–614.
Pesaran, M. A., & Shin, Y. (1999). An autoregressive distributed lag modelling approach to cointegration analysis. In S. Strom (Ed.), *Econometrics and economic theory in the 20th century: The Ragnar Frisch centennial symposium*. Cambridge University Press.
Pesaran, M. H., Shin, Y., & Smith, R. J. (2001). Bound testing approaches to the analysis of level relationships. *Journal of Applied Econometrics, 16*, 289–326.
Petzina, D. (1886). The extent and causes of unemployment in the Weimar Republic. In P. D. Stachura (Ed.), *Unemployment and the great depression in Weimar Germany*. Palgrave.
Petzina, D. (1990). Was there a crisis before the crisis? The state of the German economy in the 1920s. In J. B. von Kruedener (Ed.), *Economic crisis and political collapse: The Weimar Republic 1924–1933*. St. Martin's Press.
Peukert, D. J. (1987). *The Weimar Republic: The crisis of classical modernity*. Hill & Wang.
Ritschl, A. (1990). Zu Hohe Löhne in der Weimarer Republik? Eine Auseinandersetzung mit Holtfrerichs Berechnungen zur Lohnposition der Arbeiterschaft 1925-1932. *Geschichte und Gesellschaft, 16*, 375–402.
Ritschl, A. (1996). *Was Schacht right? Reparations, the Young plan and the great depression in Germany*. Available on line at https://personal.lse.ac.uk/ritschl/pdf_files/schacht2.pdf
Ritschl, A. (1998). Reparations transfers, the Borchardt hypothesis and the great depression in Germany, 1929–32: A guided tour for hard-headed Keynesians. *European Review of Economic History, 2*, 49–72.
Ritschl, A. (1999). Les Réparations Allemandes, 1920-1933. Une controverse revue par la théorie de jeux. *Economie Internationale, 78*, 129–154.
Ritschl, A. (2002). *Deutschlands Krise und Konjunktur, 1924–1934: Binnenkonjunktur, Auslandsverschuldung und Reparationsproblem zwischen Dawes-Plan und Transfersperre*. Akademie Verlag.
Ritschl, A. (2014). The German transfer problem, 1920-1933: A sovereign debt perspective? In A. Nutzenadel & C. Torp (Eds.), *Economic crises and global politics in the 20th century*. Routledge.
Sachs, J., & Warner, A. (1995). *Natural resource abundance and economic growth*. NBER working paper n. 5398.
Sala-i-Martin, X., & Subramanian, A. (2012). Addressing the natural resource curse: An illustration from Nigeria. *Journal of African Economies, 22*, 570–615.
Schmidt, C. T. (1934). *German business cycles, 1924–1933*. NBER.

Schremmer, E. (1987). Die badische Gewerbesteuer und die Kapitalbildung in gewerblichen Anlagen und Vorräten in Baden und in Deutschland, 1815 bis 1913. *Viertljahrschrift für Sozial-und Wirtschaftsgeschichte, 74*, 18–61.

Schuker, J. A. (1988). American 'reparations' to Germany, 1919-33: Implications for the Third-World debt crisis. Princeton Studies in International Finance, 61.

Schumpeter, J. A. ([1927]1985). *Aufsätze zur Wirtschaftspolitik*. Mohr Verlag.

Shearer, J. R. (1989). *The politics of industrial efficiency in the Weimar Republic: Technological innovation, economic efficiency and their social consequences in the Ruhr coal mining industry, 1918–1929*. Ph. D. diss., University of Pennsylvania.

Shearer, J. R. (1995). Talking about efficiency: Politics and the industrial rationalization movement in the Weimar Republic. *Central European History, 28*, 483–506.

Spoerer, M. (1994). German net investment and the cumulative real wage position 1925-1929. On a premature burial of the Borchardt debate. *Historical Social Research, 19*, 26–41.

Spoerer, M. (1997). Weimar's investment records in intertemporal and international perspective. *European Review of Economic History, 1*, 291–297.

Sweezy, M. Y. (1940). German corporate profits: 1926-1938. *Quarterly Journal of Economics, 54*, 354–398.

Temin, P. (1976). *Did monetary forces cause the great depression?* Norton & Company.

Temin, P. (2008). The German crisis of 1931. Evidence and tradition. *Cliometrica, 2*, 5–17.

Tooze, A. (2006). *The wages of destruction*. Allen Lane.

Van der Ploeg, F. (2011). Natural resource: Curse or blessing? *Journal of Economic Literature, 49*, 366–420.

Van Wijenbergen, S. (1984). The Dutch disease: A disease after all? *Economic Journal, 94*, 41–55.

Kruedener, J. B. von (1985). Die Überforderung der Weimarer Republik als Sozialstaat. *Geschichte und Gesellschaft, 11*, 358–376.

Kruedener, J. B. von (1990). Introduction: The 'Borchardt Debate' on the failure of economic policy at the end of the Weimar Republic. In J. B. von Kruedener (Ed.), *Economic crisis and political collapse: The Weimar Republic 1924–1933*. St. Martin's Press.

Voth, H. T. (1994a). Wages, investment, and the fate of the Weimar Republic: A long-term perspective. *German History, 11*, 265–292.

Voth, H. T. (1994b). Much ado about nothing? A note on investment and wage pressure in Weimar Germany, 1925-2. *Historical Social Research, 19*, 124–139.

Voth, H. T. (1995). Did high wages or high interest rates bring down the Weimar republic? A cointegration model of investment in Germany, 1925-1930. *Journal of Economic History, 55*, 801–821.

Wagenführ, R. (1933). *Die Industriewirtschaft: Entwicklungstendenzen der deutschen und internationalen Industrieproduktion 1860 bis 1932*. Verlag Hobbing.

Walter, R. (1995). *Wirtschatsgeschichte: Vom Merkantilismus bis zur Gegenwart*. Böhlau.

Weisbrod, B. (1985). Die Befriegung von den 'Tariffessein'. Deflationpolitik als Krisenstrategie der Unternehmer in der Ära Brüning. *Geschichte und Gesellschaft, 11*, 295–325.

Wixforth, H. (2003). German banks and their business strategies in the Weimar Republic: New findings and preliminary results. In M. Kasuya (Ed.), *Coping with crisis*. Oxford University Press.

Chapter 7
The Crisis of 1931 and the Collapse of the Weimar Republic

7.1 Introduction

In the 1928 elections, the SDP and DVP achieved relative success. However, the compromise between social democrats and the industrialists and bankers represented by the Deutsche Volkspartei could only last as long as the huge inflows of capital from abroad and the flourishing economy allowed the latent conflicts between the classes to be concealed.[1] These conflicts emerged forcefully starting in late 1929 when capital inflows became rarer and the German economy entered a recession. This significant slowdown in productive activity caused a marked increase in the unemployment rate and in spending on unemployment benefits. While the state's expenditures increased, its revenues, given the slowdown in the economy, decreased. Consequently, the deficit widened significantly. At the same time, capital inflows, also following the American financial crisis, were drastically reduced. In this context, unlike what happened in previous years, in the late 1920s it became very difficult for the government to obtain resources with foreign loans. The question arose as to who should bear the consequences of the economic recession.

In terms of balancing public finances, the Social Democratic Party and trade unions were in favor of tax increases and against cuts in unemployment benefits. Instead, the moderate parties' part of the government led by Müller did not share this position. In fact they were in favor of a reduction in expenditure on social services and of higher indirect taxes. Because of these different views, the Great coalition that supported the Müller government broke up (Table 7.1).

President Hindenburg, therefore, in March 1930 gave Heinrich Brüning, the leader of the Zentrum Party, the task of setting up a minority government, to which he guaranteed the possibility of making use of Article 48 of the Constitution, as done in 1923 by Stresemann. This decision, on the one hand, meant the marginalization of parliament in the country's political choices and, on the other hand, the

[1] See Petzina (1969).

G. B. Pittaluga, E. Seghezza, *An Economic Historiography of Germany, 1918-1931*, Frontiers in Economic History, https://doi.org/10.1007/978-3-031-70347-8_7

Table 7.1 German government coalition in the last period of the Weimar Republic (1928–1932)

Chancellor	Date of entry into office	USPD	SPD	Zentrum	DDP	DVP	BVP	DNVP	WP	NSDAP	Percentage of Parliament seats
Müller	6/28/1928		X	R	R	R	R				61.3
Brüning	3/20/1930			X	R	R	R				34.8[a]
Brüning	10/9/1931			X	Tolerated presidential cabinet						
Papen	6/1/1932			X	Presidential cabinet						
Schleicher (until 28 Jan. 1933)	12/3/1932			X	Presidential cabinet						

Source: Notermans (2000). Note: X, Party of Prime Minister; R, Party represented in coalition. [a] After 1930 elections 31.3%, including DNVP and excluding DDP. Legenda: USPD, Unabhangige Szialdemokratische Partei Deutschlands (Independent Social Democratic Party); SPD, Szialdemokratische Partei Deutschlands (Social Democratic Party); Zentrumpartei (Center Party: a Catholic party); DDP, Deutsche Democratische Partei (German Democratic Party: a liberal-socialist party); DVP, Deutsche Volkspartei (German People's Party: a center-right party supporting right-liberalism); BVP, Bayerische Volkspartei (Bavarian People's Party: a conservative party based mainly in Bavaria); DNVP, Deutschnationale Volkspartei (German National People's Party: an authoritarian and radical right party); WP, Wirtschaftspartei (Business Party: a tough conservative party); NSDAP, Nationalsozialistische Deutsche Arbeiterpartei (National Socialist German Workers' Party: the Nazi party)

victory of the conservative-bourgeois interest groups over the Left.[2] On the other hand, as Rosenberg (1936, p. 306) writes: "The leading Social Democrats, who were convinced that the Socialist proletariat was too weak to embark upon open warfare, indulged themselves in hopes that the existing crisis would run the same course that had been followed by the crisis of 1923. . . . If Brüning in his struggle with Hitler and Hugenberg . . . it was possible—so they argued—that some fortunate concatenation of circumstances would permit of the resuscitation of the Weimar Republic. These men forgot that in 1924 democracy in Germany was not rescued by their endeavors, but by the intervention of the New York Stock Exchange. In 1930-31, American financiers were neither willing nor able to rescue the Weimar Republic for a second time."

In fact, as Table 6.5 shows, in 1929 there was a sharp slowdown in capital inflows from abroad. This slowdown mainly affected American banks' investments. The behavior of the latter seems to be attributable not only to the boom on the New York Stock Exchange and the high capital gains it allowed,[3] but also to a loss of confidence in the economic and political stability of Germany. In late 1928 and early 1929, following the boom on the New York Stock Exchange, American banks' investments in Germany diminished significantly, determining a remarkable reduction of capital inflows into this country.[4]

In order to re-establish Germany's credibility in the international financial market, starting in July 1930, Brüning initiated a policy of fiscal austerity, aimed at rebalancing public finances. The government's spending cuts and tax increases caused a strong hostile reaction in Parliament.

President Hindenburg therefore decided to dissolve the Reichstag and call new elections. The latter was held in September 1930 and marked a clamorous success for the extreme parties, primarily the NSDAP, and a defeat for the government parties.

Regardless of the electoral result, President Hindenburg mandated Brüning to form a new government, this time supported by the Zentrum Party alone, however, with the full support of the President. This government in late 1930 and mid-1931 passed two other tax bills that cut salaries and pensions for civil servants, reduced unemployment and health insurance benefits and increased taxes.

The economic and social distress that followed these austerity measures and the ensuing recession led to a significant NSDAP success in local elections in the spring of 1931. This success in the general elections of 1932 turned into a real triumph for this party.

It is, therefore, not surprising that a large number of scholars have attributed the main cause of Hitler's rise to power to the austerity policy of the Brüning government. This thesis was contested by Borchardt according to whom Brüning, given the institutional constraints, had little margin of freedom in policy choices. This contrast

[2]On this aspect see Petzina (1969) and Maier (1975).

[3]See Temin (1971, p. 243).

[4]See Rothbard (1963, p. 131–132).

gave rise to a broad debate, the so-called "Borchardt debate," whose terms are reported in Sect. 7.7.

The pronounced slowdown of the German economy that occurred in the early 1930s was favored not only by Brüning's fiscal policy but also by the credit crunch associated with the currency and banking crisis of 1931. This crisis was brought about by a dramatic sudden stop. Already in the spring of 1929 (in correspondence with the negotiations that led to the signing of the Young Plan) and in the autumn of 1930, after the victory of the extreme parties in the political elections in September, Germany had been affected by huge outflows of capital. These outflows had led to tensions on the exchange rate and on the degree of liquidity of German banks, in particular of the large banks heavily indebted to foreign currency.

The Reichsbank had, however, managed to cauterize those crises by using part of its foreign exchange reserves and by borrowing abroad.

The German central bank, however, was unable to successfully deal with the sudden stop in mid-1931 since, on the one hand, to defend the Reichsmark it had to raise the official discount rate and, on the other hand, to safeguard the stability of the banks affected by foreign deposits' withdrawals, was forced to inject ample liquidity into the system.

There has been extensive debate on the causes of the 1931 crisis. Some scholars believe that the outflow of capital at the origin of that crisis was determined by a widespread distrust in the solvency of German banks, which were undercapitalized and had an excessive share of foreign deposits. Other scholars, on the other hand, tend to attribute the 1931 crisis to foreign policy reasons, in particular, to the distrust of the Allies regarding Germany's willingness to pay the annuities envisaged by the Young Plan. Strong tensions on the exchange rate arose from this distrust and the consequent sudden stop. These two different visions on the origin of the 1931 crisis and the alternative hypothesis that it was a twin crisis are reported in Sect. 7.5.

The fact remains that the credit crunch that followed the 1931 crisis accentuated the recessive effects of the fiscal austerity measures decided by the Brüning government, resulting in a pronounced fall in output and a dramatic increase in the unemployment rate. The resulting widespread social unrest was instrumental in Hitler's rise to power.

7.2 The Young Plan Negotiations and the Currency Crisis of 1929

In Germany between 1929 and 1931 there were three different phases of capital flight: April 1929, September 1930, and June 1931.

In April 1929, capital outflowed due to difficulties in negotiating a definitive German Reparations plan. In fact, by its nature, the Dawes Plan was a temporary measure, involving the payment of five annuities while the total amount of the

Reparations, formally speaking, remained that declared in 1921 by the London ultimatum.

The German authorities demanded a revision of the Dawes Plan that would allow them to know the final amount of the Reparations they owed the Allies. Their request had two objectives, firstly, with a revision of the Dawes Plan they sought to obtain a reduction of the annual payment and the cessation of the meddling of the General Agent of Reparations in German internal affairs, the end of supervision over the management of the railroads and of the Reichsbank, aspects that undermined German sovereignty and which, therefore, were considered extremely humiliating.[5]

For quite different reasons, the General Agent of Reparations, Parker Gilbert, also urged a revision of the Dawes Plan. By the end of 1927, in his third annual report, he had noted that Germany's fulfilment of its commitments under that Plan was due not to a virtuous fiscal policy but rather to the plentiful supply of short-term credit from American banks to Germany. Should these credits, for whatever reason, cease, it was inevitable that problems would arise in Germany's compliance with the commitments set out in the Dawes Plan.

According to Gilbert, the fixing of the global amount of the Reparations would have given Germany an incentive to put its public finances in order and would also have allowed foreign investors to better assess the risk of holding Reparation bonds, facilitating the marketing (i.e., public sale to private investors) of part of the German Reparation bonds. Thanks to the latter, European debtor countries would have been able to, at least partially, settle their war debts with the United States. All of which would have contributed to easing international tensions.

In the autumn of 1928, Gilbert had several meetings with the countries involved seeking support for his proposal, urging the appointment of a new committee of experts to revise the Dawes Plan. His proposal was welcomed by both the creditor countries and Germany, indeed it was even, somewhat unexpectedly, welcomed by the French Prime Minister Poincaré, who in the past had been absolutely intransigent on the issue of Reparations. According to Poincaré's statements, a revision of the Dawes Plan would be an opportunity to define a closer relationship between the Reparations and the inter-Ally debt. This position suggests that France, in 1929, no longer needed the German Reparations for post-war reconstruction but rather to pay off its war debts. Moreover, according to Poincaré, the revision of the Dawes Plan could have made the commercialization of the German debt possible.[6]

The start of the negotiations to revise the Dawes Plan was announced by the creditor powers and Germany in September 1928. In December of the same year, a committee of experts chaired by Owen D. Young (an American industrialist and chairman of General Electric) was appointed to draw up the new plan.[7]

---

[5] See McNeil (1986, p. 159–160).

[6] Apart from the official reasons, Poincaré was in favor of a revision of the Dawes Plan because he realized that Germany would not be able to pay anything if external credit ceased. It was therefore a question of redefining the guarantees for the payment of Reparations. See Néré (2002, p. 83).

[7] Germany, unlike the case of the Dawes Plan, also appointed representatives to this Committee.

The Young Committee held its first meeting on February 11, 1929, and remained in session for 17 weeks. This long period between the appointment of the Committee and the signing of the new Plan by the six powers on June 7, 1929, is clear evidence of the difficulties encountered during the negotiations.

The main source of difficulties arose from the presentation on 17 April by Schacht, the head of the German delegation, of a memorandum highlighting the weakness of the German economy and the consequent inability of Germany to support the payment of large annuities. He set the maximum amount at 1650 million Reichsmarks paid over 37 years and conditional on a certain performance of the German economy. He further added that in return for the payment of these annuities, Germany demanded the return of Danzig, the Polish corridor, and the German colonies (in order to be able to import raw materials at lower costs) as well as a substantial reduction of the tariffs applied by the Allies to the import of goods from Germany, factors which would have facilitated the payment of Reparations by his country.

Schacht's disagreements within the Committee of Experts[8] seemed to put the successful outcome of the conference in jeopardy. Indeed, Schacht's position was greeted with surprise by his own government headed by Müller, who called on the Reichsbank President to adopt a less aggressive attitude. Given the difficulties in reaching an agreement, in the international financial markets, a widespread distrust in the stability of the Reichsmark developed. As Fig. 7.1 shows, starting in the last week of April, the mark forward discount rate increased significantly, reaching a peak at the end of May.

The deterioration of confidence in the Reichsmark was matched by a substantial withdrawal of foreign deposits from German banks which, given the low level of domestic saving, represented a significant proportion of their deposits (Table 7.2).

Pertinently, Northrop (1938, p. 180) writes: "The German economy was far from a balanced economy; it was at all times dependent upon foreign funds which not only made central banking policy not independent but also controlled the basic structural development of the country and forced it to react quickly and disastrously to any check in the free flow of foreign capital."

The run on the foreign deposits of German banks in the spring of 1929 threatened both the stability of the Reichsmark and the solvency of the German banking system.[9] In an attempt to defend exchange rate parity, the Reichsbank used a substantial part of its gold reserves, which fell from 2553 to 1705 million Reichsmarks between the end of March and May (Fig. 7.1). Because of this, the cover ratio, which in January was 64.4, fell to 50.9 in April and 41.0 in May. In addition to using part of its reserves to defend the exchange rate, the Reichsbank tried to counteract the outflow of capital by raising the discount rate from 6.5 to 7.5% and resorting to credit

[8]These disputes concerned, in particular, who would bear the burden of the reduction in the amount they would receive. The dispute was particularly bitter between France and England.

[9]The indebtedness of the banks made the government's ability to obtain financial support from them more uncertain. See Maurer and Wengst (1980).

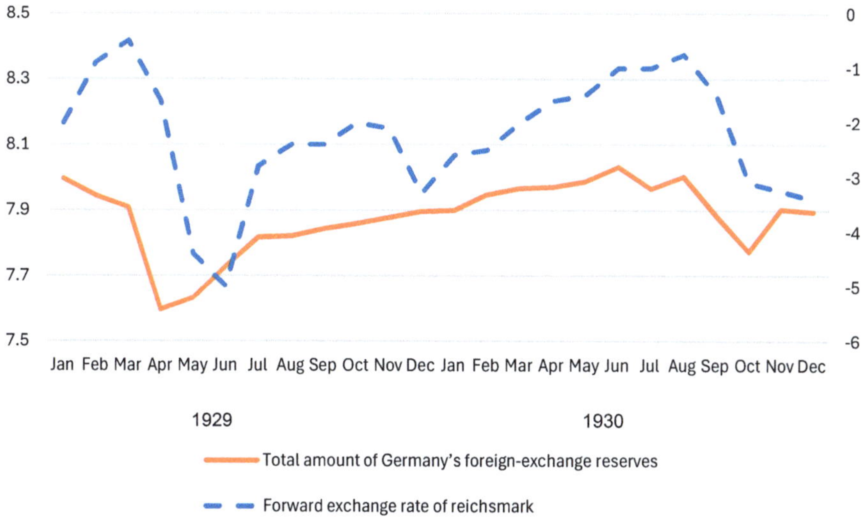

Fig. 7.1 One-month forward exchange rate and foreign exchange reserves of the Reichsbank (Jan. 1929–Dec. 1930). Source: For the exchange rate Einzig (1938), for the foreign exchange reserve Federal Reserve Monthly Bulletin. Note: Foreign exchange reserves are measured in logarithms

Table 7.2 German Credit Banks' deposits (million Reichsmarks and percentage; figures at the end of June of each year, 1925–1933)

Years	Total deposits	Foreign deposits	% share of foreign deposits on total deposits
1925	4249	837	19.7
1926	5312	1312	24.7
1927	7080	2485	35.1
1928	8682	3768	43.4
1929	10,101	4020	39.8
1930	11,312	3880	34.3
1931	8500	1530	18.0
1932	6543	615	9.4
1933	6057	527	8.7

Source: Untersuchung des Bankwesens (1933) and Balderston (1991)

restrictions. As a result, money market interest rates rose very sharply and with them bank interest rates. The agreement reached on 7 June by the Committee of Experts on the final text of the Young Plan contributed to easing tensions over the Reichsmark. However, the stop of the withdrawals of foreign deposits occurred only after a consortium of American banks led by Boston's Lee Higginson & Co. made a substantial loan to Germany.

In his memoirs, Schacht places ultimate responsibility for the 1929 exchange rate crisis on France. In particular, he accuses the French press of waging a smear

Table 7.3 The liquidity of the Great Berlin banks (1913–1930)

Year	Liquidity[a] on credits[b]	Liquidity[a] on short-term deposits
1913	53.6	12.4
1924	53.6	9.8
1925	47.4	9.8
1926	52.6	7.8
1927	47.2	9.3
1928	46.9	8.0
1929	42.4	7.8
1930	40.4	5.0

Source: Northrop (1938). Note: [a] Sum of cash, giro deposits, and deposits with other banks; [b] Sum of bills, reports and lombards

campaign against the Reichsbank and places most of the blame on French banks for the massive withdrawal of currency deposits from the large German banks. However, his position appears to be an attempt to downplay the part his contribution to the Committee of Experts for the preparation of the Young Plan had played in initiating the crisis.

The run on foreign currency deposits inevitably had an impact on bank liquidity which declined significantly (and permanently) between 1928 and 1929, as Table 7.3 shows. This resulted in a structural weakening of the German banks as they borrowed short-term funds on foreign markets and used them to grant long-term, and therefore illiquid, loans to industry.

The German government's distancing itself from Schacht's position and Young's mediation work[10] made the work of the Committee of Experts possible. The final text of the Plan, made public on June 7, 1929, stipulated the following:

(i) The annuities to be paid by Germany, starting at 1650 million gold marks and rising within 5 years to 2500 million, were set at less than 59 million. Their discounted present value corresponded to 37 billion gold marks. Each annuity was divided into a "conditional"[11] and an "unconditional"[12] component.
(ii) The resources with which Germany made the annuity payments came from two sources: the Railways and the Reich budget. From the first source came the unconditional payments, while the conditional ones were to come from the

[10]Young defined a compromise scheme based on three points: (1) The definition of a "transfer protection," dividing Germany's obligations into two categories: unconditional (i.e., payments that had to be made under all circumstances) and conditional (i.e., payments that could be postponed in case their execution could jeopardize the stability of the mark). (2) The total amount of the German Reparations was to be sufficient to cover the Allies' war debts, the service of the Dawes loan and some indemnity for war damage. (3)The creditor countries were to reduce their original demands for Reparations by 16%.

[11]That is, as specified in the previous footnote, payments that could be postponed in case their execution could jeopardise the stability of the mark.

[12]That is, the payments that had to be made under all circumstances.

second. The Dawes Plan included a "transfer protection" clause, which stated that Reparations were converted into foreign exchange if there were sufficient official reserves to prevent a collapse of the Reichsmark. This implied that in the event of low reserves commercial credits enjoyed a higher degree of seniority than Reparations.[13] With the Young Plan, the transfer protection clause was eliminated, so that Reparations were given a higher seniority than commercial credits.

(iii) The Reparations Commission was abolished and annuity payments were to be made through the new Bank of International Settlements, which was also to market German debt.

(iv) Germany's financial independence was restored; all foreign supervision of the country's monetary and fiscal policy ceased. Not only the Reparations Agent and the Transfer Committee were eliminated, but also the foreign representatives nominated in the Board of the Reichsbank and the State Railways were abolished. Since the Reparations problem was settled, Germany was guaranteed the withdrawal of the Allied military from the Rhineland.

The Young Plan was approved with only minor amendments at the first session of the Conference at the Hague on August 31, 1929, and at the second session of the same conference held between 3 and 20 January 1930 and became operational as of June 1930. In the meantime, on 7 March, after the German government had approved the Plan, Schacht resigned as president of the Reichsbank.[14]

Thanks, in part, to the success of the negotiations on the Young Plan in the summer months of 1929, a fair degree of confidence in the stability of the German currency was re-established as the trend of the forward exchange rate in Fig. 7.1 illustrates.

At the beginning of December 1929, however, the discount rate on the forward exchange rate rose once again: this rise coincided with the publication by the President of the Reichsbank of a memorandum stating that the German central bank would not contribute to the formation of the Bank for International Balance of Payments (the future Bank of International Settlements) if the payment terms of the Reparations under the Young Plan were not made less unfavorable to Germany. The effects of this memorandum are well described by Schacht himself (1955, p. 236): "I prepared a memorandum on the Young Plan which I not merely submitted

[13] See Ritschl (2002), Link (1970), and McNeil (1986).

[14] According to Mühlen (1938), Schacht, however, negotiated a substantial severance package of 3 years' salary (360,000 marks per annum). Various explanations have been given for this. According to some, Schacht believed that the crash of the New York stock market would affect Germany in disastrous terms and did not want to be involved in these events. A different motivation for Schacht's resignation is given by Ritschl (1996) according to which he was aware that with the elimination of the transfer protection under the Young Plan Germany would be exposed to overborrowing. In this case the country would have fallen into a debt crisis. A deep economic depression and political turmoil would have ensued. If indeed this was Schacht's view, it later proved to be correct.

to the government on December 6, but published in the press on the same day. It came as a bombshell."

The markets' perception of a serious conflict between the Reichsbank and the government over the implementation of the Young Plan undermined investor's confidence in the stability of the Reichsmark. Despite this, in the early part of 1930, Franco-German relations improved significantly, raising hopes of a full solution to the Reparations issue and confidence in the perspectives of the German currency which enjoyed a period of relative stability.

7.3 The Currency Crisis of 1930

Although the 1929 currency crisis eventually was resolved, the large withdrawal of foreign deposits associated with had an impact not only on the liquidity of German banks, but also on their ability to provide credit. The contraction of bank credit combined with the Reichsbank's restrictive monetary policy in defense of the Reichsmark had negative effects on the level of production and, starting in late 1929, the German economy entered a recessionary phase. The severe slowdown of the German economy led to a significant increase in unemployment, which rose between March 1929 and March 1930 from 13.3 to 20.1%.[15]

This increase in unemployment led to a sharp rise in public spending, due primarily to the payment of unemployment benefits[16] at the same time as the state's revenues were falling due to the slowdown in the growth of output. Consequently, the public deficit tended to widen at a time when, also due to the concomitant US banking crisis, the public sector's ability to finance itself on foreign markets was diminishing. Fearing that budget deficits would encourage a new inflationary process, both trade unions and the Social Democratic Party were in favor of a balanced budget. They, however, believed that this could be achieved not with public spending cuts, but by raising taxes on the propertied classes. The insistence with which the Left supported this position and its determination to defend unemployment benefits in their then-existing form contributed to the fall of the Grand Coalition government headed by Müller which included, in addition to the Social Democratic Party, two moderate parties: the Bavarian People's Party (BVP) and the liberal-conservative German National People's Party (DVP).

The German President, Hindenburg, believing that the situation was ripe for a right turn in both domestic and foreign policy,[17] offered the chancellorship to

[15]This figure refers to Trade Union members. See Bry (1960).

[16]In fact, on the basis of the law passed in 1927, the expenditure for the latter, up to a certain amount (i.e., 1.4 million unemployed), was financed out of employer and employee contributions. However, the Reich remained responsible for covering the unemployment benefits' expenditure beyond this number.

[17]See Ferguson and Temin (2003).

Heinrich Brüning, the head of the Catholic Zentrum Party, proposing that since this would be a minority government (Table 7.1), he could rely on Article 48 of the Weimar Constitution, i.e., the possibility of legislating in emergency situations by decree of the President of the Republic.[18] As Bessel (1990, p. 137) writes: "The effective suspension of parliamentary government from 1930 onwards and the increasing reliance upon emergency legislation passed with Reich President Hindenburg's signature revealed the bankruptcy of democratic politics in Weimar Germany."

Brüning, although he headed a minority government in parliament, counted, in addition to Hindenburg's institutional guarantees, on the support of a broad spectrum of interest groups, in particular of the inflation-hit middle class, the East Elbian Junkers, workers in the non-Marxist trade unions, some industrialists (in particular, small- and medium-sized firms).[19] On the other hand, it had no support from those parts of the productive process that had benefited from inflation and state-controlled prices and wages, that is, the major industries which feared the international competition.[20]

Most likely, Brüning's main goal was to restore Germany's credibility in the international financial markets. Only in this way would he be able to revitalize the capital flows from abroad that Germany desperately needed.[21] To this end, he initiated a policy of fiscal austerity, with the intention of reducing domestic absorption and improving German export performance, and, at the same time, sought to dismantle the cartels and practices, which made the setting of prices and wages a political issue rather than one left to the forces of supply and demand as is normally the case in a capitalist economy. The better allocation of resources that would have resulted from these measures would have allowed Germany to improve its level of efficiency and competitiveness and therefore to reabsorb, albeit gradually, the economic imbalances that afflicted it and reschedule its foreign and domestic obligations.

With this in mind, he issued the First Emergency Fiscal and Economic Decree in July 1930. It included both spending cuts (including a significant reduction in civil service salaries and cuts in state and municipal revenues) and increases in taxes and contributions (including a 1–4.5% increase in the insurance premium and a surcharge on income taxes for those earning more than 8000 Reichsmarks). The same

---

[18] President Hindenburg used it, as Storer (2013, p. 63) writes, to "circumvent the Reichstag and revive the political culture of the imperial elite." On this aspect, see also Feuchtwanger (1995) and Winkler (1993). Bracher (1955) was the first to draw attention to the deleterious effects, in the sense of the definitive deterioration of democratic institutions, that the presidential and authoritarian government practice established by Brüning had in predisposing the collapse of Weimar and the advent of Nazism.

[19] See Schuker (1988, p. 83).

[20] Brüning to Wihelm Sollman, Feb. 1, 1945, F206. Brüning-Sollman correspondence.

[21] See, in particular, Borchardt ([1979] 1991a), James (1986), and Ritschl (2002). Other scholars, like Holtfrerich (1986) and Winkler (1993) believe instead that Brüning intended to end the payment of Reparations as soon as possible.

Table 7.4 The Reich's budget (1929–1932)

Balance sheet items	1929	1930	1931	1932
Revenue	6980.2	7769.7	6877.4	5883.2
Expenditure	7748.5	7930.7	6521.7	5749.0
Balance	−768.2	−160.9	355.7	134.2

Source: Ritschl (2002)

decree gave the government the power to lower cartel prices. At the same time, on a strictly political level, the state representatives on the arbitration board lobbied for a reduction in the level of wages. Thanks to the measures taken by Brüning, the budget was balanced again (Table 7.4). Commenting on this presidential decree in its edition of July 27, 1930, the *New York Times* underlined the fact that it was a blatant violation of the principle of "no taxation without representation": the Brüning government that had proposed its adoption was, in fact, a minority government supported by President Hindenburg and only able to govern on the basis of Article 48 of the Constitution.

However, the Reichstag's negative reaction to Brüning's tax measures was very strong and, as a result, President Hindenburg decided to dissolve the Reichstag and call new elections. In them, held on September 14, 1930, the Social Democrat Party lost 10 seats falling to 143, Brüning's Zentrum gained 6 seats, but the other government parties, particularly the State Party and the People's Party, lost heavily. In contrast, the National Socialist Party's share of the vote rose from 2.6 to 18.3% and it increased its parliamentary representation from 12 to 107 seats, similarly the Communist Party's share rose from 10.6 to 13.1% and its number of seats from 44 to 77.[22] In the post-election environment, the coalition supporting the Brüning government had only 171 MPs out of 577, that is, 29.6%.[23]

Despite the substantial defeat of the centrist parties and the significant strengthening of the extreme political wings (both left and right) of the Reichstag, Hindenburg nonetheless mandated Brüning to form a new government.[24] The Social Democrats, caught between the National Socialist Party and the Communist Party, adopted a largely passive policy of "toleration" toward the government, i.e., they did not actively oppose it. This attitude by the Social Democratic Party, and thus by the trade unions, meant that even in a period of severe economic recession and rising unemployment the number of workers involved in strikes was relatively modest.[25]

The result of the election on 14 September was shocking and laid bare a profound polarization of the electorate. As Born (1983, p. 258) writes: "The electoral success of an intransigent and revolutionary nationalism shook the confidence of Germany's foreign creditors in the political stability and credit worthiness of the Weimar Republic." The ensuing currency crisis, mainly due to withdrawals of funds from

[22] See Falter et al. (1986).

[23] See Statistisches Jahrbuch für das Deutsche Reich (1932).

[24] See Bennett (1962).

[25] The number of workers involved in strikes had been 234,543 in 1929 and fell in 1931 to 178,223. See Flora (1987).

the country by foreign investors,[26] saw about 800 million Reichsmarks leave the country in a month and by 17 December this sum had almost doubled. This high capital outflow was partly compensated for by the improvement of the current account balance, which, having been essentially balanced in 1929, showed a surplus of more than 1600 million Reichsmarks in 1930. This surplus mitigated the Reichsbank's loss of reserves as a result of the currency crisis.

The intense capital flight that affected Germany in the autumn of 1930 can be traced back to the emergence at that time of expectations of exchange rate depreciation (Fig. 7.1). These expectations were fueled, in addition to the election result of 14 September, by other "bad" news. On 25 September, Hitler, leader of the National Socialist Party, gave a speech in Leipzig in which he declared that, when his party came to power, "heads would roll," this encouraged rumors of an imminent "putsch" by the National Socialists which were amplified by British and American newspapers. To put an end to these rumors, President Hindenburg and Chancellor Brüning were forced to issue a public denial.

At the beginning of October, further fuel for the expectations of a depreciation of the German currency came from the international instability created by the financial collapse of Brazil and the sharpening of domestic political instability after the DDP (an element of the Brüning government's coalition) was shaken by a split. The rather timid increase of the discount rate from 4 to 5% decided by the Reichsbank, dominated by the so-called Konstatierungpolitik (i.e., the assumption of keeping the policy interest rate aligned to that of London), failed to restore expectations on the Reichsmark. To defend the stability of the mark, the Reichsbank used part of its gold reserves, which fell by almost 17% between August and November 1930. At the same time, the state budget remained unbalanced despite the additional restrictive fiscal measures taken by the government, including the increase of workers' contributions to the unemployment fund and cuts in civil servants' and intergovernmental salaries. Covering this deficit was only made possible by the issuance of a $125 million loan through a syndicate headed by Lee Higginson. Although the loan initiative came from the bank's subsidiary in Paris, France hesitated to join it and delayed the successful outcome of the negotiations[27] which were concluded on October 11, 1930. Thanks also to this loan, the currency crisis came to a halt in November. To obtain it, the Brüning government pledged to introduce new fiscal austerity measures. In December, a second fiscal decree imposed further salary and pension cuts for civil servants and reduced unemployment and health insurance benefits. At the same time existing tax rates were raised and new taxes were introduced.

The exchange rate crises of spring 1929 and autumn 1930, even if overcome, had negative structural effects on the German economy. The currency crisis of spring 1929 had caused a significant loss of gold reserves for the Reichsbank and, as a result, the gold cover had fallen to close to the minimum allowed level of 40%, this

[26] See, among others, Ferguson and Temin (2003).

[27] See Banholzer and Straumann (2015).

figure had been established in the German central bank reform following the acceptance of the Dawes Plan in 1924.

The currency crisis of autumn 1930, given the current account surplus, had less of an effect on the Reichsbank's gold reserves. It did, however, lead to a pronounced decrease in the foreign deposits held in German banks (Table 7.2). This decrease had a negative impact on the balance sheet structure of these banks, especially the larger ones[28] which, by their very nature, collected short-term funds but granted long-term loans.

In the short term, the liquidity strains of the German banks as a result of the capital outflows were compensated by a significant increase in discounted bills by the Reichsbank. Between August and October 1930, the amount of the non-Treasury bills in the balance sheet of the German central bank increased by about 570 million marks from 1730 to 2301 million marks.

The ease with which commercial banks had access to central bank refinancing encouraged forms of moral hazard and therefore asset quality deteriorated not only because of the performance of the real economy, but also for this reason. This deterioration was associated with the persistent under-capitalization of the German banking system: between 1913 and 1929, the equity ratio had fallen from 19.5% to 6.7%, moreover, the average for the larger banks was traditionally lower than the overall average and clearly undercapitalized.[29]

7.4 The Crisis of 1931

Despite increasingly severe structural weaknesses, Germany's economic outlook continued to improve in early 1931 and there was a widespread belief that the autumn crisis was finally over: industrial production was increasing and the Reichsbank was again accumulating foreign exchange reserves. American Ambassador Sackett wrote in a report to the Federal Reserve Bank of New York: "I have the distinct impression that things are looking better in Germany."[30]

However, by the beginning of March, it was realized within the government that due to decreased revenues, the government budget was back in imbalance. This made meeting the Reparations payments under the Young Plan problematic and presumably made new restrictive fiscal measures essential. Brüning, realizing that further tax hikes and spending cuts would further impact his government's already much-diminished popularity, considered it advisable to adopt a more aggressive German foreign policy toward the Allies, thereby seeking to reduce the pressure from the National Socialist Party and the German Nationalists and to broaden

[28] See Schnabel (2009).

[29] In November 1929, Dresdner Bank and Danatbank, two of the leading German banks of the time, had equity ratios of 5.7 and 4.8%, respectively.

[30] Quotation in Ferguson and Temin (2003).

popular support for his government. On 18 March, the government approved the draft customs union with Austria, negotiated by Foreign Minister Curtius. This initiative aroused the indignation of France, which saw in it the prologue to the Anschluss, both the Italian and British governments also responded negatively.

After the relative stability at the beginning of the year, the situation began to deteriorate in the second quarter of 1931. Industrial production began to slow, unemployment began to rise again, and social unrest spread. At the same time, the fiscal situation had become unsustainable. To remedy this, the Brüning government decided to publish a new austerity plan on 11 May, however, on the evening of that same day the Austrian Chancellor, Otto Ender, announced the insolvency of the Osterreichische Credit Anstalt. On hearing this news Harry Siepman's, a senior official at the Bank of England, confided to a friend that in his opinion the crisis would soon spread to Germany and then the UK and that "... it may well bring down the whole house of cards in which we have been living."[31]

Several scholars have argued that the German banking crisis of 1931 was caused by the spillover effects of the failure of the large Austrian bank, among them primarily Lüke (1958) and Born (1967).[32] In agreement with this point of view is Kindleberger (1973, p. 148–149) according to which the collapse of Credit Anstalt led to runs on the banks of neighboring countries, in particular, on the German banks. Temin (1976, p. 2–3) believes that the link between the failure of the large Austrian bank and the German crisis of 1931 is to be found in the fact that "[t]he Austrian government guaranteed its [the Credit Anstalt's] liabilities and the bank's foreign creditors agreed to stop withdrawals. This meant, however, that the assets of the creditors lost liquidity. German banks were affected particularly, and their creditors started to withdraw deposits in anticipation of further trouble."

However, as emerged from figures found in the archive of the Austrian National Bank, German creditors held less than 3.4% of Credit Anstalt's overseas debt.[33]

Even if a direct link between the collapse of Credit Anstalt and the German crisis of 1931 can be excluded, it is possible that this collapse led investors to pay greater attention to the Reich's situation, in particular, to its economic and financial situation and, even more, to the absence of measures aimed at restoring the budget and paying the annuities of the Young Plan.

Actually, the weakness of the Brüning government, sustained by a slim parliamentary majority, was exacerbated by its growing unpopularity with the German public. In fact, in the elections held on 17 May in the town of Oldenburg, the National Socialist party (which in 1928 had obtained 7.5% of the vote) jumped to 37%. The German electorate was becoming increasingly polarized and on 19 May

---

[31] Quoted by Leith-Ross (1968, p. 133).

[32] See on this aspect, among others, Aguado (2001).

[33] The main shares were held by British creditors (37.7%), by American ones (33.5%), by French ones (8.7%), by Dutch ones (8.6%) and by Swiss ones (7.8%). The remaining share, equal to 3.7%, was held by other countries, including Germany. See Vienna, Archive of Oesterreichische Nationalbank. Bankatte 1536/1931.

Brüning, to regain support with the right-wing electorate, made a particularly nationalistic speech in front of a huge crowd on the subject of Reparations. His statements were a new cause for alarm in France. At the beginning of June, the German government approved a third fiscal decree which, among other measures, imposed a crisis tax as well as a further pay reduction for civil servants. At the same time, the unemployment insurance was reduced by 5%. On 6 June, when presenting these measures, Brüning made the statement that due to the fiscal crisis Germany was not able to meet the annuities under the Young Plan.[34] This stance arouded concern among the Allies. To try to remedy this situation, Brüning, accompanied by Foreign Minister Curtius, flew to London to ask for financial support from the Bank of England. While he was in talks with British Prime Minister MacDonald, the German newspapers published the measures of the tax decree and the accompanying manifesto. Part of the latter contained the following statement: "We have made every effort to meet our obligations arising from the last war. We have also made extensive use of foreign assistance towards this end. That is no longer possible. By calling on all the energies and reserves of all sections of the population, the German Government has earned the right—and makes it a duty towards its own people—to pronounce to the world: the limit of the privations which we can impose on our people has been reached. The premises on which the Young Plan was based have proved to be erroneous in the light of subsequent events. The Young Plan has failed to give the German people the relief which, according to the intentions of all concerned, it was meant to give and of which it at first held out promise. The Government realizes that the extremely precarious economic and financial situation of the Reich requires that it be relieved of the unbearable Reparation obligations. This is also a prerequisite for the economic recovery of the whole world."[35]

This statement was interpreted by the Allied countries as Germany's declaration of its intention not to fulfil its commitments under the Young Plan and aroused deep irritation not only in France but also in the United Kingdom and the United States. It was also because of this that the British government and its central bank were unwilling to grant financial assistance to the German government, marking the failure of Brüning and Curtius' mission to London.[36]

The confidence of the international markets in the stability of the Reichsmark was severely shaken.[37] A large part of the deposits of those major banks headquartered in Berlin that had extensive branch networks—like Deutsche Bank, Dresdner Bank, and Commerzbank—consisted of foreign short-term deposits. In the first week of June 1931, a huge capital outflow hit these banks.

---

[34] See Ferguson and Temin (2003).

[35] Quoted in Straumann (2019, p. 146).

[36] According to Wehler (2003), this failure was due to Brüning's reactionary and revisionist approach to foreign policy. This view is shared by Knox (2007).

[37] No wonder, then, that several scholars have expressed strong criticism of this example of Brüning's diplomacy. See, on this aspect, Eyck (1962) and Rosenberg (1936).

The withdrawal of foreign deposits led to liquidity strains, particularly extreme in the case of the Danatbank,[38] the difficulties of which had been made public by reports in the communist tabloid "Welt" claiming that it had been unable to extend a loan to the city of Berlin. Danat's situation became critical when several newspapers reported a huge write-down by the textile company Nordwolle, one of Danat's main industrial clients.

To counter exchange rate tensions, on 13 June the Reichsbank raised the discount rate from 5 to 7%. However, this increase was not enough to stabilize the exchange rate and at the same time worsened the liquidity situation of the large banks, precisely those who were most severely affected by deposit withdrawals being made by foreign investors. This, in turn, had a negative impact on the interbank market and from June onward loans to other banks fell significantly: they had been over 1 billion in December 1930, 0.867 billion in May 1931, and fell to 0.686 billion in June. Faced with a possible banking crisis, the Reichsbank expanded its commercial paper discount operations by injecting liquidity into the system. The reluctance of the German central bank to make substantial changes to the discount and money market rates made the goal of simultaneously defending the exchange rate and protecting the stability of the banks critical. In this context, the German central bank continued to lose reserves to defend the exchange rate. When it emerged on 17 June that the textile company Nordwolle's losses substantially exceeded the company's assets, the capital flight intensified.

Table 7.2 shows that at the end of June 1931, the foreign currency deposits of the German Credit Banks had fallen by 2350 million Reichsmarks compared to the same month of the previous year. Given the efforts to defend exchange rate stability in the first 2 weeks of June, the Reichsbank's loss of gold amounted to 550 million Reichsmark; at the end of the third week of the same month it rose to 1250 million Reichsmarks.[39] The pessimism that prevailed in both domestic and international business circles did not abate on hearing the news on 20 June that US President Herbert Hoover was proposing a moratorium on all war debts[40] and, when France's opposition to this arrangement became clear, in late June, withdrawals intensified again.[41] On the 29th of that month, the German central bank obtained a stand-by loan of 100 million dollars from the Bank of England, the Banque de France, the Federal Reserve Bank of New York, and the Bank of International Settlements. Also due to the modest size of this loan at the end of June, the cover ratio approached the

[38]It was a banking run as that considered by Diamond and Dybvig (1983).

[39]On this point see Murad (1932).

[40]This moratorium was mainly aimed to protect US commercial credits to Germans. See Ritschl and Sarferaz (2014, p. 353).

[41]France's position stemmed both from its concerns that the moratorium would imply a relative strengthening of Germany and from a lack of understanding of the seriousness of Germany's domestic political situation. For France this moratorium meant a net revenue loss of 16.1 million sterling compared to a net revenue loss of 53.6 million sterling for the United States, 9.6 for the United Kingdom, 1.8 for Italy and 2.4 for Belgium. Germany would have benefited from a net revenue increase of 77 million pounds sterling.

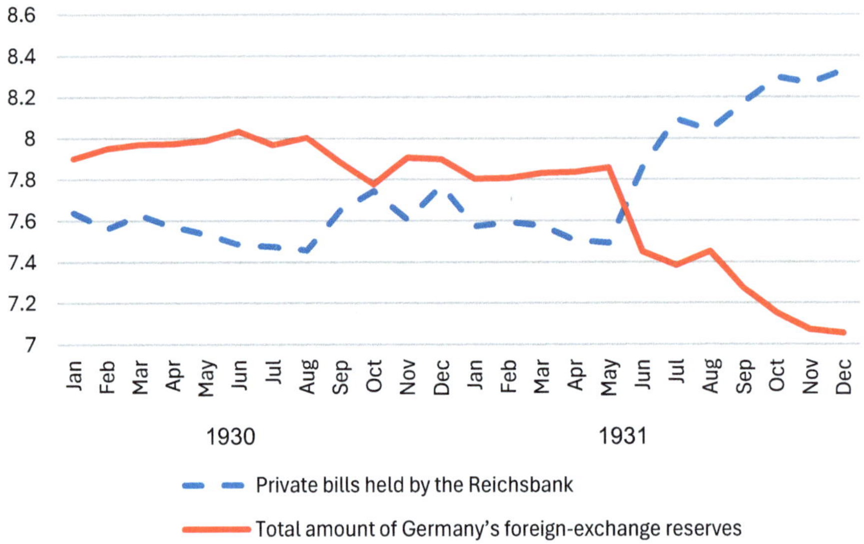

Fig. 7.2 Foreign reserves and private bills held by the Reichsbank (Jan. 1930–Dec. 1931). Source: Federal Reserve, Bulletin, several months. Notes: Both variables are measured in logarithms

minimum threshold of 40%. At the same time the money multiplier fell sharply and, as a result, the money supply decreased significantly. On 6 July, after intense negotiations, France finally approved Hoover's moratorium proposal. However, in the time between the proposal of Hoover's Plan and its acceptance by France, Germany's economic situation had deteriorated profoundly. In early July, it emerged that the Danat crisis was more serious than previously thought and confidence in the stability of the German banking system was finally undermined by the fact that other German banks first became illiquid and then insolvent.

At the beginning of July, capital flight intensified and the banking crisis became a panic that resulted in a marked trend of cash withdrawals of bank deposits.

Since June the Reichsbank started to compensate for the loss of foreign deposits by banks by injecting liquidity into the banking system through discount transactions. As a result, its balance sheet changed significantly in the second part of 1931: the decrease in gold reserves was matched by a pronounced increase in private bills in the portfolio (Fig. 7.2).

To curb the tumultuous growth of discount operations, on 22 June the Reichsbank imposed credit restrictions on these operations and constraints on the mobility of capital by stipulating that "... for any central bank credit provision it is to be ensured that it is not used by the banks to finance the purchase of foreign exchange, which have no real economic foundations ... ."[42] The measures taken by the Reichsbank

[42] See James (1998, p. 61).

Table 7.5 Gold and eligible foreign assets reserve ratio (as a percentage of total note circulation and central bank at sight liabilities, 1929–1933)

Items	1929	1930	1931	1932	1933
Gold reserves	36.7	37.6	17.2	18.6	9.4
Gold reserves and eligible foreign assets	45.5	45.8	20.1	21.1	9.6

Source: League of Nations (1931)

further negatively affected the functioning of the interbank market: in July, interbank deposits fell to 0.546 billion Reichsmarks.

The objective of bank stability increasingly tended to conflict with that of exchange rate stability. "On the one hand, the Reichsbank provided liquidity to banks throughout most of the run [of foreign deposits], allowing banks to serve withdrawing depositors. On the other, it was constrained by its legal obligation to maintain a gold coverage ratio of its notes in circulation of 40%."[43]

Therefore, the Reichsbank faced a dilemma: "... it could either continue to provide liquidity to the banking system risking a breaching of the gold cover limits prescribed by law or it could—as it in fact did—curtail lending to banks, thereby risking the collapse of the banking system."[44]

Even if the banking panic began in July 1931, after the currency crisis, "... the banking and currency problems became increasingly intertwined, as the run on the currency and the withdrawals at German banks were reinforcing each other."[45] This explains why the Reichsbank was, by then, no longer able to defend the stability of the currency and safeguard the stability of the banking system.[46]

The Reichsbank's persistent loss of reserves threatened the continued convertibility of the Reichsmark. In fact on 3 July, the cover ratio (including, in addition to gold, eligible foreign assets), fell below 40% and continued to fall thereafter, arriving close to 20% at the end of 1931 (Table 7.5).

In order to cope with the dramatic loss of foreign exchange reserves and safeguard the convertibility of the Reichsmark, Reichsbank President Luther tried to obtain a loan from other central banks, but faced opposition from Montagu Norman. The Bank of France Governor Moret took a similar position, while also the United States was reluctant to lend to Germany. The situation appeared desperate when on 12 July at a cabinet meeting with leading bankers it emerged that apart from Danat other German banks, first and foremost Dresdner, had very large losses. Luther therefore proposed a bank holiday and, overruling the protests of the bankers, the government decided to close Danat on Monday 13 July. Initially, the measure seemed to be a success, however, toward the middle of the morning of that day long queues formed in front of the banks: the run had turned into a panic. Brüning summoned the government to deal with the situation and, after Luther realized that

[43] See Blickle et al. (2022, p. A.6).

[44] See Schnabel (2004, p. 864–865).

[45] See Schnabel (2004, p. 826).

[46] See Toniolo (2005).

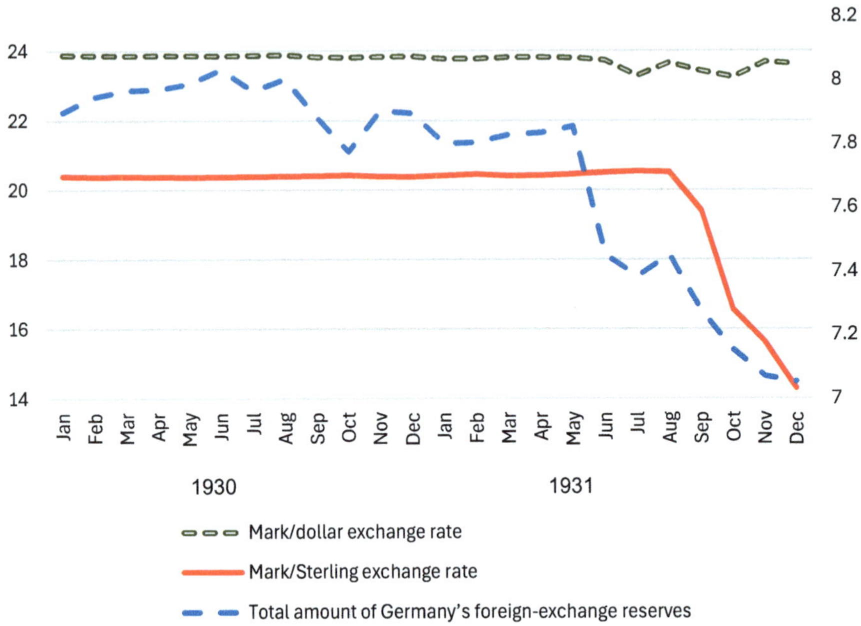

Fig. 7.3 Reichsbank foreign reserves and the mark/sterling and mark/dollar exchange rate (Jan. 1930–Dec. 1931). Source: Federal Reserve, Bulletin, several months. Note: In cents per unit of Reichsmark

the central banks of the major countries were unwilling to grant credit to Germany, it was decided to hold a 2-day general bank holiday on 14 July and the following day. However, on 15 July to stop the capital flight, the government was forced to introduce exchange controls,[47] which effectively ended the gold convertibility of the Reichsmark.

In September 1931, several currencies, starting with the pound, abandoned convertibility and devalued. Since Brüning, discarded the idea of devaluing the Reichsmark, fearing that this might trigger a new phase of hyperinflation, the German currency appreciated against currencies that had abandoned the gold exchange standard, primarily sterling (Fig. 7.3).

With the adoption of exchange rate controls, the Reichsbank regained margins of freedom with respect to the goal of preserving the stability of the banking system. However, it was not until 1932 that the banking crisis was finally halted through a far-reaching reorganization of the banking system. Underlying this was the purchase of a large amount of bank shares by the state. This measure was aimed at reconstituting the capital of these enterprises, not at controlling them, and the government's intention was to reprivatize the banks in a short time. The universal structure of the banks was maintained even though initially, on the instructions of

[47] See Schiemann (1931), Child (1958) and Irmler (1976).

Reichsbank President Luther,[48] a proposal was made to separate deposit banks from investment banks, a proposal which was strongly opposed by German bankers. After stressful negotiations, an emergency decree on the reorganization of the credit banks was issued in February 1932. According to which, the Darmstadter and the National Bank were merged with Dresdner Bank, while Commerz and Private bank acquired control of a number of important commercial banks.

7.5 The Main Interpretations of the Currency and Banking Crisis of 1931

Three aspects, at least, differentiate the 1931 crisis from the currency crises of 1929 and 1930. First, it was a banking crisis as well as a currency crisis. Second, in it, as Schnabel (2004, p. 855) observes, unlike previous crises, "[t]he German government apparently had exhausted its credit capacity", in particular the credit on the international markets that had enabled the Reichsbank and government to resolve the 1929 and 1930 crises. Third, it lasted longer than the previous crises and had devastating consequences on both output and employment, making the Great Depression in Germany particularly dramatic.

The various explanations that have been given for the 1931 crisis[49] can be divided into three main strands: those scholars who see it as a banking crisis, those who view it as a currency crisis, and a third group who refer to "twin-crises" schemes.

7.5.1 The Banking Crisis Hypothesis

Contemporaries saw the crisis of 1931 primarily as a banking crisis, caused by the structural weakness of the banks,[50] this view was later taken up by Born (1967), according to whom, after the First World War and even more so after 1924, German banks had resorted to high levels of foreign borrowing in order to expand. The share of foreign deposits of these banks rose from 1.6% in 1913 to 6.6% in 1925 and reached 19.0% in 1930. According to some scholars,[51] because of this imbalance in the structure of their liabilities when, in May 1931, the Osterreichische Credit Anstalt, a large Austrian bank, collapsed, the large withdrawal of foreign deposits (in particular, from Danatbank and Dresdner Bank), led to a banking panic.

Taking up this point of view, James (1984) traces the crisis of 1931 to a banking panic linked to the severe deterioration of the German government's finances.

[48] See Sitzung des Wirtschausschusses des Reichskabinets vom August 18, 1931.

[49] For a survey of them see Burhop (2011).

[50] See, among others, Walb (1932).

[51] See, in particular, Born (1967), Kindleberger (1984) and Kindleberger and Aliber (2005).

Table 7.6 Deposits' multiplier and annual percentage change of deposits and notes in circulation (Feb. 1931–Sep. 1931)

Month	Deposits' multiplier	Currency in circulation	Deposits	Money (M2)
February	3.31	5548	18,386	23,934
March	3.26	5614	18,317	23,931
April	3.27	5599	18,281	23,879
May	3.21	5528	17,747	23,275
June	2.90	5529	16,061	21,590
July	2.56	5885	15,059	20,944
August	2.44	5882	14,334	20,215
September	2.33	5964	13,883	19,847

Source: James (1984). Legenda: Deposits' multiplier is the deposit to currency in circulation ratio

Indeed, the German government was finding it increasingly difficult to finance its net expenditure. It could not finance itself by issuing long-term bonds since the previous experience of hyperinflation had shown this to be extremely risky. On the other hand, the Reichsbank reform of 1924 prevented it from financing the government by purchasing securities on the primary market, i.e., by printing money. Given this, the government had no choice but to borrow from the banking system and hence the increasing fragility of the German public sector budget was inevitably reflected in the banking system. According to James, Brüning's fiscal austerity policy further contributed to weakening the German banking system. In fact, this policy, by causing a slowdown in output growth, had a negative impact on the public sector's revenues and also on the balance sheets of the banks which had accumulated large loans to this sector.

As James writes (1984, p. 7) summarizing his point of view: "Here it is argued that the banking collapse was a consequence of weaknesses and difficulties in the sphere of public finance which led to a German loss of confidence in financial markets."

In order to demonstrate the plausibility of this hypothesis, James uses indicators similar to those used by Friedman and Schwartz (1963) in their analysis of the American banking crisis of the early 1930s. In this analysis he specifically refers to the deposits to currency in circulation ratio as an indicator of confidence in banks and that a decline in this ratio, that is in the deposit multiplier, indicates a loss of confidence in the solvency of the German banking system[52] and, as can be seen from Table 7.6, this ratio did in fact fall from 3.21 to 2.56 between May and July.

James' explanation of the 1931 crisis is based on two claims. First, the crisis that hit the banking sector was due to public finance imbalances and their effects on banks' solvency. Second, the loss of confidence in the banks affected Germans rather than foreigners.

[52] Sharing this view, Balderston (1993, p. 312) writes: "... the connection between the state's cash crisis of June 1931 and the banking crisis which had been developing since May is too obvious to need elaboration."

Similarities with James' explanation are presented by Fischer (1999a, 1999b), according to whom the 1931 crisis was the result of a banking panic, which in turn was provoked by a combination of local public finance and the behavior of the banks. In particular, Fischer believes that the July crisis was triggered by the collapse of Rheinische Landesbank, one of Germany's most important public banks, which was overexposed in terms of loans granted to West German cities and associations of municipalities. Again, therefore, the 1931 crisis ultimately resulted from Germany's deep public finance imbalances.

7.5.2 *The Currency Crisis Hypothesis*

The views considered in the previous sub-section lead to the conclusion that the currency crisis that provoked the de facto introduction of controls on capital movements and, thus, substantially to Germany's exit from the Gold Standard, was caused by the crisis in the German banking system which, in turn, provoked the capital flight at the root of the Reichsmark crisis. In other papers, however, this causal connection is reversed and the banking crisis is considered an effect of the currency crisis. This view can be based alternatively on the First or on the Second Generation models of currency crises.

To the Second Generation models of currency crises,[53] can be traced back to the studies according to which the German banking crisis of 1931 was the result of a loss of confidence in the stability of the mark caused by exogenous events that led to a change in expectations. According to Kindleberger, (1973), for example, the news of the bankruptcy of Credit Anstalt led foreign investors to withdraw capital from many European countries. "At the end of May 1931, Austrian financial difficulties ramified widely and led to runs on the banks of Hungary, Czechoslovakia, Romania, Poland, and Germany."[54]

Instead, the First-Generation models[55] of currency crises can be traced back to those explanations of the 1931 crisis which stress the incompatibility of the constraints of Reichsmark convertibility with Germany's high level of foreign debt. In particular, according to Eichengreen (1992), German crisis of 1931 was rooted in the structural drawbacks of the Gold Exchange Standard. This monetary system, in fact, due to the lack of cooperation between central banks, tended to widen countries' imbalances rather than reduce them. Indeed, when in 1928 the United States, in order to counter mounting stock market speculation, raised the policy interest rate, "[a] heavy adjustment burden was consequently thrust upon the debtor countries."[56]

[53] See Obstfeld (1986).

[54] See Kindleberger (1973, p. 148).

[55] See Krugman (1979).

[56] See Eichengreen (1992, p. 401).

The cost of servicing the foreign debt for these countries, in particular, Germany, which was the most indebted of them in dollars, rose considerably.

In 1929, Reparation transfers reached 15% of German exports.[57] Confidence in the stability of the Reichsmark, already weakened by these events, plummeted with the crisis and the collapse of the Credit Anstalt bank. "As storm clouds gathered . . ., American investors drew back."[58] Although the Austrian bank had little connection to the German banking system, for investors its solvency crisis was a powerful warning signal.[59] Austria's recourse to standstill agreements was an additional incentive for foreign investors to obtain liquidity by divesting themselves of their deposits in Germany.[60]

Also for Temin, Germany's problems resulted from the adoption of the Gold Standard: "Weimar Germany was a typical case of the consequences of a fixed exchange rate, not an exception"[61] and still "[t]he German crisis was in fact a simple currency crisis, best described by a first-generation model. The crisis was caused by government policies incompatible with the fixed exchange rate, not by actions of German banks."[62]

At least two observations can be made to this last hypothesis. First, in the period when the mark exchange rate was flexible, i.e., between October 1918 and June 1922, the period before hyperinflation, Germany had an average annual inflation rate of 157%. This inflation progressively eroded the financial wealth of the rentier class and seriously undermined savings and the domestic capital market. Secondly, it was thanks to adherence to the Gold Standard that Germany enjoyed large inflows of capital from abroad in the second half of the 1920s and it was these inflows that enabled it to cover the Reich's budget deficits and persistent current account deficits.

The explanations of the 1931 crisis just cited emphasize the importance of economic factors, in particular, the constraints of the Gold Exchange Standard on the policy choices of the German government. In contrast, other explanations trace the German crisis to political choices of the government, in particular, to the change in the German foreign policy that occurred in the first part of 1931. For example, Ferguson and Temin (2003) argued that Brüning on June 6, 1931, made ". . . the fatal decision to denounce Reparations and proclaim that Germany had paid all that it could," which stunned the world. The French, in particular, drew the conclusion that Germany did not want to comply with the Young Plan. These rumors encouraged a large outflow of capital, primarily from German big banks.

---

[57] See Eichengreen (1992, p.401).

[58] See Eichengreen (1992, p. 401).

[59] As the Economist wrote on June 13, 1931: "The world does not distinguish very clearly between the banking and industrial situation in Berlin and that in Vienna."

[60] Similar to Eichengreen's is Temin's (2008) explanation of the 1931 crisis.

[61] Temin (2008, p. 16).

[62] Temin (2008, p. 16).

Also according to Hardach (1984), "The event that definitively initiated the foreign exchange crisis, which had long been pending, was the announcement by the Brüning government on June 6 that Germany was unable to fulfil the Young Plan and needed a new Reparations settlement."[63] In this view, therefore, the German crisis of 1931 was therefore first and foremost a foreign exchange crisis provoked by foreign policy choices that undermined market confidence in the stability of the Reichsmark.[64]

Such a loss of confidence caused a sudden stop. The Reichsbank lost one-third of its foreign reserves in the week after the 6 June Brüning's declaration.

This hypothesis is supported, compared to the banking crisis hypothesis, by two arguments. Firstly, already between March and April 1931, a decrease in short-term deposits in the Berlin big banks was observed. This decrease is widespread across all banks and not just the riskiest ones such as Danatbank.[65] Furthermore, as Balderston (1994, p. 51) writes: "The losses in April preceded the (unexpected) news of the Credit Anstalt's failure on 8 May. Thus, the common cause for the deposit losses seems to have been the proposal for an Austro-German customs union."

Secondly, the fact that the currency crisis preceded the banking crisis is supported by the data in Table 7.6. This table, in fact, shows that the ratio of deposits to currency in circulation (col.1) fell considerably in June. However, this decrease was mainly due to a decrease in the numerator, i.e., deposits, rather than an increase in the denominator, i.e., in circulating notes, as would have happened in the case of a banking panic, when there is a replacement process of banking deposits with currency.

This seems to indicate that, contrary to what James (1984) claimed, it was initially foreigners who withdrew their deposits from German banks. Indirect confirmation of this is represented by the fact that the decrease in deposits in the month of June was particularly more pronounced for the large Berlin banks (those in which the share of foreign deposits was highest) than for the rest of the banking system, in particular, for large provincial banks and saving banks.[66]

It was only in July that the Reichsmark crisis also became a banking crisis. In fact, from that month onward, as Table 7.6 shows, the fall in deposits was associated with an increase in currency: the process of substitution of deposits for currency, which characterizes banking panics began.

[63] See Hardach (1984, p. 221).

[64] This view is shared and extended by Ferguson and Temin (2003) according to whom an abrupt change in Brüning's government's foreign policy lay at the root of Brüning's declaration.

[65] See Balderston (1994, Table 1).

[66] See Schnabel (2004, Table 7).

7.5.3 The Twin-Crises Hypothesis

In her 2004 contribution, Schnabel finds both the explanations of the 1931 crisis based on the banking hypothesis and those based on the currency hypothesis unsatisfactory, instead, based on the results obtained in an econometric test, she concludes that: "The results of the deposit equation strongly support the currency-crisis hypothesis. The variable gold cover, which measures the level of central bank reserves relative to the notes in circulation, and hence the strength of the currency, enters with a positive sign and is highly significant, implying that a strong currency was accompanied by high deposit growth (or low withdrawals). We also find that banks with higher shares of foreign deposits . . . showed significantly higher deposit withdrawals than other banks, pointing towards disproportionately high withdrawals of foreign deposits. The results also support the banking-crisis hypothesis. Most importantly, there is a positive and significant relationship between a bank's cash liquidity and its deposit growth."[67]

She believes that the 1931 crisis can be explained by reference to third-generation currency crisis models. Within these models, used in the explanations of the 1997–1998 Asian crisis, two major views can be distinguished. Firstly, a view based on the models put forward by, among others, McKinnon and Phil (1996), Krugman (1998, 1999), and Corsetti et al. (1998), according to which an unregulated financial system can lead banks to indulge in moral hazard: in particular, these firms, counting on an explicit guarantee of their solvency from the government, can engage in overborrowing, overinvestment, and trading in asset-bubble environments, even in apparently sound macroeconomic conditions. The implicit guarantee given by the government to banks constitutes a hidden public budget deficit, since rational actors expect that in the case of bank insolvency, the government will intervene to support them. From this perspective, therefore, currency crises are closely linked to banking crises: the latter implies high fiscal costs while the latter corresponds to expectations of monetization of public deficits.

The second major view of the third-generation models of currency crises emphasizes the vicious circle between currency crises and bank runs: This is stressed, in particular, by Chang and Velasco (2001) and Goldstein (2005). In these studies, on the one hand, the expected depreciation of the exchange rate has negative effects on the banks' outlook, since, it is assumed, they have foreign liabilities and domestic assets. This results in a bank run and a banking crisis, the latter leading to capital outflows and encouraging speculative attacks on the currency.

Following this second approach of the third-generation models of the currency crises Schnabel (2004) argues that the German economy in mid-1931 was affected by ". . . simultaneous occurrence of disturbances in the banking sector and currency turmoil," therefore for her, the banking and currency crises were linked through a coincidence of capital flows.[68] In this view, the banking and currency crises were

[67] See Schnabel (2004, p. 823).

[68] See, among others, Miller (1996) and Goldfajn and Valdés (1997).

closely interconnected and, indeed, the withdrawal of foreign deposits from banks entailed a loss and, thus, fostered the emergence of concerns about the stability of the Reichsmark. These concerns encouraged further deposit withdrawals which threatened the stability of the banks, these concerns then further encouraged depositors to withdraw their savings, including those held in domestic currency.

The "twin crisis" hypothesis insists primarily on internal causes of the 1931 crisis and has the great merit of emphasizing the fact that the banking crisis, induced by the withdrawal of foreign deposits, has its ultimate explanation in the structural weaknesses of the German banking system, weaknesses which were largely attributable to changes which occurred after the First World War.[69] In this period, in fact:

(i) The degree of concentration of the German banking system increased significantly. Between 1914 and 1928, the great Berlin banks swallowed several smaller banks, significantly increasing their market share so that at the end of 1929 it exceeded 20%.[70] These were universal banks: which in addition to conducting traditional banking business also undertook investment banking and international finance.
(ii) Especially in the period following hyperinflation, the share of short-term foreign-held debt of the German banks increased significantly. At the end of 1929, this amounted to 18% of total deposits overall but, in the case of the large banks, it reached as high as 42%. Because of this, the German banking system had become particularly exposed to the risk of short-term capital reversals. In this case, only refinancing efforts by the Reichsbank could have prevented liquidity crises from degenerating into solvency crises.
(iii) The increasing exposure to illiquidity risk was associated with a pronounced decrease in equity ratios. This decrease was particularly noticeable for the big banks whose equity ratios fell from 19.5 to 6.7% between 1913 and 1929. In 1929, among these banks the equity ratio of the banks that first experienced serious difficulties in 1931, Danatbank and Dresdner Bank, were particularly low.

The above gives reason to believe that the German banking system in the early 1930s was particularly fragile. This fragility had developed especially in the latter half of the 1920s after the hyperinflation of 1923, in the period of the so-called "crisis before the crisis." Given this, it is not surprising that when the international environment deteriorated, Germany was simultaneously overwhelmed by a banking and currency crisis.

Although recognizing that at some point these two types of crises came to feed on each other, Schnabel (2004, p. 855) also acknowledges that: "... observations suggest the following interpretation: As in earlier periods of political uncertainty,

---

[69] See Schnabel (2004).

[70] If measured by total assets between 1913 and 1929 the share of the great branch banks rose from 12.6 to 22.9%. See Enquête-Ausschuss (1929); Untersuchung, Deutscher Reichs und Preussische Staatsanzeiger, various dates.

Table 7.7 Principal accounts of big Berlin banks (million Reichsmarks, 1929–1931)

Items	Nov. 1929	Nov. 1930	May 1931	Nov. 1931
Cash and balances with Reichsbank	206	209	211	183
Bills portfolio	2884	2513	2548	1431
– Treasury	486	546	630	358
– Commercial	2398	1907	1918	1073
Securities	215	189	192	478
Total loans and advances	7784	7901	7235	5838
Other items	2426	2093	1942	1801
Total balance sheet	13,515	12,905	12,128	9731

Source: League of Nations (1935)

foreign and, to a lesser extent, domestic investors started to move their money out of Germany, which showed up in reserves losses at the Reichsbank. The run on the Reichsmark translated into a run on German banks, with the causality running from the currency crisis to the banking crisis. This, in fact, is the preferred interpretation of 1931 in basically all recent studies of the crisis."

7.6 The Effects of the Banking Crisis and Fiscal Austerity on the German Economy

Between November 1930 and December 1931, the deposits of German commercial banks fell notably. Underlying this was a pronounced fall in the deposit multiplier. In response to the drop in deposits and the policy of the Reichsbank, which, in an effort to defend the exchange rate, had placed limits on refinancing, the banks reduced the credit supply. The major Berlin banks, in particular, reduced their total loans and advances by more than 26% between November 1930 and November 1931 (Table 7.7).[71]

The credit squeeze took on the characteristics of a credit crunch and contributed significantly to the contraction of aggregate demand. According to an estimate by Breitenlechner et al. (2022), this represented about a quarter of the total.

The negative effects of the credit crunch on aggregate demand were combined with those of Brüning's government's fiscal austerity policy. Government expenditure between 1929 and 1930 declined markedly. Although it reached its peak with the Dietramzell Emergency Decree of 24 August 1931,[72] the austerity program

[71] Also contributing to this contraction, as shown in Table 7.7, was the tendency of banks to recompose their portfolios in favor of less risky assets.

[72] With this decree, Brüning appropriated the power to implement wage reductions and other austerity measures without having to submit them to Parliament for approval. See Mommsen (1996, p. 397).

Table 7.8 GNP, industrial production and unemployment in Germany (1926–1932)

	Gross National Product (in million marks)	Industrial Production (1913 = 100)	Unemployed (in thousand)	Rate of Unemployment (percent)
1926	51,089	87	2278	18.4
1927	56,201	110	1500	8.8
1928	57,896	113	1545	8.6
1929	56,859	114	2001	13.3
1930	52,899	99	3075	22.8
1931	45,895	82	4519	34.4
1932	42,207	66	5602	44.2

Source: For the number of unemployed Statistisches Jahrbuch für das Deutsche Reich, several years; for unemployment rate and industrial production Bry (1960); for GNP Ritschl and Spoerer (1997). Note: the unemployment rate refers to trade union members

continued and two further emergency decrees were issued on 6 October and 8 December.

With these decrees Brüning cut public spending yet further, although the reductions primarily affected capital spending, they nonetheless also hit non-capital expenditure with the reduction of pensions, other elements of the welfare state and public sector salaries and wages being particularly large. Brüning sought to garner the support of the powerful East Elbian agricultural interests by exempting subsidies to the agricultural sector from the cuts.[73] These interest groups, especially after the fall in world agricultural prices, demanded protective measures from the government, including high import tariffs. These demands clashed with those of the industrialists who were interested in expanding exports and were in favor not only of free trade, but also of maintaining a stable exchange rate in nominal terms and if possible depreciated in real terms. In light of this they agreed with the policy of fiscal austerity pursued by Brüning and its deflationary implications. Similarly, the trade unions hoped that the deflation, as indeed it did for a time, would lead to an increase in real wages.

On October 6 and December 8, 1931, the Brüning government approved two other tax bills which provided for further spending cuts and tax increases.[74] Corresponding to these measures, the collapse of public investments was particularly severe even in comparison with what happened in the United Kingdom and in the United States.[75] The effects of fiscal austerity on the German economy were added those exerted on it by the start of the global Great Depression, which caused a fall in international price levels. This fall had particularly pronounced repercussions on the

[73] Which amounted to 2 billion Reichsmarks in the 1930 government budget.

[74] Between 1928 and 1931, the effective income tax rate (the ratio of indirect taxes minus subsidies to GNP) increased from 12% to 14%. The effective sales tax rate recorded a similar increase of two percentage points over the same period.

[75] See Balderston (1983).

Table 7.9 Real earnings of German coal miners and number of unemployed (1929.I–1932.II)

Periods	Real wage	Unemployed (thousands)
1929-I	6.30	2036
1929-II	6.43	1575
1929-III	6.44	1814
1929-IV	6.49	2281
1930-I	6.60	2493
1930-II	6.72	3301
1930-III	6.64	4115
1930-IV	6.82	3507
1931-I	6.64	4393
1931-II	6.69	4162
1931-III	6.75	4839
1931-IV	6.44	5248
1932-I	6.23	5587
1932-II	6.34	5764

Source: Bry (1960)

agricultural sector, whose revenues were reduced by about a third in the early 1930s.[76]

The international context, the Brüning's fiscal policy and the credit crunch due to the 1931 crisis led to a pronounced fall in output and to a dramatic increase in the unemployment rate (Table 7.8).

Because of this deep recession price levels fell sharply: in December 1931 industrial finished products and industrial raw and semifinished products prices were, respectively, 9.1 and 11.8% lower than in the same month of the previous year.

Given that at the end of 1931, the Reichsbank's discount rate was at 7% and the day-to-day money rate at 8.45% the diminution of prices led to a remarkable increase in real interest rate: therefore, deflation triggered a process of debt deflation.[77] As shown by Fisher (1933), if the price level falls, businesses find themselves having to repay debts whose value in real terms is high. In order to meet their commitments they are forced to sell assets. By doing so, they encourage a further fall in prices of goods and assets and, by repaying part of the debt incurred, they encourage a slowing down of the velocity of circulation and a decrease in the money supply. In this context, "...[t]he more the debtors pay, the more they owe. The more the economic boat tips, the more it tends to tip. It is not tending to right itself, but is capsizing."[78]

In the second half of 1931, when the price level fell pronouncedly, the increase in the real interest rate on private discount transactions was matched by a significant increase in the number of corporate bankruptcies which, at the end of 1930 had been

[76] See Deutsch Statistische Jahrbuch, 1928–1944.

[77] The consequences of deflation, when not due to decisive improvements in factor productivity, are negative (see Bordo & Filardo, 2004).

[78] Fisher (1933, p. 344)

Table 7.10 Aggregate investment (billion Reichsmarks, 1928–1932)

Kinds of investment	1928	1929	1930	1931	1932
Gross fixed capital investment	13,676	12,786	10,372	6438	4225
Of which: State buildings	2658	2670	2082	1456	1095
Gross fixed capital investment by enterprises	11,018	10,116	8280	4982	3130
Less: Depreciation	6702	6938	6881	6363	5827
Fixed investment by enterprises	6974	5848	3491	75	−1602
Additional: Inventory	1310	360	−1740	−3130	−1520
Net investment by companies	8284	6208	1751	−3055	−3122

Source: Ritschl (2002)

1144; while at the end of 1931 this number had risen to 1692. The increase in the number of bankruptcies during 1931 implied an increase in the risk premium on German bank loans. The differential between the German and British private discount rates increased during 1931 from 2.25 to 7.41 percentage points between January and August.

In a deflationary phase, given the downward rigidity of monetary wages, real wages tend to rise.[79] As Table 7.9 shows, Germany, too, in correspondence with a fall in output and the price level, was simultaneously affected by a significant increase in the number of unemployed workers and a substantial hold in workers' real wages.

The high rigidity of German workers' real wages was largely due to the malfunctioning of the German labor market, which can be traced to both the regulation of bargaining[80] and unemployment benefits combined with changes in the degree of representation of the various trade unions. With regard to the latter, it should be noted that from 1924 onward, membership of the traditional trade unions began to decline, while from 1928 onward radical trade union groups, generally linked to the Communist Party of Germany (KPD), assumed increasing importance. These groups, known as Gewerkschaftsopposition (RGO), came to dominate workers' representation in many industries.

The unemployment insurance system also contributed to the malfunctioning of the labor market, encouraging moral hazard in the behavior of trade unions and rendering the link that normally exists between the unemployment rate and the level of wages essentially inoperative.[81]

[79]Eichengreen and Sachs (1986) showed that in the interwar period this process was particularly intense in the countries that remained in the Gold Standard.

[80]Even at the time of the Depression, the wages and conditions of a large share of workers were defined through collective bargaining. This share can be estimated at two-thirds of blue collar workers and 40% of the total workforce. For a description of the functioning of the labor market in Weimar Germany, see Bry (1960) and James (1986).

[81]No wonder, then, that at least in the first phase of the depression, despite the fall in employment, the aggregate labor income declined very little: from 42,621,000 Reichsmarks in 1928, to 43,045,000 and 39,600,000 Reichsmarks in 1929 and 1930. See Ellis (1940).

The different trends in real wages and labor productivity led to a squeeze on corporate profits,[82] which helps to explain the significant drop in private investment (Table 7.10), a drop which coincided with the pronounced reduction in public investment due to Brüning's fiscal austerity policy.[83] It was primarily the development of these components that determined the depth of the German depression.

In 1932, the German GNP was about half what it had been in 1928 and, as Table 7.8 shows, the unemployment rate had increased almost fourfold. In its intensity, the Great Depression in Germany was similar to that in the United States and was much more severe than that which hit the other advanced countries of the European continent.

The pronounced rise in unemployment due to the deep recession of the German economy led to widespread discontent in German society. In the presidential elections of March 1932, Hitler, leader of the National Socialist Party, won almost 37% in the run-off. This result convinced President Hindenburg to replace Brüning with Franz von Papen giving him the task of forming a technical government and holding parliamentary elections on July 31, 1932. In those elections, the National Socialist Party obtained almost 38% of the vote, the Communist Party almost 15%, while the parties that supported the Republic, in particular, the Social Democratic Party, suffered a significant fall. Since the National Socialist Party did not have an absolute majority and the other parties refused to collaborate with it, Hindenburg called new elections for November 1932. In those elections, the National Socialist Party was confirmed as the relative majority party. In December 1932, Schleicher took over the role of chancellor from Papen, but in January 1933, subject to attacks from various parts, including from the industrialists who had previously supported him, he resigned.

It is widely believed that in Germany the early 1930s economic crisis was particularly serious because of the fiscal austerity pursued by Brüning, who was therefore considered by many scholars to be mainly responsible for Hitler's rise to power.[84]

[82]The downward rigidity of the real wage meant that the demand for consumption remained relatively high compared to the demand for production goods: the fall in the cost of living was less pronounced than the fall in wholesale prices.

[83]Regarding Brüning's fiscal policy, Holtfrerich (2015, p. 9) writes: "Brüning, in contrast [to Hoover], although having a doctorate in economics, did not show any understanding of the circular-flow model of macroeconomics and of the necessity of sustaining demand to counteract a crisis. He was determined to balance the federal budget no matter what tax increases and drastic expenditure cuts might be required."

[84]See among others Childers (1983).

7.7 Political and Economic Causes in the Main Explanations for the Collapse of the Weimar Republic

The economic and political collapse of the Weimar Republic and the manner in which it occurred raises various questions. What were the causes of the collapse of the democratic regime established in 1919 in Germany? Were they to be traced primarily to the fiscal policy of the Brüning government and its dramatic effects on unemployment?

Most economists have traced the end of the Weimar Republic to the effects of the Great Depression and the fiscal austerity of the Brüning government and there is little doubt that the austerity measures implemented by this government between 1930 and 1932 impoverished Germany and contributed significantly to the radicalization of the German electorate,[85] a radicalization to which the banking crisis of 1931 also contributed.[86]

As Einzig argued in the 1930s,[87] the deflationary policy of the government, in creating enormous social unrest, fostered in the electorate a polarization toward the two extreme wings of the political spectrum, i.e., toward the National Socialist Party and the Communist Party, severely weakening the center. In this way, it favored Hitler's rise to power and the end of democracy. This drift could have been avoided if, in concomitance with the fall in demand due to the interruption of capital inflows, Brüning had initiated anti-cyclical fiscal policies. Instead, he pursued the goal of a balanced budget, adopted fiscal austerity measures, and was only concerned with preserving the convertibility of the Reichsmark.[88]

The abandonment of the Gold Standard would, on the other hand, have allowed Germany to regain monetary autonomy and support aggregate demand, thus preventing the unemployment rate from reaching 44.2% in 1932.[89] This view was widely shared by economists and economic historians in the years when Keynesian theory was dominant. As Balderston (1993, p. 4–5) writes: "... received opinion up to 1979 viewed the slump in Germany as the result of a combination of monetary instability and policy inaptness." And again: "A Keynesian consensus emerged among historians of economic policy: Brüning was culpable in choosing deflation

[85] Empirical confirmation of this can be found in Galorè-Vilà et al. (2021).

[86] See Doerr et al. (2021).

[87] Einzig (1938, p. 13) writes: "When the sweeping crisis of 1931 threatened the stability of the Reichsmark, the German government, instead of allowing the pressure to produce its effects, resorted to drastic deflationary measures in order to defend the stability of exchange. The result was the increase of unemployment to something like six million, and the development of a widespread discontent with the regime ... Had dr. Brüning allowed the Reichsmark to depreciate to a reasonable degree in 1931, he might have been able to remain in office .... ."

[88] See, among others, Erbe (1958), Sanmann (1965), and Ferguson and Temin (2003). The latter even argues that the fall of domestic spending occurred before the capital flows from abroad dried up. This position is contested by Falkus (1975) and Balderston (1977).

[89] See Eichengreen and Temin (2010).

when he could and should have chosen reflation, and his choice immiserated Germany and opened the floodgates to Nazism."[90]

This consensus view was challenged by the economic historian Knut Borchardt ([1979], 1991a) according to whom the difficulties of the Weimar Republic were to be traced back to the structural weaknesses, which developed in the German economy in the 1920s. In particular, to higher wages than productivity growth and consequently to a slowdown in the accumulation of capital. Based on this premise, Borchardt concluded that the Brüning government's margins of freedom to implement countercyclical policies were limited.[91]

Balderston (2002) well illustrates the connection between Borchardt's arguments and Brüning's policy options regarding:

1. Brüning government's option of devaluing the Reichsmark or adopting a flexible exchange rate (which implied regaining discretion in the management of monetary policy).
2. The possibility of the Brüning government adopting a deficit-spending policy combined with job-creation measures.

In his view option (1.) was not feasible because—with the acceptance of the Dawes Plan—Germany had, on the one hand, committed itself to keeping its currency convertible into gold and, on the other, had carried out a reform of the Reichsbank, making it independent of government influence. The German central bank was therefore statutorily prevented from financing government deficits with money. The only monetary policy instrument left to the Reichsbank was the ability to set the rediscount rate for commercial bills and refinance banks. This it did extensively during the crises of mid-1931.[92]

As a guarantee of Germany's commitment to maintain the convertibility of the Reichsmark, the central bank was also required to maintain coverage by gold or gold-based foreign currency of at least 40%. At lower coverage ratios, the Reichsbank was required to raise the discount rate.[93]

Under the Young Plan, the main features of which have just been sketched, the Reichsbank Act was an integral part of the agreements governing the payment of Reparations by Germany,[94] with supervision of the implementation of this law being the responsibility of the Executive of the Bank of International Settlement, of which the central banks of London, New York, and Paris were part.

To the various scholarly views[95] according to which the Brüning government should have devalued the Reichsmark, Borchardt (1990, 1991a) essentially raises

[90] See Balderston (2002, p. 91).

[91] See Borchardt ([1980] 1991b).

[92] See James (1985).

[93] If the degree of coverage was less than 40% but more than 25%, the discount rate was to be gradually raised to 5%. If the coverage ratio was only 25%, the discount rate was to be raised to 7%.

[94] See Postdam 31.01 No. 15576-8.

[95] See, among others, Haberler (1976), Maier (1985), and Sommariva and Tullio (1987).

two objections. Firstly, a significant devaluation of the Reichsmark would have been associated with a pronounced expansion of the currency and thus an acceleration of the rate of inflation and, understandably, a large part of German society after the experience of 1923 was fiercely opposed to any policy, which might imply an inflationary upswing. In fact, Brüning, speaking of this possibility, said: "Germany has already experienced an inflation. It would be unthinkable to inflict another inflation on the German people. It would also be impossible to maintain the currency on a level 20% below the current one."[96] The aversion to devaluation and the inflation which it would cause was pervasive in German society on both the left and the right.[97]

Secondly, neither the Dawes Plan nor the Young Plan contemplated a devaluation of the mark which would have meant an explicit violation of the agreements made on Reparations. Such a breach would have exposed Germany to retaliation, in this case, the central banks of the Allied countries could have withdrawn their credit, interrupted the Hoover moratorium, refused to extend the Standstill Agreement, and so on.

Not considering it possible to devalue the Reichsmark given the foreign constraints, Brüning pursued what today we would call a form of internal devaluation. As Schuker (1988, p. 53) writes: "Brüning did not intend to default on the commercial foreign debt. Rather, he aimed to impose Germany's export performance by subjecting prices and wages to the discipline of the market." He sought this route to maintain and, if possible, increase the competitiveness of the German economy by encouraging a decrease in the domestic price level. Since the nominal exchange rate of the Reichsmark was fixed, this would mean a depreciation of the real exchange rate and a higher level of competitiveness of German goods. In order to overcome trade union resistance to his plan, he proposed that monetary wages should only decrease in line with prices: this would have allowed workers to maintain the purchasing power of their wages intact. This proposal, however, failed.

With regard to point (2) of the criticism of Brüning, i.e., the possibility of deficit-spending policies, since covering public deficits with money was not possible for the reasons just stated, there was no alternative but to provide for their financing with debt. However, already in 1930, but especially in 1931, this possibility appeared impossible to Germany. Firstly, the financial markets were unwilling to buy German securities as both the private and public sectors were considered overly indebted. Already in 1929 both the Reich, the Landers and the Communities had stood on the verge of bankruptcy, while in October 1930 a consortium headed by Lee Higginson had only just managed to place a German loan of 125 million dollars on the market, after this there were no further loans issued.[98]

---

[96] See Akten der Reichskanzlei (ADR), nr. 502, 2 October 1931, 1782–1783. Similar arguments can be found in ADR, nr. 523, 27 October 1931, 1848–1850.

[97] On this aspect see Straumann (2009).

[98] For an analysis of the reasons for Germany's difficulty in obtaining financing on international markets see Clarke (1967) and Moggridge (1982).

This situation is well illustrated in a speech by Brüning at a meeting of the Reichstag in August 1931: "The deliberations of the Committee of Banking Experts have led to the unanimous view that a long-term loan is not possible in the foreseeable future for market reasons. We must, once and for all, be clear in our minds about one thing, that, for purely technical reasons, we have no other alternative but to grit our teeth and see how we can get through the winter."[99]

On the other hand, in the situation of illiquidity and distress in which it found itself in the summer crisis of 1931, it was unthinkable that the government could obtain financing from the banks.

Given the situation just illustrated, the only source of public deficit financing could come from the Reichsbank, whose behavior, however, was subject to the constraints previously outlined. On the basis of these arguments, Borchardt shared the view expressed in a letter sent by Prof. Bonn to State Secretary Schäffer on September 10, 1931: "The seriousness of the German situation is due to the fact that through light-minded borrowing during the boom Germany has made itself uncreditworthy during the recession."[100]

Borchardt's theses have been challenged by several scholars according to whom Brüning, having alternatives that could have been explored, was wrong to adopt a deflationary policy. Holtfrerich, in particular, has pointed out that several key government figures and senior civil servants advocated for reflationary policies.[101] Among them, the State Secretary Hans Schäffer produced a memorandum on September 02, 1931, in which he advocated an economic policy designed to check deflation and stop the decline of prices.[102] Shortly afterward, in January 1932, Ernst Wagemann, President of the Reich Statistical Office, published a plan which proposed measures to widen the Reichsbank's margins of freedom to increase the money supply and stimulate demand.[103]

James (1990) downplayed the importance of these positions, recalling how Schäffer himself later revised his position, even criticizing the Wagemann plan in the belief that the German crisis could not be countered by technical measures, since it was rooted in a shortage of domestic and foreign capital.[104]

Beyond what has been, and is, the political and technical debate on the possibilities of the Brüning government to reflate the German economy and looking beyond

[99]Brüning's speech to the Vereingte Ausschüsse of the Reichsrat, August 13, 1931. See also Brüning (1970).

[100]Letter from Prof. Bonn to State Secretary Schäffer, 10 September 1931, Ba Koblenz, NL 82 (Bonn), no. 52.

[101]See Holtfrerich (1982, 1990b).

[102]For the text of this memorandum see Schulz et al. (1980).

[103]See Bombach and Netzband (1981).

[104]Schäffer diaries: memoranda of 19 and 28 Nov. 1931; and entry of 2 Feb. 1932. 28 Jan. 1932 Schäffer to Wagemann, Schäffer papers.

the external constraints on the policy choices of this government,[105] we must not forget the internal conditions to which it was subject and the weakness inherent in a minority government. As Bessel (1990, p. 185) writes: "While examining economic policy per se it may seem logical to posit that what was possible for Hitler should have been possible for Brüning. But this overlooks the fundamental differences in their political positions." These differences primarily concerned domestic politics, the first Brüning government was a minority government while the second had less than 10% parliamentary support. The question must therefore be asked whether, beyond the institutional constraints highlighted by Borchardt, there was political scope to pursue an alternative policy.

7.8 The Escalation of Distributive Conflict and the End of German Democracy

Brüning's aim of setting market forces free to work and encouraging a fall in prices and wages that would allow Germany to gain competitiveness in international markets failed. As we have seen, the downward rigidity of monetary wages meant that even with a significant increase in unemployment, real wages increased. The government's recourse to decrees through which wages were adjusted or limits placed on the prices of goods and services, albeit unintentionally, made the German economy a centrally controlled economy, while the nationalization of the major banks, decided in 1932, led in the same direction.

The failure of the previously mentioned objective was largely due to the resistance of the various interest groups to accept the reforms necessary for the recovery of the German economy. In previous years, the distributional conflict that characterized the Weimar Republic had been cauterized in different ways, in the years of inflation it was the rentiers who had borne the costs of the growth of the economy that, while allowing low unemployment rates and maintaining social calm, implied persistent current account deficits that were unsustainable in the long run. In the second half of the 1920s, after the stabilization and the Reichstag's acceptance of the Dawes Plan, the distributional conflict subsided thanks to large inflows of capital from abroad. This allowed Germany to keep domestic absorption and living standards high. As Weisbrod (1990, p. 49) writes: "The period between 1924 and 1929 must be seen as a period of relative stability, which, in political terms, granted the embattled Weimar Republic only a temporary lease of life. The prospect of economic growth on the basis of the financial arrangements of the Dawes Plan triggered a process of accommodation with the constitutional and legal framework of the post-revolutionary settlement."

[105] Acknowledged by Eichengreen (1993, p. 26), who writes: "Countries other than Germany might free themselves from these constraints by abandoning the Gold Standard. In the German case, however, the Hague Treaty and powerful memories of hyperinflation precluded even that option."

Against this backdrop, the political class was incapable of making any real recovery plans for the German economy. On the contrary, capital inflows from abroad reflected negatively on the real and financial structure of the economy. On the one hand, the exchange rate appreciated in correspondence with large amounts of foreign financing, giving rise to a form of Dutch disease, characterized by a reallocation of capital and labor toward non-tradable sectors whose profitability was higher than that of tradables. On the other hand, the public sector, primarily the Reich and the municipalities, became heavily indebted to foreign markets. Ordinary banks, especially the larger ones, did the same.

At the end of the 1920s the inflow of capital from abroad came to a halt and in 1929, 1930, and 1931, Germany experienced a series of sudden stops and currency crises of increasing intensity. As a result of these crises and in particular, the crisis of 1931, German output decreased significantly. This decrease in output exacerbated the distributional conflict that had characterized the Weimar Republic and had been temporarily compounded, first, by inflation and then by foreign financing. No interest group was willing to bear the reduction in income resulting from the cessation of foreign borrowing and fall in aggregate income, and least of all the cost of government-imposed redistributive measures. Emblematic of this is the reactions of certain interest groups to the agricultural support measures and the attempt to control price dynamics.

As we have seen, the banking panic that followed the 1931 crisis resulted in a significant increase in the real interest rate, the negative effects of which were particularly pronounced on the most indebted economic sector, agriculture. The bank debt exposure of this sector in 1930–1931 was particularly high[106] and, following the increase in the real interest rate in 1931, the debt burden of agricultural enterprises increased significantly. This, coupled with the pronounced fall in international food prices that had begun in the late 1920s, led to the bankruptcy of many agricultural businesses. The grave economic and financial situation encouraged the landowning aristocracy to lobby the government for support, and Brüning had no choice other than to pass measures to support one of the interest groups that had supported him most loyally.

The first form of support consisted of measures to reduce or consolidate debt. Previous governments had given large estate subsidies of fairly modest overall amounts.[107] With the law of March 31, 1931 (Osthile law), the government tackled the problem of agrarian debt much more aggressively, providing farmers with 500 million Reichsmarks for debt relief. In the Fourth Emergency Decree of 8 December 1931, it was decided to reduce interest rates above 8%, in particular, those on agricultural credit. The various forms of financial support for agriculture

[106]This was mainly due to the low profitability of this sector, especially of the large estates of East Prussia. The situation was further aggravated by the pronounced fall in the world price of wheat that began in the late 1920s. See James (1986, p. 258).

[107]In 1928, foreign currency credit lines had been arranged at below-market interest rates. In 1929, a fund was set up to reschedule loans and relieve the interest burden.

limited the number of bankruptcies in the sector, which nevertheless amounted to 5765 firms in 1931 and 7060 in 1932.[108]

A second measure that helped to contain the number of agricultural bankruptcies was the use of duties on imported agricultural products. During the second half of the 1920s, these duties were gradually raised and extended to a broader spectrum of goods.

The measures to support agriculture and the property owners provoked deeply negative reactions from both industry and trade unions. In particular, the introduction of duties on agricultural products was strongly opposed by industrialists for at least two reasons. Firstly, this measure exposed Germany to retaliation by countries importing German industrial products, such as the Netherlands, Scandinavian countries, and Poland, this was a concern shared by the trade unions and the SPD.[109] Secondly, since the duties affected domestic food prices, they reduced the purchasing power of workers, causing them to demand wage increases, which increased the industrial costs.

According to the workers' unions, the wage rises represented nothing more than compensation for the protection offered by the government to the agrarian sector. This reaction was, of course, contrary to Brüning's goal of internal devaluation.

The measures to support agriculture not only aroused discontent among industrialists and workers, but also proved ineffective. Because of this, violent protests were directed by the agrarians not only against the banks, which demanded the repayment of loans, but also against Hindenburg himself, who had previously been considered by this class as a firm point of reference, and thus against Brüning and the Republic. It is certainly no coincidence that in the predominantly agricultural parts of the country, i.e., in the East Prussian provinces, the National Socialist Party enjoyed major electoral successes in the general elections of 1930 and 1932.[110]

The actions taken aimed at a simultaneous reduction of prices and wages[111] also provoked negative reactions from the interest groups that were immediately affected. The wage reductions of civil servants contained in the first tax decree aroused great hostility toward the government among these workers, while similar hostility was aroused in shopkeepers over the imposition of retail price reductions, such as those contained in the January 1931 decree. This decrease, given the relative rigidity of labor costs, affected the profit margins of small shopkeepers who thus came to believe that: "... the decent Catholic Chancellor Brüning was taking the side of modern world against the solid bourgeois values which small retailers believed that they embodied perfectly."[112] In this way, Brüning also lost the support of a large part of the petty bourgeoisie, which turned inevitably toward the National Socialist Party.

The examples just illustrated show how Brüning's measures, on the one hand, proved ineffective with respect to his goal of reducing prices and wages, and, on the

[108] See Statistisches Jahrbuch, 1933, p. 386.

[109] See James (1986, p. 268).

[110] See Bessel (1990).

[111] See James (1986, p. 244).

[112] See James (1986, p. 232).

other hand, progressively eroded the support for his government with interest groups that had initially supported him and hence contributed to a polarization of the electorate.

The intensification of the distributive conflict made it ever more difficult to satisfy these conflicting interests through a democratic process.

For a long time, an absolute aversion to the payment of Reparations had united the various different political parties. However, when, with the moratorium proposed by Hoover, this issue was effectively removed, social and political conflict flared up uncontrollably. The German electorate became yet more polarized, the political representation of the center parties weakened significantly, and a growing section of the electorate, having lost all faith in democracy, called for an authoritarian regime.

In this context, the political conflict escalated. During 1931, acts of political violence, in particular, clashes between extreme factions[113] and attacks on property,[114] increased significantly. The press helped emphasize these episodes of unrest which seemed to foreshadow the specter of civil war.[115] Brüning's government increasingly appeared unable not only to reconcile the different interests of German society but also to counter the violent chaos that pervaded the country.

Distrust in this and the subsequent governments of Papen and Schleicher eventually became a distrust of democracy and the Weimar Republic. It should, however, be noted that on a formal level the democratic mechanisms had already been compromised well before the perceived "need" for authoritarian government led, in July and November 1932, to the electoral success of the National Socialist Party. Indeed, while public support for the democratic regime was waning, the functioning of some of the institutional mechanisms that characterize such a regime had long since broken down. As mentioned previously, the Brüning governments, as also the other minority governments, operated on the basis of Article 48 of the Constitution, and between 1930 and 1932, the number of laws passed by the Reichstag fell from 98 to 5, while presidential decrees rose from 5 to 66 during the same period. The bypassing of parliament began with Brüning, but with Papen's chancellorship the "authoritarian democracy" evolved into an "authoritarian presidential government."[116] No wonder, then, that according to some scholars the end of German democracy should not be fixed with Hitler's appointment as chancellor on January 30, 1933, but rather with the breakdown of the Great Coalition on March 27, 1930. They argue, in fact, that with the institutionalization of the use of Article 48, the Weimar Republic had ceased to exist as a parliamentary democracy and had become a proto-autocratic regime,[117] with Hindenburg ruling as "protoführer."[118]

[113] See Schumann (2001).

[114] See Loberg (2014).

[115] See Fulda (2009).

[116] See McElligott (2009, p. 34–35).

[117] See Mommsen (1998).

[118] See Broszat (1987).

7.9 Conclusions

It has already been said that the German people's sense of national identity was probably weakened by the abdication of the Kaiser demanded by President Wilson. The Republic, also because of this, was supported by some interest groups but opposed by others who blamed it for accepting to pay Reparations. In this context, as always happens when the sense of national identity is weak, the distributive conflict was bitter for the whole period that the Republic and the democratic regime lasted.

This conflict, however, for much of the 1920s was cushioned initially, until 1923, by inflation that allowed the state to enjoy a large amount of seigniorage, and after hyperinflation and the acceptance of the Dawes Plan, by large inflows of capital from abroad that allowed the government to cover both public and current account deficits in the balance of payments. From 1929 onward, however, the flow of capital from abroad was drastically reduced and maintaining the convertibility of the Reichsmark became problematic. An early warning of this problem occurred in the spring of 1929 during the negotiations in Paris of a committee of experts, chaired by the American financier Owen Young, entrusted with the task of finding a definitive solution to the Reparations problem, thus completing the Dawes Plan. In the course of these negotiations, Reichsbank President Schacht, a delegate of the German government, took a very aggressive stance toward the Allied powers, claiming that Germany could only support an annual German payment in the amount of 1650 million marks given a revision of some important points of the Versailles Treaty. As a result of this stance, the negotiations reached an impasse, which was perceived by the markets as a failure of the talks. Confidence in the stability of the Reichsmark was severely weakened and the resulting flight of capital obliged the Reichsbank to use part of its gold reserves to defend the Reichsmark. These interventions were accompanied by a tightening of monetary policy. Currency tensions eased when Germany received a loan from a group of foreign banks led by the Lee Higginson Bank. The crisis of the spring 1929 highlighted the fragility of Germany's financial situation. The scarcity of capital flows from abroad meant that it was impossible for the country to maintain a persistent budget and current account imbalances. In this context, if the convertibility of the Reichsmark was to be maintained, it was necessary to reduce domestic absorption through restrictive fiscal measures. The lack of consensus on the nature and extent of these measures led to the fall of the Great Coalition government headed by the Social Democrat Hermann Müller in March 1930 which was succeeded by a minority government, without SPD support, chaired by the Center Party leader Heinrich Brüning.

This government in the course of 1930 adopted a series of decrees that introduced expenditure cuts and tax increases which, issued as emergency decrees according to Article 48 of the Constitution, did not require parliamentary approval. These measures led to a drastic fall in domestic demand. Brüning's attempt to compensate for this fall with an increase in exports failed because his attempt to simultaneously reduce wages and prices was unsuccessful, with non-market mechanisms prevailing in the determination of these variables which were rigidly downward. As a result of this and the international recession, German exports decreased rather than increased. Over the course of the 1930s, in line with the decrease in aggregate demand, output contracted and the unemployment rate rose sharply.

The resulting widespread social discontent contributed to a resounding victory by extremist parties, in particular, the Communist and National Socialist Parties, in the elections of 14 September of that year. The political polarization sanctioned by the elections and the political instability that ensued fostered a new wave of distrust in the possibility of a stabilization of the German economy. This resulted in a new phase of capital outflow, in particular, of foreign deposits from German banks, and a downward speculation on the Reichsmark. As a result, the Reichsbank intervened in the foreign exchange market to defend the convertibility of the German currency. At the same time, however, it was forced to compensate the banks' loss of liquid resources with extensive discounting of commercial paper. In this crisis, therefore, a trade-off emerged in Reichsbank policy that would take dramatic form in the 1931 crisis.

The Reichsbank acted to stabilize the exchange rate while, at the same time trying to provide liquidity to attempt to ensure the stability of the banking system, this liquidity was used by the banks to provide loans to their clients some of whom were possibly involved in speculating on the currency market.

As in the case of the 1929 crisis, the 1930 crisis was overcome thanks to a loan (from a consortium led by the Lee Higginson Bank) and a few months of calm followed.

In the early part of 1931, however, as a new budget imbalance emerged, the government adopted new fiscal austerity measures. Brüning, realizing the resulting growing unpopularity of his government and trying to gain the support of the nationalists, took an increasingly aggressive foreign policy approach. He, therefore, supported Foreign Minister Curtius' attempt to create a customs union between Germany and Austria, despite this being a blatant violation of the Treaty of Versailles.[119] Opinion at home and abroad greeted the project as the prelude to a political union; and the alarm was raised in those countries, notably France and Czechoslovakia, to whom the idea of such a union was intolerable.

In early June, when presenting a new tax decree, Brüning made a dramatic appeal to the Allied powers, the so-called Tribute Appeal, in which he stated that the economic conditions of the Reich make "... relieving Germany of the unbearable Reparations payments imperative necessity," adding that the "limit of what we can impose on our people"[120] had been reached. This stance by the German Chancellor led to the belief in the markets that Germany was unable to pay the annuities stipulated under the Young Plan. This conviction, even more than the failure of the Austrian bank Credit Anstalt, encouraged a massive withdrawal of foreign deposits, a withdrawal which intensified with the news of Danat Bank's critical

[119] See Orde (1980).

[120] Quoted in Mommsen (1996, p. 387).

situation. The Reichsbank, in an attempt to defend the stability of the Reichsmark, lost a large part of its reserves. Given the strong dependence of German banks on foreign capital, the withdrawal of deposits by non-residents led to a shortage of funds on the interbank market and, as a result, these banks found themselves in a solvency crisis. The currency crisis turned into a banking panic. The risk of a chain of bank failures prompted the government to proclaim a bank holiday for 14 and 15 July. On these 2 days, it passed a reform involving strong state participation in the ownership of the big German banks.

The recurring fiscal austerity measures and the credit crunch following the banking crisis had a dramatic impact on the growth of German output and unemployment. The social turmoil that resulted from the poor performance of the German economy and Brüning government's fiscal measures fostered the emergence of a widespread distrust of democracy and fueled the demand for an authoritarian regime, paving the way for Hitler's rise.

A wide range of scholars attribute National Socialism's rise to power to the Brüning government's policy of fiscal austerity. The assumption underlying this view is that if Brüning had somehow stimulated aggregate demand, the unemployment rate would not have risen dramatically, social discontent would have remained contained and the National Socialist Party would not have become the relative majority party in the country. This view was criticized by Borchardt according to whom, taking into account the constraints imposed by the Dawes Plan and Germany's difficulties in obtaining foreign funding, as was the case in the second half of the 1920s, Brüning government's margins of freedom in conducting economic policy were very limited. The debate that followed Borchardt's analysis highlighted that at the beginning of the 1930s, the German economy had accumulated major structural weaknesses: a public budget persistently in deficit as well as the current account balance, non-market price, and wage setting mechanisms, a banking system with a very low degree of capitalization and highly dependent on foreign deposits. These weaknesses were rooted in the high level of distributional conflict that characterized Germany after the First World War and which the Weimar Republic was unable to resolve. After the defeat, the abdication of the Kaiser and the establishment of the Republic, the sense of national identity was attenuated: no interest group was willing to accept the sacrifices necessary to stabilize the German economy. The possibility of settling the social conflict by resorting to the redistributive effects of inflation and later the Dawes Plan, thanks to the massive inflow of capital from abroad, had been exhausted. Due to the persistence of this social conflict, the stabilization of the German economy had proved impracticable even when the international conditions facilitating it existed, i.e., between 1920 and 1921. It could therefore hardly be achieved at a time when the rest of the world was entering a deep recession and the weaknesses of the German economy, which had developed during the inflation and overborrowing phases, were emerging in all their gravity.

When US President Hoover proposed a moratorium on war debts, the last bond that held the various interest groups together, namely their opposition to the Allied powers on the issue of Reparations, was removed. The remaining trust in the

Republic and the ability of a democratic system to settle social conflict dissolved and the Weimar Republic collapsed.

References

Aguado, G. (2001). The Creditanstalt crisis of 1931 and the failure of Austro-German customs union project. *The Historical Journal, 44*, 199–221.

Balderston, T. (1977). The German business cycle in the 1920s. *Economic History Review, 30*, 159–171.

Balderston, T. (1983). The beginning of the depression in Germany 1924-30: Investment and the capital market. *Economic History Review, 36*, 395–415.

Balderston, T. (1991). German banking between the wars: The crisis of the credit banks. *Business History Review, 66*, 565–581.

Balderston, T. (1993). *The origins and course of the German economic crisis: November 1923 to May 1932*. Haude & Spener.

Balderston, T. (1994). The banks and the gold standard in the German financial crisis of 1931. *Financial History Review, 1*, 43–68.

Balderston, T. (2002). *Economics and politics in the Weimar Republic*. Cambridge University Press.

Banholzer, S., & Straumann, T. (2015). Why the French said "non": Creditor-debtor politics and the German financial crises of 1930 and 1931. *Journal of Contemporary History, 56*, 1040–1060.

Bennett, E. W. (1962). *Germany and the diplomacy of the financial crisis, 1931*. Harvard University Press.

Bessel, R. (1990). Why did the Weimar Republic collapse? In I. Kershaw (Ed.), *Weimar: Why did German democracy fail?* St. Martin's Press.

Blickle, K., Beunnermeier, M., & Luck, S. (2022). *Who can tell which banks will fail?* NBER working paper n. 29753.

Bombach, G., & Netzband, K. B. (1981). *Der Keynesianismus III. Die geld- und beschäftigungs-theoretische Diskussion in Deutschland zur Zeit von Keynes. Dokumente und Analysen.* Springer-Verlag.

Borchardt, K. (1990). A decade of debate about Brüning's economic policy. In J. B. von Kruedener (Ed.), *Economic crisis and political collapse. The Weimar Republic 1924–1933*. St. Martin's Press.

Borchardt, K. ([1979], 1991a). Constraints and room for manoeuvre in the Great Depression of the early Thirties: towards a revision of the received historical picture. In K. Borchardt (Ed.), *Perspectives on Modern German Economic History and Policy*, Cambridge University Press. English translation from K. Borchardt (1979), Zwangslagen und Handlungsspielr*ä*ume in der *großen* Wirtschaftskrise der frühen drei*ß*iger Jahre: zur Revision des *ü*berlieferten Geschichtsbildes. *Jahrbuch der Bayerischen Akademie der Wissenschaften, 72*, 85–132. Reprinted in 1982 in K. Borchardt (Ed.), *Wachstum, Krisen, und Hundlungsspielräume der Wirrschuftspolitik*. Vandenhoeck & Ruprecht.

Borchardt, K. ([1980], 1991b). The economic causes of the collapse of the Weimar Republic. In K. Borchardt (Ed.), *Perspectives on Modern German Economic History and Policy*, Cambridge University Press. English translation from K. Borchardt (1980), Wirtschaftliche Ursachen des Scheiterns der Weimarer Republik, in K.D. Erdmann, & H. Schulze (Eds.), *Weimar, Selbstpreisgabe eimer Demokratie. Eine Bilanz heute*, Droste. Reprinted in 1982 in K. Borchardt (Ed.), *Wachstum, Krisen, und Hundlungsspielräume der Wirtschaftspolitik*. Vandenhoeck & Ruprecht.

Bordo, M., & Filardo, A. (2004). *Deflation and monetary policy in a historical perspective: Remembering the past or being condemned to repeat it?* NBER working paper n. 10833.

Born, K. E. (1967). *Die deutsche Bankenrise 1931*. Piper.

Born, K. E. (1983). *International banking in the 19th and 20th centuries*. Berg Publishers.

Bracher, K. D. (1955). *Die Auflösung der Weimarer Republik: eine Studie zum Problem des Machtverfalls in der Demokratie*. Ring-Verlag.

Breitenlechner, M., Gründler, D., Mathy, G. P., & Scharler, J. (2022). Credit supply shocks and the great depression in Germany. *European Review of Economic History, 26*, 1–37.

Broszat, M. (1987). *Hitler and the collapse of Weimar Germany*. Leamington.

Brüning, H. (1970). *Memoiren 1918-1934*. Deutsche Verlagsanstalt.

Bry, G. (1960). *Wages in Germany 1871–1945*. Princeton University Press.

Burhop, C. (2011). The historiography of the 1931 crisis in Germany. *Jahrbuch für Wirtschaftsgeschichte/Economic History Yearbook, 52*, 9–27.

Chang, R., & Velasco, A. (2001). A model of financial crises in emerging markets. *Quarterly Journal of Economics, 116*, 489–517.

Child, F. C. (1958). *The theory and practice of exchange control in Germany*. Martinus Nijhoff.

Childers, T. (1983). *The Nazi voter. The social foundations of fascism in Germany, 1919–1933*. University of North Carolina Press.

Clarke, S. O. (1967). *Central bank cooperation 1924–1931*. Federal Reserve Bank of New York.

Corsetti, G., Pesenti, P., & Roubini, N. (1998). Paper tigers? A model of Asian crisis. *European Economic Review, 43*, 1211–1216.

Diamond, D., & Dybvig, P. (1983). Bank runs, deposit insurance, and liquidity. *Journal of Political Economy, 91*, 401–419.

Doerr, S., Gissler, S., Peydro, J. L., & Voth, H. J. (2021). *Financial crises and political radicalization: How failing banks paved Hitler's path to power*. BIS working paper n. 928.

Eichengreen, B. (1992). *Golden fetters: The gold standard and the great depression*. Oxford University Press.

Eichengreen, B. (1993). *Perspectives on the Borchardt debate*. University of California Department of Economics working paper n. 93/20.

Eichengreen, B., & Sachs, J. (1986). Competitive devaluations and the great depression: A theoretical reassessment. *Economic Letters, 22*, 67–71.

Eichengreen, B., & Temin, P. (2010). Fetters of gold and paper. *Oxford Review of Economic Policy, 26*, 370–384.

Einzig, P. (1938). Finance and foreign policy. *Virginia Quarterly Review, 14*, 1–16.

Ellis, H. S. (1940). Exchange control in Germany. *Quarterly Journal of Economics, 54*, 1–217.

Enquête-Ausschuß. (1929). *Die Reichsbank. Verhandlungen und Berichte des Unterausschusses für Geld-, Kredit- und Finanzwesen*. Mittler & Sohn.

Erbe, R. (1958). *Die nationalsozialistische Wirtschaftspolitik 1933–1939 im Lichte der modernen Theorie*. Polygraphischer Verlag.

Eyck, E. (1962). *Geschichte der Weimarer Republik*. Eugen Rentsch.

Falkus, M. E. (1975). The German business cycle in the 1920s. *Economic History Review, 28*, 451–465.

Falter, J. W., Lindenberger, T., & Schumann, S. (1986). *Wahlen und Abstimmungen in der Weimarer Republik: Materialen zum Wahlverhalten, 1919–1933*. Verlag C.H. Beck.

Ferguson, T., & Temin, P. (2003). Made in Germany: The German currency crisis of July 1931. *Research in Economic History, 21*, 1–53.

Feuchtwanger, E. (1995). *From Weimar to Hitler: Germany, 1918–33*. Palgrave.

Fischer, A. (1999a). Der Kollaps vor dem Kollaps. Zwei Akzentverschiebungen in Sachen Bankerise. *Bankhistorisches Archiv, 25*, 5–22.

Fischer, A. (1999b). Schuld und Schicksal in der Bankenkrise - eine westdeutsche Perspektive. *Vierteljahrschrift für Sozial und Wirtschaftsgeschichte, 86*, 181–209.

Fisher, I. (1933). Debt-deflation theory of great depressions. *Econometrica, 4*, 337–357.

Flora, P., Alber, J., Eichenberg, R., Kohl, J., Kraus, F., Pfenning, W., & Seebohm, K. (1987). *State, economy, and society in Western Europe 1815–1975*. Macmillan.

Friedman, M., & Schwartz, A. (1963). *A monetary history of the United States 1867 to 1960*. Princeton University Press.

Fulda, B. (2009). *Press and politics in the Weimar Republic*. Oxford University Press.

Galofré-Vilà, G., Meissner, C. M., McKee, M., & Stuckler, D. (2021). Austerity and the rise of the Nazi Party. *Journal of Economic History, 81*, 81–113.

Goldfajn, I., & Valdés, R. O. (1997). *Capital flows and the twin crises: The role of liquidity*. IMF working paper n. WP/97/87.

Goldstein, I. (2005). Strategic complementarities and the twin crises. *Economic Journal, 115*, 368–390.

Haberler, G. (1976). *The world economy, money and the great depression, 1919–1939*. American Economic Institute for Public Policy Research.

Hardach, G. (1984). Banking and industry in Germany in the interwar period 1919-1939. *Journal of European Economic History, 13*, 203–234.

Holtfrerich, C. L. (1982). Alternativen zu Brünings Wirtschaftspolitik in der Weltwirtschaftskrise? *Historische Zeitschrift, 235*, 605–631.

Holtfrerich, C. L. (1986). *The German inflation 1914–1923: Causes and effects in international perspective*. De Gruyter.

Holtfrerich, C. L. (1990a). Was the policy of deflation in Germany unavoidable? In J. V. von Kruedener (Ed.), *Economic crisis and the political collapse. The Weimar Republic 1924–33*. Berg Publishers.

Holtfrerich, C. L. (1990b). Economic policy options and the end of the Weimar Republic. In I. Kershaw (Ed.), *Weimar: Why did German democracy fail?* St. Martin's Press.

Holtfrerich, C. L. (2015). *Austerity: Views of chancellor Brüning's and president Hoover's fiscal policies across the Atlantic, 1930–32*. Helmut Schmidt Prize Lecture, German Historical Institute at Washington, December, 10.

Irmler, H. (1976). Bankenkrise und Vollbeschäftigungspolitik (1931-1936). Deutsche Bundesbank (Ed.), *Währung und Wirtschaft in Deutschland 1876-1975*.

James, H. (1984). The causes of the German banking crisis of 1931. *Economic History Review, 37*, 68–87.

James, H. (1985). *The Reichsbank and public finance in Germany: 1924–1933*. Knapp.

James, H. (1986). *The German slump, politics and economics, 1924–36*. Clarendon Press.

James, H. (1990). Economic reasons for the collapse of the Weimar republic. In I. Kershaw (Ed.), *Weimar: Why did German democracy fail?* St. Martin's Press.

James, A. (1998). Die Reichsbank 1876 bis 1945. In D. Bundesbank (Ed.), *Fünfzig Jahre Deutsche Mark: Notenbank und Währung in Deutschland seit 1948*. Verlag C.H. Beck.

Kindleberger, C. (1973). *The world in depression*. University of California Press.

Kindleberger, C. (1984). *A financial history of Western Europe*. Allen & Unwin.

Kindleberger, C., & Aliber, R. (2005). *Manias, panics and crashes. A history of financial crises*. Wiley.

Knox, M. (2007). *To the threshold of power, 1922/33*. Cambridge University Press.

Krugman, P. (1979). A model of balance-of-payments crisis. *Journal of Money, Credit and Banking, 11*, 311–325.

Krugman, P. (1998). *What happened to Asia?* https://web.mit.edu/krugman/www/DISINTER.html.

Krugman, P. (1999). Balance sheets, the transfer problem, and financial crises. *International Tax and Public Finance, 6*, 459–472.

League of Nations. (1931). *Memorandum on commercial banks, 1919–1929*. League of Nations.

League of Nations (1935). Commercial banks, The Economic Intelligence Service of the League of Nations, Geneva.

Leith-Ross, F. (1968). *Money talks: Fifty years of international finance: The autobiography of Sir Frederick Leith-Ross*. Hutchinson.

Link, W. (1970). *Die amerikanische Stabilizierungspolitik in Deutschland, 1921–1932*. Verlag Droste.

Loberg, M. (2014). Fortress shop: Consumer culture, violence, and security in Weimar Berlin. *Journal of Contemporary History, 49*, 675–701.
Lüke, R. E. (1958). *Von der Stabilisierung zur Krise*. Polygraphischer Verlag.
Maier, C. S. (1975). *Recasting bourgeois Europe: Stabilization in France, Germany and in Italy in the decade after world war I*. Princeton University Press.
Maier, C. (1985). Die Nicht-determinierheit ökonomischer Modelle. Überlegungen zu Knut Borchardts these von der 'kranken Wirtschaft' der Weimarer Republik. *Geschichte und Gesellschaft, 11*, 275–294.
Maurer, I., & Wengst, U. (1980). *Politik und Wirtschaft in der Krise 1930–1932. Quellen zur Ära Brüning*. Verlag Droste.
McElligott, A. (2009). *Weimar Germany*. Oxford University Press.
McKinnon, R., & Phil, H. (1996). Credible liberalization and international capital flows: The 'Overborrowing syndrome'. In T. Ito & A. Kruger (Eds.), *Financial deregulation and integration in East Asia*. University of Chicago Press.
McNeil, W. C. (1986). *American money and the Weimar Republic: Economics and politics on the eve of the great depression*. Columbia University Press.
Miller, V. (1996). Speculative currency attacks with endogenously induced commercial bank crises. *Journal of International Money and Finance, 15*, 383–403.
Moggridge, D. E. (1982). Policy in the crises of 1920 and 1929. In C. Kindleberger & J. P. Laffargue (Eds.), *Crises, theory, history and policy*. Cambridge University Press.
Mommsen, H. (1996). *The rise and fall of Weimar democracy*. University of North Carolina Press.
Mommsen, W. J. (1998). Max Weber and the peace Treaty of Versailles. In M. F. Boemke, G. D. Feldman, & E. Glaser (Eds.), *The Treaty of Versailles. A reassessment after 75 years*. Cambridge University Press.
Mühlen, N. (1938). *Hitler's magician: Schacht*. Routledge.
Murad, A. (1932). The Reichsbank in the financial crisis of 1931. *Journal of Business of the University of Chicago, 5*, 175–191.
Néré, J. (2002). *The foreign policy of France from 1914 to 1945*. Routledge.
Northrop, M. B. (1938). *Control policies of the Reichsbank, 1924–1933*. Columbia University Press.
Notermans, T. (2000). *Money, markets and the state*. Cambridge University Press.
Obstfeld, M. (1986). Rational and self-fulfilling balance-of-payments crises. *American Economic Review, 76*, 72–81.
Orde, A. (1980). The origins of the German-Austrian customs union affair of 1931. *Central European History, 13*, 34–59.
Petzina, D. (1969). Germany and the great depression. *Journal of Contemporary History, 4*, 59–74.
Ritschl, A. (1996). *Was Schacht right? Reparations, the Young plan and the great depression in Germany*. Available on line at https://personal.lse.ac.uk/ritschl/pdf_files/schacht2.pdf
Ritschl, A. (2002). *Deutschlands Krise und Konjunktur, 1924–1934: Binnenkonjunktur, Auslandsverschuldung und Reparationsproblem zwischen Dawes-Plan und Transfersperre*. Akademie Verlag.
Ritschl, A., & Sarferaz, S. (2014). Currency versus banking in the German debt crisis of 1931. *International Economic Review, 55*, 349–373.
Ritschl, A., & Spoerer. (1997). Das Bruttosozialprodukt in Deutschland nach den amtlichen Volkseinkommens- und Sozialproduktsstatistiken 1901-1995. *Jahrbuch für Wirtschaftsgeschichte/ Economic History Yearbook, 38*, 27–54.
Rosenberg, A. (1936). *A history of the German Republic*. Methuen and Co..
Rothbard, M. N. (1963). *America's great depression*. Mises Institute.
Sanmann, H. (1965). Daten und Alternativen der deutschen Wirtschafts und Finanzpolitik in der Ära Brüning. *Hamburger Jahrbuch für Wirtschafts und Gesellschaftspolitik, 10*, 109–140.
Schacht, H. (1955). *My first seventy-six years: The autobiography of Hjalmer Schacht*. Allan Wingate.
Schiemann, J. (1931). *Die Deutsche Währung in der Weltwirtschaftskrise 1929–1933*. Paul Haupt.

Schnabel, I. (2004). The German twin crisis of 1931. *Journal of Economic History, 64*, 822–871.
Schnabel, I. (2009). The role of liquidity and implicit guarantees in the German twin crisis of 1931. *Journal of International Money and Finance, 28*, 1–25.
Schuker, J. A. (1988). American 'reparations' to Germany, 1919-33: Implications for the Third-World debt crisis. Princeton Studies in International Finance, 61.
Schulz, G., Maurer, I., Wengst, U., & Heideking, T. (1980). *Politik und Wirtschaft in der Krise 1930–1932. Quellen zur Ära Brüning*. Droste Verlag.
Schumann, D. (2001). *Political violence in the Weimar Republic, 1918–1933*. Beghahn Books.
Sommariva, A., & Tullio, G. (1987). *German macroeconomic history, 1880–1979*. Palgrave Macmillan.
Storer, C. (2013). *A short history of the Weimar Republic*. Tauris.
Straumann, T. (2009). Rule rather than exception: Brüning's fear of devaluation in comparative perspective. *Journal of Contemporary History, 44*, 603–617.
Straumann, T. (2019). *1931: Debt, crisis, and the rise of Hitler*. Oxford University Press.
Temin, P. (1971). Beginning of the depression in Germany. *Economic History Review, 24*, 240–248.
Temin, P. (1976). *Did monetary forces cause the great depression?* Norton & Company.
Temin, P. (2008). The German crisis of 1931. Evidence and tradition. *Cliometrica, 2*, 5–17.
Toniolo, G. (2005). *Central bank co-operation and the BIS, 1930–1973*. Cambridge University Press.
Walb, E. (1932). Die Bankekrise von 1931. *Zeitschrift für handelswissenschaftliche Forschung, 26*, 2–28.
Wehler, H. U. (2003). *Deutsche Gesellschaftsgeschichte, Bd. 4: Vom Beginn des Ersten Weltkriegs bis zur Gründung der beiden deutschen Staaten 1914–1949*. Beck Verlag.
Weisbrod, B. (1990). Industrial crisis strategy in the great depression. In J. B. von Kruedener (Ed.), *Economic crisis and political collapse: The Weimar Republic 1924–1933*. St. Martin's Press.
Winkler, H. A. (1993). *Weimar 1918–33. Die Geschichte der ersten deutschen Demokratie*. Verlag Beck.

Chapter 8
Conclusions

In many studies, the collapse of the Weimar Republic is traced to dramatic economic events. Thus, according to some, the hyperinflation of 1923 by destroying the middle class and strengthening interest groups opposed to the Republic, primarily big business, eroded the foundations of the German democratic regime.

For others, the collapse of the Weimar Republic was due to the crisis of 1931 and the concomitant fiscal austerity measures introduced by the Brüning government. The crisis combined with these measures led to pronounced deflation, GDP collapsed and the unemployment rate rose dramatically. The resulting economic and social malaise paved the way for National Socialism and Hitler's rise to power.

In reality, the hyperinflation of 1923, the crisis of 1931, and the austerity policies of the Brüning government were the outcome, not the cause, of a profound political disorder that undermined the republican regime at its foundations. This disorder was rooted in the fact that the German elite and masses had been unable to accept the reality and consequences of defeat in the First World War. Symptomatic of this was the widespread acceptance by the German public of the "stabbed in the back myth" which claimed that the German army had not been defeated on the battlefield but rather its effectiveness had been compromised by the sabotage of "traitors" within German society, the "culprits" being identified as pacifists, Jews, and communists. From this perspective, the politicians who had accepted the armistice and the Treaty of Versailles were viewed as traitors.

In the 1920s, the only shared element in German society was a widespread sentiment opposing the Versailles treaty. This sentiment neither promoted social cohesion nor was it an identifying factor.

The widespread idea among the masses was that by rejecting the Treaty and eliminating Reparations Germany would return to the pre-war situation, this illusion prevented governments from taking the necessary measures for an orderly demobilization and a solid path of economic reconstruction of the country.

In the absence of a unifying point of reference, social and political conflicts reached extreme levels with each interest group exerting pressure on the government to maximize their position.

G. B. Pittaluga, E. Seghezza, *An Economic Historiography of Germany, 1918-1931*, Frontiers in Economic History, https://doi.org/10.1007/978-3-031-70347-8_8

In the early 1920s social conflict was calmed by keeping public spending and domestic demand high. This economic policy was supported principally by industrialists, who were concerned that unchecked economic and social conflict would encourage the spread of the ideas of the radical left amongst disillusioned workers. Given a "war of attrition" between the various conflicting interest groups, it was politically impossible to address growing public expenditure through orderly management of the public budget and, infact, Erzberger's tax reforms were undermined and rendered fruitless during their implementation.[1]

The fear of a Bolshevik revolution similar to the one that had taken place in Russia in 1917 led Stinnes, the President of the German Confederation of German Industry, to believe that inflation was a political necessity.[2] Recourse to inflation enabled the German governments of the early 1920s to obtain high resources from seigniorage and keep public spending, especially current account spending, high. High public spending helped to keep domestic demand high and through this to maintain high levels of employment.

The expansive fiscal policy approach allowed the political elite and the Republic to limit the growth of support for the radical Left. Also contributing to this containment effort was the limited opposition of big industry to the trade unions' objective of restoring workers' real wages to their pre-war levels.

An economic environment emerged in the early 1920s in which high domestic absorption led to current account imbalances. These imbalances were followed by phases of intense depreciation of the mark, which were triggered by bad news about the Reparations. The depreciation of the German currency was followed by phases of pronounced price increases and, with some delay, wage levels were adjusted accordingly.

As high inflation became a structural fact of the German economy, workers learned to demand increasingly frequent adjustments of wages to price rises. Rising prices took on the characteristics of inertial inflation "... the self-replicating pattern of wage and price inflation" which "... once it is built into the system in a consistent manner it continues very much on its own."[3]

The way this self-replicating process evolves depends on the lag with which wages adjust to prices. As inflation rises this lag is reduced, price growth assumes an accelerated pattern that at some point becomes explosive, as it did in the case of Germany from the summer of 1922 onward. As was the case with previous phases of price acceleration from 1919 onward, the onset of hyperinflation resulted from a sudden stop. After the assassination of Rathenau, foreign investors who had bought assets denominated in marks began to sell them and withdraw their currency deposits from German banks.

[1] Hefeker (2001) has shown that the failure of Erzberger fiscal reform was due not only to the conflict between capital and labor, but also between center and states.

[2] See Feldman (1993, p. 447).

[3] See Tobin (1981, p. 23).

Corresponding to this massive outflow of capital, the mark's exchange rate depreciated pronouncedly in a short time. This depreciation of the German currency was followed by a rise in wholesale prices and the cost of living. Trade unions' demands for ever more efficient forms of wage indexation added impetus to the increase in prices, creating an uncontrollable spiral between exchange rates, prices, and wages. The Reichsbank facilitated this process by adjusting the money supply, albeit belatedly.

From this perspective, hyperinflation can clearly be seen as the continuity of the high inflation of the preceding years, of which it represents the final degeneration. Its ultimate cause, as suggested by Kindleberger's structural hypothesis, was the intense distributive conflict and the Weimar governments' attempt to manage it by seconding an implicit alliance between the productive classes who benefited from the redistributive effects of inflation.

Despite the explosive price growth and its distorting consequences on the allocation of resources and the distribution of income and wealth, no stabilization measures were taken until October 1923. This delay was largely due to the fears of industry that they would cause an increase in unemployment and in taxes for both companies and personal income. "Finally the government and representatives of industry accepted a stabilization program once the alternative appeared grave communist-led unrest and once depression threatened as credit dried up in the summer and fall of 1923."[4] In brief, the productive classes and especially industry accepted stabilization measures only when the income redistribution favored by inflation had exhausted its effect, that is in the extreme impoverishment of holders of financial assets (and those living on fixed incomes) and the costs of rising prices had become significant even for the productive classes.

A decree in mid-October 1923 introduced a new currency, the Rentenmark, which although not convertible into gold was nonetheless indexed to it. By the same decree, the Reichsbank was prohibited from financing Reich overdrafts.

Between November and December 1923, the mark exchange rate stabilized and price rises came to an end. Given the speed with which the German economy was stabilized, various scholars have spoken of a "Rentenmark miracle" and there was much debate about the reasons for this miracle. Some insisted on the positive psychological effects of the introduction of a new currency on the behavior of individuals. Others, such as Sargent (1982), insisted that a regime change, such as the measures decided by the government in October 1923, brought about a change in the inflationary expectations of individuals and stabilized an economy with only modest economic and social costs.

In reality, the stabilization of German hyperinflation seems to have resulted from measures to stabilize the exchange rate. In addition to the creation of the Rentenmark and the adoption of fiscal correction measures, these measures consisted of an extremely restrictive monetary policy stance. This approach discouraged downward speculation on the German currency. The mark exchange rate stabilized completely in December and, with it, domestic price levels also stabilized.

[4]See Maier (1987, p. 203).

Thanks to the stabilization of the mark and domestic prices, it was possible to eliminate the public deficit thanks to a pronounced increase in the Reich's revenue, due primarily to the Olivera-Tanzi effect.

As is generally the case with exchange-rate-based stabilization, price stabilization was followed by an appreciation of the exchange rate in real terms, an increase in domestic demand and in foreign debt. The economic and social costs of stabilization were, in themselves, moderate. Hyperinflation, however, had distorting effects of a structural nature on the German economy. Businesses, given the low cost of credit in real terms, had made investments that turned out to be unproductive, the domestic financial market was to a large extent destroyed, and the banks had been severely weakened in terms of capital coverage. These distortions could only be reabsorbed over time. In the immediate, there was concern from part of the political class that the restrictive measures taken would lead to deflation. At the beginning of 1924, monetary policy became accommodative again and, as a result, the mark showed signs of instability. The fear of a new phase of exchange rate depreciation and inflation led the Reichsbank to return to a restrictive monetary policy.

The stabilization of the German economy was consolidated with the Dawes Plan, made public in 1924. This Plan, in addition to defining the Reparations, established the convertibility of the German currency, the Reichsmark, and the political independence of the Reichsbank.

Thanks to the Dawes Plan and the provisions that it envisaged, Germany once again became part of the international financial circuit. Between 1924 and 1929 inflows of foreign capital into Germany were extraordinarily high, exceeding the Reparation annuities set by the Plan. This huge inflow of capital allowed Germany to maintain a large and persistent budget and current account deficits in the second half of the 1920s. These deficits, high public expenditure and the high internal absorption that were at the root of them allowed the political elite to reduce the distributive conflict and maintain relative social harmony.

Although the huge inflow of foreign capital had beneficial effects (that is it allowed the survival of the Republic), it also had at least two distorting effects. Firstly, it caused the German economy to suffer from Dutch disease-like effects, i.e., an appreciation of the real exchange rate and price increases of non-tradable goods compared to those of tradables. As a result, there was an increasing tendency to shift capital and labor to the non-tradable sector where profits and wages were higher.

This process inevitably had negative effects on total productivity and in particular on labor productivity. German output growth suffered as a result, to the extent that the years 1924–1929 were referred to as the "crisis before the crisis." While Holtfrerich and other Keynesian economists insist on the negative effects of high interest rates on investment demand, Borchardt and other scholars traced this low growth in German output to the pressing demands of high wages on the part of the industrial trade unions and the low profits of companies.

However, it would seem important to attribute this phase of relative stagnation of the German economy to a form of reverse Balassa-Samuelson[5] effect whereby wage

[5]See Balassa (1964) and Samuelson (1964).

increases in the non-tradable sector were transmitted to the tradable sector, weakening its competitiveness in international markets.

The large inflows of capital from abroad not only allowed the German government a persistently expansive fiscal policy but also provided Germany with resources to compensate for the reduction in domestic savings resulting from hyperinflation. It was, in particular, the large Berlin banks that benefited in the second half of the 1920s from the high levels of non-resident currency deposits. While this provided these banks with ample resources, it also made them fragile, exposing them to sudden stops.

The first episode of capital flight occurred in the spring of 1929 when Schacht, the President of the Reichsbank, during the Paris negotiations for the Young Plan (which was intended to settle the Reparations problem once and for all) made a series of demands that were considered almost a provocation by the delegates of the Allied countries. To counter capital flight and defend the convertibility of the Reichsmark, the German central bank used part of its gold reserves but the currency crisis was only finally averted thanks to a loan from foreign banks.

Especially after the New York Stock Exchange crisis of October 1929 the flow of foreign capital to Germany slowed noticeably, coming to a complete halt in 1930.

In the absence of foreign funding, the German government was no longer able to conduct an economic policy that had been characterized by twin deficits for much of the second half of the 1920s.

Faced with the need to implement fiscal adjustment measures, the SPD withdrew its support from the grand coalition government headed by Muller and, in March 1930, this government was succeeded by a new government headed by Brüning. President Hindenburg effectively granted this minority government power to act through Article 48 of the Constitution. This allowed it to issue economic decrees without having to submit them to Parliament for approval.

As early as June 1930, the Brüning government issued a first tax decree that included tax increases and spending cuts. However, faced with forceful opposition to the decree from within parliament, President Hindenburg decided to dissolve the government and call new elections. In these elections, held on September 13, 1930, the governing parties lost both votes and seats to extremist parties, in particular, the National Socialist Party and the Communist Party.

Distrust of Germany's ability to implement virtuous economic policy again led some foreign investors to withdraw deposits from German banks and sell Reichsmarks. This crisis, like that of 1929, was countered by the Reichsbank and resolved by a loan from an international consortium of banks.

In March 1931, faced with falling state revenues mainly due to falling output, the Brüning government decided to initiate new fiscal austerity measures. In the face of the growing unpopularity of these measures and seeking to retain support from the right wing of the political spectrum, Brüning chose to pursue a more aggressive foreign policy toward the Allies. It was in this context that he announced his support for the planned customs union with Austria, led by Foreign Minister Curtius, and made his radical speech in early June at the presentation of the new tax decree. These actions were perceived as an official declaration that Germany did not intend to comply with the Young Plan: i.e., that it was refusing to pay the annuities specified by the plan.

Following the declaration, the withdrawal of currency deposits from large German banks, which had started with the news of the bankruptcy of the Credit Anstalt Bank, became massive. The Reichsbank thus found itself in the difficult position of having to defend the convertibility of the Reichsmark while simultaneously supporting the banking system by offering liquidity through the discounting of commercial paper. These two objectives, however, were at odds, since although by providing liquidity to the banks it guaranteed their continued solvency, it also financed their supply of credit lines which were often being used for exchange rate speculation against the Reichsmark.

To escape from this vicious circle, in June the Reichsbank resorted to banking credit restrictions. The bank's liquidity situation worsened further with the news that Danat Bank, Germany's second-largest bank, had essentially gone bankrupt. A banking panic ensued that threatened the solvency of the German banking system. The foreign exchange crisis, which had started with a sudden stop in early June 1931, turned into a banking crisis. This crisis was cauterized by the government proclaiming 2 days of bank holiday on 14 and 15 July and then outlining a proposed reform involving the nationalization of a large part of the German banking system.

As the world economy was hit by an ever-worsening recession, Brüning government's fiscal austerity and the credit crunch that followed the banking crisis contributed to a particularly pronounced fall in German output, which was matched by a dramatic increase in unemployment. The economic and social malaise that followed accentuated the polarization of the electorate and contributed to the rise of National Socialism to power.

In the immediate aftermath of the Second World War, various scholars blamed Hitler's seizure of power on the irresponsible fiscal austerity chosen and implemented by the Brüning government arguing that an expansive fiscal policy aimed at stimulating domestic demand would have prevented Germany from the tragic Nazi experience.

This view has been heavily criticized from the late 1970s onward by Borchardt and other scholars arguing that the Brüning government's room for maneuver was extremely limited.[6] It could not conduct a policy of deficit spending because it could not provide monetary coverage for it (since under the Dawes Plan the Reichsbank could not buy government bonds on the primary market). Moreover, both the workers' unions and the industrialists, after the experience of hyperinflation, were utterly averse to any form of money creation that might have inflationary outcomes. On the other hand, it was not possible to cover public deficits with debt, as capital inflows from abroad had dried up and domestic savings were scarce. Nor could Brüning stimulate aggregate demand by devaluing the mark since the Dawes Plan required its convertibility.

[6]For a survey of this debate see Borchardt (1990).

Its difficulties of action stemmed from the legacy of past failures, from the fact that the Republic had survived thanks to mechanisms that had procured a temporary social peace. With these mechanisms exhausted, Germany's unresolved problems emerged with extreme force.

From a strictly economic point of view, given his narrow margins of action, Brüning pursued a kind of internal devaluation, i.e. a simultaneous reduction of prices and wages. The recovery of the German industry's competitiveness through a depreciation of the real exchange rate would have made it possible to increase the support of aggregate demand in this way. In addition, returning the task of setting prices and wages to market forces would have fostered an improvement in the efficiency of allocating resources and, at the same time, it would have allowed the government greater freedom rather than being confined to adopt purely redistributive measures.

Brüning did not succeed in realizing these goals. He was, once again, prevented from doing so by the intense distributive conflict in German society and, above all, by the fierce defense of their own interests and privileges by big industry and its cartels, and by most trade unions, entrenched in a strenuous defense of workers' real wages.

In conclusion, we are led to share Feldman's opinion, according to which it seems appropriate to consider the Weimar Republic, rather than as an experiment, "... as a gamble which stood virtually no chance of success."[7] The most surprising thing, therefore, is not the fact that the Weimar Republic collapsed at a certain point, but rather the fact that, due to a series of circumstances that we have tried to clarify in this book, it lasted so long.[8]

References

Balassa, B. (1964). The purchasing power parity doctrine: A reappraisal. *Journal of Political Economy, 72*, 584–596.

Bessel, R. (1990). Why did the Weimar Republic collapse? In I. Kershaw (Ed.), *Weimar: Why did German democracy fail?* St. Martin's Press.

Borchardt, K. (1990). A decade of debate about Brüning economic policy. In J. B. von Kruedener (Ed.), *Economic crisis and political collapse. The Weimar Republic 1924-1933*. St. Martin's Press.

Feldman, G. D. (1985). Weimar from inflation to depression: Experimenter gamble? In G. D. Feldman & E. Müller-Luckner E. (Eds.), *Sie Nachwirkungen der Inflation auf die Deutsche Geschichte, 1924–33*. Oldenbourg Verlag.

Feldman, G. D. (1993). *The great disorder: Politics, economics, and society in the German Inflation, 1914–1924*. Oxford University Press.

Hefeker, C. (2001). The agony of central power: Fiscal federalism in the German Reich. *European Economic History Review, 5*, 119–142.

[7] See Feldman (1985, p. 4).

[8] See Bessel (1990, p. 148).

Maier, C. (1987). *In search of stability*. Cambridge University Press.
Samuelson, P. (1964). Theoretical notes on trade problems. *Review of Economics and Statistics, 46*, 145–154.
Sargent, T. J. (1982). The ends of four big hyperinflations. In R. E. Hall (Ed.), *Inflation: Causes and effects*. University of Chicago Press.
Tobin, J. (1981). Diagnosing inflation: A taxonomy. In M. J. Flanders & A. Razin (Eds.), *Development in an inflationary world*. Academic Press.

Index of Authors

G. B. Pittaluga, E. Seghezza, *An Economic Historiography of Germany, 1918-1931*, Frontiers in Economic History , https://doi.org/10.1007/978-3-031-70347-8

Index of Subjects

G. B. Pittaluga, E. Seghezza, *An Economic Historiography of Germany, 1918-1931*, Frontiers in Economic History , https://doi.org/10.1007/978-3-031-70347-8

MIX
Papier aus verantwortungsvollen Quellen
Paper from responsible sources
FSC® C105338

If you have any concerns about our products,
you can contact us on
ProductSafety@springernature.com

In case Publisher is established outside the EU,
the EU authorized representative is:
Springer Nature Customer Service Center GmbH
Europaplatz 3, 69115 Heidelberg, Germany

Printed by Libri Plureos GmbH
in Hamburg, Germany